TAKING SIDES

Clashing Views on

Moral Issues

ELEVENTH EDITION

TAKING SIDES

Clashing Views on

Moral Issues

FIFVENTH EDITION

Selected, Edited, and with Introductions by

Stephen Satris
Clemson University

Contemporary Learning Series
2460 Kerper Blvd., Dubuque, IA 52001

Visit us on the Internet
http://www.mhcls.com

To the memory of my mother and father

Photo Acknowledgment
Cover image: Chase Jarvis/Getty Images

Cover Acknowledgment
Maggie Lytle

Manufactured in the United States of America

Eleventh Edition

123456789DOCDOC987

Library of Congress Cataloging-in-Publication Data
Main entry under title:
Taking sides: clashing views on moral issues/selected, edited, and
with introductions by Stephen Satris.—11th ed.
Includes bibliographical references and index.
1. Ethics. 2. Social Ethics. I.Satris, Stephen, *comp.*
170'.22

MHID: 0-07-339715-6
ISBN: 978-0-07-339715-3
ISSN: 1094-7604

Printed on Recycled Paper

Preface

This text contains 34 essays, arranged in pro and con pairs, that address 17 controversial issues in morality and moral philosophy. Each of the issues is expressed in terms of a single question in order to draw the lines of debate more clearly.

Some of the questions that are included here have been in the mainstream of moral philosophy for hundreds (or even thousands) of years and are central to the discipline. I have not shied away from abstract questions about relativism and the relationship between morality and religion. Other questions relate to specific topics of contemporary concern, such as human cloning, abortion, affirmative action, and drug legalization.

The authors of the selections included here take a strong stand on a given issue and provide their own best defenses of a pro or con position. The selections were chosen for their usefulness in defending a position and for their accessibility to students. The authors are philosophers, scientists, and social critics from a wide variety of backgrounds. Each presents us with a determinant answer on an issue—even if we ultimately cannot accept the answer as our own.

Each issue is accompanied by an *introduction*, which sets the stage for the debate, and each issue concludes with a *postscript* that summarizes the debate, considers other views on the issue, and suggests additional readings. The introductions and postscripts do not preempt what is the reader's own task: to achieve a critical and informed view of the issue at stake. I have also provided relevant Internet site addresses (URLs) on the Internet References page that accompanies each part opener. And at the back of the book is a list of all the *contributors to this volume*, which provides information on the philosophers and social commentators whose views are debated here.

Taking Sides: Clashing Views on Moral Issues is a tool to encourage critical thought on important moral issues. Readers should not feel confined to the views expressed in the selections. Some readers may see important points on both sides of an issue and may construct for themselves a new and creative approach, which may incorporate the best of both sides or provide an entirely new vantage point for understanding.

Changes to this edition   This new edition is significantly different from the tenth edition. There are four completely new issues: "Is Ayn Rand's Ethical Egoism Correct?" (Issue 3); "Is Cloning Pets Ethically Justified?" (Issue 8); "Is Gambling Immoral?" (Issue 11); and "Is Torture Ever Justified?" (Issue 15). In addition, one issue was given a new article: "Is Moral Relativism Correct?" (Issue 1); one issue was rephrased and given a new article: "Does Morality Require Vegetarianism?" (Issue 17), and another issue was rephrased and given two new articles: "Is Physician-Assisted Suicide Wrong?" (Issue 16).

A word to the instructor   An *Instructor's* Resource Guide *With Test Questions* (multiple-choice and essay) is available through the publisher for the instructor using *Taking Sides* in the classroom. A general guidebook, *Using Taking Sides in the Classroom,* which discusses methods and techniques for using the pro-con approach in any classroom setting, is also available. An online version of *Using Taking Sides in the Classroom* and a correspondence service for *Taking Sides* adopters can be found at http://www.mhcls.com/usingts.

  Taking Sides: Clashing Views on Moral Issues is only one title in the Taking Sides series. If you are interested in seeing the table of contents for any of the other titles, please visit the Taking Sides Web site at http://www.mhcls.com/takingsides/.

Acknowledgments   Finally, a unique debt of thanks is owed to those who tolerated my strange hours and the time spent away from them as this book was being prepared and revised: Kim, Angela, and Michelle.

Stephen Satris
Clemson University

Contents In Brief

Contents

Ayn Rand argues against the idea that morality is something that is for the good of *others*, and thus something that requires self-sacrifice. Here, in her novel *Atlas Shrugged*, she has the leading character speak in favor of moral egoism—the idea that one should look after *oneself* and one's own happiness. Louis Pojman argues that Rand has confused the concept of *selfishness* with that of *self-interest*. Since she thinks of selfishness as a virtue, this leads her to devalue altruism, or acting for others, as a vice. His own account aims to establish some middle ground between complete altruism and complete egoism.

Professor of philosophy Don Marquis argues that abortion is generally wrong for the same reason that killing an innocent adult human being is generally wrong: it deprives the individual of a future that he or she would otherwise have. Philosopher Jane English (1947–1978) asserts that there is no well-defined line dividing persons from nonpersons. She maintains that both the conservative and the liberal positions are too extreme and that some abortions are morally justifiable and some are not.

Philosopher Vincent C. Punzo maintains that the special intimacy of sex requires a serious commitment that is for the most part not required in other human activities. Philosopher Alan H. Goldman argues for a view of sex that is completely separate from any cultural or moral ideology that might be attached to it.

Jonathan Rauch argues that same-sex marriage would provide a stabilizing effect on gay relationships and would benefit children. He argues that society has a stake in encouraging these stabilizing relationships and in benefitting children, and should therefore support same-sex marriage. Jeff Jordan considers various "models" of marriage. In issues of same-sex marriage, these models clash. Jordan uses these

James F. Childress, professor of ethics and professor of medical education, argues that a free market would cause the loss of important altruistic motivations and would turn organs into commodities; moreover, such an untried market might make fewer—not more—organs available.

Issue 10. Should Drugs Be Legalized? 175

Political analyst David Boaz argues that in a free country, people have the right to ingest whatever substances they choose without governmental interference. Moreover, as our national experience with Prohibition shows, attempts at restricting substances create more problems than they solve. The Drug Enforcement Administration presents the case that drugs are illegal for good reason—they are harmful. If the legalization proponents were heeded, we as a society would be much worse off. We should be concentrating harder on fighting drug use and drug trafficking where there is significant progress.

Issue 11. Is Gambling Immoral? 197

Lisa Newton, a philosopher at Fairfield University, argues that gambling is immoral on the grounds that it violates stewardship (and not on the grounds that it violates anyone's rights or that it leads to negative results). Most of the paper examines the concept of stewardship and how it relates to gambling. Stewardship, which is an old concept that is known to us primarily through religious tradition, can also be given a modern secular form. Peter Collins, a British philosopher, argues that gambling is not immoral. He addresses gambling from both traditional utilitarian (or consequentialist) and Kantian perspectives—and finds the critiques from these perspectives lacking. He then specifically considers the more recent criticism that is based on the idea of stewardship—this too he finds lacking. Collins concludes with the idea of true happiness, and expresses the judgment that although gambling is not necessarily a part of a truly happy life, it is morally trivial.

Issue 12. Is Affirmative Action Fair? 221

Professor of philosophy Albert G. Mosley argues that affirmative action is a continuation of the history of black progress since the Brown v. Board of Education desegregation decision of 1954 and the Civil Rights Act of

1964. He defends affirmative action as a "benign use of race." Professor of philosophy Louis P. Pojman contends that affirmative action violates the moral principle that maintains that each person is to be treated as an individual, not as representative of a group. He stresses that individual merit needs to be appreciated and that respect should be given to each person on an individual basis.

as if their own arguments are merely a harmless exercise of reason, detached from actual events in Guantanamo, Abu Graib, etc.

Issue 16. Is Physician-Assisted Suicide Wrong? 326

YES: **Richard Doerflinger,** from "Assisted Suicide: Pro-Choice or Anti-Life?" *Hastings Center Report* (January/February 1989) *328*

NO: **David T. Watts and Timothy Howell,** from "Assisted Suicide Is not Voluntary Active Euthanasia," *Journal of the American Geriatrics Society* (October 1992) *335*

Admitting that religiously based grounds for the wrongness of killing an innocent person are not convincing to many people, Doerflinger argues on mainly secular grounds having to do with inconsistencies in the arguments of supporters of physician-assisted suicide. He examines the idea of autonomy, and the tendency for something like physician-assisted suicide to spread once it becomes initially accepted in a limited way. Watts and Howell first claim that it is very important to distinguish between *assisted suicide* and *voluntary active euthanasia*. Basically, the first of these is suicide or killing oneself; the second involves being killing by someone else (e.g., a physician). Watts and Howell argue that most of the opposition to physician-assisted suicide turns out to be really opposition to voluntary active euthanasia; furthermore, they argue that physician-assisted suicide would not have the dire consequence that its opponents predict.

UNIT 4 HUMAN BEINGS AND OTHER SPECIES 345

Issue 17. Does Morality Require Vegetarianism? 346

YES: **Jordan Curnutt,** from "A New Argument for Vegetarianism," *Journal of Social Philosophy* (Winter 1997) *348*

NO: **Holmes Rolston III,** from *Environmental Ethics* (Temple University Press, 1988) *359*

Jordan Curnutt specifically rejects the two major lines of thought that have led to the philosophical support of vegetarianism, utilitarian ideas (based on animal suffering) and deontological ideas (based on animal rights). Curnutt offers what he calls a new argument for vegetarianism, based on the harm of killing animals, and the weakness of the reasons that people might propose for causing that harm. Environmental thinker Holmes Rolston III maintains that meat eating by humans is a natural part of the ecosystem. He states that it is important that animals do not suffer needlessly, but it would be a mistake to think that animals, like humans, are members of a culture. Rolston concludes that people too readily project human nature on animal nature.

Introduction

Thinking About Moral Issues

Stephen Satris

Getting Started

If you were asked in your biology class to give the number of bones in the average human foot, you could consult your textbook, you could go to the library and have the librarian track down the answer, you could search the Internet, or you could ask your friend who always gets A's in biology. Most likely you have not previously had any reason to consider this question, but you do know for certain that it has one right answer, which you will be expected to provide for the final exam.

What do you do, however, when faced with a moral question like one of the ones raised in this text? Whereas it is a relatively straightforward matter to find out how many bones there are in the human foot, in addressing moral issues, understanding cannot be acquired as easily. Someone cannot report back to you on the right answer. You will have to discuss the ideas raised by these moral questions and determine the answers for yourself. And you will have to arrive at an answer through reason and careful thought; you cannot just rely on your *feelings* to answer these questions. Keep in mind, too, that these are questions you will be facing your entire life—understanding will not end with the final exam.

In approaching the issues in this book, you should maintain an open mind toward both sides of the question. Otherwise, it will be more difficult for you to see, appreciate, and, most importantly, *learn* from the opposing position. Therefore, you should first ask yourself what your own assumptions are about an issue and become aware of any preconceived notions you may have. And then, after such reflection, you should assume the posture of an impartial judge. If you have a strong prior attachment to one side, do not let it prevent you from giving a sympathetic ear to the opposing side.

Once the arguments have been laid out and you have given them careful consideration, do not remain suspended in the middle. Now is the time for informed judgment.

A natural dramatic sequence is played out for each of the 17 issues discussed in *Taking Sides: Clashing Views on Moral Issues*. A question is posed, and you must open yourself to hear each author's arguments, reasons, and examples, which are meant to persuade you to take the author's viewpoint. But then comes the second part of the drama. Having heard and considered both sides of an issue, what will *you* say? What understanding of the issue can *you* achieve?

You can choose aspects of the "yes" answer and aspects of the "no" answer and weave them together to construct a coherent whole. You can accept one answer and build some qualifications or limitations into it. Or you might be stimulated to think of a completely new angle on the issue.

Be aware of three dangers. The first is a premature judgment or fixed opinion that rules out a fair hearing of the opposing side. The second danger is in many ways like the first, but is somewhat more insidious. It is an unconscious assumption (or set of assumptions) that makes it impossible to hear the other side correctly. (The best antidote for this is to be able to give a fair and accurate account of the issue as it appears to someone on the opposing side.) Finally, the third danger is to lack a judgment after having considered the issue. In this case, two contrary positions simply cannot both be right, and it is up to the reader to make an effort to distinguish what is acceptable from what is unacceptable in the arguments and positions that have been defended.

Fundamental Issues in Morality

The 17 issues in this book are divided into four sections, or parts. The first part deals with fundamental questions about morality as a whole. In this context, it might be said that "morality is a religious matter" or perhaps, that "it's all relative." The issues in the first part do not directly confront specific moral problems; they question the nature of morality itself.

Already in Unit 1, we see something that is a recurring feature of moral thought and of this book: Moral issues are interrelated. Suppose, for example, that you answer the question "Is Moral Relativism Correct?" (Issue 1) in the affirmative and also answer the question "Does Morality Need Religion?" (Issue 2) in the affirmative. How can these two answers fit together? A positive answer to the second question is generally thought to involve a source for morality that is supernatural, beyond the customs and traditions of any one particular social group. But an affirmative answer to the first question suggests that morality is grounded in what is cultural and *not* supernatural. (It may be possible to maintain affirmative answers to both of these questions, but a person who does so owes us an explanation as to how these two ideas fit together.) Many other issues that at first sight might seem distinct have connections among one another.

Another point, and one that applies not only to the issues in Unit 1 but to controversial issues in general, is this: In evaluating any position, you should do so on the merits (or lack of merit) of the specific case that is made. Do not accept or reject a position on the basis of what the position (supposedly) tells you about the author, and do not criticize or defend a position by reducing it to simplistic slogans. The loss of articulation and sophistication that occurs when a complex position is reduced to a simple slogan is significant and real. For example, a "no" answer to the question "Does Morality Need Religion?" might be superficially labeled as "antireligion," and a "yes" answer might seem as "proreligion." Yet Saint Thomas Aquinas, who has always been regarded as the foremost theologian of the Christian tradition, would respond with a "no" to that question. Moral questions are complex, and the reduction of answers to simple reactions or superficial slogans will not be helpful. The questions and issues that are raised here require careful analysis, examination, and argumentation.

Gender, Sex, and Reproduction

Unit 2 includes several questions that have to do with ways of looking at society, especially sex roles, sexual relationships, and reproduction. In many ways, the issues in this section are basic to an understanding of our own place in society, our relation to others, and what we expect of men and women.

Specific issues considered in Unit 2 are "Is Abortion Immoral?", "Must Sex Involve Commitment?", "Should Same-Sex Marriage Be Allowed?", and "Should Human Cloning Be Banned?"

The question "Is Abortion Immoral?" (Issue 4) is not at all new, threatening to polarize people into pro life and pro-choice camps. But it is best to leave such labels and superficial slogans behind. Whenever an issue seems to demand answers very quickly, as this one might, it is better to go slowly and to first consider the arguments, examples, and rationale of each position before making up your mind. Both of the writers on this topic, for example, stay away from religious arguments—which could very quickly polarize people.

The question "Must Sex Involve Commitment?" (Issue 5) has traditionally been answered in the positive—the conservative answer certainly tends to be positive. But after the social changes that have liberalized society's sexual attitudes, does the traditional answer still stand? What, exactly, has changed in people's attitudes? Have people come to see premarital sex as morally permissible (where it was once thought to be immoral)? Or, do people still see it as immoral, but they are no longer shocked by its widespread occurrence in real life, films, etc.? The word *must* in "Must sex involve commitment?" is moral. The view that sex must involve commitment is not intended to be one that reflects how things actually are. In fact, those who answer this question positively would probably think that how things actually are is not at all how they should be.

The question "Should Same-Sex Marriage Be Allowed?" (Issue 6) arises in a social context of changing practices and values. Certainly, same-sex relationships are more widely tolerated now than in the past. Some people may think that this shows a moral decline and would naturally be against same-sex marriage. But even some people who think of this increased tolerance as a good thing are hesitant to accept same-sex marriage. Marriage is something for a man and a woman, they might say. Of course, traditionally, this has in fact been so. But the question now arises whether any changes should be made to this idea. Is marriage different? Is it for heterosexual unions only? And if same-sex marriage is allowed, what would be the social repercussions?

The question "Should Human Cloning Be Banned?" (Issue 7) has arisen because technology may exist that could clone human beings. Some people think that science would be going too far here and that cloning people would be akin to "playing God." They also feel that not everything that technology makes possible should actually be done. Others see no problem with proceeding with experimentation toward human cloning. Is cloning just a case of using science to manipulate natural facts and achieve some desired results, or are the results here not to be desired?

Law and Society

Unit 3 focuses on questions that involve our social nature. We ask what particular arrangements will (or will not) be tolerated in society. We also ask what laws we should have (or not have).

This section considers the questions: "Is Cloning Pets Ethically Justified?", "Should Congress Allow the Buying and Selling of Human Organs?", "Should Drugs Be Legalized?", "Is Gambling Immoral?", "Is Affirmative Action Fair?", "Should Handguns Be Banned?", "Should the Death Penalty Be Abolished?", and "Is Torture Ever Justified?".

The first question, "Is Cloning Pets Ethically Justified?" (Issue 8), raises many of the same questions that arise in the case of cloning human beings. People may have unrealistic expectations of cloning in both cases. And in both cases the cloned individual may be held to those expectations. On the other hand, it may be felt that human beings are in a class by themselves and should not be cloned—while we can do virtually anything in the case of animals. Yet, here again, objectors to cloning stress the failures of the technique and the problems that it always seems to bring with it. If our pets really are at our mercy (unlike human beings), perhaps it is not right to treat them in ways that seem to be problematic.

The second question, "Should Congress Allow the Buying and Selling of Human Organs?" (Issue 9) is one that might initially sound quite gruesome. But the fact is that there are many more people needing organs—such as kidneys—than there are organs available for transplant. Part of the problem with the shortage of organs—again, we focus specifically on kidneys here—is that there is no financial incentive for donors to provide kidneys. Doctors and hospitals are compensated for their roles in the organ transplant process, but the donor—by law—cannot be compensated. There cannot be payment for organs. Yet there is a demand for organs on the part of those in need. Would a market in which there was buying and selling help? Is this even something we should think about?

Asking "Should Drugs Be Legalized" (Issue 10) raises a number of points that require consideration. Here we ask about the future and what kind of society is worth aiming for. Should we strive for a society in which certain substances are available on the open market to consumers who choose them, or should we aim to eliminate certain substances and legally punish drug dealers and users? This is one of several issues in which we are drawn to two incompatible values; in this case, the values are complete liberty and social order. It seems impossible to have both.

The question "Is Gambling Immoral?" (Issue 11) is puzzling for at least one reason. Gambling has traditionally been counted as a vice, and many people today think it is wrong, but if gambling is immoral, it is surprisingly difficult to articulate just what is wrong with it. Even a traditional view of gambling as wrong usually allows that such activities as church bingo, etc., are not wrong. State lotteries are also another strange case. We might feel the positive pull toward lotteries as a useful means of raising state revenue (without increasing taxes), and at the same time have an uneasy feeling about the fact that the state has always forbidden "games of chance"—but now lets itself run one of the games it forbids to all others. Gambling is definitely a strange area, and one that needs some clear thinking!

The question, "Is Affirmative Action Fair?" (Issue 12) confronts a policy that is intended to address problems arising from the history and the current state of race relations in the United States. Most arguments in favor of affirmative action can be seen as either backward-looking or forward-looking. Arguments that regard affirmative action as a form of compensation or as a response to previous injustices are backward-looking because they focus on prior events. Arguments that regard affirmative action as a means of achieving integration or diversity or as a means of providing minority role models are forward looking because they point to the future. Critics of programs of affirmative action, however, have charged that such programs lead to reverse discrimination and unfairly focus on "group rights," whereas the only actual rights are rights of individuals.

The question, "Should Handguns Be Banned?" (Issue 13) is raised largely in response to the very high number of murders that are committed with handguns in the United States. According to an affirmative answer to this question, the crime problem could be largely solved, while shotguns would still be allowed for hunting and other legal purposes. But some people who give a negative answer to this question see the strong arm of the government coming into play and fear that individual rights would be at stake. Others argue that banning handguns would not stop criminals from committing crimes; in fact, they argue, it may encourage them since criminals could count on law-abiding citizens as being without handguns.

Many subsidiary questions enter into the issue of "Should the Death Penalty Be Abolished?" (Issue 14). Does the death penalty deter crime? Is it the only way to give some criminals what they deserve? Does it fall unfairly on minorities and the poor? How much should we be concerned about errors? Is there a worldwide contemporary movement away from capital punishment? And, finally, even if we had the answers to all these questions, could we use those answers to address the overarching question of whether or not the death penalty should be retained?

The question "Is Torture Ever Justified?" (Issue 15) was, until 9/11, mainly a hypothetical question. Now, it is asked by government interrogators—who have suspects and want answers, and by concerned citizens as well, who might feel that torture makes us no better than the terrorists. The problem is that arguments on both sides seem fairly strong. To use torture against terrorists who have killed some innocent Americans and may want to kill us too does not seem very far from self-defense. On the other hand, if we engage in torture, then we seem to be the very devils we are said by the terrorists to be. But aren't American supposed to be the "good guys"? With torture, we seem to be stooping to the same level as the terrorists.

The question "Is Physician-Assisted Suicide Wrong?" (Issue 16) is another question about life or death, but this time the person who would die would not be regarded as a criminal. Such a person, who may have a terminal illness and perhaps be in great pain, requests the physician's assistance in killing himself. (Why would such assistance even be needed? Some people may be so bad off as not to be able to do it themselves; still others may be better off—but might end up botching things and making the situation worse. Hence, the physician is asked to lend expertise and assistance.) The question is whether this request should be fulfilled. If so, the end comes quickly. If not, the end will come, but not so quickly. But is helping to bring the situation to a quick end something that physicians should do?

Human Beings and Other Species

Unit 4 has only one question: "Does Morality Require Vegetarianism?" (Issue 17). This is a question that probably would not have been taken seriously in earlier times. However, today there are people and organizations that promote vegetarianism on moral grounds. The simplest idea here is that animals are beings that can be harmed, and they generally do suffer when they are raised and killed for meat. Most people can live without eating meat, so meat-eating seems to be a cultural practice that we have in our power to change. Of course, many people *like* meat-eating and are very reluctant to change. From their point of view, animals are part of nature, human beings are part of nature, and meat-eating—where one species eats another—is also part of nature. But the meat-eating question remains and forces itself upon people, who pride themselves on their knowledge—knowledge that includes awareness of the fact that they share the planet with other species.

Internet References . . .

The Internet Encyclopedia of Philosophy

This is a very useful reference tool for the serious philosophy student. It contains an excellent collection of readings from classic philosophy texts and original contributions by professional philosophers around the Internet.

http://www.utm.edu/research/iep/

Ethics Updates

Ethics Updates is an online resource edited by Lawrence M. Hinman, a well-respected ethicist at the University of San Diego. The site includes definitions of basic ideas, online articles, audio files, video files, discussion boards, and sophisticated search engines. There is a wide variety of subject matter, running from ethical theory to applied ethics, and the site offers frequent opportunities for user input.

http://ethics.sandiego.edu

Internet Philosophical Resources on Moral Relativism

This *Ethics Updates* site contains discussion questions and Internet resources devoted to moral, cultural, and ethical relativism.

http://ethics.sandiego.edu/theories/Relativism/index.asp

Fundamental Issues
in Morality

*E*ven *before confronting particular moral issues, we find that there are several conflicting assertions that have been made about morality considered as a whole. Some people state that there is no such thing as objective moral knowledge and that morality can provide no answers. Among them, relativists contend that all moral talk is simply the expression of subjective feelings or cultural norms, and these vary from case to case. Others maintain that morality does not have a source in purely human experience and interaction. Religion, they say, is the ground of morality. These and other ideas are discussed in this section.*

- Is Moral Relativism Correct?

- Does Morality Need Religion?

- Is Ayn Rand's Ethical Egoism Correct?

ISSUE 1

Is Moral Relativism Correct?

YES: **Gilbert Harman**, from "Moral Relativism," in Gilbert Harman and Judith Jarvis Thomson, eds., *Moral Relativism and Moral Objectivity* (Blackwell, 1996)

NO: **Louis P. Pojman**, from "The Case against Moral Relativism," in Louis P. Pojman and Lewis Vaughn, eds., *The Moral Life: An Introductory Reader in Ethics and Literature* (Oxford University Press, 2007)

ISSUE SUMMARY

YES: Philosopher Gilbert Harman argues that relativism is true for morality—much as Einstein proved it was true for motion. Just as motion always presupposes some framework in which it occurs (and something can be in motion relative to one person but not to another), morality too always presupposes some framework.

NO: Louis Pojman carefully distinguishes what he calls the diversity thesis—that moral rules differ from society to society—from ethical relativism. The diversity thesis is a straightforward description of what are acknowledged differences in the moral beliefs and practices of various human groups. But he argues that moral relativism does not follow from this diversity.

Many people are drawn to the idea that moral relativism is correct, but most people who have thought and written about this issue think that it is not. As a result, the supporters of moral relativism are in the minority. Among those, however, who think moral relativism is correct, Gilbert Harman's work—excerpted here—stands out.

Harman draws attention to what is probably one of the most common sources of the idea of moral relativism, namely, the fact that there is vast diversity among the moral views of different people at different times and places; furthermore, he emphasizes there is even a diversity of moral views among people in the very same society.

Diversity of views by itself proves nothing, and Harman acknowledges this. Consider the fact that among people of different times and places, there is also a diversity of views about many other things (e.g., about the origin of the earth, whether thunder is caused by Zeus, and so on). But no one would say that there is no truth of the matter, or that such matters are relative.

Of course, one might argue that *beliefs* are relative, at least in the following sense. If you time-traveled back to ancient Greece and asked people whether it was Zeus who caused thunder, you'd receive a large number of affirmative answers, whereas asking the same question of almost anyone today would most probably yield negative answers. So the *beliefs* might be in some sense relative. Both Harman and Pojman would agree that their own disagreement is not over what the beliefs of people would be but what the situation actually is.

As for the belief that Zeus causes thunder, we can probably chalk that one up to the lack of scientific sophistication of the ancient Greeks. But it is also worthwhile considering a more modern question—such as the origin and nature of black holes. There may be competing theories about black holes, and (unlike the case of thunder) the matter might not be settled at all. But no one would say that the nature of thunder or black holes is *relative*. There's a definite truth there to find out. In the case of thunder, we may know the truth; in the case of black holes, we may not. So here is a case in which we ourselves may lack the knowledge. But that doesn't mean that the matter is relative.

From Pojman's point of view, he could easily grant that the views of the people of different times and places are different. Nevertheless, he might say, what different people (e.g., the ancient Greeks and modern day scientists) say or believe about something may have little or nothing to do with the truth of the matter. Perhaps one of these groups is correct. Perhaps neither is correct. But in any case, the truth of the matter does not depend on what they might say or believe.

Likewise, an opponent of relativism, such as Pojman himself, will insist that the same holds true for moral belief and for physical belief. In any case, the moral objectivist (or non-relativist) will certainly hold that moral judgments are not dependent on cultural acceptance for their validity. So, it's possible for some people to promote a certain moral position, and for that moral position to be correct, while the majority of the population rejects the position. Pojman would admit that in some cases it's *hard* to see the validity, or lack of validity, behind a moral point of view. (Perhaps many controversial ideas—like those in this book—are *hard* in this sense.) Of course, in some cases it's quite easy to see whether or not we have moral validity. (For example, consider an obvious wrong like rape. No one defends rape, it's not controversial, and there is no issue about it in this book.)

In the following essays, Gilbert Harman first defends relativism, invoking, in fact, Einstein's relativistic theory about physical phenomena. Louis Pojman, a supporter of moral objectivism, then argues that moral relativism is not correct.

YES

Gilbert Harman

Moral Relativism

Introduction

Motion is a relative matter. Motion is always relative to a choice of spatio-temporal framework. Something that is moving in relation to one spatio-temporal framework can be at rest in relation to another. And no spatio-temporal framework can be singled out as the one and only framework that captures the truth about whether something is in motion.

According to Einstein's Theory of Relativity even an object's mass is relative to a choice of spatio-temporal framework. An object can have one mass in relation to one such framework and a different mass in relation to another. Again, there is no privileged spatio-temporal framework that determines the real mass of an object.

I am going to argue for a similar claim about moral right and wrong. That is, . . . I am going to defend *moral relativism*. I am going to argue that moral right and wrong (good and bad, justice and injustice, virtue and vice, etc.) are always relative to a choice of moral framework. What is morally right in relation to one moral framework can be morally wrong in relation to a different moral framework. And no moral framework is objectively privileged as the one true morality.

Einstein's relativistic conception of mass involves the following claim about the truth conditions of judgments of mass.

> (1) For the purposes of assigning truth conditions, a judgment of the form, *the mass of X is M* has to be understood as elliptical for a judgment of the form, *in relation to spatio-temporal framework F the mass of X is M.*

The word *elliptical* might be misleading here. Einstein's Theory of Relativity does not involve a claim about meaning or about what people intend to be claiming when they make judgments about an object's mass. The point is, rather, that the only truth there is in this area is relative truth.

Before Einstein, judgments about mass were not intended as relative judgments. But it would be mean-spirited to invoke an "error theory" and conclude that these pre-Einsteinian judgments were all false![1] Better to suppose that such a judgment was true to the extent that an object had the

From MORAL RELATIVISM AND MORAL OBJECTIVITY, 1996, pp. 3–6, 8–15, 17–19. Copyright © 1996 by Blackwell Publishing, Ltd. Reprinted by permission.

relevant mass in relation to a spatio-temporal framework that was conspicu-
ous to the person making the judgment, for example, a framework in which
that person was at rest.

Similarly, the moral relativism I will argue for is not a claim what people
mean by their moral judgments. Moral relativism does not claim that people
intend their moral judgments to be "elliptical" in the suggested way; just as
relativism about mass does not claim that people intend their judgments
about mass to make implicit reference to a spatio-temporal framework.

To a first approximation, moral relativism makes the following claim
about moral judgments.

> (2) For the purposes of assigning truth conditions, a judgment of the
> form, *it would be morally wrong of P to D,* has to be understood as
> elliptical for a judgment of the form, *in relation to moral framework
> M, it would be morally wrong of P to D.* Similarly for other moral
> judgments.[2]

As before, it is important not to put too much stress on the word *elliptical.*
The moral relativism I will argue for is no more a claim about what people
mean by their moral judgments than relativism about mass is a claim about
what people mean when they make judgments about mass. Moral relativism
does not claim that people intend their moral judgments to be "elliptical" in the
suggested way; just as relativism about mass does not claim that people intend
their judgments about mass to make implicit reference to a spatio-temporal
framework. . . .

⁓ ⦿ ⦿⁓

(2) is only part of a definition of moral relativism because it is important to
distinguish moral relativism both from moral absolutism on the one side and
from moral nihilism on the other side. Moral absolutism holds that there is a
single true morality. Moral relativism claims instead:

> (3) There is no single true morality. There are many different moral
> frameworks, none of which is more correct than the others.

Moral nihilism agrees with (3) and takes that conclusion to be a reason to
reject morality altogether including any sort of relative morality.

Moral nihilism can be compared to religious nihilism. Religious nihilism would be a natural response to the conclusion that there is no single true
religion but only many different religious outlooks, none of which is more
correct than the others. Such a conclusion would seem to provide a reason to
reject religion and religious judgments altogether, rather than a reason to
accept "religious relativism." It might then be possible to assign objective
truth conditions to religious judgments in relation to one or another religious
framework, but it is hard to see how such relative religious judgments could
play a serious role in religious practices. Moral nihilism argues that the same

is true of morality: given (3), there is no point to engaging in morality and moral judgment.

Moral relativism rejects moral nihilism and asserts instead

(4) Morality should not be abanboned.

Furthermore, moral relativism insists. . . .

(5) Relative moral judgments can continue to play a serious role in moral thinking. . . .

Explaining Moral Diversity

In this and the following section I argue that the following claim is a reasonable inference from the most plausible explanation of moral diversity.

> There is no single true morality. There are many different moral frameworks, none of which is more correct than the others.

I begin by mentioning data to be explained: the nature and extent of moral diversity.

Members of different cultures often have very different beliefs about right and wrong and often act quite differently on their beliefs. To take a seemingly trivial example, different cultures have different rules of politeness and etiquette: burping after eating is polite in one culture, impolite in another. Less trivially, some people are cannibals, others find cannibalism abhorrent.

The institution of marriage takes different forms in different societies. In some, a man is permitted to have several wives, in others bigamy is forbidden. More generally, the moral status of women varies greatly from one society to another in many different ways.

Some societies allow slavery, some have caste systems, which they take to be morally satisfactory, others reject both slavery and caste systems as grossly unjust.

It is unlikely that any nontrivial moral principles are universally accepted in all societies. The anthropologist George Silberbauer (1993, p. 15) is able to say only that "there are values which can be seen as common to nearly all societies," a remark limited by the phrases "can be seen as" and "nearly all." He further limits this claim by adding, "there are sometimes strong contrasts in the ways in which [these values] are expressed in precepts, principles and evaluations of behaviour."

Some say that there is a universally recognized central core of morality consisting of prohibitions against killing and harming others, against stealing, and against lying to others. Walzer (1987, p. 24) offers a more limited list of universal prohibitions: "murder, deception, betrayal and gross cruelty." It makes sense for Walzer to leave theft off the list, since some societies do not recognize private property, so they would have no rules against stealing.

(Without property, there can be no such thing as stealing. It is trivial to say that all societies that recognize private property have rules against stealing, because having such rules is a necessary condition of recognizing private property!)

It may be that *murder* is always considered wrong, if murder is defined as "wrongful killing." But few societies accept *general* moral prohibitions on killing or harming other people. There are societies in which a "master" is thought to have an absolute right to treat his slaves in any way he chooses, including arbitrarily beating and killing them. Similarly, there may be no limitations on what a husband can do to his wife, or a father to his young children. Infanticide is considered acceptable in some societies. When moral prohibitions on harming and killing and lying exist, they are sometimes supposed to apply only with respect to the local group and not with respect to outsiders. A person who is able successfully to cheat outsiders may be treated as an admirable person. Similarly for someone who is able to harm and kill outsiders.

Any universally accepted principle in this area must verge on triviality, saying, for example, that one must not kill or harm members of a certain group, namely the group of people one must not kill or harm![3]

Thomson (1990) appears to disagree. She states certain principles and says of them, "it is not at all clear how their negations could be accommodated into what would be recognizable as a moral code" (Thomson, 1990, p. 20). The principles she mentions are, "Other things being equal, one ought not act rudely," "Other things being equal, one ought to do what one promised," "Other things being equal, one ought not cause others pain," and "One ought not torture babies to death for fun."

On the contrary, it is clear that many moral codes have accommodated the negations of all these general principles by accepting instead principles restricted to insiders. And, if the phrase "other things being equal" is supposed to include a restriction to insiders, then triviality looms in the manner I have already mentioned.

Now, mere moral diversity is not a disproof of moral absolutism. Where there are differences in custom, there are often differences in circumstance. Indeed, differences in custom are themselves differences in circumstance that can affect what is right or wrong without entailing moral relativism. You do not need to be a moral relativist to recognize that in England it is wrong to drive on the right, whereas in France it is not wrong to drive on the right.

Even where circumstances are relevantly the same, mere differences in moral opinion no more refute moral absolutism than scientic differences in opinion about the cause of canal-like features on the surface of Mars establish that there is no truth to that matter.

But, even though the rejection of moral absolutism is not an immediate logical consequence of the existence of moral diversity, it is a reasonable inference from the most *plausible explanation* of the range of moral diversity that actually exists (Wong, 1984).

One of the most important things to explain about moral diversity is that it occurs not just between societies but also within societies and in a way that leads to seemingly intractable moral disagreements. In the contemporary United States, deep moral differences often seem to rest on differences in basic values rather than on differences in circumstance or information. Moral vegetarians, who believe that it is wrong to raise animals for food, exist in the same community as nonvegetarians, even in the same family. A disagreement between moral vegetarians and nonvegetarians can survive full discussion and full information and certainly appears to rest on a difference in the significance assigned to animals as compared with humans. Is there a nonrelative truth concerning the moral importance of animals? How might that "truth" be discovered?

In a similar way, disagreements about the moral acceptability of abortion or euthanasia survive extensive discussion and awareness of all relevant information about abortion. Such disagreements appear to depend on basic disagreements concerning the intrinsic value or "sanctity" of human life as compared with the value of the things that life makes possible, such as pleasurable experience and fulfilling activity (Dworkin, 1993).

There are similarly intractable disagreements about the relative value of artifacts of culture as compared with human life. Some people think that it is worse when terrorists bomb famous old museums than when they bomb crowded city streets; others feel that the loss of human life is worse than the loss of architecture and art. Again, there are disagreements about how much help one person should be prepared to give to others. Is it morally wrong to purchase a new record player instead of trying to help people who cannot afford food? Singer (1972) says yes; others say no. There are intractable disputes about whether it is morally worse to kill someone than it is to let that person die (Rachels, 1975) and about the relative importance of liberty versus equality in assessing the justice of social arrangements (Rawls, 1971; Nozick, 1972). . . .

It is hard to see how to account for all moral disagreements in terms of differences in situation or beliefs about nonmoral facts. Many moral disagreements seem to rest instead on basic differences in moral outlook.

Explaining Basic Differences

Suppose that many moral disagreements do indeed rest on basic differences in moral outlook rather than on differences in situation or beliefs about nonmoral facts. What explanation might there be for that?

An "absolutist" explanation might be that some people are simply not well placed to discover the right answers to moral questions.[4] The point to this response is not just that different people have different evidence but that what one makes of evidence depends on one's antecedent beliefs, so that starting out with some beliefs can help one reach the truth, whereas starting out with other beliefs can prevent one from reaching the truth. Rational change in belief tends to be conservative. It is rational to make the least change in one's view that is necessary in order to obtain greater coherence in what one believes (Goodman, 1965; Rawls, 1971; Harman, 1986). Different people with different starting points will rationally respond in different ways to the same evidence. There is no guarantee that people who start sufficiently far apart in belief will tend to converge in view as the evidence comes in. Someone whose initial view is relatively close to the truth may be led by the evidence to come closer to the truth. Someone who starts further away from the truth may be led even further away by the same evidence. Such a person is simply not well placed to discover the truth.

Here then is one absolutist's explanation of why moral disagreements that rest on basic differences in moral outlook cannot be rationally resolved, supposing that is in fact the case.

Moral relativists instead see an analogy with other kinds of relativity.

Consider the ancient question whether the earth moves or the sun moves. Here the relativistic answer is correct. Motion is a relative matter. Something can be in motion relative to one system of spatio-temporal coordinates and not in motion relative to another system. The particular motion an object exhibits will differ from one system to another. There is no such thing as absolute motion, apart from one or another system of coordinates.

A relativistic answer is also plausible in the moral case. Moral right and wrong are relative matters. A given act can be right with respect to one system of moral coordinates and wrong with respect to another system of moral coordinates. And nothing is absolutely right or wrong, apart from any system of moral coordinates.

By "a moral system of coordinates" I mean a set of values (standards, principles, etc.), perhaps on the model of the laws of one or another state. Whether something is wrong in relation to a given system of coordinates is to [be] determined by the system together with the facts of the case in something like the way in which whether something is illegal in a given jurisdiction is determined by the laws of that jurisdiction together with the facts of the case.

Why does it seem (to some people) that there are objective nonrelative facts about moral right and wrong? Well, why does it seem to some people that there [are] objective nonrelative facts about motion or mass? In the case of motion or mass, one particular system of coordinates is so salient that it seems to have a special status. Facts about motion or mass in relation to the salient system of coordinates are treated as nonrelational facts.

In a similar way, the system of moral coordinates that is determined by a person's own values can be so salient that it can seem to that person to have a special status. Facts about what is right or wrong in relation to that system of coordinates can be misidentified as objective nonrelational facts.

To be sure, the system of moral coordinates that is determined by a given person's values cannot in general be *identified* with all and only exactly those very values. Otherwise a person could never be mistaken about moral issues (in relation to the relevant system of coordinates) except by being mistaken about his or her own values!

For the same reason, a legal system cannot be simply identified with existing legislation, the record of prior court decisions, and the principles currently accepted by judges. Otherwise legislation could not be unconstitutional and judges could not be mistaken in the legal principles they accept or the decisions they reach. . . .

Evaluative Relativity: "Good For"

We might compare the relativity of moral wrongness with the way in which something that is good for one person may not be good for another person. If Tom has bet on a horse that runs well in the rain and Sue has bet on a horse that does not run well in the rain, then rain is good for Tom and bad for Sue. This is an uncontroversial example of evaluative relativity. The rain is good in relation to Tom's goals and bad in relation to Sue's.

Similarly, abortion can be immoral with respect to (the moral coordinates determined by) Tom's values and not immoral with respect to Sue's. Moral relativists sometimes express this by saying that abortion is immoral "for Tom" and not immoral "for Sue." Of course, what is meant here is not that abortion is bad for Tom but not bad for Sue in the sense of harmful to one but not the other, not is it just to say that Tom may think abortion immoral and Sue may think it moral. The rain might be good for Tom even if he doesn't realize it and abortion might be immoral for Tom whether or not he realizes that it is.

Notice, by the way that a speaker does not always have to make explicit for whom a given situation is good. In particular, if Max has bet on the same horse as Alice and he is speaking to Alice, out of the hearing of Sue, he can say simply. "This rain is bad," meaning that it is bad for him and Alice.

Similarly, a moral relativist talking to another moral relativist can suppress reference to a particular set of values if the judgment is supposed to hold in relation both to the (moral coordinates determined by the) values accepted by the speaker and to the (moral coordinates determined by the) values accepted by the hearer. If Sue and Arthur both have values with the same implications for abortion, and Tom isn't listening, Sue might say simply, "Abortion is not morally wrong", meaning that it is not wrong in relation to her and Arthur's values. It is not wrong for either of them. . . .

Relativity Theory

Something that is good for some people is bad for others, indifferent to yet others. Moral relativism says that the same is true of moral values and moral norms. According to moral relativism whether something is morally good, right, or just is always relative to a set of moral coordinates, a set of values or moral standards, a certain moral point of view. . . .

[Moral] relativism makes the following claim about moral judgments:

> For the purpose of assigning truth conditions, a judgment of the form, it would be morally wrong of P to D, has to be understood as elliptical for a judgment of the form, in relation to moral framework M, it would be morally wrong of P to D. Similarly for other moral judgments.

Recall that moral relativism is not by itself a claim about meaning. It does not say that speakers always *intend* their moral judgments to be relational in this respect. It is clear that many speakers do not. Moral relativism is a thesis about how things are and a thesis about how things aren't! Moral relativism claims that there is no such thing as objectively absolute good, absolute right, or absolute justice; there is only what is good, right, or just in relation to this or that moral framework. What someone takes to be absolute rightness is only rightness in relation to (a system of moral coordinates determined by) that person's values.

Earlier, I compared moral relativism with Einstein's theory of relativity in physics, which says that physical magnitudes, like mass, length, or temporal duration, are relative to a frame of reference, so that two events that are simultaneous with respect to one frame of reference can fail to be simultaneous with respect to another. In saying this, Einstein's theory does not make a claim about speakers' intentions. It does not claim that speakers intend to be making relational judgments when they speak of mass or simultaneity. The claim is, rather, that there is no such thing as absolute simultaneity or absolute mass. There is only simultaneity or mass with respect to one or another frame of reference. What someone might take to be absolute magnitudes are really relative magnitudes: magnitudes that are relative to that person's frame of reference.

Imagine a difference of opinion about whether event E precedes event F. According to Einstein's theory of relativity, there may be no uniform answer to this question: perhaps, in relation to one framework E precedes F, while in relation to a different framework E does not precede F.

Similarly, consider a moral disagreement about whether we are right to raise animals for food. Moral relativism holds that there is no uniform answer to this question: in relation to (the system of moral coordinates determined by) one person's values it is permissible to raise animals for food and in relation to (the system of moral coordinates determined by) a different person's values it is not permissible to raise animals for food. To repeat: what someone takes to be absolute rightness is only rightness in relation to (a system of moral coordinates determined by) that person's values.

Moral relativism does not claim that moral differences by themselves entail moral relativism, any more than Einstein claimed that differences in opinion about simultaneity by themselves entailed relativistic physics. We have to consider what differences there are or could be and why this might be so. How are we to explain the sorts of moral differences that actually occur? Can we seriously suppose that there is an answer to the question about the justice of our treatment of animals that is independent of one or another moral framework? What is the best explanation of differences in this and other areas of seeming intractability?

I emphasize again that moral relativism does not identify what is right in relation to a given moral framework with whatever is taken to be right by those who accept that framework. That would be like saying Einstein's theory of relativity treats two events as simultaneous with respect to a given coordinate system if people at rest with respect to the coordinate system believe the events are simultaneous.

Notes

1. Mackie, 1977, chapter one, advocates an error theory of this sort about ordinary moral judgments.

2. So, for example, a judgment of the form, *P ought morally to D,* has to be understood as elliptical for a judgment of the form, *in relation to moral framework M, P ought morally to D.*

3. There will be universal truths about moralities just as there are universal truths about spatio-temporal frameworks. Perhaps all spatio-temporal frameworks must admit of motion and rest. And perhaps all moralities have some rules against killing, harm, and deception. The existence of universal features of spatio-temporal frameworks is compatible with and is even required by Einstein's Theory of Relativity and the existence of universal features of morality is compatible with moral relativism.

4. I am indebted to Nicholas Sturgeon for this suggestion.

Bibliography

Dworkin, R. (1993). *Life's Dominion,* New York: Knopf.

Goodman, N. (1965). *Fact, Fiction, and Forecast.* Cambridge, Mass.: Harvard University Press.

Harman, G. (1986). *Change in View: Principles of Reasoning,* Cambridge, Massachusetts: Bradford Books/MIT Press.

Mackie, J. (1977). *Ethics: Inventing Right and Wrong,* London: Penguin Books.

Nozick, R. (1972). *Anarchy, State, and Utopia,* New York: Basic Books.

Rachels, J. (1975). "Active and passive euthanasia," *New England Journal of Medicine* **292**.

Rawls, J. (1971). *A Theory of Justice,* Cambridge, Mass.: Harvard University Press.

Silberbauer, G. (1993). "Ethics in small-scale societies," *A Companion to Ethics,* ed. Peter Singer, Oxford: Blackwell.

Singer, P. (1972). "Famine, affluence, and morality," *Philosophy and Public Affairs* **1**.

Thomson, J. (1990). *The Realm of Rights,* Cambridge, Mass.: Harvard University Press.

Walzer, M. (1987). *Interpretation and Social Criticism.* Cambridge, Massachusetts: Harvard University Press.

Wong, D. B. (1984). *Moral Relativity,* Berkeley, California: University of California Press.

Louis P. Pojman

 **NO**

The Case Against Moral Relativism

"Who's to Judge What's Right or Wrong?"

> Like many people, I have always been instinctively a moral relativist. As far
> back as I can remember . . . it has always seemed to be obvious that the dic-
> tates of morality arise from some sort of convention or understanding
> among people, that different people arrive at different understandings, and
> that there are no basic moral demands that apply to everyone. This seemed
> so obvious to me I assumed it was everyone's instinctive view, or at least
> everyone who gave the matter any thought in this day and age.
>
> —Gilbert Harman[1]

> Ethical relativism is the doctrine that the moral rightness and wrongness
> of actions vary from society to society and that there are not absolute uni-
> versal moral standards on all men at all times. Accordingly, it holds that
> whether or not it is right for an individual to act in a certain way depends
> on or is relative to the society to which he belongs.
>
> —John Ladd[2]

Gilbert Harman's intuitions about the self-evidence of ethical relativism contrast strikingly with Plato's or Kant's equal certainty about the truth of objectivism, the doctrine that universally valid or true ethical principles exist. . . . "Two
things fill the soul with ever new and increasing wonder and reverence the
oftener and more fervently reflection ponders on it: the starry heavens above
and the moral law within," wrote Kant. On the basis of polls taken in my ethics
and introduction to philosophy classes in recent years, Harman's views may
signal a shift in contemporary society's moral understanding. The polls show
a two-to-one ratio in favor of moral relativism over moral absolutism, with
fewer than five percent of the respondents recognizing that a third position
between these two polar opposites might exist. Of course, I'm not suggesting
that all of these students had a clear understanding of what relativism entails,
for many who said they were relativists also contended in the same polls that
abortion except to save the mother's life is always wrong, that capital punishment is always wrong, or that suicide is never morally permissible. . . .

1. An Analysis of Relativism

Let us examine the theses contained in John Ladd's succinct statement on ethical (conventional) relativism that appears at the beginning of this essay. If we analyze it, we derive the following argument:

1. Moral rightness and wrongness of actions vary from society to society, so there are no universal moral standards held by all societies.
2. Whether or not it is right for individuals to act in a certain way depends on (or is relative to) the society to which they belong.
3. Therefore, there are no absolute or objective moral standards that apply to all people everywhere.

1. The first thesis, which may be called the *diversity thesis,* is simply a description that acknowledges the fact that moral rules differ from society to society. The Spartans of ancient Greece and the Dobu of New Guinea believe that stealing is morally right, but we believe it is wrong. The Roman father had the power of life and death . . . over his children, whereas we condemn parents for abusing their children. A tribe in East Africa once threw deformed infants to the hippopotamuses, and in ancient Greece and Rome infants were regularly exposed, while we abhor infanticide. Ruth Benedict describes a tribe in Melanesia that views cooperation and kindness as vices, whereas we see them as virtues. While in ancient Greece, Rome, China and Korea parricide was condemned as "the most execrable of crimes," among Northern Indians aged persons, persons who were no longer capable of walking, were left alone to starve. Among the California Gallinomero, when fathers became feeble, a burden to their sons, "the poor old wretch is not infrequently thrown down on his back and securely held while a stick is placed across his throat, and two of them seat themselves on the ends of it until he ceases to breathe."[3] Sexual practices vary over time and place. Some cultures permit homosexual behavior, while others condemn it. Some cultures practice polygamy, while others view it as immoral. Some cultures condone while others condemn premarital sex. Some cultures accept cannibalism, while the very idea revolts us. Some West African tribes perform clitoridectomies on girls, whereas we deplore such practices. Cultural relativism is well documented, and "custom is the king o'er all." There may or may not be moral principles that are held in common by every society, but if there are any, they seem to be few at best. Certainly it would be very difficult to derive any single "true" morality by observing various societies' moral standards.

2. The second thesis, *the dependency thesis,* asserts that individual acts are right or wrong depending on the nature of the society from which they emanate. Morality does not occur in a vacuum, and what is considered morally right or wrong must be seen in a context that depends on the goals, wants, beliefs, history, and environment of the society in question. As William G. Sumner says,

> We learn the morals as unconsciously as we learn to walk and hear and breathe, and [we] never know any reason why the [morals] are what they

are. The justification of them is that when we wake to consciousness of life
we find them facts which already hold us in the bonds of tradition, custom,
and habit.[4]

Trying to see things from an independent, noncultural point of view
would be like taking out our eyes in order to examine their contours and
qualities. There is no "innocent eye." We are simply culturally determined
beings.

We could, of course, distinguish between a weak and a strong thesis of
dependency, for the nonrelativist can accept a certain degree of relativity in the
way moral principles are *applied* in various cultures, depending on beliefs, history, and environment. For example, Jewish men express reverence for God by
covering their heads when entering places of worship, whereas Christian men
uncover their heads when entering places of worship. Westerners shake hands
upon greeting each other, whereas Hindus place their hands together and point
them toward the person to be greeted. Both sides adhere to principles of reverence and respect but apply them differently. But the ethical relativist must
maintain a stronger thesis, one that insists that the moral principles themselves
are products of the cultures and may vary from society to society." The ethical
relativist contends that even beyond environmental factors and differences in
beliefs, a fundamental disagreement exists among societies. . . .

In a sense we all live in radically different worlds. But the relativist wants
to go further and maintain that there is something conventional about *any*
morality, so that every morality really depends on a level of social acceptance.
Not only do various societies adhere to different moral systems, but the very
same society could (and often does) change its moral views over place and
time. For example, the majority of people in the southern United States now
view slavery as immoral, whereas one hundred and forty years ago they did
not. Our society's views on divorce, sexuality, abortion, and assisted suicide
have changed somewhat as well—and they are still changing.

3. The conclusion that there are no absolute or objective moral standards binding on all people follows from the first two propositions. Combining cultural relativism (*the diversity thesis*) with *the dependency thesis* yields
ethical relativism in its classic form. If there are different moral principles
from culture to culture and if all morality is rooted in culture, then it follows
that there are no universal moral principles that are valid (or true) for all
cultures and peoples at all times.

2. Subjectivism

Some people think that this conclusion is still too tame, and they maintain that
morality is dependent not on the society but rather on the individual. As my
students sometimes maintain, "Morality is in the eye of the beholder." They treat
morality like taste or aesthetic judgments—person relative. This form of moral
subjectivism has the sorry consequence that it makes morality a very useless
concept, for, on its premises, little or no interpersonal criticism or judgment is
logically possible. Suppose that you are repulsed by observing John torturing
a child. You cannot condemn him if one of his principles is "torture little

children for the fun of it." The only basis for judging him wrong might be that he was a hypocrite who condemned others for torturing. But suppose that another of his principles is that hypocrisy is morally permissible (for him); thus we cannot condemn him for condemning others for doing what he does.

On the basis of subjectivism Adolf Hitler and the serial murderer Ted Bundy could be considered as moral as Gandhi, so long as each lived by his own standards, whatever those might be. . . .

Notions of good and bad, or right and wrong, cease to have interpersonal evaluative meaning. We might be revulsed by the views of Ted Bundy, but that is just a matter of taste. A student might not like it when her teacher gives her an F on a test paper, while he gives another student an A for a similar paper, but there is no way to criticize him for injustice, because justice is not one of his chosen principles.

Absurd consequences follow from subjectivism. If it is correct, then morality reduces to aesthetic tastes about which there can be neither argument nor interpersonal judgment. Although many students say they espouse subjectivism, there is evidence that it conflicts with other of their moral views. They typically condemn Hitler as an evil man for his genocidal policies. A contradiction seems to exist between subjectivism and the very concept of morality, which it is supposed to characterize, for morality has to do with *proper* resolution of interpersonal conflict and the amelioration of the human predicament. . . . Whatever else it does, morality has a minimal aim of preventing a Hobbesian state of nature . . . , wherein life is "solitary, poor, nasty, brutish, and short. But if so, subjectivism is no help at all, for it rests neither on social agreement of principle (as the conventionalist maintains) nor on an objectively independent set of norms that bind all people for the common good. If there were only one person on earth, there would be no occasion for morality, because there wouldn't be any interpersonal conflicts to resolve or others whose suffering he or she would have a duty to ameliorate. Subjectivism implicitly assumes something of this solipsism, an atomism in which isolated individuals make up separate universes.

Subjectivism treats individuals like billiard balls on a societal pool table where they meet only in radical collisions, each aimed at his or her own goal and striving to do in the others before they themselves are done in. This atomistic view of personality is belied by the facts that we develop in families and mutually dependent communities in which we share a common language, common institutions, and similar rituals and habits, and that we often feel one another's joys and sorrows. As the poet John Donne wrote, "No man is an island, entire of itself; every man is a piece of the continent."

Radical individualistic ethical relativism is incoherent. If so, it follows that the only plausible view of ethical relativism must be one that grounds morality in the group or culture. This form is called *conventionalism.*

3. Conventionalism

Conventional ethical relativism, the view that there are no objective moral principles but that all valid moral principles are justified (or are made true) by virtue of their cultural acceptance, recognizes the social nature of morality. That is precisely its power and virtue. It does not seem subject to the same absurd consequences which plague subjectivism. Recognizing the importance of our social environment in generating customs and beliefs, many people suppose that ethical relativism is the correct metaethical theory. Furthermore, they are drawn to it for its liberal philosophical stance. It seems to be an enlightened response to the sin of ethnocentricity, and it seems to entail or strongly imply an attitude of tolerance toward other cultures. Anthropologist Ruth Benedict says, that in recognizing ethical relativity, "We shall arrive at a more realistic social faith, accepting as grounds of hope and as new bases for tolerance the coexisting and equally valid patterns of life which mankind has created for itself from the raw materials of existence."[5] The most famous of those holding this position is the anthropologist Melville Herskovits, who argues even more explicitly than Benedict that ethical relativism entails intercultural tolerance.

1. If morality is relative to its culture, then there is no independent basis for criticizing the morality of any other culture but one's own.
2. If there is no independent way of criticizing any other culture, we ought to be *tolerant* of the moralities of other cultures.
3. Morality is relative to its culture. Therefore,
4. We ought to be *tolerant* of the moralities of other cultures.[6]

Tolerance is certainly a virtue, but is this a good argument for it? I think not. If morality simply is relative to each culture, then if the culture in question does not have a principle of tolerance, its members have no obligation to be tolerant. Herskovits seems to be treating the *principle of tolerance* as the one exception to his relativism. He seems to be treating it as an absolute moral principle. But from a relativistic point of view there is no more reason to be tolerant than to be intolerant and neither stance is objectively morally better than the other.

Not only do relativists fail to offer a basis for criticizing those who are intolerant, but they cannot rationally criticize anyone who espouses what they might regard as a heinous principle. If, as seems to be the case, valid criticism supposes an objective or impartial standard, relativists cannot morally criticize anyone outside their own culture. Adolf Hitler's genocidal actions, so long as they are culturally accepted, are as morally legitimate as Mother Teresa's works of mercy. If Conventional Relativism is accepted, racism, genocide of unpopular minorities, oppression of the poor, slavery, and even the advocacy of war for its own sake are as equally moral as their opposites. And if a subculture decided that starting a nuclear war was somehow morally acceptable, we could not morally criticize these people. Any actual morality, whatever its content, is as valid as every other, and more valid than ideal moralities—since the latter aren't adhered to by any culture.

There are other disturbing consequences of ethical relativism. It seems to entail that reformers are always (morally) wrong since they go against the tide of cultural standards. William Wilberforce was wrong in the eighteenth century to oppose slavery; the British were immoral in opposing *suttee* in India (the burning of widows, which is now illegal in India). The early Christians were wrong in refusing to serve in the Roman army or to bow down to Caesar, since the majority in the Roman Empire believed that these two acts were moral duties. In fact, Jesus himself was immoral in breaking the law of His day by healing on the Sabbath day and by advocating the principles of the Sermon on the Mount, since it is clear that few in His time (or in ours) accepted them.

Yet we normally feel just the opposite, that the reformer is a courageous innovator who is right, who has the truth, against the mindless majority. Sometimes the individual must stand alone with the truth, risking social censure and persecution. . . . Yet if relativism is correct, the opposite is necessarily the case. Truth is with the crowd and error with the individual. . . .

There is an even more basic problem with the notion that morality is dependent on cultural acceptance for its validity. The problem is that the notion of a *culture* or *society* is notoriously difficult to define. This is especially so in a pluralistic society like our own where the notion seems to be vague with unclear boundary lines. One person may belong to several societies (subcultures) with different value emphases and arrangements of principles. A person may belong to the nation as a single society with certain values of patriotism, honor, courage, laws (including some which are controversial but have majority acceptance, such as the current law on abortion). But he or she may also belong to a church which opposes some of the laws of the State. He may also be an integral member of a socially mixed community where different principles hold sway, and he may belong to clubs and a family where still other rules are adhered to. Relativism would seem to tell us that where he is a member of societies with conflicting moralities he must be judged both wrong and not-wrong whatever he does. For example, if Mary is a U.S. citizen and a member of the Roman Catholic Church, she is wrong (qua Catholic) if she chooses to have an abortion and not-wrong (qua citizen of the U.S.A.) if she acts against the teaching of the Church on abortion. As a member of a racist university fraternity, KKK, John has no obligation to treat his fellow Black student as an equal, but as a member of the university community itself (where the principle of equal rights is accepted) he does have the obligation; but as a member of the surrounding community (which may reject the principle of equal rights) he again has no such obligation; but then again as a member of the nation at large (which accepts the principle) he is obligated to treat his fellow with respect. What is the morally right thing for John to do? The question no longer makes much sense in this moral Babel. It has lost its action-guiding function.

Perhaps the relativist would adhere to a principle which says that in such cases the individual may choose which group to belong to as primary. If Mary chooses to have an abortion, she is choosing to belong to the general society relative to that principle. And John must likewise choose among groups. The trouble with this option is that it seems to lead back to counter-intuitive results. If Murder Mike of Murder, Incorporated, feels like killing Bank President Ortcutt and wants to feel good about it, he identifies with the Murder, Incorporated society rather than the general public morality. Does this justify the killing? In fact, couldn't one justify anything simply by forming a small subculture that approved of it? Ted Bundy would be morally pure in raping and killing innocents simply by virtue of forming a little coterie. How large must the group be in order to be a legitimate subculture or society?

Does it need ten or fifteen people? How about just three? Come to think about it, why can't my burglary partner and I found our own society with a morality of its own? Of course, if my partner dies, I could still claim that I was acting from an originally social set of norms. But why can't I dispense with the interpersonal agreements altogether and invent my own morality—since morality, on this view, is only an invention anyway? Conventionalist relativism seems to reduce to subjectivism. And subjectivism leads, as we have seen, to moral solipsism, to the demise of morality altogether. . . .

. . . I don't think you can stop the move from conventionalism to subjectivism. The essential force of the validity of the chosen moral principle is that it is dependent on *choice.* The conventionalist holds that it is the choice of the group, but why should I accept the group's silly choice, when my own is better (for me)? Why should anyone give such august authority to a culture of society? If this is all morality comes to, why not reject it altogether—even though one might want to adhere to its directives when others are looking in order to escape sanctions?

4. A Critique of Ethical Relativism

However, while we may fear the demise of morality, as we have known it, this in itself may not be a good reason for rejecting relativism. That is, for judging it false. Alas, truth may not always be edifying. But the consequences of this position are sufficiently alarming to prompt us to look carefully for some weakness in the relativist's argument. So let us examine the premises and conclusion listed at the beginning of this essay as the three theses of relativism.

1. *The Diversity Thesis.* What is considered morally right and wrong varies from society to society, so that there are no moral principles accepted by all societies.
2. *The Dependency Thesis.* All moral principles derive their validity from cultural acceptance.
3. *Ethical Relativism.* Therefore, there are no universally valid moral principles, objective standards which apply to all people everywhere and at all times.

Does any one of these seem problematic? Let us consider the first thesis, the diversity thesis, which we have also called cultural relativism. Perhaps there is not as much diversity as anthropologists like Sumner and Benedict suppose. One can also see great similarities between the moral codes of various cultures. E. O. Wilson has identified over a score of common features,[7] and before him Clyde Kluckhohn has noted much significant common ground between cultures.

> Every culture has a concept of murder, distinguishing this from execution, killing in war, and other "justifiable homicides." The notions of incest and other regulations upon sexual behavior, the prohibitions upon untruth under defined circumstances, of restitution and reciprocity, of mutual obligations between parents and children—these and many other moral concepts are altogether universal.[8]

Colin Turnbull's description of the sadistic, semidisplaced, disintegrating Ik in Northern Uganda supports the view that a people without principles of kindness, loyalty, and cooperation will degenerate into a Hobbesian state of nature.[9] But he has also produced evidence that underneath the surface of this dying society, there is a deeper moral code from a time when the tribe flourished, which occasionally surfaces and shows its nobler face.

On the other hand, there is enormous cultural diversity and many societies have radically different moral codes. Cultural relativism seems to be a fact, but, even if it is, it does not by itself establish the truth of ethical relativism. Cultural diversity in itself is neutral between theories. For the objectivist could concede complete cultural relativism, but still defend a form of universalism; for he or she could argue that some cultures simply lack correct moral principles.

On the other hand, a denial of complete cultural relativism (i.e., an admission of some universal principles) does not disprove ethical relativism. For even if we did find one or more universal principles, this would not prove that they had any objective status. We could still *imagine* a culture that was an exception to the rule and be unable to criticize it. So the first premise doesn't by itself imply ethical relativism and its denial doesn't disprove ethical relativism.

We turn to the crucial second thesis, the dependency thesis. Morality does not occur in a vacuum, but rather what is considered morally right or wrong must be seen in a context, depending on the goals, wants, beliefs, history, and environment of the society in question. We distinguished a *weak* and a *strong* thesis of dependency. The weak thesis says that the application of principles depends on the particular cultural predicament, whereas the strong thesis affirms that the principles themselves depend on that predicament. The nonrelativist can accept a certain relativity in the way moral principles are *applied* in various cultures, depending on beliefs, history, and environment. For example, a raw environment with scarce natural resources may justify the Eskimos' brand of euthanasia to the objectivist, who in another environment would consistently reject that practice. The members of a tribe in the Sudan throw their deformed children into the river because of their belief that such infants *belong* to the hippopotamus, the god of the river. We believe that they have a false belief about this, but the point is that the same principles of respect for property and respect for human life are operative in these contrary practices. They differ with us only in belief, not in substantive moral principle. This is an illustration of how nonmoral beliefs (e.g., deformed children belong to the hippopotamus) when applied to common moral principles (e.g., give to each his due) generate different actions in different cultures. In our own culture the difference in the nonmoral belief about the status of a fetus generates opposite moral prescriptions. The major difference between pro-choicers and pro-lifers is not whether we should kill persons but whether fetuses are really persons. It is a debate about the facts of the matter, not the principle of killing innocent persons.

So the fact that moral principles are weakly dependent doesn't show that ethical relativism is valid. In spite of this weak dependency on nonmoral factors, there could still be a set of general moral norms applicable to all cultures and even recognized in most, which are disregarded at a culture's own expense.

What the relativist needs is a strong thesis of dependency, that somehow all principles are essentially cultural inventions. But why should we choose to view morality this way? Is there anything to recommend the strong thesis over the weak thesis of dependency? The relativist may argue that in fact we don't have an obvious impartial standard from which to judge. "Who's to say which culture is right and which is wrong?" But this seems to be dubious. We can reason and perform thought experiments in order to make a case for one system over another. We may not be able to *know* with certainty that our moral beliefs are closer to the truth than those of another culture or those of others within our own culture, but we may be *justified* in believing that they are. If we can be closer to the truth regarding factual or scientific matters, why can't we be closer to the truth on moral matters? Why can't a culture be simply confused or wrong about its moral perceptions? Why can't we say that the society like the Ik which sees nothing wrong with enjoying watching its own children fall into fires is less moral in that regard than the culture that cherishes children and grants them protection and equal rights? To take such a stand is not to commit the fallacy of ethnocentricism, for we are seeking to derive principles through critical reason, not simply uncritical acceptance of one's own mores.

Many relativists embrace relativism as a default position. Objectivism makes no sense to them. I think this is Ladd and Harman's position, as the latter's quotation at the beginning of this article seems to indicate. Objectivism has insuperable problems, so the answer must be relativism. . . .

In conclusion I have argued (1) that cultural relativism (the fact that there are cultural differences regarding moral principles) does not entail ethical relativism (the thesis that there are no objectively valid universal moral principles) [and] (2) that the dependency thesis (that morality derives its legitimacy from individual cultural acceptance) is mistaken. . . .

So "Who's to judge what's right or wrong?" We are. We are to do so on the basis of the best reasoning we can bring forth, and with sympathy and understanding.[10]

Notes

1. Gilbert Harman, "Is There a Single True Morality?" in *Morality, Reason and Truth*, eds. David Copp and David Zimmerman (Rowman & Allenheld, 1984).

2. John Ladd, *Ethical Relativism* (Wadsworth, 1973).

3. Reported by the anthropologist Powers, *Tribes of California*, p. 178. Quoted in E. Westermarck, *Origin and Development of Moral Ideals* (London, 1906), p. 386. This work is a mine of examples of cultural diversity.

4. W. G. Sumner, *Folkways* (Ginn & Co., 1906), p. 76.

5. Ruth Benedict, *Patterns of Culture* (New American Library, 1934), p, 257.

6. Melville Herskovits, *Cultural Relativism* (Random House, 1972).

7. E. O. Wilson, *On Human Nature* (Bantam Books, 1979), pp. 22–23.

8. Clyde Kluckhohn, "Ethical Relativity: Sic et Non," *Journal of Philosophy*, LII (1955).

9. Colin Turnbull, *The Mountain People* (New York: Simon & Schuster, 1972).

10. Bruce Russell, Morton Winston, Edward Sherline, and an anonymous reviewer made important criticisms on earlier versions of this article, issuing in this revision.

POSTSCRIPT

Is Moral Relativism Correct?

One important feature about this issue is that there is a difference between the well-known and widely recognized facts about moral diversity and the claim of moral relativism. Harman's claim goes beyond the observed facts about moral diversity. He claims that moral diversity can be *explained* by moral relativism; it's not identical with it. In fact, he admits that the existence of moral diversity doesn't by itself disprove moral absolutism.

Harman draws an analogy between physical (or Einsteinian) relativism and moral relativism. Just as Einstein has showed that there is no absolute motion, and something may be in motion according to one framework but not according to another, Harman suggests that there is no such thing as absolute good, but that something can be good according to one framework but not another.

If Harman is correct about good and bad (and right and wrong, etc.), then it is very important to be able to identify the *frameworks* that he says are involved. Note that these are not simply people's moral beliefs—as if believing that something is good would make it good! (Compare, for example, the idea of believing that something is in motion—the belief doesn't mean that it's really in motion.) Harman specifically rejects the idea of identifying the framework with a person's own values. If we did make such an identification, then—unless a person could be mistaken about his or her own values—we would all be right whenever we made moral claims. We'd be infallible when it comes to moral belief—but this is absurd. *Some* moral claims are mistaken. (One way to see this is to imagine that you held some moral belief in the past that you now regard as wrong; this is quite different from merely liking or disliking something, where your tastes could change without "right" and "wrong" coming in to it at all.) Harman draws an analogy to law. The law is not infallible either. The view of "separate but equal" may have been the law in the past, but we see now that this is wrong, and we have changed our ways.

An objectivist like Pojman would want to focus on the part that says "we see that this is wrong." In order to see that something is wrong, it would have to be objectively wrong. Sometimes—and civil rights may provide a good example—we do see that something in the law that needs to be changed. The Constitution, which is the highest law in the land, has been amended numerous times. There are several different possibilities as to what is going on when we amend the Constitution. One possibility is that things just come into fashion and go out of fashion. At one time, the Constitution allowed for slavery, for instance, and now it doesn't. Is slavery something that just came into fashion at one time and then passed out of fashion at another? A second possibility is that slavery was thought to be objectively wrong—and so egregiously wrong that it need to be ruled out by the Constitution.

In some sense, Harman would be prepared for these considerations, since the Constitution could function similarly to his idea of a *framework*. He runs into a problem when we are changing frameworks (for example, when the Constitution is amended, or even when the Congress is just talking about the value of amending it). When we are "in between frameworks," as it were, relativism seems to make little sense.

Another difficulty comes about when we have a great number of frameworks, for example, as we do in a multicultural and pluralistic society. Here, any single individual may look at things in terms of religious, political, regional, generational, etc. frameworks. Someone may simultaneously belong to groups that use a number of frameworks. And not all of these frameworks will agree. Relativism seems to provide no way to get a handle on the kind of uncertainty that a person may have in choosing between the ways of his church, his family, his friends, his country, etc.

Strangely, it is just this kind of uncertainly in the face of diverse views that has cast doubt on the idea of moral objectivity, but moral relativism seems to fare no better.

Issues associated with moral relativism and absolutism, and the relation of all this to cultural variation and diversity, are quite complex. See Peter Kreeft, *A Refutation of Moral Relativism: Interviews With an Absolutist* (Ignatius Press, 1999); John Cook, *Morality and Cultural Differences* (Oxford University Press, 1999); Paul K. Moser and Thomas L. Carson, eds., *Moral Relativism: A Reader* (Oxford University Press, 2000); Neil Levy, *Moral Relativism: A Short Introduction* (OneWorld Publications, 2002); and Maria Baghramian, *Relativism* (Routledge, 2004; and Michael C. Brannigan, *Ethics across Cultures* (McGraw-Hill, 2005).

ISSUE 2

Does Morality Need Religion?

YES: C. Stephen Layman, from *The Shape of the Good: Christian Reflections on the Foundations of Ethics* (University of Notre Dame Press, 1991)

NO: John Arthur, from "Religion, Morality, and Conscience," in John Arthur, ed., *Morality and Moral Controversies,* 4th ed. (Prentice Hall, 1996)

ISSUE SUMMARY

YES: Philosopher C. Stephen Layman argues that morality makes the most sense from a theistic perspective and that a purely secular perspective is insufficient. The secular perspective, Layman asserts, does not adequately deal with secret violations, and it does not allow for the possibility of fulfillment of people's deepest needs in an afterlife.

NO: Philosopher John Arthur counters that morality is logically independent of religion, although there are historical connections. Religion, he believes, is not necessary for moral guidance or moral answers; morality is social.

There is a widespread feeling that morality and religion are connected. One view is that religion provides a ground for morality, so without religion there is no morality. Thus, a falling away from religion implies a falling away from morality.

Such thoughts have troubled many people. The Russian novelist Dosoyevsky (1821–1881) wrote, "If there is no God, then everything is permitted." Many Americans today also believe that religious faith is important. They often maintain that even if doctrines and dogmas cannot be known for certain, religion nevertheless leads to morality and good behavior. President Dwight D. Eisenhower is reputed to have said that everyone should have a religious faith but that it did not matter what that faith was. And many daily newspapers throughout the country advise their readers to attend the church or synagogue of their choice. Apparently, the main reason why people think it is important to subscribe to a religion is that only in this way will one be

24

able to attain morality. If there is no God, then everything is permitted and there is moral chaos. Moral chaos can be played out in societies and, on a smaller scale, within the minds of individuals. Thus, if you do not believe in God, then you will confront moral chaos; you will be liable to permit (and permit yourself to do) anything, and you will have no moral bearings at all.

Such a view seems to face several problems, however. For example, what are we to say of the morally good atheist or of the morally good but completely nonreligious person? A true follower of the view that morality derives from religion might reply that we are simply begging the question if we believe that such people *could* be morally good. Such people might do things that are morally right and thus might *seem* good, the reply would go, but they would not be acting for the right reason (obedience to God). Such people would not have the same anchor or root for their seemingly moral attitudes that religious persons do.

Another problem for the view that links morality with religion comes from the following considerations: If you hold this view, what do you say of devoutly religious people who belong to religious traditions and who support moralities that are different from your own? If morality is indeed derived from religion, if different people are thus led to follow different moralities, and if the original religions are not themselves subject to judgment, then it is understandable how different people arrive at different moral views. But the views will still be different and perhaps even incompatible. If so, the statement that morality derives from religion must mean that one can derive *a* morality from *a* religion (and not that one derives morality itself from religion). The problem is that by allowing this variation among religions and moralities back into the picture, we seem to allow moral chaos back in, too.

The view that what God commands is good, what God prohibits is evil, and without divine commands and prohibitions nothing is either good or bad in itself is called the *divine command theory*, or the *divine imperative view*. This view resists the recognition of any source of good or evil that is not tied to criteria or standards of God's own creation. Such a recognition is thought to go against the idea of God's omnipotence. A moral law that applied to God but was not of God's own creation would seem to limit God in a way in which he cannot be limited. But, on the other hand, this line of thought (that no moral law outside of God's own making should apply to him) seems contrary to the orthodox Christian view that God is good. For if good means something in accordance with God's will, then when we say that God is good, we are only saying that he acts in accordance with his own will—and this just does not seem to be enough.

In the following selections, C. Stephen Layman argues that a religious perspective makes better sense of moral commitment than a secular perspective. Indeed, in his view, it is not even clear that a secular individual who followed the dictates of morality would be rational. John Arthur asserts that morality does not need a religious foundation at all and that morality is social.

YES

C. Stephen Layman

Ethics and the Kingdom of God

Why build a theory of ethics on the assumption that there is a God? Why not simply endorse a view of ethics along . . . secular lines . . . ? I shall respond to these questions in [two] stages. First, I contrast the secular and religious perspectives on morality. Second, I explain why I think the moral life makes more sense from the point of view of theism [belief in God] than from that of atheism. . . .

❦

As I conceive it, the modern secular perspective on morality involves at least two elements. First, there is no afterlife; each individual human life ends at death. It follows that the only goods available to an individual are those he or she can obtain this side of death.[1]

Second, on the secular view, moral value is an *emergent* phenomenon. That is, moral value is "a feature of certain effects though it is not a feature of their causes" (as wetness is a feature of H_2O, but not of hydrogen or oxygen).[2] Thus, the typical contemporary secular view has it that moral value emerges only with the arrival of very complex nervous systems (viz., human brains), late in the evolutionary process. There is no Mind "behind the scenes" on the secular view, no intelligent Creator concerned with the affairs of human existence. As one advocate of the secular view puts it, "Ethics, though not consciously created [either by humans or by God], is a product of social life which has the function of promoting values common to the members of society."[3]

By way of contrast, the religious point of view (in my use of the phrase) includes a belief in God and in life after death. God is defined as an eternal being who is almighty and perfectly morally good. Thus, from the religious point of view, morality is not an emergent phenomenon, for God's goodness has always been in existence, and is not the product of nonmoral causes. Moreover, from the religious point of view, there are goods available after death. Specifically, there awaits the satisfaction of improved relations with God and with redeemed creatures.

It is important to note that, from the religious perspective, *the existence of God and life after death* are not independent hypotheses. If God exists, then at least two lines of reasoning lend support to the idea that death is not final. While I cannot here scrutinize these lines of reasoning, I believe it will be useful to sketch them.[4] (1) It has often been noted that we humans seem unable to find complete fulfillment in the present life. Even those having abundant material possessions and living in the happiest of circumstances find themselves, upon reflection, profoundly unsatisfied. . . . [I]f this earthly life is the whole story, it appears that our deepest longings will remain unfulfilled. But if God is good, He surely will not leave our deepest longings unfulfilled provided He is able to fulfill them—at least to the extent that we are willing to accept His gracious aid. So, since our innermost yearnings are not satisfied in this life, it is likely that they will be satisfied after death.

(2) Human history has been one long story of injustice, of the oppression of the poor and weak by the rich and powerful. The lives of relatively good people are often miserable, while the wicked prosper. Now, if God exists, He is able to correct such injustices, though He does not correct all of them in the present life. But if God is also good, He will not leave such injustices forever unrectified. It thus appears that He will rectify matters at some point after death. This will involve benefits for some in the afterlife—it may involve penalties for others. (However, the . . . possibility of post-mortem punishment does not necessarily imply the possibility of hell *as standardly conceived*.)

We might sum up the main difference between the secular and religious views by saying that the only goods available from a secular perspective are *earthly* goods. Earthly goods include such things as physical health, friendship, pleasure, self-esteem, knowledge, enjoyable activities, an adequate standard of living, etc. The religious or theistic perspective recognizes these earthly goods *as good*, but it insists that there are non-earthly or *transcendent* goods. These are goods available only if God exists and there is life after death for humans. Transcendent goods include harmonious relations with God prior to death as well as the joys of the afterlife—right relations with both God and redeemed creatures.

⋅⟨⊙⟩⋅

[One secular] defense of the virtues amounts to showing that society cannot function well unless individuals have moral virtue. If we ask, "Why should we as individuals care about society?", the answer will presumably be along the following lines: "Individuals cannot flourish apart from a well-functioning society, *so morality pays for the individual.*"

This defense of morality raises two questions we must now consider. First, is it misguided to defend morality by an appeal to self-interest? Many people feel that morality and self-interest are fundamentally at odds: "If you perform an act because you see that it is in your interest to do so, then you aren't doing the right thing *just because it's right*. A successful defense of morality must be a defense of duty for duty's sake. Thus, the appeal to self-interest is completely misguided." Second, *does* morality really pay for the individual? More particularly, does morality always pay in terms of earthly goods? Let us take these questions up in turn.

(1) Do we desert the moral point of view if we defend morality on the grounds that it pays? Consider an analogy with etiquette. Why should one bother with etiquette? Should one do the well-mannered thing simply for its own sake? Do we keep our elbows off the table or refrain from belching just because these things are "proper"?

To answer this question we must distinguish between the *justification of an institution* and *the justification of a particular act within that institution.* (By 'institution' I refer to any system of activities specified by rules.) This distinction can be illustrated in the case of the game (institution) of baseball. If we ask a player why he performs a particular act during a game, he will probably give an answer such as, "To put my opponent out" or "To get a home run." These answers obviously would not be relevant if the question were, "Why play baseball at all?" Relevant answers to this second question would name some advantage for the individual player, e.g., "Baseball is fun" or "It's good exercise." Thus, a justification of the institution of baseball (e.g., "It's good exercise") is quite different from a justification of a particular act within the institution (e.g., "To get a home run").

Now let's apply this distinction to our question about etiquette. If our question concerns the justification of a particular act within the institution of etiquette, then the answer may reasonably be, in effect, "This is what's proper. This is what the rules of etiquette prescribe." . . .

But plainly there are deeper questions we can ask about etiquette. Who hasn't wondered, at times, what the point of the institution of etiquette is? Why do we have these quirky rules, some of which seem to make little sense? When these more fundamental questions concerning the entire institution of etiquette are being asked, it makes no sense to urge etiquette for etiquette's sake. What is needed is a description of the human *ends* the institution fulfills— ends which play a justificatory role similar to fun or good exercise in the case of baseball. And it is not difficult to identify some of these ends. For example, the rules of etiquette seem designed, in part, to facilitate social interaction; things just go more smoothly if there are agreed upon ways of greeting, eating, conversing, etc.

If anyone asks, "Why should I as an individual bother about etiquette?", an initial reply might be: "Because if you frequently violate the rules of etiquette, people will shun you." If anyone wonders why he should care about being shunned, we will presumably reply that good social relations are essential to human flourishing, and hence that a person is jeopardizing his own best interests if he places no value at all on etiquette. Thus, in the end, a defense of the institution of etiquette seems to involve the claim that the institution of etiquette *pays* for those who participate in it; it would not be illuminating to answer the question, "Why bother about etiquette?" by saying that etiquette is to be valued for its own sake.

Now, just as we distinguish between justifying the institution of etiquette (or baseball) and justifying a particular act within the institution, so we must distinguish between justifying the institution of morality and justifying a particular act within the institution. When choosing a particular course of action we may simply want to know what's right. But a more ultimate question also cries out for an answer: "What is the point of the institution of morality, anyway? Why should one bother with it?" It is natural to respond by saying that society cannot function well without morality, and individuals cannot flourish apart from a well-functioning society. In short, defending the institution of morality involves claiming that morality pays for the individual in the long run. It seems obscurantist to preach duty for duty's sake, once the more fundamental question about the point of the institution of morality has been raised.

But if morality is defended on the grounds that it pays, doesn't this distort moral motivation? Won't it mean that we no longer do things because they are right, but rather because they are in our self-interest? No. We must bear in mind our distinction between the reasons that justify a particular act within an institution and the reasons that justify the institution itself. A baseball player performs a given act in order to get on base or put an opponent out; he does not calculate whether this particular swing of the bat (or throw of the ball) is fun or good exercise. A well-mannered person is not constantly calculating whether a given act will improve her relations with others, she simply does "the proper thing." Similarly, even if we defend morality on the grounds that it pays, it does not follow that the motive for each moral act becomes, "It will pay" for we are not constantly thinking of the philosophical issues concerning the justification of the entire system of morality; for the most part we simply do things because they are right, honest, fair, loving, etc. Nevertheless, our willingness to plunge wholeheartedly into "the moral game" is apt to be vitiated should it become clear to us that the game does not pay.

At this point it appears that the institution of morality is justified only if it pays for the individuals who participate in it. For if being moral does not pay for individuals, it is difficult to see why they should bother with it. The appeal to duty for duty's sake is irrelevant when we are asking for a justification of the institution of morality itself.

(2.) But we must now ask, "Does morality in fact pay?" There are at least four reasons for supposing that morality does not pay from a *secular* perspective. (a) One problem for the secular view arises from the fact that the moral point of view involves a concern for *all* human beings—or at least for all humans affected by one's actions. Thus, within Christian theology, the parable of the good Samaritan is well known for its expansion of the category of "my neighbor." But human societies seem able to get along well without extending full moral concern to all outsiders; this is the essence of tribal morality. Thus, explorers in the 1700s found that the Sioux Indians followed a strict code in dealing with each other, but regarded themselves as free to steal horses from the Crow. Later on, American whites repeatedly broke treaties with the American Indians in a way that would not have been possible had the Indians been regarded as equals. It is no exaggeration to say that throughout much of human history tribal morality has been the morality humans lived by.

And so, while one must agree . . . that the virtues are necessary for the existence of society, it is not clear that this amounts to anything more than a defense of tribal morality. . . . From a purely secular point of view, it is unclear why the scope of moral concern must extend beyond one's society—or, more precisely, why one's concern must extend to groups of people outside of one's society *who are powerless and stand in the way of things one's society wants.* Why should the members of a modern industrial state extend full moral consideration to a tiny Amazonian tribe? . . .

(b) A second problem for secular views concerns the possibility of secret violations of moral rules. What becomes of conscientiousness when one can break the rules in secret, without anyone knowing? After all, if I can break the rules in secret, I will not cause any social disharmony. Of course, there can be no breaking of the rules in secret if there is a God of the Christian type, who knows every human thought as well as every human act. But there are cases in which it is extraordinarily unlikely that any *humans* will discover one's rule breaking. Hence, from a secular perspective, there are cases in which secret violations of morality are possible.

Consider the following case. Suppose *A* has borrowed some money from *B,* but *A* discovers that *B* has made a mistake in his records. Because of the mistake, *B* believes that *A* has already paid the money back. *B* even goes out of his way to thank *A* for prompt payment on the loan. Let us further suppose that *B* is quite wealthy, and hence not in need of the money. Is it in *A*'s interest to pay the money back? Not paying the money back would be morally wrong; but would it be irrational, from a secular point of view? Not necessarily. Granted, it might be irrational in some cases, e.g., if *A* would have intense guilt feelings should he fail to repay the loan. But suppose *A* will not feel guilty because he really needs the money (and knows that *B* does not need it), and because he understands that secret violations belong to a special and rare category of action. Then, from a secular point of view, it is doubtful that paying the loan would be in *A*'s interest.

The point is not that theists never cheat or lie. Unfortunately they do. The point is rather that secret violations of morality arguably pay off from a secular point of view. And so, once again, it seems that there is a "game" that pays off better (in terms of earthly goods) than the relatively idealistic morality endorsed by the great ethicists, viz., one allowing secret "violations."

(c) Even supposing that morality pays for some people, does it pay for *everyone* on the secular view? Can't there be well-functioning societies in which some of the members are "moral freeloaders"? In fact, don't all actual societies have members who maintain an appearance of decency, but are in fact highly manipulative of others? How would one show, on secular grounds, that it is in the interest of these persons to be moral? Furthermore, according to psychiatrists, some people are highly amoral, virtually without feelings of guilt or shame. Yet in numerous cases these amoral types appear to be happy. These "successful egoists" are often intelligent, charming, and able to evade legal penalties for their unconventional behavior.[5] How could one show, on secular grounds, that it is in the interests of such successful egoists to be moral? They seem to find their amoral lives amply rewarding.

(d) Another problem from the secular perspective stems from the fact that in some cases morality demands that one risk death. Since death cuts one off from all earthly goods, what sense does it make to be moral (in a given case) if the risk of death is high?

This point must be stated with care. In many cases it makes sense, from a secular point of view, to risk one's life. For example, it makes sense if the risk is small and the earthly good to be gained is great; after all, one risks one's life driving to work. Or again, risking one's life makes sense from a secular point of view if failing to do so will probably lead to profound and enduring earthly unhappiness. Thus, a woman might take an enormous risk to save her child from an attacker. She might believe that she would be "unable to live with herself" afterward if she stood by and let the attacker kill or maim her child. Similarly, a man might be willing to die for his country, because he could not bear the dishonor resulting from a failure to act courageously.

But failing to risk one's life does not always lead to profound and enduring earthly unhappiness. Many soldiers play it safe in battle when risk taking is essential for victory; they may judge that victory is not worth the personal risks. And many subjects of ruthless tyrants entirely avoid the risks involved in resistance and reform. Though it may be unpleasant for such persons to find themselves regarded as cowards, this unpleasantness does not necessarily lead to profound and enduring earthly unhappiness. It seems strained to claim that what is commonly regarded as moral courage always pays in terms of earthly goods.

At this point it appears that the institution of morality cannot be justified from a secular point of view. For, as we have seen, the institution of morality is justified only if it pays (in the long run) for the individuals who participate in it. But if by "morality" we mean the relatively idealistic code urged on us by the great moralists, it appears that the institution of morality does not pay, according to the secular point of view. This is not to say that no moral code could pay off in terms of earthly goods; a tribal morality of some sort might pay for most people, especially if it were to include conventions which skirt the problems inherent in my "secret violation" and "risk of death" cases. But such a morality would be a far cry from the morality most of us actually endorse.

Defenders of secular morality may claim that these difficulties evaporate if we look at morality from an evolutionary point of view. The survival of the species depends on the sacrifice of individuals in some cases, and the end of morality is the survival of the species. Hence, it is not surprising that being highly moral will not always pay off for individuals.

This answer is confused for two reasons. First, even if morality does have survival value for the species, we have seen that this does not by itself justify the individual's involvement in the institution of morality. In fact, it does not justify such involvement if what is best for the species is not what is best for the individual member of the species. And I have been arguing that, from a secular point of view, the interests of the species and the individual diverge.

Second, while evolution might explain why humans *feel* obligated to make sacrifices, it is wholly unable to account for genuine moral obligation. If we did not feel obligated to make sacrifices for others, it might be that the species would have died out long ago. So, moral *feelings* may have survival value. However, *feeling obligated* is not the same thing as *being obligated*. . . . Thus, to show that moral feelings have survival value is not to show that there are any actual moral obligations at all. . . . The point is, the evolutionary picture does not require the existence of real obligations; it demands only the existence of moral feelings or beliefs. Moral feelings or beliefs w ould motivate action even if there were in actuality no moral obligations. For example, the belief that human life is sacred may very well have survival value even if human life is not sacred. Moral obligation, as opposed to moral feeling, is thus an unnecessary postulate from the standpoint of evolution.

At this point defenders of the secular view typically make one of two moves: (i) They claim that even if morality does not pay, there remain moral truths which we must live up to; or (ii) they may claim that morality pays in subtle ways which we have so far overlooked. Let us take these claims up in turn.

(i) It may be claimed that moral obligation is just a fact of life, woven into the structure of reality. Morality may not always pay, but certain moral standards remain true, e.g., "Lying is wrong" or "Human life is sacred." These are not made true by evolution or God, but are necessary truths, independent of concrete existence, like "$1 + 1 = 2$" or "There are no triangular circles."

There are at least three difficulties with this suggestion. First, assuming that there are such necessary truths about morality, why should we care about them or pay them any attention? We may grant that an act is correct from the moral point of view and yet wonder whether we have good reason to participate in the institution of morality. So, even if we grant that various statements of the form "One ought to do X" are necessarily true, this does not show that the institution of morality pays off. It just says that morality is a "game" whose rules are necessary truths. . . . To defend the institution of morality simply on the grounds that certain moral statements are necessarily true is to urge duty for duty's sake. And . . . this is not an acceptable defense of the institution of morality.

Second, the idea that some moral truths are necessary comports poorly with the usual secular account. As Mavrodes points out, necessary moral truths seem to be what Plato had in mind when he spoke about the Form of the Good. And Plato's view, though not contradicted by modern science, receives no support from it either. Plato's Form of the Good is not an emergent phenomenon, but is rather woven into the very structure of reality, independently of physical processes such as evolution. So, Plato's view is incompatible with the typically modern secular view that moral value is an emergent phenomenon, coming into existence with the arrival of the human nervous system. For this reason, Plato's views have "often been taken to be congenial . . . to a religious understanding of the world."[6]

Third, it is very doubtful that there are any necessary truths of the form "One ought to do X." We have seen that the institution of morality stands unjustified if participation in it does not pay (in the long run) for individuals. And why should we suppose that there are *any* necessary moral truths if the institution of morality is unjustified? . . . [S]tatements of the form "One ought to do X" are not *necessary* truths, though they may be true *if* certain conditions are met. . . . Hence, if there are any necessary moral truths, they appear to be conditional (if-then) in form: If certain conditions exist, one ought to do X. Among the conditions, as we have seen, is the condition that doing X pays for the individual in the long run. So, it is very doubtful that there are any necessary moral truths of the form "One ought to do X."[7] The upshot is that morality is partly grounded in those features of reality which guarantee that morality pays; and the secular view lacks the metaphysical resources for making such a guarantee. . . .

(ii) But some have claimed that, if we look closely at human psychology, we can see that morality does pay *in terms of earthly goods.* For example, Plato suggested that only a highly moral person could have harmony between the various elements of his soul (such as reason and desire). Others have claimed that being highly moral is the only means to inner satisfaction. We humans are just so constituted that violations of morality never leave us with a net gain. Sure, we may gain earthly goods of one sort or another by lying, stealing, etc., but these are always outweighed by inner discord or a sense of dissatisfaction with ourselves.

There are several problems with this. First, some may doubt that moral virtue is the best route to inner peace. After all, one may experience profound inner discord when one has done what is right. It can be especially upsetting to stand up for what is right when doing so is unpopular; indeed, many people avoid "making waves" precisely because it upsets their inner peace. . . .

Second, how good is the evidence that inner peace *always* outweighs the benefits achievable through unethical action? Perhaps guilt feelings and inner discord are a reasonable price to pay for certain earthly goods. If a cowardly act enables me to stay alive, or a dishonest act makes me wealthy, I may judge that my gains are worth the accompanying guilt feelings. A quiet conscience is not everything.

Third, if inner discord or a sense of dissatisfaction stems from a feeling of having done wrong, why not reassess my standards? Therapists are familiar with the phenomenon of false guilt. For example, a married woman may feel guilty for having sex with her spouse. The cure will involve enabling the patient to view sex as a legitimate means of expressing affection. The point is that just because I feel a certain type of act is wrong, it does not follow that the only route to inner peace is to avoid the action. I also have the option of revising my standards, which may enable me to pursue self-interested goals in a less inhibited fashion. Why drag along any unnecessary moral baggage? How could it be shown, on secular grounds, that it is in my interest to maintain the more idealistic standards endorsed by the great moralists? Certainly, some people have much less idealistic standards than others, and yet seem no less happy.

By way of contrast with the secular view, it is not difficult to see how morality might pay if there is a God of the Christian type. First, God loves all humans and wants all included in his kingdom. So, a tribal morality would violate his demands, and to violate his demands is to strain one's most important personal relationship. Second, there are no secret violations of morality if God exists. Since God is omniscient, willful wrongdoing of any sort will estrange the wrongdoer from God. Third, while earthly society may be able to function pretty well even though there exists a small number of "moral freeloaders," the freeloaders themselves are certainly not attaining harmonious relations with God. Accordingly, their ultimate fulfillment is in jeopardy. Fourth, death is the end of earthly life, but it is not the end of conscious existence, according to Christianity. Therefore, death does not end one's opportunity for personal fulfillment; indeed, if God is perfectly good and omnipotent, we can only assume that the afterlife will result in the fulfillment of our deepest needs—unless we willfully reject God's efforts to supply those needs.

So, it seems to me that the moral life makes more sense from a theistic perspective than from a secular perspective. Of course, I do not claim that I have proved the existence of God, and a full discussion of this metaphysical issue would take us too far from matters at hand.[8] But if I have shown that the moral life makes more sense from a theistic perspective than from a secular one, then I have provided an important piece of evidence in favor of the rationality of belief in God. Moreover, I believe that I have turned back one objection to the Christian teleological view, namely, the allegation that theism is unnecessary metaphysical baggage.

Notes

1. It can be argued that, even from a secular perspective, some benefits and harms are available after death. For example, vindicating the reputation of a deceased person may be seen as benefiting that person. See, for example, Thomas Nagel, *Mortal Questions* (London: Cambridge University Press, 1979), pp. 1–10. But even if we grant that these are goods for the deceased, it is obvious that, from the secular point of view, such post-mortem goods cannot be consciously enjoyed by the deceased. They are not available in the sense that he will never take pleasure in them.

2. George Mavrodes, "Religion and the Queerness of Morality," in *Rationality, Religious Belief, and Moral Commitment,* ed. Robert Audi and William J. Wainwright (Ithaca, N.Y.: Cornell University Press, 1986), p. 223.

3. Peter Singer, *Practical Ethics* (London: Cambridge University Press, 1970), p. 209.

4. For an excellent discussion of arguments for immortality, see William J. Wainwright, *Philosophy of Religion* (Belmont, Calif.: Wadsworth, 1988), pp. 99–111.

5. My source for these claims about "happy psychopaths" is Singer, *Practical Ethics,* pp. 214–216. Singer in turn is drawing from Hervey Cleckley, *The Mask of Sanity, (An Attempt to Clarify Some Issues About the So-Called Psychopathic Personality)*, 5th ed. (St. Louis, Mo.: E. S. Cleckley, 1988).

6. Mavrodes, "Religion and the Queerness of Morality," p. 224. I am borrowing from Mavrodes throughout this paragraph.

7. Those acquainted with modal logic may have a question here. By a principle of modal logic, if p is a necessary truth and p necessarily implies q, then q is a necessary truth. So, if it is necessarily true that "certain conditions are met" and necessarily true that "If they are met, one ought to X," then, "One ought to do X" is a necessary truth. But I assume it is not *necessarily true* that "certain conditions are met." In my judgment it would be most implausible to suppose, e.g., that "Morality pays for humans" is a necessary truth.

8. Two fine discussions of moral arguments for theism are Robert Merrihew Adams, "Moral Arguments for Theistic Belief," in *Rationality and Religious Belief,* ed. C. F. Delaney (Notre Dame, Ind.: University of Notre Dame Press, 1979), pp. 116–140, and J. L. Mackie, *The Miracle of Theism* (Oxford: Oxford University Press, 1982), pp. 102–118.

 **NO**

Religion, Morality, and Conscience

My first and prime concern in this paper is to explore the connections, if any, between morality and religion. I will argue that in fact religion is not necessary for morality. Yet despite the lack of any logical or other necessary connection, I will claim, there remain important respects in which the two are related. In the concluding section I will discuss the notion of moral conscience, and then look briefly at the various respects in which morality is "social" and the implications of that idea for moral education. First, however, I want to say something about the subjects: just what are we referring to when we speak of morality and of religion?

Morality and Religion

A useful way to approach the first question—the nature of morality—is to ask what it would mean for a society to exist without a social moral code. How would such people think and behave? What would that society look like? First, it seems clear that such people would never feel guilt or resentment. For example, the notions that I ought to remember my parent's anniversary, that he has a moral responsibility to help care for his children after the divorce, that she has a right to equal pay for equal work, and that discrimination on the basis of race is unfair would be absent in such a society. Notions of duty, rights, and obligations would not be present, except perhaps in the legal sense; concepts of justice and fairness would also be foreign to these people. In short, people would have no tendency to evaluate or criticize the behavior of others, nor to feel remorse about their own behavior. Children would not be taught to be ashamed when they steal or hurt others, nor would they be allowed to complain when others treat them badly. (People might, however, feel regret at a decision that didn't turn out as they had hoped; but that would only be because their expectations were frustrated, not because they feel guilty.)

Such a society lacks a moral code. What, then, of religion? Is it possible that a people lacking a morality would nonetheless have religious beliefs? It seems clear that it is possible. Suppose every day these same people file into their place of worship to pay homage to God (they may believe in many gods or in one all-powerful creator of heaven and earth). Often they can be heard praying to God for help in dealing with their problems and thanking Him for their good fortune. Frequently they give sacrifices to God, sometimes in the

From MORALITY AND MORAL CONTROVERSIES, 4th ed., 1991, pp. 21–28. Copyright © 1991 by John Arthur. Reprinted by permission.

form of money spent to build beautiful temples and churches, other times by performing actions they believe God would approve such as helping those in need. These practices might also be institutionalized, in the sense that certain people are assigned important leadership roles. Specific texts might also be taken as authoritative, indicating the ways God has acted in history and His role in their lives or the lives of their ancestors.

To have a moral code, then, is to tend to evaluate (perhaps without even expressing it) the behavior of others and to feel guilt at certain actions when we perform them. Religion, on the other hand, involves beliefs in supernatural power(s) that created and perhaps also control nature, the tendency to worship and pray to those supernatural forces or beings, and the presence of organizational structures and authoritative texts. The practices of morality and religion are thus importantly different. One involves our attitudes toward various forms of behavior (lying and killing, for example), typically expressed using the notions of rules, rights, and obligations. The other, religion, typically involves prayer, worship, beliefs about the supernatural, institutional forms and authoritative texts.

We come, then, to the central question: What is the connection, if any, between a society's moral code and its religious practices and beliefs? Many people have felt that morality is in some way dependent on religion or religious truths. But what sort of "dependence" might there be? In what follows I distinguish various ways in which one might claim that religion is necessary for morality, arguing against those who claim morality depends in some way on religion. I will also suggest, however, some other important ways in which the two are related, concluding with a brief discussion of conscience and moral education.

Religious Motivation and Guidance

One possible role that religion might play in morality relates to motives people have. Religion, it is often said, is necessary so that people will DO right. Typically, the argument begins with the important point that doing what is right often has costs: refusing to shoplift or cheat can mean people go without some good or fail a test; returning a billfold means they don't get the contents. Religion is therefore said to be necessary in that it provides motivation to do the right thing. God rewards those who follow His commands by providing for them a place in heaven or by insuring that they prosper and are happy on earth. He also punishes those who violate the moral law. Others emphasize less self-interested ways in which religious motives may encourage people to act rightly. Since God is the creator of the universe and has ordained that His plan should be followed, they point out, it is important to live one's life in accord with this divinely ordained plan. Only by living a moral life, it is said, can people live in harmony with the larger, divinely created order.

The first claim, then, is that religion is necessary to provide moral motivation. The problem with that argument, however, is that religious motives are far from the only ones people have. For most of us, a decision to do the right thing (if that is our decision) is made for a variety of reasons: "What if I get caught? What if somebody sees me—what will he or she think? How will I feel afterwards? Will I regret it?" Or maybe the thought of cheating just doesn't arise. We were raised to be a decent person, and that's what we are—period. Behaving fairly and treating others well is more important than whatever we might gain from stealing or cheating, let alone seriously harming another person. So it seems clear that many motives for doing the right thing have nothing whatsoever to do with religion. Most of us, in fact, do worry about getting caught, being blamed, and being looked down on by others. We also may do what is right just because it's right, or because we don't want to hurt others or embarrass family and friends. To say that we need religion to act morally is mistaken; indeed it seems to me that many of us, when it really gets down to it, don't give much of a thought to religion when making moral decisions. All those other reasons are the ones which we tend to consider, or else we just don't consider cheating and stealing at all. So far, then, there seems to be no reason to suppose that people can't be moral yet irreligious at the same time.

A second argument that is available for those who think religion is necessary to morality, however, focuses on moral guidance and knowledge rather than on people's motives. However much people may want to do the right thing, according to this view, we cannot ever know for certain what is right without the guidance of religious teaching. Human understanding is simply inadequate to this difficult and controversial task; morality involves immensely complex problems, and so we must consult religious revelation for help.

Again, however, this argument fails. First, consider how much we would need to know about religion and revelation in order for religion to provide moral guidance. Besides being sure that there is a God, we'd also have to think about which of the many religions is true. How can anybody be sure his or her religion is the right one? But even if we assume the Judeo-Christian God is the real one, we still need to find out just what it is He wants us to do, which means we must think about revelation.

Revelation comes in at least two forms, and not even all Christians agree on which is the best way to understand revelation. Some hold that revelation occurs when God tells us what he wants by providing us with His words: The Ten Commandments are an example. Many even believe, as evangelist Billy Graham once said, that the entire *Bible* was written by God using 39 secretaries. Others, however, doubt that the "word of God" refers literally to the words God has spoken, but believe instead that the *Bible* is an historical document, written by human beings, of the events or occasions in which God revealed Himself. It is an especially important document, of course, but nothing more than that. So on this second view revelation is not understood as *statements* made by God but rather as His *acts* such as leading His people from Egypt, testing Job, and sending His son as an example of the ideal life. The *Bible* is not itself revelation, it's the historical account of revelatory actions.

If we are to use revelation as a moral guide, then, we must first know what is to count as revelation—words given us by God, historical events, or both? But even supposing that we could somehow answer those questions, the problems of relying on revelation are still not over since we still must interpret that revelation. Some feel, for example, that the *Bible* justifies various forms of killing, including war and capital punishment, on the basis of such statements as "An eye for an eye." Others, emphasizing such sayings as "Judge not lest ye be judged" and "Thou shalt not kill," believe the *Bible* demands absolute pacifism. How are we to know which interpretation is correct? It is likely, of course, that the answer people give to such religious questions will be influenced in part at least by their own moral beliefs: if capital punishment is thought to be unjust, for example, then an interpreter will seek to read the *Bible* in a way that is consistent with that moral truth. That is not, however, a happy conclusion for those wishing to rest morality on revelation, for it means that their understanding of what God has revealed is itself dependent on their prior moral views. Rather than revelation serving as a guide for morality, morality is serving as a guide for how we interpret revelation.

So my general conclusion is that far from providing a short-cut to moral understanding, looking to revelation for guidance often creates more questions and problems. It seems wiser under the circumstances to address complex moral problems like abortion, capital punishment, and affirmative action directly, considering the pros and cons of each side, rather than to seek answers through the much more controversial and difficult route of revelation.

The Divine Command Theory

It may seem, however, that we have still not really gotten to the heart of the matter. Even if religion is not necessary for moral motivation or guidance, it is often claimed, religion is necessary in another more fundamental sense. According to this view, religion is necessary for morality because without God there could BE no right or wrong. God, in other words, provides the foundation or bedrock on which morality is grounded. This idea was expressed by Bishop R. C. Mortimer:

> "God made us and all the world. Because of that He has an absolute claim
> on our obedience. . . . From [this]it follows that a thing is not right simply
> because we think it is. It is right because God commands it."[1]

What Bishop Mortimer has in mind can be seen by comparing moral rules with legal ones. Legal statutes, we know, are created by legislatures; if the state assembly of New York had not passed a law limiting speed people can travel, then there would be no such legal obligation. Without the statutory enactments, such a law simply would not exist. Mortimer's view, the *divine command theory,* would mean that God has the same sort of relation to moral law as legislature has to statutes it enacts: without God's commands there would be no moral rules, just as without a legislature there would be no statutes.

Defenders of the divine command theory often add to this a further claim, that only by assuming God sits at the foundation of morality can we explain the objective difference between right and wrong. This point was forcefully argued by F. C. Copleston in a 1948 British Broadcasting Corporation radio debate with Bertrand Russell.

Copleston: . . . The validity of such an interpretation of man's conduct depends on the recognition of God's existence, obviously. . . . Let's take a look at the Commandant of the [Nazi] concentration camp at Belsen. That appears to you as undesirable and evil and to me too. To Adolf Hitler we suppose it appeared as something good and desirable. I suppose you'd have to admit that for Hitler it was good and for you it is evil.

Russell: No, I shouldn't go so far as that. I mean, I think people can make mistakes in that as they can in other things. If you have jaundice you see things yellow that are not yellow. You're making a mistake.

Copleston: Yes, one can make mistakes, but can you make a mistake if it's simply a question of reference to a feeling or emotion? Surely Hitler would be the only possible judge of what appealed to his emotions.

Russell: . . . You can say various things about that; among others, that if that sort of thing makes that sort of appeal to Hitler's emotions, then Hitler makes quite a different appeal to my emotions.

Copleston: Granted. But there's no objective criterion outside feeling then for condemning the conduct of the Commandant of Belsen, in your view. . . . The human being's idea of the content of the moral law depends certainly to a large extent on education and environment, and a man has to use his reason in assessing the validity of the actual moral ideas of his social group. But the possibility of criticizing the accepted moral code presupposes that there is an objective standard, that there is an ideal moral order, which imposes itself. . . . It implies the existence of a real foundation of God.[2]

Against those who, like Bertrand Russell, seek to ground morality in feelings and attitudes, Copleston argues that there must be a more solid foundation if we are to be able to claim truly that the Nazis were evil. God, according to Copleston, is able to provide the objective basis for the distinction, which we all know to exist, between right and wrong. Without divine commands at the root of human obligations, we would have no real reason for condemning the behavior of anybody, even Nazis. Morality, Copleston thinks, would then be nothing more than an expression of personal feeling.

To begin assessing the divine command theory, let's first consider this last point. Is it really true that only the commands of God can provide an objective basis for moral judgments? Certainly many philosophers have felt that morality rests on its own perfectly sound footing, be it reason, human nature, or natural sentiments. It seems wrong to conclude, automatically, that morality cannot rest on anything but religion. And it is also possible that morality doesn't have any foundation or basis at all, so that its claims should be ignored in favor of whatever serves our own self-interest.

In addition to these problems with Copleston's argument, the divine command theory faces other problems as well. First, we would need to say much more about the relationship between morality and divine commands. Certainly the expressions "is commanded by God" and "is morally required" do not *mean* the same thing. People and even whole societies can use moral concepts without understanding them to make any reference to God. And while it is true that God (or any other moral being for that matter) would tend to want others to do the right thing, this hardly shows that being right and being commanded by God are the same thing. Parents want their children to do the right thing, too, but that doesn't mean parents, or anybody else, can make a thing right just by commanding it!

I think that, in fact, theists should reject the divine command theory. One reason is what it implies. Suppose we were to grant (just for the sake of argument) that the divine command theory is correct, so that actions are right just because they are commanded by God. The same, of course, can be said about those deeds that we believe are wrong. If God hadn't commanded us not to do them, they would not be wrong.

But now notice this consequence of the divine command theory. Since God is all-powerful, and since right is determined solely by His commands, is it not possible that He might change the rules and make what we now think of as wrong into right? It would seem that according to the divine command theory the answer is "yes": it is theoretically possible that tomorrow God would decree that virtues such as kindness and courage have become vices while actions that show cruelty and cowardice will henceforth be the right actions. (Recall the analogy with a legislature and the power it has to change law.) So now rather than it being right for people to help each other out and prevent innocent people from suffering unnecessarily, it would be right (God having changed His mind) to create as much pain among innocent children as we possibly can! To adopt the divine command theory therefore commits its advocate to the seemingly absurd position that even the greatest atrocities might be not only acceptable but morally required if God were to command them.

Plato made a similar point in the dialogue *Euthyphro*. Socrates is asking Euthyphro what it is that makes the virtue of holiness a virtue, just as we have been asking what makes kindness and courage virtues. Euthyphro has suggested that holiness is just whatever all the gods love.

Socrates: Well, then, Euthyphro, what do we say about holiness? Is it not loved by all the gods, according to your definition?

Euthyphro: Yes.

Socrates: Because it is holy, or for some other reason?

Euthyphro: No, because it is holy.

Socrates: Then it is loved by the gods because it is holy: it is not holy because it is loved by them?

Euthyphro: It seems so.

Socrates: . . . Then holiness is not what is pleasing to the gods, and what is pleasing to the gods is not holy as you say, Euthyphro. They are different things.

Euthyphro: And why, Socrates?

Socrates: Because we are agreed that the gods love holiness because it is holy: and that it is not holy because they love it.[3]

This raises an interesting question: Why, having claimed at first that virtues are merely what is loved (or commanded) by the gods, would Euthyphro so quickly contradict this and agree that the gods love holiness *because* it's holy, rather than the reverse? One likely possibility is that Euthyphro believes that whenever the gods love something they do so with good reason, not without justification and arbitrarily. To deny this, and say that it is merely the gods' love that makes holiness a virtue, would mean that the gods have no basis for their attitudes, that they are arbitrary in what they love. Yet—and this is the crucial point—it's far from clear that a religious person would want to say that God is arbitrary in that way. If we say that it is simply God's loving something that makes it right, then what sense would it make to say God wants us to do right? All that could mean, it seems, is that God wants us to do what He wants us to do; He would have no reason for wanting it. Similarly "God is good" would mean little more than "God does what He pleases." The divine command theory therefore leads us to the results that God is morally arbitrary, and that His wishing us to do good or even God's being just mean nothing more than that God does what He does and wants whatever He wants. Religious people who reject that consequence would also, I am suggesting, have reason to reject the divine command theory itself, seeking a different understanding of morality.

This now raises another problem, however. If God approves kindness because it is a virtue and hates the Nazis because they were evil, then it seems that God discovers morality rather than inventing it. So haven't we then identified a limitation on God's power, since He now, being a good God, must love kindness and command us not to be cruel? Without the divine command theory, in other words, what is left of God's omnipotence?

But why, we may ask, is such a limitation on God unacceptable? It is not at all clear that God really can do anything at all. Can God, for example, destroy Himself? Or make a rock so heavy that He cannot lift it? Or create a universe which was never created by Him? Many have thought that God cannot do these things, but also that His inability to do them does not constitute a serious limitation on His power since these are things that cannot be done at all: to do them would violate the laws of logic. Christianity's most influential theologian, Thomas Aquinas, wrote in this regard that "whatever implies contradiction does not come within the scope of divine omnipotence, because it cannot have the aspect of possibility. Hence it is more appropriate to say that such things cannot be done than that God cannot do them."[4]

How, then, ought we to understand God's relationship to morality if we reject the divine command theory? Can religious people consistently maintain their faith in God the Creator and yet deny that what is right is right because He commands it? I think the answer to this is "yes." Making cruelty good is not like making a universe that wasn't made, of course. It's a moral limit on God rather than a logical one. But why suppose that God's limits are only logical?

One final point about this. Even if we agree that God loves justice or kindness because of their nature, not arbitrarily, there still remains a sense in which God could change morality even having rejected the divine command theory. That's because if we assume, plausibly I think, that morality depends in part on how we reason, what we desire and need, and the circumstances in which we find ourselves, then morality will still be under God's control since God could have constructed us or our environment very differently. Suppose, for instance, that he created us so that we couldn't be hurt by others or didn't care about freedom. Or perhaps our natural environment were created differently, so that all we have to do is ask and anything we want is given to us. If God had created either nature or us that way, then it seems likely our morality might also be different in important ways from the one we now think correct. In that sense, then, morality depends on God whether or not one supports the divine command theory.

"Morality Is Social"

I have argued here that religion is not necessary in providing moral motivation or guidance, and against the divine command theory's claim that God is necessary for there to be morality at all. In this last section, I want first to look briefly at how religion and morality sometimes *do* influence each other. Then I will consider the development of moral conscience and the important ways in which morality might correctly be thought to be "social."

Nothing I have said so far means that morality and religion are independent of each other. But in what ways are they related, assuming I am correct in claiming morality does not *depend* on religion? First, of course, we should note the historical influence religions have had on the development of morality as well as on politics and law. Many of the important leaders of the abolitionist and civil rights movements were religious leaders, as are many current members of the pro-life movement. The relationship is not, however, one-sided: morality has also influenced religion, as the current debate within the Catholic church over the role of women, abortion, and other social issues shows. In reality, then, it seems clear that the practices of morality and religion have historically each exerted an influence on the other.

But just as the two have shaped each other historically, so, too, do they interact at the personal level. I have already suggested how people's understanding of revelation, for instance, is often shaped by morality as they seek the best interpretations of revealed texts. Whether trying to understand a work of art, a legal statute, or a religious text, interpreters regularly seek to understand them in the best light—to make them as good as they can be, which requires that they bring moral judgment to the task of religious interpretation and understanding.

The relationship can go the other direction as well, however, as people's moral views are shaped by their religious training and beliefs. These relationships between morality and religion are often complex, hidden even from ourselves, but it does seem clear that our views on important moral issues, from sexual morality and war to welfare and capital punishment, are often influenced by our religious outlook. So not only are religious and moral practices and understandings historically linked, but for many religious people the relationship extends to the personal level—to their understanding of moral obligations as well as their sense of who they are and their vision of who they wish to be.

Morality, then, is influenced by religion (as is religion by morality), but morality's social character extends deeper even than that, I want to argue. First, of course, we possess a socially acquired language within which we think about our various choices and the alternatives we ought to follow, including whether a possible course of action is the right thing to do. Second, morality is social in that it governs relationships among people, defining our responsibilities to others and theirs to us. Morality provides the standards we rely on in gauging our interactions with family, lovers, friends, fellow citizens, and even strangers. Third, morality is social in the sense that we are, in fact, subject to criticism by others for our actions. We discuss with others what we should do, and often hear from them concerning whether our decisions were acceptable. Blame and praise are a central feature of morality.

While not disputing any of this, John Dewey has stressed another, less obvious aspect of morality's social character. Consider then the following comments regarding the origins of morality and conscience in an article he titled "Morality Is Social":

> In language and imagination we rehearse the responses of others just as we dramatically enact other consequences. We foreknow how others will act, and the foreknowledge is the beginning of judgment passed on action. We know *with* them; there is conscience. An assembly is formed within our breast which discusses and appraises proposed and performed acts. The community without becomes a forum and tribunal within, a judgmentseat of charges, assessments and exculpations. Our thoughts of our own actions are saturated with the ideas that others entertain about them. . . . Explicit recognition of this fact is a prerequisite of improvement in moral education. . . . Reflection is morally indispensable.[5]

To appreciate fully the role of society in shaping morality and influencing people's sense of responsibility, Dewey is arguing, requires appreciating the fact that to think from the moral point of view, as opposed to the selfish one, for instance, means rejecting our private, subjective perspective in favor of the view of others, envisioning how they might respond to various choices we might make. Far from being private and unrelated to others, moral conscience is in that sense "public." To consider a decision from the moral perspective, says Dewey, requires that we envision an "assembly of others" that is "formed within our breast." In that way, our moral conscience cannot be sharply distinguished from our nature as social beings since conscience invariably brings with it, or constitutes, the perspective of the other. "Is this right?" and "What would this look like were I to have to defend it to others?" are not entirely separable questions.[6]

It is important not to confuse Dewey's point here, however. He is *not* saying that what is right is finally to be determined by the reactions of actually existing other people, or even by the reaction of society as a whole. What is right or fair can never be finally decided by a vote, and might not meet the approval of any specific others. But what then might Dewey mean in speaking of such an "assembly of others" as the basis of morality? The answer is that rather than actual people or groups, the assembly Dewey envisions is hypothetical or "ideal." The "community without" is thus transformed into a "forum and tribunal within, a judgment seat of charges, assessments and exculpations." So it is through the powers of our imagination that we can meet our moral responsibilities and exercise moral judgment, using these powers to determine what morality requires by imagining the reaction of Dewey's "assembly of others."

Morality is therefore *inherently* social, in a variety of ways. It depends on socially learned language, is learned from interactions with others, and governs our interactions with others in society. But it also demands, as Dewey put it, that we know "with" others, envisioning for ourselves what their points of view would require along with our own. Conscience demands we occupy the positions of others.

Viewed in this light, God would play a role in a religious person's moral reflection and conscience since it is unlikely a religious person would wish to exclude God from the "forum and tribunal" that constitutes conscience. Rather, for the religious person conscience would almost certainly include the imagined reaction of God along with the reactions of others who might be affected by the action. Other people are also important, however, since it is often an open question just what God's reaction would be; revelation's meaning, as I have argued, is subject to interpretation. So it seems that for a religious person morality and God's will cannot be separated, though the connection between them is not the one envisioned by defenders of the divine command theory.

Which leads to my final point, about moral education. If Dewey is correct, then it seems clear there is an important sense in which morality not only can be taught but must be. Besides early moral training, moral thinking depends on our ability to imagine others' reactions and to imaginatively put ourselves into their shoes. "What would somebody (including, perhaps, God) think if this got out?"expresses more than a concern with being embarrassed or punished; it is also the voice of conscience and indeed of morality itself. But that would mean, thinking of education, that listening to others, reading about what others think and do, and reflecting within ourselves about our actions and whether we could defend them to others are part of the practice of morality itself. Morality cannot exist without the broader, social perspective introduced by others, and this social nature ties it, in that way, with education and with public discussion, both actual and imagined. "Private" moral reflection taking place independent of the social world would be no moral reflection at all; and moral education is not only possible, but essential.

Notes

1. R. C. Mortimer, *Christian Ethics* (London: Hutchinson's University Library, 1950), pp. 7–8.

2. This debate was broadcast on the "Third Program" of the British Broadcasting Corporation in 1948.
3. Plato, *Euthyphro,* tr. H. N. Fowler (Cambridge MA: Harvard University Press, 1947).
4. Thomas Aquinas, *Summa Theologica,* Part I, Q.25, Art. 3.
5. John Dewey, "Morality Is Social" in *The Moral Writings of John Dewey,* revised edition, ed. James Gouinlock (Amherst, NY: Prometheus Books, 1994), pp. 182–184.
6. Obligations to animals raise an interesting problem for this conception of morality. Is it wrong to torture animals only because other *people* could be expected to disapprove? Or is it that the animal itself would disapprove? Or, perhaps, duties to animals rest on sympathy and compassion while human moral relations are more like Dewey describes, resting on morality's inherently social nature and on the dictates of conscience viewed as an assembly of others?

POSTSCRIPT

Does Morality Need Religion?

As Arthur notes, some of the earliest—and indeed some of the best—arguments on this issue can be found in Plato's dialogue *Euthyphro*, which was written in the fourth century B.C. His arguments were in terms of Greek religious practices and Greek gods, but we can reformulate the points and elaborate on the arguments in monotheistic terms.

One key dilemma in the original Greek version asks us to consider whether holy things (i) are holy because they please the gods or (ii) please the gods because they are holy. In monotheistic terms, the dilemma would be whether holy things (i) are holy because they please God or (ii) please God because they are holy. The question can then be broadened and the dilemma posed in terms of good things in general. We then ask whether good things are (i) good because God wills them or (ii) willed by God because they are good.

Plato believed that the gods love what is holy because it is holy (i.e., he believed the second option above), just as Christians have traditionally believed that God wills good things because they are good. Traditionally, a contrast is drawn between God, an infinite and all-good being who always wills the good, and humans, finite beings who are not all-good and do not always will the good.

We might also consider a parallel dilemma concerning truths. Are things true because God knows them, or does God know them because they are true? The traditional view is that God is all-knowing. God knows all truths because they are truths (and no truths lie outside divine knowledge), whereas people do not know all truths (and many truths lie outside human knowledge).

Nevertheless, there has also been in Christianity a tradition that the almighty power of God is not to be constrained by anything—even if we imagine that what constrains God are good things. This view holds that God creates not only good things but the very fact that a good thing (such as honesty) is good while another thing (such as false witness against your neighbor) is not. Thus, in this view, God in his power determines what is good and what is bad.

These topics are further discussed in Glenn Tinder, "Can We Be Good Without God? On the Political Meaning of Christianity" *The Atlantic Monthly* (December 1989); Richard J. Mouw, *The God Who Commands: A Study in Divine Command Ethics* (University of Notre Dame Press, 1990); E. M. Adams, *Religion and Cultural Freedom* (Temple University Press, 1993); D. Z. Phillips, ed., *Religion and Morality* (St. Martin's Press, 1996); and Paul Chamberlain, *Can We Be Good Without God? A Conversation About Truth, Morality, Culture, and a Few Other Things That Matter* (InterVarsity Press, 1996).

ISSUE 3

Is Ayn Rand's Ethical Egoism Correct?

YES: Ayn Rand, from *Atlas Shrugged* (The Penguin Group, 1992)

NO: Louis P. Pojman, from "Egoism and Altruism: A Critique of Ayn Rand," in Louis P. Pojman and Lewis Vaughn, eds., *The Moral Life: An Introductory Reader in Ethics and Literature,* 3d ed. (Oxford University Press, 2007)

ISSUE SUMMARY

YES: Ayn Rand argues against the idea that morality is something that is for the good of *others,* and thus something that requires self-sacrifice. Here, in her novel *Atlas Shrugged,* she has the leading character speak in favor of moral egoism—the idea that one should look after *oneself* and one's own happiness.

NO: Louis Pojman argues that Rand has confused the concept of *selfishness* with that of *self-interest.* Since she thinks of selfishness as a virtue, this leads her to devalue altruism, or acting for others, as a vice. His own account aims to establish some middle ground between complete altruism and complete egoism.

First of all, we might begin by making a couple of linguistic observations, since "ethical egoism" might sound strange to the ear. *Ethical* egoism is usually distinguished from *psychological* egoism. Psychological egoism holds that each person will always look out for his or her own self-interest. (Even seeming counter-examples to this, like the case of the hero, are dismissed because heroes are doing only what they most want to do anyway, so they aren't really "heroes" in the conventional sense.) Ethical egoism, by contrast, is the view that people do sometimes act altruistically, for the interest of other people, and sometimes follow their own self-interest, but the best thing that a person could do is to follow his or her own self-interest and not to be misled (by social or religious demands) into acting altruistically or for the welfare of others. This is going to sound odd to us, and Rand is well aware that it will sound odd, but she believes that people have largely been misled by social demands, by religious upbringing, etc., into thinking that acting morally means acting for the benefit of *others,* and that acting for one's own personal benefit is selfish and wrong.

47

In fact, Rand has a book entitled *The Virtue of Selfishness*, because in her view, selfishness *is* a virtue. The character who is speaking delivers her message. He makes a speech against social and "mystical" (religious) ideas of what is good, and issues a call for individuals to reject the moral values that are imposed on them from external sources and to use their powers as rational beings to take responsibility for their own lives, to value self-interest, and to achieve happiness. According to ethical egoism, this is exactly the thing to do: One should concentrate on oneself and on one's own happiness.

Opponents of Rand's egoism, such as Pojman, argue that Rand has set up a false dilemma between altruism and egoism. She seems to consider only the most extreme cases. A person who sacrifices his or her own life for others is an extreme case—not all ordinary people or even ordinary altruists would be willing to go this far. But Rand seems to assume that the altruist's primary goal is one of sacrificing his or her life. This totally neglects the happiness and welfare of "number one." But since the happiness and welfare of "number one" is the goal of any rational creature, Rand concludes that altruism must be rejected and egoism must be embraced.

Note that this goes beyond the idea of looking out for "number one," for even those who value this idea can agree that a person could go overboard and be too self-concerned and self-centered. But since most people (and even most animals) naturally have a desire to look after "number one," the idea of altruism has to be stressed to us so as to counter-balance inborn self-concern. Perhaps, it might be suggested, the trick is to find some middle ground between complete egoism and complete altruism.

But the ethical egoist is not interested in any such compromise. According to Rand, our greatest goal and good in life is to find happiness, and if we are rational beings, we will see that altruism serves the happiness of *others,* and therefore gets in the way of our highest goal.

People generally agree with the idea of happiness. But one point that is often pointed out is what is called "the paradox of hedonism." Hedonism is the pursuit of pleasure, and the paradox is that it is generally the case that the best way to achieve fulfillment in this regard is to do the things you like. If people achieve what they are seeking, they will be happy—and that's the paradox of hedonism. People gain pleasure not from setting out to seek and achieve it directly, but from doing the things they enjoy. Then the pleasure follows. Likewise, it might be thought, people might achieve their own happiness and well-being in connection with promoting the happiness and well-being of other people, at least to some degree.

Some interesting ideas from evolutionary psychology (and what used to be called sociobiology) might be relevant here. Groups of human beings have developed survival strategies that involve both individual self-regarding behavior and altruistic other-regarding behavior. A group of totally selfish individuals would seem unable to survive. And a group of totally self-sacrificing individuals would also be unable to survive.

In the following essay, Ayn Rand first has the hero of her novel *Atlas Shrugged* propound a forceful ethical egoism. Louis Pojman then raises several criticisms against ethical egoism.

48

YES

Ayn Rand

Excerpts from *Atlas Shrugged*

"Yes, this *is* an age of moral crisis. Yes, you *are* bearing punishment for your evil. But it is not man who is now on trial and it is not human nature that will take the blame. It is your moral code that's through, this time. Your moral code has reached its climax, the blind alley at the end of its course. And if you wish to go on living, what you now need is not to *return* to morality—you who have never known any—but to *discover* it.

"You have heard no concepts of morality but the mystical or the social. You have been taught that morality is a code of behavior imposed on you by whim, the whim of a supernatural power or the whim of society, to serve God's purpose or your neighbor's welfare, to please an authority beyond the grave or else next door—but not to serve *your* life or pleasure. Your pleasure, you have been taught, is to be found in immorality, your interests would best be served by evil, and any moral code must be designed not *for* you, but *against* you, not to further your life, but to drain it.

"For centuries, the battle of morality was fought between those who claimed that your life belongs to God and those who claimed that it belongs to your neighbors—between those who preached that the good is self sacrifice for the sake of ghosts in heaven and those who preached that the good is self-sacrifice for the sake of incompetents on earth. And no one came to say that your life belongs to you and that the good is to live it.

"Both sides agreed that morality demands the surrender of your self-interest and of your mind, that the moral and the practical are opposites, that morality is not the province of reason, but the province of faith and force. Both sides agreed that no rational morality is possible, that there is no right or wrong in reason—that in reason there's no reason to be moral.

"Whatever else they fought about, it was against man's mind that all your moralists have stood united. It was man's mind that all their schemes and systems were intended to despoil and destroy. Now choose to perish or to learn that the anti-mind is the anti-life.

"Man's mind is his basic tool of survival. Life is given to him, survival is not. His body is given to him, its sustenance is not. His mind is given to him, its content is not. To remain alive, he must act, and before he can act he must know the nature and purpose of his action. He cannot obtain his food without

From ATLAS SHRUGGED, 1957, 1985, 1992, pp. 570–579, pp. 1011–1034, 1052–1053, 1059. Copyright © 1992 by Penguin Group (USA) Inc. Reprinted by permission.

a knowledge of food and of the way to obtain it. He cannot dig a ditch—or build a cyclotron—without a knowledge of his aim and of the means to achieve it. To remain alive, he must think.

"But to think is an act of choice. The key to what you so recklessly call 'human nature,' the open secret you live with, yet dread to name, is the fact that *man is a being of volitional consciousness.* Reason does not work automatically; thinking is not a mechanical process; the connections of logic are not made by instinct. The function of your stomach, lungs or heart is automatic; the function of your mind is not. In any hour and issue of your life, you are free to think or to evade that effort. But you are not free to escape from your nature, from the fact that *reason* is your means of survival—so that for *you*, who are a human being, the question 'to be or not to be' is the question 'to think or not to think.'

"A being of volitional consciousness has no automatic course of behavior. He needs a code of values to guide his actions. 'Value' is that which one acts to gain and keep, 'virtue' is the action by which one gains and keeps it. 'Value' presupposes an answer to the question: of value to whom and for what? 'Value' presupposes a standard, a purpose and the necessity of action in the face of an alternative. Where there are no alternatives, no values are possible.

"There is only one fundamental alternative in the universe: existence or non-existence—and it pertains to a single class of entities: to living organisms. The existence of inanimate matter is unconditional, the existence of life is not: it depends on a specific course of action. Matter is indestructible, it changes its forms, but it cannot cease to exist. It is only a living organism that faces a constant alternative: the issue of life or death. Life is a process of self-sustaining and self-generated action. If an organism fails in that action, it dies; its chemical elements remain, but its life goes out of existence. It is only the concept of 'Life' that makes the concept of 'Value' possible. It is only to a living entity that things can be good or evil.

"A plant must feed itself in order to live; the sunlight, the water, the chemicals it needs are the values its nature has set it to pursue; its life is the standard of value directing its actions. But a plant has no choice of action; there are alternatives in the conditions it encounters, but there is no alternative in its function: it acts automatically to further its life, it cannot act for its own destruction.

"An animal is equipped for sustaining its life; its senses provide it with an automatic code of action, an automatic knowledge of what is good for it or evil. It has no power to extend its knowledge or to evade it. In conditions where its knowledge proves inadequate, it dies. But so long as it lives, it acts on its knowledge, with automatic safety and no power of choice, it is unable to ignore its own good, unable to decide to choose the evil and act as its own destroyer.

"Man has no automatic code of survival. His particular distinction from all other living species is the necessity to act in the face of alternatives by means of *volitional choice.* He has no automatic knowledge of what is good for him or evil, what values his life depends on, what course of action it requires. Are you prattling about an instinct of self-preservation? An *instinct* of self-preservation is precisely what man does not possess. An 'instinct' is an unerring and automatic form of knowledge. A desire is not an instinct. A desire to live does not give you the knowledge required for living. And even man's desire to live is not automatic: your secret evil today is that *that* is the desire you do not hold. Your fear of death is not a love for life and will not give you the knowledge needed to keep it. Man must obtain his knowledge and choose his actions by a process of thinking, which nature will not force him to perform. Man has the power to act as his own destroyer—and that is the way he has acted through most of his history.

"A living entity that regarded its means of survival as evil, would not survive. A plant that struggled to mangle its roots, a bird that fought to break its wings would not remain for long in the existence they affronted. But the history of man has been a struggle to deny and to destroy his mind.

"Man has been called a rational being, but rationality is a matter of choice—and the alternative his nature offers him is: rational being or suicidal animal. Man has to be man—by choice; he has to hold his life as a value—by choice; he has to learn to sustain it—by choice; he has to discover the values it requires and practice his virtues—by choice.

"A code of values accepted by choice is a code of morality.

"Whoever you are, you who are hearing me now, I am speaking to whatever living remnant is left uncorrupted within you, to the remnant of the human, to your *mind*, and I say: There *is* a morality of reason, a morality proper to man, and *Man's Life* is its standard of value.

"All that which is proper to the life of a rational being is the good; all that which destroys it is the evil.

"Man's life, as required by his nature, is not the life of a mindless brute, of a looting thug or a mooching mystic, but the life of a thinking being—not life by means of force or fraud, but life by means of achievement—not survival at any price, since there's only one price that pays for man's survival: reason.

"Man's life is the *standard* of morality, but your own life is its *purpose*. If existence on earth is your goal, you must choose your actions and values by the standard of that which is proper to man—for the purpose of preserving, fulfilling and enjoying the irreplaceable value which is your life.

"Since life requires a specific course of action, any other course will destroy it. A being who does not hold his own life as the motive and goal of his actions, is acting on the motive and standard of *death*. Such a being is a metaphysical monstrosity, struggling to oppose, negate and contradict the fact of his own existence, running blindly amuck on a trail of destruction, capable of nothing but pain.

"Happiness is the successful state of life, pain is an agent of death. Happiness is that state of consciousness which proceeds from the achievement of one's values. A morality that dares to tell you to find happiness in the renunciation of your happiness—to value the failure of your values—is an insolent negation of morality. A doctrine that gives you, as an ideal, the role of a sacrificial animal seeking slaughter on the altars of others, is giving you *death* as your standard. By the grace of reality and the nature of life, man—every man—is an end in himself, he exists for his own sake, and the achievement of his own happiness is his highest moral purpose.

"But neither life nor happiness can be achieved by the pursuit of irrational whims. Just as man is free to attempt to survive in any random manner, but will perish unless he lives as his nature requires, so he is free to seek his happiness in any mindless fraud, but the torture of frustration is all he will find, unless he seeks the happiness proper to man. The purpose of morality is to teach you, not to suffer and die, but to enjoy yourself and live.

"Sweep aside those parasites of subsidized classrooms, who live on the profits of the mind of others and proclaim that man needs no morality, no values, no code of behavior. They, who pose as scientists and claim that man is only an animal, do not grant him inclusion in the law of existence they have granted to the lowest of insects. They recognize that every living species has a way of survival demanded by its nature, they do not claim that a fish can live out of water or that a dog can live without its sense of smell—but man, they claim, the most complex of beings, man can survive in any way whatever, man has no identity, no nature, and there's no practical reason why he cannot live with his means of survival destroyed, with his mind throttled and placed at the disposal of any orders *they* might care to issue.

"Sweep aside those hatred-eaten mystics, who pose as friends of humanity and preach that the highest virtue man can practice is to hold his own life as of no value. Do they tell you that the purpose of morality is to curb man's instinct of self-preservation? It is for the purpose of self-preservation that man needs a code of morality. The only man who desires to be moral is the man who desires to live.

"No, you do not have to live; it is your basic act of choice; but if you choose to live, you must live as a man—by the work and the judgment of your mind.

"No, you do not have to live as a man; it is an act of moral choice. But you cannot live as anything else—and the alternative is that state of living death which you now see within you and around you, the state of a thing unfit for existence, no longer human and less than animal, a thing that knows nothing but pain and drags itself through its span of years in the agony of unthinking self-destruction.

"No, you do not have to think; it is an act of moral choice. But someone had to think to keep you alive; if you choose to default, you default on existence and you pass the deficit to some moral man, expecting him to sacrifice his good for the sake of letting you survive by your evil. . . .

"This much is true: the most *selfish* of all things is the independent mind that recognizes no authority higher than its own and no value higher than its judgment of truth. You are asked to sacrifice your intellectual integrity, your logic, your reason, your standard of truth—in favor of becoming a prostitute whose standard is the greatest good for the greatest number.

"If you search your code for guidance, for an answer to the question: 'What *is* the good?'—the only answer you will find is *'The good of others.'* The good is whatever others wish, whatever you feel they feel they wish, or whatever you feel they ought to feel. 'The good of others' is a magic formula that transforms anything into gold, a formula to be recited as a guarantee of moral glory and as a fumigator for any action, even the slaughter of a continent. Your standard of virtue is not an object, not an act, not a principle, but an *intention*.

You need no proof, no reasons, no success, you need not achieve *in fact* the good of others—all you need to know is that your motive was the good of others, *not* your own. Your only definition of the good is a negation: the good is the 'non-good for me.'

"Your code—which boasts that it upholds eternal, absolute, objective moral values and scorns the conditional, the relative and the subjective—your code hands out, as its version of the absolute, the following rule of moral conduct: If *you* wish it, it's evil; if others wish it, it's good; if the motive of your action is *your* welfare, don't do it; if the motive is the welfare of others, then anything goes.

"As this double-jointed, double-standard morality splits you in half, so it splits mankind into two enemy camps: one is *you,* the other is all the rest of humanity. *You* are the only outcast who has no right to wish or live. *You* are the only servant, the rest are the masters, *you* are the only giver, the rest are the takers, *you* are the eternal debtor, the rest are the creditors never to be paid off. You must not question their right to your sacrifice, or the nature of their wishes and their needs: their right is conferred upon them by a negative, by the fact that they are 'non-you.'

"For those of you who might ask questions, your code provides a consolation prize and booby-trap: it is for your own happiness, it says, that you must serve the happiness of others, the only way to achieve your joy is to give it up to others, the only way to achieve your prosperity is to surrender your wealth to others, the only way to protect your life is to protect all men except yourself—and if you find no joy in this procedure, it is your own fault and the proof of your evil; if you were good, you would find your happiness in providing a banquet for others, and your dignity in existing on such crumbs as *they* might care to toss you.

"You who have no standard of self-esteem, accept the guilt and dare not ask the questions. But you know the unadmitted answer, refusing to acknowledge what you see, what hidden premise moves your world. You know it, not in honest statement, but as a dark uneasiness within you, while you flounder between guiltily cheating and grudgingly practicing a principle too vicious to name.

"I, who do not accept the unearned, neither in values nor in *guilt,* am here to ask the questions you evaded. Why is it moral to serve the happiness of others, but not your own? If enjoyment is a value, why is it moral when experienced by others, but immoral when experienced by you? If the sensation of eating a cake is a value, why is it an immoral indulgence in your stomach, but a moral goal for you to achieve in the stomach of others? Why is it immoral for you to desire, but moral for others to do so? Why is it immoral to produce a value and keep it, but moral to give it away? And if it is not moral for you to keep a value, why is it moral for others to accept it? If you are selfless and virtuous when you give it, are they not selfish and vicious when they take it? Does virtue consist of serving vice? Is the moral purpose of those who are good, self-immolation for the sake of those who are evil? . . .

"Under a morality of sacrifice, the first value you sacrifice is morality; the next is self-esteem. When need is the standard, every man is both victim and parasite. As a victim, he must labor to fill the needs of others, leaving himself in the position of a parasite whose needs must be filled by others. He cannot approach his fellow men except in one of two disgraceful roles: he is both a beggar and a sucker.

"You fear the man who has a dollar less than you, that dollar is rightfully his, he makes you feel like a moral defrauder. You hate the man who has a dollar more than you, that dollar is rightfully yours, he makes you feel that you are morally defrauded. The man below is a source of your guilt, the man above is a source of your frustration. You do not know what to surrender or demand, when to give and when to grab, what pleasure in life is rightfully yours and what debt is still unpaid to others—you struggle to evade, as 'theory,' the knowledge that by the moral standard you've accepted you are guilty every moment of your life, there is no mouthful of food you swallow that is not *needed* by someone somewhere on earth—and you give up the problem in blind resentment, you conclude that moral perfection is not to be achieved *or desired,* that you will muddle through by snatching as snatch can and by avoiding the eyes of the young, of those who look at you as if self-esteem were possible and they expected you to have it. Guilt is all that you retain within your soul—and so does every other man, as he goes past, avoiding *your* eyes. Do you wonder why your morality has not achieved brotherhood on earth or the good will of man to man?

"The justification of sacrifice, that your morality propounds, is more corrupt than the corruption it purports to justify. The motive of your sacrifice, it tells you, should be *love*—the love you ought to feel for every man. A morality that professes the belief that the values of the spirit are more precious than matter, a morality that teaches you to scorn a whore who gives her body indiscriminately to all men—this same morality demands that you surrender your soul to promiscuous love for all comers.

"As there can be no causeless wealth, so there can be no causeless love or any sort of causeless emotion. An emotion is a response to a fact of reality, an estimate dictated by your standards. To love is to *value.* The man who tells you that it is possible to value without values, to love those whom you appraise as worthless, is the man who tells you that it is possible to grow rich by consuming without producing and that paper money is as valuable as gold.

"Observe that he does not expect you to feel a causeless fear. When his kind get into power, they are expert at contriving means of terror, at giving you ample cause to feel the fear by which they desire to rule you. But when it comes to love, the highest of emotions, you permit them to shriek at you accusingly that you are a moral delinquent if you're incapable of feeling causeless love. When a man feels fear without reason, you call him to the attention of a psychiatrist; you are not so careful to protect the meaning, the nature and the dignity of love.

"Love is the expression of one's values, the greatest reward you can earn for the moral qualities you have achieved in your character and person, the emotional price paid by one man for the joy he receives from the virtues of another. Your morality demands that you divorce your love from values and hand it down to any vagrant, not as response to his worth, but as response to his *need,* not as reward, but as alms, not as a payment for virtues, but as a blank check on vices. Your morality tells you that the purpose of love is to set you free of the bonds of morality, that love is superior to moral judgment, that true love transcends, forgives and survives every manner of evil in its object, and the greater the love the greater the depravity it permits to the loved. To love a man for his virtues is paltry and human, it tells you; to love him for his flaws is divine. To love those who are worthy of it is self-interest; to love the unworthy is sacrifice. Yon owe your love to those who don't deserve it, and the less they deserve it, the more love you owe them—the more loathsome the object, the nobler your love—the more unfastidious your love, the greater your virtue—and if you can bring your soul to the state of a dump heap that welcomes anything on equal terms, if you can cease to value moral values, you have achieved the state of moral perfection.

"Such is your morality of sacrifice and such are the twin ideals it offers: to refashion the life of your body in the image of a human stockyards, and the life of your spirit in the image of a dump. . . .

"Since childhood, you have been hiding the guilty secret that you feel no desire to be moral, no desire to seek self-immolation, that you dread and hate your code, but dare not say it even to yourself, that you're devoid of those moral 'instincts' which others profess to feel. The less you felt, the louder you proclaimed your selfless love and servitude to others, in dread of ever letting them discover your own self, the self that you betrayed, the self that you kept in concealment, like a skeleton in the closet of your body. And they, who were at once your dupes and your deceivers, they listened and voiced their loud approval, in dread of ever letting you discover that they were harboring the same unspoken secret. Existence among you is a giant pretense, an act you all perform for one another, each feeling that he is the only guilty freak, each placing his moral authority in the unknowable known only to others, each faking the reality he feels they expect him to fake, none having the courage to break the vicious circle.

"No matter what dishonorable compromise you've made with your impracticable creed, no matter what miserable balance, half-cynicism, half-superstition, you now manage to maintain, you still preserve the root, the lethal tenet: the belief that the moral and the practical are opposites. Since childhood, you have been running from the terror of a choice you have never dared fully to identify: If the *practical,* whatever you must practice to exist, whatever works, succeeds, achieves your purpose, whatever brings you food and joy, whatever profits you, is evil—and if the good, the moral, is the *impractical,* whatever fails, destroys, frustrates, whatever injures you and brings you loss or pain—then your choice is to be moral or to live.

"The sole result of that murderous doctrine was to remove morality from life. You grew up to believe that moral laws bear no relation to the job of living, except as an impediment and threat, that man's existence is an amoral jungle where anything goes and anything works. And in that fog of switching definitions which descends upon a frozen mind, you have forgotten that the evils damned by your creed were the virtues required for living, and you have come to believe that actual evils are the *practical* means of existence. Forgetting that the impractical 'good' was self-sacrifice, you believe that self-esteem is impractical; forgetting that the practical 'evil' was production, you believe that robbery is practical. . . .

"Accept the fact that the achievement of your happiness is the only *moral* purpose of your life, and that *happiness*—not pain or mindless self-indulgence— is the proof of your moral integrity, since it is the proof and the result of your loyalty to the achievement of your values. Happiness was the responsibility you dreaded, it required the kind of rational discipline you did not value yourself enough to assume—and the anxious staleness of your days is the monument to your evasion of the knowledge that there is no moral substitute for happiness, that there is no more despicable coward than the man who deserted the battle for his joy, fearing to assert his right to existence, lacking the courage and the loyalty to life of a bird or a flower reaching for the sun. Discard the protective rags of that vice which you called a virtue: humility— learn to value yourself, which means: to fight for your happiness—and when you learn that *pride* is the sum of all virtues, you will learn to live like a man.

"As a basic step of self-esteem, learn to treat as the mark of a cannibal any man's *demand* for your help. To demand it is to claim that your life is *his* property—and loathsome as such claim might be, there's something still more loathsome: your agreement. Do you ask if it's ever proper to help another man? No—if he claims it as his right or as a moral duty that you owe him. Yes—if such is your own desire based on your own selfish pleasure in the value of his person and his struggle. . . ."

Louis P. Pojman

 **NO**

Egoism and Altruism: A Critique of Ayn Rand

*U*niversal *ethical egoism* is the theory that everyone ought always to serve his or her own self-interest. That is, everyone ought to do what will maximize one's own expected utility or bring about one's own greatest happiness, even if it requires harming others. Ethical egoism is utilitarianism reduced to the pinpoint of the single individual ego. Instead of advocating the greatest happiness for the greatest number, as utilitarianism does, it advocates the greatest happiness for myself, whoever I may be. It is a self-preoccupied prudence, urging one to postpone enjoyment today for long-term benefits. In its more sophisticated form, it compares life to a competitive game, perhaps a war-game, and urges each person to *try* to win in the game of life.

In her books *The Virtue of Selfishness* and *Atlas Shrugged*, Ayn Rand argues that selfishness is a virtue and altruism a vice, a totally destructive idea that leads to the undermining of individual worth. She defines *altruism* as the view that

> any action taken for the benefit of others is good, and any action taken for one's own benefit is evil. Thus, the *beneficiary* of an action is the only criterion of moral value—and so long as the beneficiary is anybody other than oneself, anything goes.[1]

As such, altruism is suicidal:

> If a man accepts the ethics of altruism, his first concern is not how to live his life, but how to sacrifice it. . . . Altruism erodes men's capacity to grasp the value of an individual life; it reveals a mind from which the reality of a human being has been wiped out.

Since finding happiness is the highest goal and good in life, altruism, which calls on us to sacrifice our happiness for the good of others, is contrary to our highest good.

From THE MORAL LIFE: An Introductory Reader in Ethics and Literature, 2006, pp. 580–587. Copyright © 2007 by Oxford University Press. Reprinted by permission.

Her argument seems to go like this:

1. The perfection of one's abilities in a state of happiness is the highest goal for humans. We have a moral duty to attempt to reach this goal.
2. The ethics of altruism prescribes that we sacrifice our interests and lives for the good of others.
3. Therefore, the ethics of altruism is incompatible with the goal of happiness.
4. Ethical egoism prescribes that we seek our own happiness exclusively, and as such it is consistent with the happiness goal.
5. Therefore ethical egoism is the correct moral theory.

Ayn Rand's argument for the virtue of selfishness is flawed by the fallacy of a false dilemma. It simplistically assumes that absolute altruism and absolute egoism are the only alternatives. But this is an extreme view of the matter. There are plenty of options between these two positions. Even a predominant egoist would admit that (analogous to the paradox of hedonism) sometimes the best way to reach self-fulfillment is for us to forget about ourselves and strive to live for goals, causes, or other persons. Even if altruism is not required (as a duty), it may be permissible in many cases. Furthermore, self-interest may not be incompatible with other-regarding motivation. Even the Second Great Commandment set forth by Moses and Jesus states not that you must always sacrifice yourself for the other person, but that you ought to love your neighbor *as* yourself (Lev. 19:19; Matt. 23). Self-interest and self-love are morally good things, but not at the expense of other people's legitimate interests. When there is moral conflict of interests, a fair process of adjudication needs to take place.

But Rand's version of egoism is only one of many. We need to go to the heart of ethical egoism: the thesis that our highest moral duty is always to promote our individual interests. Let us focus on the alleged problems of this thesis.

Four Criticisms of Ethical Egoism

The Inconsistent Outcomes Argument

Brian Medlin argues that ethical egoism cannot be true because it fails to meet a necessary condition of morality, that of being a guide to action. He claims that it will be like advising people to do inconsistent things based on incompatible desires.[2] His argument goes like this:

1. Moral principles must be universal and categorical.
2. I must universalize my egoist desire to come out on top over Tom, Dick, and Harry.
3. But I must also prescribe Tom's egoist desire to come out on top over Dick, Harry, and me (and so on).
4. Therefore I have prescribed incompatible outcomes and have not provided a way of adjudicating conflicts of desire. In effect, I have said nothing.

The proper response to this is that of Jesse Kalin, who argues that we can separate our beliefs about ethical situations from our desires.[3] He likens the situation to a competitive sports event, in which you believe that your opponent has a right to try to win as much as you, but you desire that you, not he, will in fact win. An even better example is that of the chess game in which you recognize that your opponent ought to move her bishop to prepare for checkmate, but you hope she won't see the move. Belief that A ought to do Y does not commit you to wanting A to do Y.

The Publicity Argument

On the one hand, in order for something to be a moral theory it seems necessary that its moral principles be publicized. Unless principles are put forth as universal prescriptions that are accessible to the public, they cannot serve as guides to action or as aids in resolving conflicts of interest. But on the other hand, it is not in the egoist's self-interest to publicize them. Egoists would rather that the rest of us be altruists. (Why did Nietzsche and Rand write books announcing their positions? Were the royalties taken in by announcing ethical egoism worth the price of letting the cat out of the bag?)

Thus it would be self-defeating for the egoist to argue for her position, and even worse that she should convince others of it. But it is perfectly possible to have a private morality that does not resolve conflicts of interest. So the egoist should publicly advocate standard principles of traditional morality—so that society doesn't break down—while adhering to a private, nonstandard, solely self regarding morality. So, if you're willing to pay the price, you can accept the solipsistic-directed norms of egoism.

If the egoist is prepared to pay the price, egoism could be a consistent system that has some limitations. Although the egoist can cooperate with others in limited ways and perhaps even have friends—so long as their interests don't conflict with his—he has to be very careful about preserving his isolation. The egoist can't give advice or argue about his position—not sincerely at least. He must act alone, atomistically or solipsistically in moral isolation, for to announce his adherence to the principle of egoism would be dangerous to his project. He can't teach his children the true morality or justify himself to others or forgive others.

The Paradox of Egoism

The situation may be even worse than the sophisticated, self-conscious egoist supposes. Could the egoist have friends? And if limited friendship is possible, could he or she ever be in love or experience deep friendship? Suppose the egoist discovers that in the pursuit of the happiness goal, deep friendship is in his best interest. Can he become a friend? What is necessary to deep friendship? A true friend is one who is not always preoccupied about his own interest in the relationship but who forgets about himself altogether, at least sometimes, in order to serve or enhance the other person's interest. "Love seeketh not its own." It is an altruistic disposition, the very opposite of egoism. So the *paradox of egoism* is that in order to reach the goal of egoism one must give up egoism and become (to some extent) an altruist, the very antithesis of egoism.

The Argument from Counterintuitive Consequences

The final argument against ethical egoism is that it is an absolute ethics that not only permits egoistic behavior but demands it. Helping others at one's own expense is not only not required, it is morally wrong. Whenever I do not have good evidence that my helping you will end up to my advantage, I must refrain from helping you. If I can save the whole of Europe and Africa from destruction by pressing a button, then so long as there is nothing for me to gain by it, it is wrong for me to press that button. The Good Samaritan was, by this logic, morally wrong in helping the injured victim and not collecting payment for his troubles. It is certainly hard to see why the egoist should be concerned about environmental matters if he or she is profiting from polluting the environment. (For example, if the egoist gains 40 hedons in producing P, which produces pollution that in turn causes others 1,000 dolors—units of suffering—but suffers only 10 of those dolors himself, then by an agent-maximizing calculus he is morally obligated to produce P.) There is certainly no obligation to preserve scarce natural resources for future generations. "Why should I do anything for posterity?" the egoist asks "What has posterity ever done for me?"

In conclusion, we see that ethical egoism has a number of serious problems. It cannot consistently publicize itself, nor often argue its case. It tends towards solipsism and the exclusion of many of the deepest human values, such as love and deep friendship. It violates the principle of fairness, and, most of all, it entails an absolute prohibition on altruistic behavior, which we intuitively sense as morally required (or, at least, permissible).

Evolution and Altruism

If sheer unadulterated egoism is an inadequate moral theory, does that mean we ought to aim at complete altruism, total self-effacement for the sake of others? What is the role of self-love in morality? An interesting place to start answering these queries is with the new field of sociobiology, which theorizes that social structures and behavioral patterns, including morality, have a biological base, explained by evolutionary theory.

In the past, linking ethics to evolution meant justifying exploitation. Social Darwinism justified imperialism and the principle that "Might makes right" by saying that survival of the fittest is a law of nature. This philosophy lent itself to a promotion of ruthless egoism. This is nature's law, "nature red in tooth and claw." Against this view ethologists such as Robert Ardrey and Konrad Lorenz argued for a more benign view of the animal kingdom—one reminiscent of Rudyard Kipling's, in which the animal kingdom survives by cooperation, which is at least as important as competition. On Ardrey's and Lorenz's view it is the group or the species, not the individual, that is of primary importance.

With the development of sociobiology—in the work of E. O. Wilson but particularly the work of Robert Trivers, J. Maynard Smith, and Richard Dawkins—a theory has come to the fore that combines radical individualism with limited altruism. It is not the group or the species that is of evolutionary importance but the gene, or, more precisely, the gene type. Genes—the parts of the chromosomes that carry the blueprints for all our natural traits (e.g., height, hair color, skin color, intelligence)—copy themselves as they divide and multiply. At conception they combine with the genes of a member of the opposite sex to form a new individual.

In his fascinating sociobiological study, Richard Dawkins describes human behavior as determined evolutionarily by stable strategies set to replicate the gene.[4] This is not done consciously, of course, but by the invisible hand that drives consciousness. We are essentially gene machines.

Morality—that is, successful morality—can be seen as an evolutionary strategy for gene replication. Here's an example: Birds are afflicted with life-endangering parasites. Because they lack limbs to enable them to pick the parasites off their heads, they—like much of the animal kingdom—depend on the ritual of mutual grooming. It turns out that nature has evolved two basic types of birds in this regard: those who are disposed to groom anyone (the nonprejudiced type?), and those who refuse to groom anyone but who present themselves for grooming. The former type of bird Dawkins calls "Suckers" and the latter "Cheaters."

In a geographical area containing harmful parasites and where there are only Suckers or Cheaters, Suckers will do fairly well, but Cheaters will not survive, for want of cooperation. However, in a Sucker population in which a mutant Cheater arises, the Cheater will prosper, and the Cheater gene type will multiply. As the Suckers are exploited, they will gradually die out. But if and when they become too few to groom the Cheaters, the Cheaters will start to die off too and eventually become extinct.

Why don't birds all die off, then? Well, somehow nature has come up with a third type, call them "Grudgers." Grudgers groom all and only those who reciprocate in grooming them. They groom each other and Suckers, but not Cheaters. In fact, once caught, a Cheater is marked forever. There is no forgiveness. It turns out then that unless there are a lot of Suckers around, Cheaters have a hard time of it—harder even than Suckers. However, it is the Grudgers that prosper. Unlike Suckers, they don't waste time messing with unappreciative Cheaters, so they are not exploited and have ample energy to gather food and build better nests for their loved ones.

J. L. Mackie argues that the real name for Suckers is "Christian," one who believes in complete altruism, even turning the other cheek to one's assailant and loving one's enemy. Cheaters are ruthless egoists who can survive only if there are enough naive altruists around. Whereas Grudgers are *reciprocal* altruists who have a rational morality based on cooperative self-interest, Suckers, such as Socrates and Jesus, advocate "turning the other cheek and repaying evil with good."[5] Instead of a Rule of Reciprocity, "I'll scratch your back if you'll scratch mine," the extreme altruist substitutes the Golden Rule, "If you want the other fellow to scratch your back, you scratch his—even if he won't reciprocate."

The moral of the story is this: Altruist morality (so interpreted) is only rational given the payoff of eternal life (with a scorekeeper, as Woody Allen says). Take that away; and it looks like a Sucker system. What replaces the "Christian" vision of submission and saintliness is the reciprocal altruist with a tit-for-tat morality, someone who is willing to share with those willing to cooperate.

Mackie may caricature the position of the religious altruist, but he misses the subtleties of wisdom involved (Jesus said, "Be as wise as serpents but as harmless as doves"). Nevertheless, he does remind us that there is a difference between core morality and complete altruism. We have duties to cooperate and reciprocate, but no duty to serve those who manipulate us nor an obvious duty to sacrifice ourselves for people outside our domain of special responsibility. We have a special duty of high altruism toward those in the close circle of our concern, namely, our family and friends.

Conclusion

Martin Luther once said that humanity is like a man who, when mounting a horse, always falls off on the opposite side, especially when he tries to over-compensate for his previous exaggerations. So it is with ethical egoism. Trying to compensate for an irrational, guilt-ridden, Sucker altruism of the morality of self-effacement, it falls off the horse on the other side, embracing a Cheater's preoccupation with self-exaltation that robs the self of the deepest joys in life. Only the person who mounts properly, avoiding both extremes, is likely to ride the horse of happiness to its goal.

Notes

1. Ayn Rand, *The Virtue of Selfishness* (New American Library, 1964), pp. vii and 27–32; 80ff.

2. Brian Medlin, "Ultimate Principles and Ethical Egoism," *Australasian Journal of Philosophy* (1957), pp: 111–118; reprinted in Louis Pojman, *Ethical Theory,* pp. 91–95.

3. See Jesse Kalin, "In Defense of Egoism," in *Ethical Theory,* 4th ed., ed. Louis Pojman (Wadsworth, 2002), p. 95f.

4. Richard Dawkins, *The Selfish Gene* (Oxford University Press, 1976), Ch. 10.

5. J. L. Mackie, "The Law of the Jungle: Moral Alternatives and Principles of Evolution," *Philosophy* 53 (1978).

POSTSCRIPT

Is Ayn Rand's Ethical Egoism Correct?

There are several concerns here. One is whether ethical egoism is a viable moral theory at all. To some people, it seems not to be one. One reason is the following. Suppose that Peter and Paul are both parties to a contract that some work is to be done (by Peter) in exchange for some payment (by Paul). Suppose these parties then come to disagree. Peter says that he has done the work (on time, satisfactorily, etc.) and that Paul owes him money. But Paul says that the work is unacceptable and that he doesn't owe Peter any money. When Peter consults ethical egoism, it seems to find in his favor and he is encouraged to pursue his own interest and press for payment. But when Paul consults it, it finds in *his* favor and he is encouraged to withhold payment. Thus, ethical egoism fails to solve the problem between Peter and Paul and instead reinforces that problem. But we naturally expect an ethical theory to *solve* the problem, not to reinforce it.

Nevertheless, there remains strong interest in ethical egoism, even on the part of many thinkers who reject it. There seems to be something common-sensical and right about the idea that "charity begins at home" and that I first of all have to look out for "number one." And if ethical egoism is correct, and is incompatible with most widespread secular and religious views, then it would refute all of them with a single blow. And even if it is not correct, it is at least a worrying threat that needs to be argued against and refuted in order to make way for whatever *is* correct. Thus, either way, ethical egoism demands attention.

Further resources on ethical egoism are the entry for "egoism" in Lawrence C. Becker and Charlotte B. Becker, eds., *Encyclopedia of Ethics,* 2nd ed. (Routledge, 2001) and chapter 5 of James Rachels and Stuart Rachels, *The Elements of Moral Philosophy,* 5th ed. (McGraw-Hill, 2007). A classic article is Jesse Kalin, "In Defense of Egoism," in David Gauthier, ed., *Morality and Rational Self-Interest* (Prentice Hall, 1970), pp. 64–87. The philosophy of Ayn Rand is specifically discussed in Craig Biddle, *Loving Life: The Morality of Self-Interest and the Facts that Support It* (Glen Allen Press, 2002). See also Ayn Rand's *The Virtue of Selfishness: A New Concept of Egoism* (Signet, 1964). Ayn Rand is discussed quite favorable in Leonard Piekoff, *Objectivism: The Philosophy of Ayn Rand* (E.P. Dutton, 1991). An interesting and more critical academically serious *engagement* with Rand's ideas can be found in the essay "On the Randian Argument" in Robert Nozick, *Socratic Puzzles* (Harvard University Press, 1997). But, on the whole, academic books dealing with Ayn Rand have been few, especially considering her popular influence. Nevertheless, recent academic books include Tara Smith, *Viable Values* (Rowman & Littlefield, 2000) and Tara Smith, *Ayn Rand's Normative Ethics: The Virtuous Egoist* (Cambridge University Press, 2007).

Internet References . . .

National Abortion and Reproductive Rights Action League

This is the home page of the National Abortion and Reproductive Rights Action League (NARAL), an organization that works to promote reproductive freedom and dignity for women and their families.

http://www.naral.org/index.cfm

Pro-Life Action League

This site is pro-life with respect to abortion, but some of the links also concern euthanasia and related topics.

www.prolifeaction.org/

Pro-Life News

This site contains many links to news items and information on abortion, euthanasia, etc.

http://www.lifenews.com/

Literature on Cloning and Reproductive Technologies

This *Ethics Updates* site contains many links to articles, interviews, associations, and other resources that are concerned with cloning and reproductive technologies.

http://ethics.sandiego.edu/applied/bioethics/index.asp

Gender, Sex, and Reproduction

*H*umans *are sexual, reproductive, social beings. Given this fact, it is imperative to have some idea of what is socially acceptable and what is not, as well as what is expected of males and females, and what is not.*

The issues in this section do not presuppose that there is anything morally questionable about sex itself, but they do raise questions about how, in today's society, we should think about sex roles and matters of sex and reproduction.

- Is Abortion Immoral?

- Must Sex Involve Commitment?

- Should Same-Sex Marriage Be Allowed?

- Should Human Cloning Be Banned?

ISSUE 4

Is Abortion Immoral?

YES: Don Marquis, from "Why Abortion Is Immoral," *The Journal of Philosophy* (April 1989)

NO: Jane English, from "Abortion and the Concept of a Person," *Canadian Journal of Philosophy* (October 1975)

ISSUE SUMMARY

YES: Professor of philosophy Don Marquis argues that abortion is generally wrong for the same reason that killing an innocent adult human being is generally wrong: it deprives the individual of a future that he or she would otherwise have.

NO: Philosopher Jane English (1947–1978) asserts that there is no well-defined line dividing persons from nonpersons. She maintains that both the conservative and the liberal positions are too extreme and that some abortions are morally justifiable and some are not.

Abortion is a divisive topic, and discussions can easily become polarized. Here we will briefly consider some of the biological facts associated with abortion and review some relevant historical and legal matters. The selections themselves will then look at the moral issues raised by abortion.

Conception occurs when the spermatozoon of a male unites with the ovum of a female. The single cell thus formed is called a zygote. In a normal pregnancy, this zygote will multiply into several cells, travel through the fallopian tube, enter the uterus, and implant itself in the uterine wall. When implantation is complete, one to two weeks after fertilization (as the original conception is also called), we can say that the pregnancy is established and that the zygote has become an embryo. Once the placenta and umbilical cord are established, the embryo takes nourishment by means of these from the blood of the pregnant woman and quickly grows primitive limbs and organs. At eight weeks from conception, the first brain waves can be detected and the embryo is now called a fetus. So-called quickening, the first felt spontaneous movement of the fetus, occurs at around 14 or 15 weeks. The threshold of viability (the point at which the fetus can be kept alive outside the uterus) is dependent upon many factors, especially the development of the cardiopulmonary system. Depending on the level of available medical technology, viability can be reached sometime between 20 and 28 weeks. Birth generally takes place about 38 to 40 weeks after conception, although here too there is significant variation.

There are other possibilities once the spermatozoon and ovum unite. The fertilized ovum, for example, might never be implanted in the wall of the uterus and might be expelled uneventfully, and even without notice, from the body. Or the zygote might implant itself somewhere other than inside the uterus, resulting in an ectopic pregnancy. The embryo will not grow properly outside the uterus, and this kind of pregnancy can be dangerous to the mother. (In the case of an ectopic pregnancy, the Roman Catholic Church will permit an abortion to save the pregnant woman's life.) Another possibility is that the pregnancy will develop normally for a while but then end in miscarriage; this is sometimes called a spontaneous abortion.

The historic *Roe v. Wade* case, decided in 1973 by the U.S. Supreme Court in a split decision of 7 2, ruled that the nineteenth-century Texas statutes against abortion were unconstitutional. The Court divided the normal pregnancy into three trimesters and ruled as follows:

> For the stage prior to approximately the end of the first trimester, the abortion decision and its effectuation must be left to the medical judgment of the pregnant woman's attending physician. For the stage subsequent to approximately the end of the first trimester, the State, in promoting its interest in the health of the mother, may, if it chooses, regulate the abortion procedure in ways that are reasonably related to maternal health. For the stages subsequent to viability, the State, in promoting its interest in the potentiality of human life, may, if it chooses, regulate, and even proscribe, abortion except where it is necessary, in appropriate medical judgment, for the preservation of the life or health of the mother. (410 U.S.113, 93 S. Ct. 705 [1973])

Before *Roe v. Wade*, some states permitted abortion only if a woman's life was in danger; abortion for any other reason or consideration was illegal and punishable by law. *Roe v. Wade* ruled that states do not have the right to regulate abortion procedures in any way during the first trimester of pregnancy. It is important to note that neither the Supreme Court nor the Texas statutes said anything about the relation of the woman to the fetus (or embryo) or about the reasons a woman might have for seeking an abortion.

In the following selections, Don Marquis constructs a secular argument to show that abortion is immoral. He focuses not on the present status of the fetus, but on the future status. This avoids the divisive question of whether or not the fetus is a person. Jane English counters that this question has no determinate answer. In her view, neither the standard conservative position nor the standard liberal position adequately addresses the issue of abortion.

YES

Don Marquis

Why Abortion Is Immoral

The view that abortion is, with rare exceptions, seriously immoral has received little support in the recent philosophical literature. No doubt most philosophers affiliated with secular institutions of higher education believe that the anti-abortion position is either a symptom of irrational religious dogma or a conclusion generated by seriously confused philosophical argument. The purpose of this essay is to undermine this general belief. This essay sets out an argument that purports to show, as well as any argument in ethics can show, that abortion is, except possibly in rare cases, seriously immoral, that it is in the same moral category as killing an innocent adult human being.

The argument is based on a major assumption. Many of the most insightful and careful writers on the ethics of abortion—such as Joel Feinberg, Michael Tooley, Mary Anne Warren, H. Tristram Engelhardt, Jr., L. W. Sumner, John T. Noonan, Jr., and Philip Devine[1]—believe that whether or not abortion is morally permissible stands or falls on whether or not a fetus is the sort of being whose life it is seriously wrong to end. The argument of this essay will assume, but not argue, that they are correct.

Also, this essay will neglect issues of great importance to a complete ethics of abortion. Some anti-abortionists will allow that certain abortions, such as abortion before implantation or abortion when the life of a woman is threatened by a pregnancy or abortion after rape, may be morally permissible. This essay will not explore the casuistry of these hard cases. The purpose of this essay is to develop a general argument for the claim that the overwhelming majority of deliberate abortions are seriously immoral.

A sketch of standard anti-abortion and pro-choice arguments exhibits how those arguments possess certain symmetries that explain why partisans of those positions are so convinced of the correctness of their own positions, why they are not successful in convincing their opponents, and why, to others, this issue seems to be unresolvable. An analysis of the nature of this standoff suggests a strategy for surmounting it.

Consider the way a typical anti-abortionist argues. She will argue or assert that life is present from the moment of conception or that fetuses look like babies or that fetuses possess a characteristic such as a genetic code that is

From *Journal of Philosophy*, vol. 86, no. 4, April 1989. Copyright © 1989 by Journal of Philosophy, Inc. Reprinted by permission.

both necessary and sufficient for being human. Anti-abortionists seem to believe that (1) the truth of all of these claims is quite obvious, and (2) establishing any of these claims is sufficient to show that abortion is morally akin to murder.

A standard pro-choice strategy exhibits similarities. The pro-choicer will argue or assert that fetuses are not persons or that fetuses are not rational agents or that fetuses are not social beings. Pro-choicers seem to believe that (1) the truth of any of these claims is quite obvious, and (2) establishing any of these claims is sufficient to show that an abortion is not a wrongful killing.

In fact, both the pro-choice and the anti-abortion claims do seem to be true, although the "it looks like a baby" claim is more difficult to establish the earlier the pregnancy. We seem to have a standoff. How can it be resolved?

As everyone who has taken a bit of logic knows, if any of these arguments concerning abortion is a good argument, it requires not only some claim characterizing fetuses, but also some general moral principle that ties a characteristic of fetuses to having or not having the right to life or to some other moral characteristic that will generate the obligation or the lack of obligation not to end the life of a fetus. Accordingly, the arguments of the anti-abortionist and the pro-choicer need a bit of filling in to be regarded as adequate.

Note what each partisan will say. The anti-abortionist will claim that her position is supported by such generally accepted moral principles as "It is always prima facie seriously wrong to take a human life" or "It is always prima facie seriously wrong to end the life of a baby." Since these are generally accepted moral principles, her position is certainly not obviously wrong. The pro-choicer will claim that her position is supported by such plausible moral principles as "Being a person is what gives an individual intrinsic moral worth" or "It is only seriously prima facie wrong to take the life of a member of the human community." Since these are generally accepted moral principles, the pro-choice position is certainly not obviously wrong. Unfortunately, we have again arrived at a standoff.

Now, how might one deal with this standoff? The standard approach is to try to show how the moral principles of one's opponent lose their plausibility under analysis. It is easy to see how this is possible. On the one hand, the anti-abortionist will defend a moral principle concerning the wrongness of killing which tends to be broad in scope in order that even fetuses at an early stage of pregnancy will fall under it. The problem with broad principles is that they often embrace too much. In this particular instance, the principle "It is always prima facie wrong to take a human life" seems to entail that it is wrong to end the existence of a living human cancer-cell culture, on the grounds that the culture is both living and human. Therefore, it seems that the anti-abortionist's favored principle is too broad.

On the other hand, the pro-choicer wants to find a moral principle concerning the wrongness of killing which tends to be narrow in scope in order that fetuses will *not* fall under it. The problem with narrow principles is that they often do not embrace enough. Hence, the needed principles such as "It is prima facie seriously wrong to kill only persons" or "It is prima facie wrong to kill only rational agents" do not explain why it is wrong to kill infants or young children or the severely retarded or even perhaps the severely mentally ill. Therefore, we seem again to have a standoff. The anti-abortionist charges, not unreasonably, that pro-choice principles concerning killing are too narrow to be acceptable; the pro-choicer charges, not unreasonably, that anti-abortionist principles concerning killing are too broad to be acceptable.

Attempts by both sides to patch up the difficulties in their positions run into further difficulties. The anti-abortionist will try to remove the problem in her position by reformulating her principle concerning killing in terms of human beings. Now we end up with: "It is always prima facie seriously wrong to end the life of a human being." This principle has the advantage of avoiding the problem of the human cancer-cell culture counterexample. But this advantage is purchased at a high price. For although it is clear that a fetus is both human and alive, it is not at all clear that a fetus is a human *being*. There is at least something to be said for the view that something becomes a human being only after a process of development, and that therefore first trimester fetuses and perhaps all fetuses are not yet human beings. Hence, the anti-abortionist, by this move, has merely exchanged one problem for another.[2]

The pro-choicer fares no better. She may attempt to find reasons why killing infants, young children, and the severely retarded is wrong which are independent of her major principle that is supposed to explain the wrongness of taking human life, but which will not also make abortion immoral. This is no easy task. Appeals to social utility will seem satisfactory only to those who resolve not to think of the enormous difficulties with a utilitarian account of the wrongness of killing and the significant social costs of preserving the lives of the unproductive.[3] A pro-choice strategy that extends the definition of 'person' to infants or even to young children seems just as arbitrary as an anti-abortion strategy that extends the definition of 'human being' to fetuses. Again, we find symmetries in the two positions and we arrive at a standoff.

There are even further problems that reflect symmetries in the two positions. In addition to counterexample problems, or the arbitrary application problems that can be exchanged for them, the standard anti-abortionist principle "It is prima facie seriously wrong to kill a human being," or one of its variants, can be objected to on the grounds of ambiguity. If 'human being' is taken to be a *biological* category, then the anti-abortionist is left with the problem of explaining why a merely biological category should make a moral difference. Why, it is asked, is it any more reasonable to base a moral conclusion on the number of chromosomes in one's cells than on the color of one's skin?[4] If 'human being', on the other hand, is taken to be a *moral* category, then the claim that a fetus is a human being cannot be taken to be a premise in the anti-abortion argument, for it is precisely what needs to be established. Hence, either the anti-abortionist's main category is a morally irrelevant, merely biological category, or it is of no use to the anti-abortionist in establishing (non-circularly, of course) that abortion is wrong.

Although this problem with the anti-abortionist position is often noticed, it is less often noticed that the pro-choice position suffers from an analogous problem. The principle "Only persons have the right to life" also suffers from an ambiguity. The term 'person' is typically defined in terms of psychological characteristics, although there will certainly be disagreement concerning which characteristics are most important. Supposing that this matter can be settled, the pro-choicer is left with the problem of explaining why *psychological* characteristics should make a *moral* difference. If the pro-choicer should attempt to deal with this problem by claiming that an explanation is not necessary, that in fact we do treat such a cluster of psychological properties as having moral significance, the sharp-witted anti-abortionist should have a ready response. We do treat being both living and human as having moral significance. If it is legitimate for the pro-choicer to demand that the anti-abortionist provide an explanation of the connection between the biological character of being a human being and the wrongness of being killed (even though people accept this connection), then it is legitimate for the anti-abortionist to demand that the pro-choicer provide an explanation of the connection between psychological criteria for being a person and the wrongness of being killed (even though that connection is accepted).[5] . . .

[T]he pro-choicer cannot any more escape her problem by making person a purely moral category than the anti-abortionist could escape by the analogous move. For if person is a moral category, then the pro-choicer is left without the resources for establishing (noncircularly, of course) the claim that a fetus is not a person, which is an essential premise in her argument. Again, we have both a symmetry and a standoff between pro-choice and anti-abortion views.

Passions in the abortion debate run high. There are both plausibilities and difficulties with the standard positions. Accordingly, it is hardly surprising that partisans of either side embrace with fervor the moral generalizations that support the conclusions they preanalytically favor, and reject with disdain the moral generalizations of their opponents as being subject to inescapable difficulties. It is easy to believe that the counterexamples to one's own moral principles are merely temporary difficulties that will dissolve in the wake of further philosophical research, and that the counterexamples to the principles of one's opponents are . . . straightforward. . . . This might suggest to an impartial observer (if there are any) that the abortion issue is unresolvable.

There is a way out of this apparent dialectical quandary. The moral generalizations of both sides are not quite correct. The generalizations hold for the most part, for the usual cases. This suggests that they are all *accidental* generalizations, that the moral claims made by those on both sides of the dispute do not touch on the *essence* of the matter.

This use of the distinction between essence and accident is not meant to invoke obscure metaphysical categories. Rather, it is intended to reflect the rather atheoretical nature of the abortion discussion. If the generalization a partisan in the abortion dispute adopts were derived from the reason why ending the life of a human being is wrong, then there could not be exceptions to that generalization unless some special case obtains in which there are even more powerful countervailing reasons. Such generalizations would not be merely accidental generalizations; they would point to, or be based upon, the essence of the wrongness of killing, what it is that makes killing wrong. All this suggests that a necessary condition of resolving the abortion controversy is a more theoretical account of the wrongness of killing. After all, if we merely believe, but do not understand, why killing adult human beings such as ourselves is wrong, how could we conceivably show that abortion is either immoral or permissible?

⋅◦⊙◦⋅

In order to develop such an account, we can start from the following unproblematic assumption concerning our own case: it is wrong to kill *us*. Why is it wrong? . . .

What primarily makes killing wrong is neither its effect on the murderer nor its effect on the victim's friends and relatives, but its effect on the victim. The loss of one's life is one of the greatest losses one can suffer. The loss of one's life deprives one of all the experiences, activities, projects, and enjoyments that would otherwise have constituted one's future. Therefore, killing someone is wrong, primarily because the killing inflicts (one of) the greatest possible losses on the victim. To describe this as the loss of life can be misleading, however. The change in my biological state does not by itself make killing me wrong. The effect of the loss of my biological life is the loss to me of all those activities, projects, experiences, and enjoyments which would otherwise have constituted my future personal life. These activities, projects, experiences, and enjoyments are either valuable for their own sakes or are means to something else that is valuable for its own sake. Some parts of my future are not valued by me now, but will come to be valued by me as I grow older and as my values and capacities change. When I am killed, I am deprived both of what I now value which would have been part of my future personal life, but also what I would come to value. Therefore, when I die, I am deprived of all of the value of my future. Inflicting this loss on me is ultimately what makes killing me wrong. This being the case, it would seem that what makes killing *any* adult human being prima facie seriously wrong is the loss of his or her future.[6] . . .

The claim that what makes killing wrong is the loss of the victim's future is directly supported by two considerations. In the first place, this theory explains why we regard killing as one of the worst of crimes. Killing is especially wrong, because it deprives the victim of more than perhaps any other crime. In the second place, people with AIDS or cancer who know they are dying believe, of course, that dying is a very bad thing for them. They believe that the loss of a future to them that they would otherwise have experienced is what makes their premature death a very bad thing for them. A better theory of the wrongness of killing would require a different natural property associated with killing which better fits with the attitudes of the dying. What could it be?

The view that what makes killing wrong is the loss to the victim of the value of the victim's future gains additional support when some of its implications are examined. In the first place, it is incompatible with the view that it is wrong to kill only beings who are biologically human. It is possible that there exists a different species from another planet whose members have a future like ours. Since having a future like that is what makes killing someone wrong, this theory entails that it would be wrong to kill members of such a species. Hence, this theory is opposed to the claim that only life that is biologically human has great moral worth, a claim which many anti-abortionists have seemed to adopt. This opposition, which this theory has in common with personhood theories, seems to be a merit of the theory.

In the second place, the claim that the loss of one's future is the wrong-making feature of one's being killed entails the possibility that the futures of some actual nonhuman mammals on our own planet are sufficiently like ours that it is seriously wrong to kill them also. Whether some animals do have the same right to life as human beings depends on adding to the account of the wrongness of killing some additional account of just what it is about my future or the futures of other adult human beings which makes it wrong to kill us. No such additional account will be offered in this essay. Undoubtedly, the provision of such an account would be a very difficult matter. Undoubtedly, any such account would be quite controversial. Hence, it surely should not reflect badly on this sketch of an elementary theory of the wrongness of killing that it is indeterminate with respect to some very difficult issues regarding animal rights.

In the third place, the claim that the loss of one's future is the wrong-making feature of one's being killed does not entail, as sanctity of human life theories do, that active euthanasia is wrong. Persons who are severely and incurably ill, who face a future of pain and despair, and who wish to die will not have suffered a loss if they are killed. It is, strictly speaking, the value of a human's future which makes killing wrong in this theory. This being so, killing does not necessarily wrong some persons who are sick and dying. Of course, there may be other reasons for a prohibition of active euthanasia, but that is another matter. Sanctity-of-human-life theories seem to hold that active euthanasia is seriously wrong even in an individual case where there seems to be good reason for it independently of public policy considerations. This consequence is most implausible, and it is a plus for the claim that the loss of a future of value is what makes killing wrong that it does not share this consequence.

In the fourth place, the account of the wrongness of killing defended in this essay does straightforwardly entail that it is prima facie seriously wrong to kill children and infants, for we do presume that they have futures of value. Since we do believe that it is wrong to kill defenseless little babies, it is important that a theory of the wrongness of killing easily account for this. Personhood theories of the wrongness of killing, on the other hand, cannot straightforwardly account for the wrongness of killing infants and young children.[7] Hence, such theories must add special ad hoc accounts of the wrongness of killing the young. The plausibility of such ad hoc theories seems to be a function of how desperately one wants such theories to work. The claim that the primary wrong-making feature of a killing is the loss to the victim of the value of its future accounts for the wrongness of killing young children and infants directly; it makes the wrongness of such acts as obvious as we actually think it is. This is a further merit of this theory. Accordingly, it seems that this value of a future-like-ours theory of the wrongness of killing shares strengths of both sanctity-of-life and personhood accounts while avoiding weaknesses of both. In addition, it meshes with a central intuition concerning what makes killing wrong.

The claim that the primary wrong-making feature of a killing is the loss to the victim of the value of its future has obvious consequences for the ethics of abortion. The future of a standard fetus includes a set of experiences, projects, activities, and such which are identical with the futures of adult human beings and are identical with the futures of young children. Since the reason that is sufficient to explain why it is wrong to kill human beings after the time of birth is a reason that also applies to fetuses, it follows that abortion is prima facie seriously morally wrong. . . .

How complete an account of the wrongness of killing does the value of a future-like-ours account have to be in order that the wrongness of abortion is a consequence? This account does not have to be an account of the necessary conditions for the wrongness of killing. Some persons in nursing homes may lack valuable human futures, yet it may be wrong to kill them for other reasons. Furthermore, this account does not obviously have to be the sole reason killing is wrong where the victim did have a valuable future. This analysis claims only that, for any killing where the victim did have a valuable future like ours, having that future by itself is sufficient to create the strong presumption that the killing is seriously wrong. . . .

In this essay, it has been argued that the correct ethic of the wrongness of killing can be extended to fetal life and used to show that there is a strong presumption that any abortion is morally impermissible. If the ethic of killing adopted here entails, however, that contraception is also seriously immoral, then there would appear to be a difficulty with the analysis of this essay.

But this analysis does not entail that contraception is wrong. Of course, contraception prevents the actualization of a possible future of value. Hence, it follows from the claim that futures of value should be maximized that contraception is prima facie immoral. This obligation to maximize does not exist, however; furthermore, nothing in the ethics of killing in this paper entails that it does. The ethics of killing in this essay would entail that contraception is wrong only if something were denied a human future of value by contraception. Nothing at all is denied such a future by contraception, however. . . .

At the time of contraception, there are hundreds of millions of sperm, one (released) ovum and millions of possible combinations of all of these. There is no actual combination at all. Is the subject of the loss to be a merely possible combination? Which one? This alternative does not yield an actual subject of harm either. Accordingly, the immorality of contraception is not entailed by the loss of a future-like-ours argument simply because there is no nonarbitrarily identifiable subject of the loss in the case of contraception.

❧◉❧

The purpose of this essay has been to set out an argument for the serious presumptive wrongness of abortion subject to the assumption that the moral permissibility of abortion stands or falls on the moral status of the fetus. Since a fetus possesses a property, the possession of which in adult human beings is sufficient to make killing an adult human being wrong, abortion is wrong. This way of dealing with the problem of abortion seems superior to other approaches to the ethics of abortion, because it rests on an ethics of killing which is close to self-evident, because the crucial morally relevant property clearly applies to fetuses, and because the argument avoids the usual equivocations on 'human life', 'human being', or 'person'. The argument rests neither on religious claims nor on Papal dogma. It is not subject to the objection of "speciesism." Its soundness is compatible with the moral permissibility of euthanasia and contraception. It deals with our intuitions concerning young children.

Finally, this analysis can be viewed as resolving a standard problem—indeed, *the* standard problem—concerning the ethics of abortion. Clearly, it is wrong to kill adult human beings. Clearly, it is not wrong to end the life of some arbitrarily chosen single human cell. Fetuses seem to be like arbitrarily chosen human cells in some respects and like adult humans in other respects. The problem of the ethics of abortion is the problem of determining the fetal property that settles this moral controversy. The thesis of this essay is that the problem of the ethics of abortion, so understood, is solvable.

Notes

1. Feinberg, "Abortion," in *Matters of Life and Death: New Introductory Essays in Moral Philosophy,* Tom Regan, ed. (New York: Random House, 1986), pp. 256–293; Tooley, "Abortion and Infanticide," *Philosophy and Public Affairs,* II, 1 (1972): 37–65; Tooley, *Abortion and Infanticide* (New York: Oxford, 1984); Warren, "On the Moral and Legal Status of Abortion," *The Monist,* I.VII, 1 (1973): 43–61; Engelhardt, "The Ontology of Abortion," *Ethics,* I, XXXIV, 3 (1974): 217–234; Sumner, *Abortion and Moral Theory* (Princeton: University Press, 1981); Noonan, "An Almost Absolute Value in History," in *The Morality of Abortion: Legal and Historical Perspectives,* Noonan, ed. (Cambridge: Harvard, 1970); and Devine, *The Ethics of Homicide* (Ithaca: Cornell, 1978).

2. For interesting discussions of this issue, see Warren Quinn, "Abortion: Identity and Loss," *Philosophy and Public Affairs,* XIII, 1 (1984): 24–54; and Lawrence C. Becker, "Human Being: The Boundaries of the Concept," *Philosophy and Public Affairs,* IV, 4 (1975): 334–359.

3. For example, see my "Ethics and the Elderly: Some Problems," in Stuart Spicker, Kathleen Woodward, and David Van Tassel, eds., *Aging and the Elderly: Humanistic Perspectives in Gerontology* (Atlantic Highlands, NJ: Humanities, 1978), pp. 341–355.

4. See Warren, *op.cit.,* and Tooley, "Abortion and Infanticide."

5. This seems to be the fatal flaw in Warren's treatment of this issue.

6. I have been most influenced on this matter by Jonathan Glover, *Causing Death and Saving Lives* (New York: Penguin, 1977), ch. 3; and Robert Young, "What Is So Wrong with Killing People?" *Philosophy,* LIV, 210 (1979): 515–528.

7. Feinberg, Tooley, Warren, and Engelhardt have all dealt with this problem.

Jane English  **NO**

Abortion and the Concept of a Person

The abortion debate rages on. Yet the two most popular positions seem to be clearly mistaken. Conservatives maintain that a human life begins at conception and that therefore abortion must be wrong because it is murder. But not all killings of humans are murders. Most notably, self-defense may justify even the killing of an innocent person.

Liberals, on the other hand, are just as mistaken in their argument that since a fetus does not become a person until birth, a woman may do whatever she pleases in and to her own body. First, you cannot do to as you please with your own body if it affects other people adversely.[1] Second, if a fetus is not a person, that does not imply that you can do to it anything you wish. Animals, for example, are not persons, yet to kill or torture them for no reason at all is wrong.

At the center of the storm has been the issue of just when it is between ovulation and adulthood that a person appears on the scene. Conservatives draw the line at conception, liberals at birth. In this paper I first examine our concept of a person and conclude that no single criterion can capture the concept of a person and no sharp line can be drawn. Next I argue that if a fetus is a person, abortion is still justifiable in many cases; and if a fetus is not a person, killing it is still wrong in many cases. To a large extent, these two solutions are in agreement. I conclude that our concept of a person cannot and need not bear the weight that the abortion controversy has thrust upon it.

The several factions in the abortion argument have drawn battle lines around various proposed criteria for determining what is and what is not a person. For example, Mary Anne Warren[2] lists five features (capacities for reasoning, self-awareness, complex communication, etc.) as her criteria for personhood and argues for the permissibility of abortion because a fetus falls outside this concept. Baruch Brody[3] uses brain waves. Michael Tooley[4] picks having-a-concept-of-self as his criterion and concludes that infanticide and abortion are justifiable, while the killing of adult animals is not. On the other side, Paul Ramsey[5] claims a certain gene structure is the defining characteristic. John Noonan[6] prefers conceived-of-humans and presents counterexamples to various other candidate criteria. For instance, he argues against viability as the criterion because the newborn and infirm would then be nonpersons, since they cannot live without the aid of others. He rejects any criterion that calls upon the sorts of sentiments a being can evoke in adults on the grounds

From *Canadian Journal of Philosophy*, October 1975, vol. 5, no. 2, pp. 233–243. Copyright © 1975 by Canadian Journal of Philosophy. Reprinted by permission of Canadian Journal of Philosophy via the Copyright Clearance Center.

that this would allow us to exclude other races as nonpersons if we could just view them sufficiently unsentimentally.

These approaches are typical: foes of abortion propose sufficient conditions for personhood which fetuses satisfy, while friends of abortion counter with necessary conditions for personhood which fetuses lack. But these both presuppose that the concept of a person can be captured in a straitjacket of necessary and/or sufficient conditions.[7] Rather, "person" is a cluster of features, of which rationality, having a self concept and being conceived of humans are only part.

What is typical of persons? Within our concept of a person we include, first, certain biological factors: descended from humans, having a certain genetic makeup, having a head, hands, arms, eyes, capable of locomotion, breathing, eating, sleeping. There are psychological factors: sentience, perception, having a concept of self and of one's own interests and desires, the ability to use tools, the ability to use language or symbol systems, the ability to joke, to be angry, to doubt. There are rationality factors: the ability to reason and draw conclusions, the ability to generalize and to learn from past experience, the ability to sacrifice present interests for greater gains in the future. There are social factors: the ability to work in groups and respond to peer pressure, the ability to recognize and consider as valuable the interests of others, seeing oneself as one among "other minds," the ability to sympathize, encourage, love, the ability to evoke from others the responses of sympathy, encouragement, love, the ability to work with others for mutual advantage. Then there are legal factors: being subject to the law and protected by it, having the ability to sue and enter contracts, being counted in the census, having a name and citizenship, the ability to own property, inherit, and so forth.

Now the point is not that this list is incomplete, or that you can find counterinstances to each of its points. People typically exhibit rationality, for instance, but someone who was irrational would not thereby fail to qualify as a person. On the other hand, something could exhibit the majority of these features and still fail to be a person, as an advanced robot might. There is no single core of necessary and sufficient features which we can draw upon with the assurance that they constitute what really makes a person; there are only features that are more or less typical.

This is not to say that no necessary or sufficient conditions can be given. Being alive is a necessary condition for being a person, and being a U.S. Senator is sufficient. But rather than falling inside a sufficient condition or outside a necessary one, a fetus lies in the penumbra region where our concept of a person is not so simple. For this reason I think a conclusive answer to the question whether a fetus is a person is unattainable.

Here we might note a family of simple fallacies that proceed by stating a necessary condition for personhood and showing that a fetus has that characteristic. This is a form of the fallacy of affirming the consequent. For example, some have mistakenly reasoned from the premise that a fetus is human (after all, it is a human fetus rather than, say, a canine fetus), to the conclusion that it is a human. Adding an equivocation on "being," we get the fallacious argument that since a fetus is something both living and human, it is a human being.

Nonetheless, it does seem clear that a fetus has very few of the above family of characteristics, whereas a newborn baby exhibits a much larger proportion of them—and a two-year-old has even more. Note that one traditional antiabortion argument has centered on pointing out the many ways in which a fetus resembles a baby. They emphasize its development ("It already has ten fingers . . .") without mentioning its dissimilarities to adults (it still has gills and a tail). They also try to evoke the sort of sympathy on our part that we only feel toward other persons ("Never to laugh . . . or feel the sunshine?"). This all seems to be a relevant way to argue, since its purpose is to persuade us that a fetus satisfies so many of the important features on the list that it ought to be treated as a person. Also note that a fetus near the time of birth satisfies many more of these factors than a fetus in the early months of development. This could provide reason for making distinctions among the different stages of pregnancy, as the U.S. Supreme Court has done.[8]

Historically, the time at which a person has been said to come into existence has varied widely. Muslims date personhood from fourteen days after conception. Some medievals followed Aristotle in placing ensoulment at forty days after conception for a male fetus and eighty days for a female fetus.[9] In European common law since the seventeenth century, abortion was considered the killing of a person only after quickening, the time when a pregnant woman first feels the fetus move on its own. Nor is this variety of opinions surprising. Biologically, a human being develops gradually. We shouldn't expect there to be any specific time or sharp dividing point when a person appears on the scene.

For these reasons I believe our concept of a person is not sharp or decisive enough to bear the weight of a solution to the abortion controversy. To use it to solve that problem is to clarify *obscurum per obscurius* [to clarify what is obscure by what is more obscure].

Next let us consider what follows if a fetus is a person after all. Judith Jarvis Thomson's landmark article, "A Defense of Abortion,"[10] correctly points out that some additional argumentation is needed at this point in the conservative argument to bridge the gap between the premise that a fetus is an innocent person and the conclusion that killing it is always wrong. To arrive at this conclusion, we would need the additional premise that killing an innocent person is always wrong. But killing an innocent person is sometimes permissible, most notably in self-defense. Some examples may help draw out our intuitions or ordinary judgments about self-defense.

Suppose a mad scientist, for instance, hypnotized innocent people to jump out of the bushes and attack innocent passers-by with knives. If you are so attacked, we agree you have a right to kill the attacker in self-defense, if killing him is the only way to protect your life or to save yourself from serious injury. It does not seem to matter here that the attacker is not malicious but himself an innocent pawn, for your killing of him is not done in a spirit of retribution but only in self-defense.

How severe an injury may you inflict in self-defense? In part this depends upon the severity of the injury to be avoided: you may not shoot someone merely to avoid having your clothes torn. This might lead one to the mistaken conclusion that the defense may only equal the threatened injury in severity; that to avoid death you may kill, but to avoid a black eye you may only inflict a black eye or the equivalent. Rather, our laws and customs seem to say that you may create an injury somewhat, but not enormously, greater than the injury to be avoided. To fend off an attack whose outcome would be as serious as rape, a severe beating or the loss of a finger, you may shoot; to avoid having your clothes torn, you may blacken an eye. . . .

Some cases of pregnancy present a parallel situation. Though the fetus is itself innocent, it may pose a threat to the pregnant woman's well-being, life prospects or health, mental or physical. If the pregnancy presents a slight threat to her interests, it seems self-defense cannot justify abortion. But if the threat is on a par with a serious beating or the loss of a finger, she may kill the fetus that poses such a threat, even if it is an innocent person. If a lesser harm to the fetus could have the same defensive effect, killing it would not be justified. It is unfortunate that the only way to free the woman from the pregnancy entails the death of the fetus (except in very late stages of pregnancy). Thus a self-defense model supports Thomson's point that the woman has a right only to be freed from the fetus, not a right to demand its death.[11] . . .

Thanks to modern technology, the cases are rare in which pregnancy poses as clear a threat to a woman's bodily health as an attacker brandishing a switchblade. How does self-defense fare when more subtle, complex and long-range harms are involved?

To consider a somewhat fanciful example, suppose you are a highly trained surgeon when you are kidnapped by the hypnotic attacker. He says he does not intend to harm you but to take you back to the mad scientist who, it turns out, plans to hypnotize you to have a permanent mental block against all your knowledge of medicine. This would automatically destroy your career which would in turn have a serious adverse impact on your family, your personal relationships and your happiness. It seems to me that if the only way you can avoid this outcome is to shoot the innocent attacker, you are justified in so doing. You are defending yourself from a drastic injury to your life prospects. I think it is no exaggeration to claim that unwanted pregnancies (most obviously among teenagers) often have such adverse life-long consequences as the surgeon's loss of livelihood.

Several parallels arise between various views on abortion and the self-defense model. Let's suppose further that these hypnotized attackers only operate at night, so that it is well known that they can be avoided completely by the considerable inconvenience of never leaving your house after dark. One view is that since you could stay home at night, therefore if you go out and are selected by one of these hypnotized people, you have no right to defend yourself. This parallels the view that abstinence is the only acceptable way to avoid pregnancy. Others might hold that you ought to take along some defense such as Mace which will deter the hypnotized person without killing him, but that if this defense fails, you are obliged to submit to the resulting injury, no matter how severe it is. This parallels the view that contraception is all right but abortion is always wrong, even in cases of contraceptive failure.

A third view is that you may kill the hypnotized person only if he will actually kill you, but not if he will only injure you. This is like the position that abortion is permissible only if it is required to save a woman's life. Finally we have the view that it is all right to kill the attacker, even if only to avoid a very slight inconvenience to yourself and even if you knowingly walked down the very street where all these incidents have been taking place without taking along any Mace or protective escort. If we assume that a fetus is a person, this is the analogue of the view that abortion is always justifiable, "on demand."

The self-defense model allows us to see an important difference that exists between abortion and infanticide, even if a fetus is a person from conception. Many have argued that the only way to justify abortion without justifying infanticide would be to find some characteristic of personhood that is acquired at birth. Michael Tooley, for one, claims infanticide is justifiable because the really significant characteristics of person [hood] are acquired some time after birth. But all such approaches look to characteristics of the developing human and ignore the relation between the fetus and the woman. What if, after birth, the presence of an infant or the need to support it posed a grave threat to the woman's sanity or life prospects? She could escape this threat by the simple expedient of running away. So a solution that does not entail the death of the infant is available. Before birth, such solutions are not available because of the biological dependence of the fetus on the woman. Birth is the crucial point not because of any characteristics the fetus gains, but because after birth the woman can defend herself by a means less drastic than killing the infant. Hence self-defense can only be used to justify abortion without necessarily thereby justifying infanticide.

On the other hand, supposing a fetus is not after all a person, would abortion always be morally permissible? Some opponents of abortion seem worried that if a fetus is not a full-fledged person, then we are justified in treating it in any way at all. However, this does not follow. Nonpersons do get some consideration in our moral code, though of course they do not have the same rights as persons have (and in general they do not have moral responsibilities), and though their interests may be overridden by the interests of persons. Still, we cannot just treat them in any way at all.

Treatment of animals is a case in point. It is wrong to torture dogs for fun or to kill wild birds for no reason at all. It is wrong Period, even though dogs and birds do not have the same rights persons do. However, few people think it is wrong to use dogs as experimental animals, causing them considerable suffering in some cases, provided that the resulting research will probably bring discoveries of great benefit to people. And most of us think it all right to kill birds for food or to protect our crops. People's rights are different from the consideration we give to animals, then, for it is wrong to experiment on people, even if others might later benefit a great deal as a result of their suffering. You might volunteer to be a subject, but this would be supererogatory; you certainly have a right to refuse to be a medical guinea pig.

But how do we decide what you may or may not do to nonpersons? This is a difficult problem, one for which I believe no adequate account exists. You do not want to say, for instance, that torturing dogs is all right whenever the sum of its effects on people is good—when it doesn't warp the sensibilities of the torturer so much that he mistreats people. If that were the case, it would be all right to torture dogs if you did it in private, or if the torturer lived on a desert island or died soon afterward, so that his actions had no effect on people. This is an inadequate account, because whatever moral consideration animals get, it has to be indefeasible, too. It will have to be a general proscription of certain actions, not merely a weighing of the impact on people on a case-by-case basis. . . .

An ethical theory must operate by generating a set of sympathies and attitudes toward others which reinforces the functioning of . . . moral principles. Our prohibition against killing people operates by means of certain moral sentiments including sympathy, compassion and guilt. But if these attitudes are to form a coherent set, they carry us further; we tend to perform supererogatory actions, and we tend to feel similar compassion toward person-like nonpersons.

It is crucial that psychological facts play a role here. Our psychological constitution makes it the case that for our ethical theory to work, it must prohibit certain treatment of nonpersons which are significantly person-like. If our moral rules allowed people to treat some person-like nonpersons in ways we do not want people to be treated, this would undermine the system of sympathies and attitudes that makes the ethical system work. . . . Thus it makes sense that it is those animals whose appearance and behavior are most like those people that get the most consideration in our moral scheme.

It is because of "coherence of attitudes," I think, that the similarity of a fetus to a baby is very significant. A fetus one week before birth is so much like a newborn baby in our psychological space that we cannot allow any cavalier treatment of the former while expecting full sympathy and nurturative support for the latter. Thus, I think that antiabortion forces are indeed giving their strongest arguments when they point to the similarities between a fetus and a baby, and when they try to evoke our emotional attachment to and sympathy for the fetus. An early horror story from New York about nurses who were expected to alternate between caring for six-week premature infants and disposing of viable 24-week aborted fetuses is just that—a horror story. These beings are so much alike that no one can be asked to draw a distinction and treat them so very differently.

Remember, however, that in the early weeks after conception, a fetus is very much unlike a person. It is hard to develop these feelings for a set of genes which doesn't yet have a head, hands, beating heart, response to touch or the ability to move by itself. Thus it seems to me that the alleged "slippery slope" between conception and birth is not so very slippery. In the early stages of pregnancy, abortion can hardly be compared to murder for psychological reasons, but in the latest stages it is psychologically akin to murder.

Another source of similarity is the bodily continuity between fetus and adult. Bodies play a surprisingly central role in our attitudes toward persons. One has only to think of the philosophical literature on how far physical identity suffices for personal identity or Wittgenstein's remark that the best picture of the human soul is the human body. Even after death, when all agree the body is no longer a person, we will observe elaborate customs of respect for the human body; like people who torture dogs, necrophiliacs are not to be trusted with people.[12] So it is appropriate that we show respect to a fetus as the body continuous with the body of the person. This is a degree of resemblance to persons that animals cannot rival. . . .

Even if a fetus is not a person, abortion is not always permissible, because of the resemblance of a fetus to a person. I agree with Thomson that it would be wrong for a woman who is seven months pregnant to have an abortion just to avoid having to postpone a trip to Europe. In the early months of pregnancy when the fetus hardly resembles a baby at all, then, abortion is permissible whenever it is in the interests of the pregnant woman or her family. The reasons would only need to outweigh the pain and inconvenience of the abortion itself. In the middle months, when the fetus comes to resemble a person, abortion would be justifiable only when the continuation of the pregnancy or the birth of the child would cause harms—physical, psychological, economic or social—to the woman. In the late months of pregnancy, even on our current assumption that a fetus is not a person, abortion seems to be wrong except to save a woman from significant injury or death.

The Supreme Court has recognized similar gradations in the alleged slippery slope stretching between conception and birth. To this point, the present paper has been a discussion of the moral status of abortion only, not its legal status. In view of the great physical, financial and sometimes psychological costs of abortion, perhaps the legal arrangement most compatible with the proposed moral solution would be the absence of restrictions, that is, so-called abortion "on demand."

So I conclude, first, that application of our concept of a person will not suffice to settle the abortion issue. After all, the biological development of a human being is gradual. Second, whether a fetus is a person or not, abortion is justifiable early in pregnancy to avoid modest harms and seldom justifiable late in pregnancy except to avoid significant injury or death.[13]

Notes

1. We also have paternalistic laws which keep us from harming our own bodies even when no one else is affected. Ironically, antiabortion laws were originally designed to protect pregnant women from a dangerous but tempting procedure.

2. Mary Anne Warren, "On the Moral and Legal Status of Abortion," *Monist* 57 (1973), p. 55.

3. Baruch Brody, "Fetal Humanity and the Theory of Essentialism, "in Robert Baker and Frederick Elliston, eds., *Philosophy and Sex* (Buffalo, N. Y., 1975).

4. Michael Tolley, "Abortion and Infanticide, "*Philosophy and Public Affairs* 2 (1982).

5. Paul Ramsey, "The Morality of Abortion," in James Rachels, ed., *Moral Problems* (New York, 1971).

6. John Noonan, "Abortion and the Catholic Church: A Summary History," *Natural Law Forum* 12 (1967), pp. 125–131.

7. Wittgenstein has argued against the possibility of so capturing the concept of a game, *Philosophical Investigations* (New York, 1958), § 66.

8. Not because the fetus is partly a person and so has some of the rights of persons, but rather because of the rights of person-like nonpersons. This I discuss . . . below.

9. Aristotle himself was concerned, however, with the different question of when the soul takes form. For historical data, see Jimmye Kimmey, "How the Abortion Laws Happened," Ms. 1 (April 1973), pp. 48ff, and John Noonan, *loc. cit.*

10. J. J. Thomson, "A Defense of Abortion, "*Philosophy and Public Affairs* 1 (1971).

11. *Ibid.,* p. 62.

12. On the other hand, if they can be trusted with people, then our moral customs are mistaken. It all depends on the facts of psychology.

13. I am deeply indebted to Larry Crocker and Arthur Kuflik for their constructive comments.

POSTSCRIPT

Is Abortion Immoral?

Whether or not a fetus can be considered a person is often at the center of the abortion issue. Marquis, however, does not find that a direct approach to this question breaks the deadlock that is characteristic of many discussions of the morality of abortion. Instead he argues that the effect of aborting a fetus, which is the loss of that fetus's future experiences, is the reason why abortion is immoral. Marquis considers this loss of future experiences to be the reason why killing adult human beings is wrong, and he carries the logic over to fetuses.

English also does not consider the question, Is a fetus a person? to be a key one, because, first, even if the fetus is *not* a person, this does not imply that we may do anything to it that we like. Second, even if it *is* a person, this does not mean that abortion may always be ruled out. Not only is the question not decisive, English asserts, but it has no *right* answer. She does not mean that there really is a right answer but we do not know it; she means instead that our concepts (including the concept of a person) do not have clear boundaries. Likewise, we might ask, when does a baby become a child? Again, there is no right answer. The problem is not that babies turn into children without our being able to catch them in the act. There is no right answer because the concepts in our language (such as *baby* and *child*) do not have sharply defined boundaries. Thus, when we ask whether or not a fetus is a person, instead of finding out that it is or is not, we find out that it has some of the features of a person but that it lacks other features.

Judith Jarvis Thomson, in her ground-breaking article "In Defense of Abortion," *Philosophy and Public Affairs* (Fall 1971), argues that, from the premise that the fetus is a person with a right to life, it does not follow that a woman cannot disconnect herself from it and terminate an unwanted pregnancy. Suppose, she says, that you wake up one day to find yourself medically attached to a famous violinist who would die if you detached yourself. A violinist is a person and has a right to life. Does it then follow, asks Thomson, that you may not detach yourself from this unwanted arrangement?

Further readings on this issue are Joel Feinberg, *The Problem of Abortion*, 2d ed. (Wadsworth, 1984); Laurence Tribe, *Abortion: The Clash of Absolutes* (W. W. Norton, 1990); Bonnie Steinbock, *Life Before Birth: The Moral and Legal Status of Embryos and Fetuses* (Oxford University Press, 1992); Frances Myrna Kamm, *Creation and Abortion: An Essay in Moral and Legal Philosophy* (Oxford University Press, 1992); Robert M. Baird and Stuart E. Rosenbaum, eds., *The Ethics of Abortion: Pro-Life vs. Pro-Choice,* 2d ed. (Prometheus Books, 1993); Eva R. Rubin, ed., *The Abortion Controversy: A Documentary History* (Greenwood Press, 1994); Bhavani Sitaraman, *The Middleground: The American Public and the Abortion Debate* (Garland, 1994); Laurie Shrage, *Moral Dilemmas of Feminism:*

Prostitution, Adultery, and Abortion (Routledge, 1994); Ian Shapiro, ed., *Abortion: The Supreme Court Decisions* (Hackett, 1995); Peter Korn, *Lovejoy: A Year in the Life of an Abortion Clinic* (Atlantic Monthly Press, 1996); Patrick Lee, *Abortion and Unborn Human Life* (Catholic University of America Press, 1996); Janet Hadley, *Abortion: Between Freedom and Necessity* (Temple University Press, 1996); Eileen McDonagh, *Breaking the Abortion Deadlock: From Choice to Consent* (Oxford University Press, 1996); Kathy Rudy, *Beyond Pro-Life and Pro-Choice: Moral Diversity in the Abortion Debate* (Beacon Press, 1997); Donald T. Chitchlow, ed., *The Politics of Abortion in Historical Perspective* (Pennsylvania State Press, 1996); Katha Pollitt, "Abortion in American History," *The Atlantic Monthly* (May 1997); and Louis Pojman and Francis Beckwith, eds., *The Abortion Controversy: 25 Years After Roe v. Wade: A Reader,* 2d ed. (Wadsworth Publishing Company, 1998).

On RU-486 (sometimes called the "abortion pill"), see Janice G. Raymond, Renate Klein, and Lynette J. Dumble, *RU 486: Myths, Misconceptions, and Morals* (Institute on Women and Technology, 1991), and Lawrence Ladder, *A Private Matter: RU-486 and the Abortion Crisis* (Prometheus Books, 1995).

A CD-ROM on abortion is J. Douglas Butler, ed., *Abortion and Reproductive Rights* (J. Douglas Butler, Inc., 1997).

Recent publications include Lawrence Becker et al., eds., *Encyclopedia of Ethics,* 2d ed. (Routledge, 2002); Edwin C. Hui, *At the Beginning of Life: Dilemmas in Theological Bioethics* (InterVarsity Press, 2002); David Boonin, *A Defense of Abortion* (Cambridge University Press, 2002); and Laurie J. Shrage, *Abortion and Social Responsibility: Depolarizing the Debate* (Oxford University Press, 2003).

ISSUE 5

Must Sex Involve Commitment?

YES: Vincent C. Punzo, from *Reflective Naturalism* (Macmillan, 1969)

NO: Alan H. Goldman, from "Plain Sex," *Philosophy and Public Affairs* (Spring 1977)

ISSUE SUMMARY

YES: Philosopher Vincent C. Punzo maintains that the special intimacy of sex requires a serious commitment that is for the most part not required in other human activities.

NO: Philosopher Alan H. Goldman argues for a view of sex that is completely separate from any cultural or moral ideology that might be attached to it.

For many people, sex and morality are interconnected. Some complain that talk about sex, such as in sex education classes, is worse than worthless—it is downright corrupt—if it is divorced from talk about morality. Yet, with the exception of specialized concepts such as sexual harassment, most contemporary moral philosophers have very little to say about sex. In part, this may be due to the modern idea that many traditional beliefs about sex are steeped in superstitious, prejudiced, or misguided views that are in need of scientific correction.

In the traditional thought of ancient and medieval times, the stage of the world contains a large backdrop that is intended to make sense of the place of humans in the world. Ancient Greek philosophers created metaphysical theories and medieval theologians created religious theories to explain the role and purpose of humankind. According to both ancient and medieval views, humans are different from animals and thought to possess traits beyond the physical, which ground this difference. However, the modern and scientific view is that humans have no special metaphysical or supernatural standing above animals. Humans are simply a part of nature. This is not an attempt to provide another backdrop, but instead an attempt to eliminate all backdrops, so that people can be viewed in a more realistic manner. This view supports the idea that sexual urges are simply a part of our nature.

Consider a different example. Eating habits are also considered to be a part of our nature, but traditionalists would remind us that we have to eat the correct foods from a nutritional standpoint. We have to direct our eating habits with reason—we cannot simply eat whatever we feel like whenever we want to. Traditionalists view eating as something beyond the process of digestion. Sexual intercourse has its own physical processes, and, like eating, also involves more than just the physical. Sex involves the use of self-control and reason.

Modernists may argue that in many ways the analogy with eating fails. In the past, eating habits were only minimally affected by superstitious or false ideas, whereas sexual practices were greatly affected.

What we are left with today are elements of ancient, medieval, and modern thought. When it comes to sex, it is clear that modern scientific views have a contribution to make; but it is not clear whether we can simply do away with all previous ideas about sex.

In the following selections, Vincent C. Punzo argues for the view that sex, since it involves the highest level of human intimacy, must involve commitment. Alan H. Goldman counters that a concept of "plain sex" helps us to understand sex for what it is—something that does not need moral ideas attached to it.

YES

Vincent C. Punzo

Morality and Human Sexuality

If one sees man's moral task as being simply that of not harming anyone, that is if one sees this task in purely negative terms, he will certainly not accept the argument to be presented in the following section. However, if one accepts the notion of the morality of aspiration, if one accepts the view that man's moral task involves the positive attempt to live up to what is best in man, to give reality to what he sees to be the perfection of himself as a human subject, the argument may be acceptable.

Sexuality and the Human Subject

[Previous discussion] has left us with the question as to whether sexual intercourse is a type of activity that is similar to choosing a dinner from a menu. The question is of utmost significance in that one's view of the morality of premarital intercourse seems to depend on the significance that one gives to the sexual encounter in human life. Those such as [John] Wilson and [Eustace] Chesser who see nothing immoral about the premarital character of sexual intercourse seem to see sexual intercourse as being no different from myriad of other purely aesthetic matters. This point is seen in Chesser's questioning of the reason for demanding permanence in the relationship of sexual partners when we do not see such permanence as being important to other human relationships.[1] It is also seen in his asking why we raise a moral issue about premarital coition when two people may engage in it, with the resulting social and psychological consequences being no different than if they had gone to a movie.[2]

Wilson most explicitly makes a case for the view that sexual intercourse does not differ significantly from other human activities. He holds that people think that there is a logical difference between the question "Will you engage in sexual intercourse with me?" and the question, "Will you play tennis with me?" only because they are influenced by the acquisitive character of contemporary society.[3] Granted that the two questions may be identical from the purely formal perspective of logic, the ethician must move beyond this perspective to a consideration of their content. Men and women find themselves involved in many different relationships: for example, as buyer-seller,

Punzo, REFLECTIVE NATURALISM. 1st Edition, © 1969. Reprinted by permission of Pearson Education, Inc., Upper Saddle River, NJ.

employer-employee, teacher-student, lawyer-client, and partners or competitors in certain games such as tennis or bridge. Is there any morally significant difference between these relationships and sexual intercourse? We cannot examine all the possible relationships into which a man and woman can enter, but we will consider the employer-employee relationship in order to get some perspective on the distinctive character of the sexual relationship.

A man pays a woman to act as his secretary. What rights does he have over her in such a situation? The woman agrees to work a certain number of hours during the day taking dictation, typing letters, filing reports, arranging appointments and flight schedules, and greeting clients and competitors. In short, we can say that the man has rights to certain of the woman's services or skills. The use of the word "services" may lead some to conclude that this relationship is not significantly different from the relationship between a prostitute and her client in that the prostitute also offers her "services."

It is true that we sometimes speak euphemistically of a prostitute offering her services to a man for a sum of money, but if we are serious about our quest for the difference between the sexual encounter and other types of human relationships, it is necessary to drop euphemisms and face the issue directly. The man and woman who engage in sexual intercourse are giving their bodies, the most intimate physical expression of themselves, over to the other. Unlike the man who plays tennis with a woman, the man who has sexual relations with her has literally entered her. A man and woman engaging in sexual intercourse have united themselves as intimately and as totally as is physically possible for two human beings. Their union is not simply a union of organs, but is as intimate and as total a physical union of two selves as is possible of achievement. Granted the character of this union, it seems strange to imply that there is no need for a man and woman to give any more thought to the question of whether they should engage in sexual intercourse than to the question of whether they should play tennis.

In opposition to Wilson, I think that it is the acquisitive character of our society that has blinded us to the distinction between the two activities. Wilson's and Chesser's positions seem to imply that exactly the same moral considerations ought to apply to a situation in which a housewife is bartering with a butcher for a few pounds of pork chops and the situation in which two human beings are deciding whether sexual intercourse ought to be an ingredient of their relationship. So long as the butcher does not put his thumb on the scale in the weighing process, so long as he is truthful in stating that the meat is actually pork, so long as the woman pays the proper amount with the proper currency, the trade is perfectly moral. Reflecting on sexual intercourse from the same sort of economic perspective, one can say that so long as the sexual partners are truthful in reporting their freedom from contagious venereal diseases and so long as they are truthful in reporting that they are interested in the activity for the mere pleasure of it or to try out their sexual techniques, there is nothing immoral about such activity. That in the one case pork chops are being exchanged for money whereas in the other the decision concerns the most complete and intimate merging of one's self with another makes no difference to the moral evaluation of the respective cases.

It is not surprising that such a reductionistic outlook should pervade our thinking on sexual matters, since in our society sexuality is used to sell everything from shave cream to underarm deodorants, to soap, to mouthwash, to cigarettes, and to automobiles. Sexuality has come to play so large a role in our commercial lives that it is not surprising that our sexuality should itself come to be treated as a commodity governed by the same moral rules that govern any other economic transaction.

Once sexuality is taken out of this commercial framework, once the character of the sexual encounter is faced directly and squarely, we will come to see that Doctor Mary Calderone has brought out the type of questions that ought to be asked by those contemplating the introduction of sexual intercourse into their relationships: "How many times, and how casually, are you willing to invest a portion of your total self, and to be the custodian of a like investment from the other person, without the sureness of knowing that these investments are being made for keeps?"[4] These questions come out of the recognition that the sexual encounter is a definitive experience, one in which the physical intimacy and merging involves also a merging of the nonphysical dimensions of the partners. With these questions, man moves beyond the negative concern with avoiding his or another's physical and psychological harm to the question of what he is making of himself and what he is contributing to the existential formation of his partner as a human subject.

If we are to make a start toward responding to Calderone's questions we must cease talking about human selfhood in abstraction. The human self is an historical as well as a physical being. He is a being who is capable of making at least a portion of his past an object of his consciousness and thus is able to make this past play a conscious role in his present and in his looking toward the future. He is also a being who looks to the future, who faces tomorrow with plans, ideals, hopes, and fears. The very being of a human self involves his past and his movement toward the future. Moreover, the human self is not completely shut off in his own past and future. Men and women are capable of consciously and purposively uniting themselves in a common career and venture. They can commit themselves to sharing the future with another, sharing it in all its aspects—in its fortunes and misfortunes, in its times of happiness and times of tragedy. Within the lives of those who have so committed themselves to each other, sexual intercourse is a way of asserting and confirming the fullness and totality of their mutual commitment.

Unlike those who have made such a commitment and who come together in the sexual act in the fullness of their selfhood, those who engage in premarital sexual unions and who have made no such commitment act as though they can amputate their bodily existence and the most intimate physical expression of their selfhood from their existence as historical beings. Granting that there may be honesty on the verbal level in that two people engaging in premarital intercourse openly state that they are interested only in the pleasure of the activity, the fact remains that such unions are morally deficient because they lack existential integrity in that there is a total merging and union on a physical level, on the one hand, and a conscious decision not to unite any other dimension of themselves, on the other hand. Their sexual union thus involves a "depersonalization" of their bodily existence, an attempt to cut off the most intimate physical expression of their respective selves from their very selfhood. The mutual agreement of premarital sex partners is an agreement to merge with the other not as a self, but as a body which one takes unto oneself, which one possesses in a most intimate and total fashion for one's own pleasure or designs, allowing the other to treat oneself in the same way. It may be true that no physical or psychological harm may result from such unions, but such partners have failed to existentially incorporate human sexuality, which is at the very least the most intimate physical expression of the human self, into the character of this selfhood.

In so far as premarital sexual unions separate the intimate and total physical union that is sexual intercourse from any commitment to the self in his historicity, human sexuality, and consequently the human body, have been fashioned into external things or objects to be handed over totally to someone else, whenever one feels that he can get possession of another's body, which he can use for his own purposes.[5] The human body has thus been treated no differently from the pork chops spoken of previously or from any other object or commodity, which human beings exchange and haggle over in their day-to-day transactions. One hesitates to use the word that might be used to capture the moral value that has been sacrificed in premarital unions because in our day the word has taken on a completely negative meaning at best, and, at worst, it has become a word used by "sophisticates" to mock or deride certain attitudes toward human sexuality. However, because the word "chastity" has been thus abused is no reason to leave it in the hands of those who have misrepresented the human value to which it gives expression.

The chaste person has often been described as one intent on denying his sexuality. The value of chastity as conceived in this section is in direct opposition to this description. It is the unchaste person who is separating himself from his sexuality, who is willing to exchange human bodies as one would exchange money for tickets to a baseball game—honestly and with no commitment of self to self. Against this alienation of one's sexuality from one's self, an alienation that makes one's sexuality an object, which is to be given to another in exchange for his objectified sexuality, chastity affirms the integrity of the self in his bodily and historical existence. The sexuality of man is seen as an integral part of his subjectivity. Hence, the chaste man rejects depersonalized sexual relations as a reduction of man in his most intimate physical being to the status of an object or pure instrument for another. He asserts that man is a subject and end in himself, not in some trans-temporal, nonphysical world, but in the historical-physical world in which he carries on his moral task and where he finds his fellow man. He will not freely make of himself in his bodily existence a thing to be handed over to another's possession, nor will he ask that another treat his own body in this way. The total physical intimacy of sexual intercourse will be an expression of total union with the other self on all levels of their beings. Seen from this perspective, chastity is one aspect of man's attempt to attain existential integrity, to accept his body as a dimension of his total personality.

In concluding this section, it should be noted that I have tried to make a case against the morality of premarital sexual intercourse even in those cases in which the partners are completely honest with each other. There is reason to question whether the complete honesty, to which those who see nothing immoral in such unions refer, is as a matter of fact actually found very often among premarital sex partners. We may well have been dealing with textbook cases which present these unions in their best light. One may be pardoned for wondering whether sexual intercourse often occurs under the following conditions: "Hello, my name is Josiah. I am interested in having a sexual experience with you. I can assure you that I am good at it and that I have no communicable disease. If it sounds good to you and if you have taken the proper contraceptive precautions, we might have a go at it. Of course, I want to make it clear to you that I am interested only in the sexual experience and that I have no intention of making any long-range commitment to you." If those, who defend the morality of premarital sexual unions so long as they are honestly entered into, think that I have misrepresented what they mean by honesty, then they must specify what they mean by an honest premarital union. . . .

Marriage as a Total Human Commitment

The preceding argument against the morality of premarital sexual unions was not based on the view that the moral character of marriage rests on a legal certificate or on a legal or religious ceremony. The argument was not directed against "preceremonial" intercourse, but against premarital intercourse. Morally speaking, a man and woman are married when they make the mutual and total commitment to share the problems and prospects of their historical existence in the world. Although marriages are not to be identified with ceremonies, the words used in marriage ceremonies have captured the character of marriage in the promise which the partners make to each other to join their lives "for better, for worse, for richer, for poorer, in sickness and in health, till death do us part."

. . . The commitment that constitutes marriage is a total commitment of one person to another person of the opposite sex. To understand the character of such commitment, it is necessary to know something about the being of those involved in the commitment; for if it is to be truly total, the commitment must be as rich as the being of those who have made it. It is at this point that the historical character of the human self's existence becomes important. A total commitment to another means a commitment to him in his historical existence. Such a commitment is not simply a matter of words or of feelings, however strong. It involves a full existential sharing on the part of two beings of the burdens, opportunities, and challenges of their historical existence.

Granted the importance that the character of their commitment to each other plays in determining the moral quality of a couple's sexual encounter, it is clear that there may be nothing immoral in the behavior of couples who engage in sexual intercourse before participating in the marriage ceremony. For example, it is foolish to say that two people who are totally committed to each other and who have made all the arrangements to live this commitment are immoral if they engage in sexual intercourse the night before the marriage ceremony.

Admittedly this position can be abused by those who have made a purely verbal commitment, a commitment which will be carried out in some vague and ill-defined future. At some time or other, they will unite their two lives totally by setting up house together and by actually undertaking the task of meeting the economic, social, legal, medical responsibilities that are involved in living this commitment. Apart from the reference to a vague and amorphous future time when they will share the full responsibility for each other, their commitment presently realizes itself in going to dances, sharing a box of popcorn at Saturday night movies, and sharing their bodies whenever they can do so without taking too great a risk of having the girl become pregnant.

Having acknowledged that the position advanced in this section can be abused by those who would use the word "commitment" to rationalize what is an interest only in the body of the other person, it must be pointed out that neither the ethician nor any other human being can tell two people whether they actually have made the commitment that is marriage or are mistaking a "warm glow" for such a commitment. There comes a time when this issue falls out of the area of moral philosophy and into the area of practical wisdom. . . .

The characterization of marriage as a total commitment between two human beings may lead some to conclude that the marriage ceremony is a wholly superfluous affair. It must be admitted that people may be morally married without having engaged in a marriage ceremony. However, to conclude from this point that the ceremony is totally meaningless is to lose sight of the social character of human beings. The couple contemplating marriage do not exist in a vacuum, although there may be times when they think they do. Their existences reach out beyond their union to include other human beings. By making their commitment a matter of public record, by solemnly expressing it before the law and in the presence of their respective families and friends and, if they are religious people, in the presence of God and one of his ministers, they sink the roots of their commitment more deeply and extensively in the world in which they live, thus taking steps to provide for the future growth of their commitment to each other. The public expression of this commitment makes it more fully and more explicitly a part of a couple's lives and of the world in which they live.

Notes

1. Eustace Chesser, *Unmarried Love* (New York: Pocket Books, 1965), p. 29.
2. *Op. cit.,* pp. 35–36; see also p. 66.
3. John Wilson, *Logic and Sexual Morality* (Baltimore, Md.: Penguin Books, 1965), p. 67, note 1.
4. Mary Steichen Calderone, "The Case for Chastity," *Sex in America,* ed. by Henry Anatole Grunwald (New York: Bantam Books, 1964), p. 147.
5. The psychoanalyst Rollo May makes an excellent point in calling attention to the tendency in contemporary society to exploit the human body as if it were only a machine. Rollo May, "The New Puritanism," *Sex in America,* pp. 161–164.

Alan H. Goldman  **NO**

Plain Sex

Several recent articles on sex herald its acceptance as a legitimate topic for analytic philosophers (although it has been a topic in philosophy since Plato). One might have thought conceptual analysis unnecessary in this area; despite the notorious struggles of judges and legislators to define pornography suitably, we all might be expected to know what sex is and to be able to identify at least paradigm sexual desires and activities without much difficulty. Philosophy is nevertheless of relevance here if for no other reason than that the concept of sex remains at the center of moral and social consciousness in our, and perhaps any, society. Before we can get a sensible view of the relation of sex to morality, . . . social regulation, and marriage, we require a sensible analysis of the concept itself; one which neither understates its animal pleasure nor overstates its importance within a theory or system of value. I say "before," but the order is not quite so clear, for questions in this area, as elsewhere in moral philosophy, are both conceptual and normative at the same time. Our concept of sex will partially determine our moral view of it, but as philosophers we should formulate a concept that will accord with its proper moral status. What we require here, as elsewhere, is "reflective equilibrium," a goal not achieved by traditional and recent analyses together with their moral implications. Because sexual activity, like other natural functions such as eating or exercising, has become imbedded in layers of cultural, moral, and superstitious superstructure, it is hard to conceive it in its simplest terms. But partially for this reason, it is only by thinking about plain sex that we can begin to achieve this conceptual equilibrium.

I shall suggest here that sex continues to be misrepresented in recent writings, at least in philosophical writings, and I shall criticize the predominant form of analysis which I term "means-end analysis." Such conceptions attribute a necessary external goal or purpose to sexual activity, whether it be reproduction, the expression of love, simple communication, or interpersonal awareness. They analyze sexual activity as a means to one of these ends, implying that sexual desire is a desire to reproduce, to love or be loved, or to communicate with others. All definitions of this type suggest false views of the relation of sex to . . . morality by implying that sex which does not fit one of these models or fulfill one of these functions is in some way deviant or incomplete.

The alternative, simpler analysis with which I will begin is that sexual desire is desire for contact with another person's body and for the pleasure

From Philosophy and Public Affairs, vol. 6, no. 3, Spring 1977, pp. 367–275, 280–281, 283.

which such contact produces; sexual activity is activity which tends to fulfill such desire of the agent. Whereas Aristotle and [others] were correct in holding that pleasure is normally a byproduct rather than a goal of purposeful action, in the case of sex this is not so clear. The desire for another's body is, principally among other things, the desire for the pleasure that physical contact brings. On the other hand, it is not a desire for a particular sensation detachable from its causal context, a sensation which can be derived in other ways. This definition in terms of the general goal of sexual desire appears preferable to an attempt to more explicitly list or define specific sexual activities, for many activities such as kissing, embracing, massaging, or holding hands may or may not be sexual, depending upon the context and more specifically upon the purposes, needs, or desires into which such activities fit. The generality of the definition also represents a refusal (common in recent psychological texts) to overemphasize orgasm as the goal of sexual desire or genital sex as the only norm of sexual activity. . . .

Central to the definition is the fact that the goal of sexual desire and activity is the physical contact itself, rather than something else which this contact might express. By contrast, what I term "means-end analyses" posit ends which I take to be extraneous to plain sex, and they view sex as a means to these ends. Their fault lies not in defining sex in terms of its general goal, but in seeing plain sex as merely a means to other separable ends. I term these "means-end analyses" for convenience, although "means-separable-end analyses," while too cumbersome, might be more fully explanatory. The desire for physical contact with another person is a minimal criterion for (normal) sexual desire, but is both necessary and sufficient to qualify normal desire as sexual. Of course, we may want to express other feelings through sexual acts in various contexts; but without the desire for the physical contact in and for itself, or when it is sought for other reasons, activities in which contact is involved are not predominantly sexual. Furthermore, the desire for physical contact in itself, without the wish to express affection or other feelings through it, is sufficient to render sexual the activity of the agent which fulfills it. Various activities with this goal alone, such as kissing and caressing in certain contexts, qualify as sexual even without the presence of genital symptoms of sexual excitement. The latter are not therefore necessary criteria for sexual activity. . . .

Our definition of sex in terms of the desire for physical contact may appear too narrow in that a person's personality, not merely her or his body, may be sexually attractive to another, and in that looking or conversing in a certain way can be sexual in a given context without bodily contact. Nevertheless, it is not the contents of one's thoughts per se that are sexually appealing, but one's personality as embodied in certain manners of behavior. Furthermore, if a person is sexually attracted by another's personality, he or she will desire not just further conversation, but actual sexual contact. While looki⌐ at or conversing with someone can be interpreted as sexual in given it is so when intended as preliminary to, and hence parasitic ⸗ sexual interest. Voyeurism or viewing a pornographic movie qt ual activity, but only as an imaginative substitute for the real th.

a deviation from the norm as expressed in our definition). The same is true of masturbation as a sexual activity without a partner.

That the initial definition indicates at least an ingredient of sexual desire and activity is too obvious to argue. We all know what sex is, at least in obvious cases, and do not need philosophers to tell us. My preliminary analysis is meant to serve as a contrast to what sex is not, at least, not necessarily. I concentrate upon the physically manifested desire for another's body, and I take as central the immersion in the physical aspect of one's own existence and attention to the physical embodiment of the other. One may derive pleasure in a sex act from expressing certain feelings to one's partner or from awareness of the attitude of one's partner, but sexual desire is essentially desire for physical contact itself: it is a bodily desire for the body of another that dominates our mental life for more or less brief periods. Traditional writings were correct to emphasize the purely physical or animal aspect of sex; they were wrong only in condemning it. This characterization of sex as an intensely pleasurable physical activity and acute physical desire may seem to some to capture only its barest level. But it is worth distinguishing and focusing upon this least common denominator in order to avoid the false views of sexual morality . . . which emerge from thinking that sex is essentially something else.

One common position views sex as essentially an expression of love or affection between the partners. It is generally recognized that there are other types of love besides sexual, but sex itself is taken as an expression of one type, sometimes termed "romantic" love.[1] Various factors again ought to weaken this identification. First, there are other types of love besides that which it is appropriate to express sexually, and "romantic" love itself can be expressed in many other ways. I am not denying that sex can take on heightened value and meaning when it becomes a vehicle for the expression of feelings of love or tenderness, but so can many other usually mundane activities such as getting up early to make breakfast on Sunday, cleaning the house, and so on. Second, sex itself can be used to communicate many other emotions besides love, and, as I will argue below, can communicate nothing in particular and still be good sex.

On a deeper level, an internal tension is bound to result from an identification of sex, which I have described as a physical-psychological desire, with love as a long-term, deep emotional relationship between two individuals. As this type of relationship, love is permanent, at least in intent, and more or less exclusive. A normal person cannot deeply love more than a few individuals even in a lifetime. We may be suspicious that those who attempt or claim to love many love them weakly if at all. Yet, fleeting sexual desire can arise in relation to a variety of other individuals one finds sexually attractive. It may even be, as some have claimed, that sexual desire in humans naturally seeks variety, while this is obviously false of love. For this reason, monogamous sex, even if justified, almost always represents a sacrifice or the exercise of self-control on the part of the spouses, while monogamous love generally does not. There is no such thing as casual love in the sense in which I intend the term "love." It may occasionally happen that a spouse falls deeply in love with someone else (especially when sex is conceived in terms of love), but this is relatively rare in comparison to passing sexual desires for others; and while the former often indicates a weakness or fault in the marriage relation, the latter does not.

If love is indeed more exclusive in its objects than is sexual desire, this explains why those who view sex as essentially an expression of love would again tend to hold a repressive or restrictive sexual ethic. . . . [T]here may be good reasons for reserving the total commitment of deep love to the context of marriage and family—the normal personality may not withstand additional divisions of ultimate commitment and allegiance. There is no question that marriage itself is best sustained by a deep relation of love and affection; and even if love is not naturally monogamous, the benefits of family units to children provide additional reason to avoid serious commitments elsewhere which weaken family ties. It can be argued similarly that monogamous sex strengthens families by restricting and at the same time guaranteeing an outlet for sexual desire in marriage. But there is more force to the argument that recognition of a clear distinction between sex and love in society would help avoid disastrous marriages which result from adolescent confusion of the two when sexual desire is mistaken for permanent love, and would weaken damaging jealousies which arise in marriages in relation to passing sexual desires. The love and affection of a sound marriage certainly differs from the adolescent romantic variety, which is often a mere substitute for sex in the context of a repressive sexual ethic.

In fact, the restrictive sexual ethic tied to the means-end analysis in terms of love . . . has failed to be consistent. At least, it has not been applied consistently, but forms part of the double standard which has curtailed the freedom of women. The inconsistency in the sexual ethic typically attached to the sex-love analysis, according to which it has generally been taken with a grain of salt when applied to men, is simply another example of the impossibility of tailoring a plausible moral theory in this area to a conception of sex which builds in conceptually extraneous factors.

I am not suggesting here that sex ought never to be connected with love or that it is not a more significant and valuable activity when it is. Nor am I denying that individuals need love as much as sex and perhaps emotionally need at least one complete relationship which encompasses both. Just as sex can express love and take on heightened significance when it does, so love is often naturally accompanied by an intermittent desire for sex. But again love is accompanied appropriately by desires for other shared activities as well. What makes the desire for sex seem more intimately connected with love is the intimacy which is seen to be a natural feature of mutual sex acts. Like love, sex is held to lay one bare psychologically as well as physically. Sex is unquestionably intimate, but beyond that the psychological toll often attached may be a function of the restrictive sexual ethic itself, rather than a legitimate apology for it. The intimacy involved in love is psychologically consuming in a generally healthy way, while the psychological tolls of sexual relations, often including embarrassment as a correlate of intimacy, are too often the result of artificial sexual ethics and taboos. The intimacy involved in both love and sex is insufficient in any case in light of previous points to render a means-end analysis in these terms appropriate.

. . . To the question of what morality might be implied by my analysis, the answer is that there are no moral implications whatever. Any analysis of sex which imputes a moral character to sex acts in themselves is wrong for that reason. There is no morality intrinsic to sex, although general moral rules apply to the treatment of others in sex acts as they apply to all human relations. We can speak of a sexual ethic as we can speak of a business ethic, without implying that business in itself is either moral or immoral or that special rules are required to judge business practices which are not derived from rules that apply elsewhere as well. Sex is not in itself a moral category, although like business it invariably places us into relations with others in which moral rules apply. It gives us opportunity to do what is otherwise recognized as wrong, to harm others, deceive them or manipulate them against their wills. Just as the fact that an act is sexual in itself never renders it wrong or adds to its wrongness if it is wrong on other grounds (sexual acts towards minors are wrong on other grounds, as will be argued below), so no wrong act is to be excused because done from a sexual motive. If a "crime of passion" is to be excused, it would have to be on grounds of temporary insanity rather than sexual context (whether insanity does constitute a legitimate excuse for certain actions is too big a topic to argue here). Sexual motives are among others which may become deranged, and the fact that they are sexual has no bearing in itself on the moral character, whether negative or exculpatory, of the actions deriving from them. Whatever might be true of war, it is certainly not the case that all's fair in love or sex.

Our first conclusion regarding morality and sex is therefore that no conduct otherwise immoral should be excused because it is sexual conduct, and nothing in sex is immoral unless condemned by rules which apply elsewhere as well. The last clause requires further clarification. Sexual conduct can be governed by particular rules relating only to sex itself. But these precepts must be implied by general moral rules when these are applied to specific sexual relations or types of conduct. The same is true of rules of fair business, ethical medicine, or courtesy in driving a car. In the latter case, particular acts on the road may be reprehensible, such as tailgating or passing on the right, which seem to bear no resemblance as actions to any outside the context of highway safety. Nevertheless their immorality derives from the fact that they place others in danger, a circumstance which, when avoidable, is to be condemned in any context. This structure of general and specifically applicable rules describes a reasonable sexual ethic as well. To take an extreme case, rape is always a sexual act and it is always immoral. A rule against rape can therefore be considered an obvious part of sexual morality which has no bearing on nonsexual conduct. But the immorality of rape derives from its being an extreme violation of a person's body, of the right not to be humiliated, and of the general moral prohibition against using other persons against their wills, not from the fact that it is a sexual act.

The application elsewhere of general moral rules to sexual conduct is further complicated by the fact that it will be relative to the particular desires and preferences of one's partner (these may be influenced by and hence in some sense include misguided beliefs about sexual morality itself). This means that there will be fewer specific rules in the area of sexual ethics than in other areas of conduct, such as driving cars, where the relativity of preference is irrelevant to the prohibition of objectively dangerous conduct. More reliance will have to be placed upon the general moral rule, which in this area holds simply that the preferences, desires, and interests of one's partner or potential partner ought to be taken into account. This rule is certainly not specifically formulated to govern sexual relations; it is a form of the central principle of morality itself. But when applied to sex, it prohibits certain actions, such as molestation of children, which cannot be categorized as violations of the rule without at the same time being classified as sexual. I believe this last case is the closest we can come to an action which is wrong *because* it is sexual, but even here its wrongness is better characterized as deriving from the detrimental effects such behavior can have on the future emotional and sexual life of the naive victims, and from the fact that such behavior therefore involves manipulation of innocent persons without regard for their interests. Hence, this case also involves violation of a general moral rule which applies elsewhere as well. . . .

I suggested earlier that in addition to generating confusion regarding the rightness or wrongness of sex acts, false conceptual analyses of the means-end form cause confusion about the value of sex to the individual. My account recognizes the satisfaction of desire and the pleasure this brings as the central psychological function of the sex act for the individual. Sex affords us a paradigm of pleasure, but not a cornerstone of value. For most of us it is not only a needed outlet for desire but also the most enjoyable form of recreation we know. Its value is nevertheless easily mistaken by being confused with that of love, when it is taken as essentially an expression of that emotion. Although intense, the pleasures of sex are brief and repetitive rather than cumulative. They give value to the specific acts which generate them, but not the lasting kind of value which enhances one's whole life. The briefness of these pleasures contributes to their intensity (or perhaps their intensity makes them necessarily brief), but it also relegates them to the periphery of most rational plans for the good life.

By contrast, love typically develops over a long term relation; while its pleasures may be less intense and physical, they are of more cumulative value. The importance of love to the individual may well be central in a rational system of value. And it has perhaps an even deeper moral significance relating to the identification with the interests of another person, which broadens one's possible relationships with others as well. Marriage is again important in preserving this relation between adults and children, which seems as important to the adults as it is to the children in broadening concerns which have a tendency to become selfish. Sexual desire, by contrast, is desire for another which is nevertheless essentially self-regarding. Sexual pleasure is certainly a good for the individual, and for many it may be necessary in order for them to function in a reasonably cheerful way. But it bears little relation to those other values just discussed, to which some analyses falsely suggest a conceptual connection. . . .

The position I have taken in this paper against those concepts is not totally new. Something similar to it is found in Freud's view of sex, which of course was genuinely revolutionary, and in the body of writings deriving from Freud to the present time. But in his revolt against romanticized and repressive conceptions, Freud went too far—from a refusal to view sex as merely a means to a view of it as the end of all human behavior, although sometimes an elaborately disguised end. This pansexualism led to the thesis (among others)that repression was indeed an inevitable and necessary part of social regulation of any form, a strange consequence of a position that began by opposing the repressive aspects of the means-end view. Perhaps the time finally has arrived when we can achieve a reasonable middle ground in this area, at least in philosophy if not in society.

Note

1.   Even Bertrand Russell, whose writing in this area was a model of rationality, at least for its period, tends to make this identification and to condemn plain sex in the absence of love: "sex intercourse apart from love has little value, and is to be regarded primarily as experimentation with a view to love." *Marriage and Morals* (New York: Bantam, 1959), p. 87.

POSTSCRIPT

Must Sex Involve Commitment?

It is clear that Punzo and Goldman differ fundamentally in their approach to sex and commitment. Goldman maintains that a concept of "plain sex" can be used to view sex without cultural and moral ideology. Punzo's approach counters the idea that an important human concept like sex can be separated from ideology.

A further question is whether men and women regard this issue in different ways. Traditionally, there has been a cultural demand that commitment is required before engaging in sex. However, a "double standard" exists that lets men practice sex in the absence of commitment without cultural disapproval. On the other hand, women are more likely to be viewed as "immoral" if they engage in sex without commitment. If the double standard is to be replaced by a unified standard, should this be one that includes commitment?

Sources relevant to this topic include Russell Vannoy, *Sex Without Love: A Philosophical Exploration* (Prometheus Books, 1981); G. Sidney Buchanan, *Morality, Sex and the Constitution: A Christian Perspective on the Power of Government to Regulate Private Sexual Conduct Between Consenting Adults* (University Press of America, 1985); G. Frankson, *Sex and Morality* (Todd & Honeywell, 1987); Joseph Monti, *Arguing About Sex: The Rhetoric of Christian Sexual Morality* (State University of New York Press, 1995); John Marshall Townsend, *What Women Want—What Men Want: Why the Sexes Still See Love and Commitment So Differently* (Oxford University Press, 1998); and J. Gordon Muir, *Sex, Politics, and the End of Morality* (Pentland Press, 1998).

ISSUE 6

Should Same-Sex Marriage Be Allowed?

YES: Jonathan Rauch, from *Gay Marriage: Why It Is Good for Gays, Good for Straights, and Good for America* (Times Books, 2004)

NO: Jeff Jordan, from "Contra Same-Sex Marriage," in Robert M. Baird and Stuart E. Rosenbaum, eds., *Same-Sex Marriage: The Moral and Legal Debate,* 2nd ed. (Blackwell, 2004)

ISSUE SUMMARY

YES: Jonathan Rauch argues that same-sex marriage would provide a stabilizing effect on gay relationships and would benefit children. He argues that society has a stake in encouraging these stabilizing relationships and in benefitting children, and should therefore support same-sex marriage.

NO: Jeff Jordan considers various "models" of marriage. In issues of same-sex marriage, these models clash. Jordan uses these models in order to argue that extension of marriage to same-sex couples actually violates the foundations of a liberal society—a society composed of free and equal individuals.

Homosexuality exists in all known human societies, and also among some animals. This, however, has not prevented homosexual behavior from being condemned by virtually all world religions. In some societies, this behavior exists in a hidden, socially unacceptable way; in others, it has been tolerated and even highly esteemed. (The variation here among both existing and historical societies is amazingly wide-ranging.)

Homosexuality is receiving more acceptance in our society. One way this can be seen is in the extension of insurance and other benefits to same-sex "domestic partners." But whereas married heterosexuals can state that they are indeed legally married, homosexual couples cannot. The status of homosexual relationships is somewhat unclear as far as the law is concerned. Of course, heterosexuals sometimes have unmarried sexual relationships too—but is that type of relationship the heterosexual counterpart of unmarried homosexual relationships? In a way, it is, since there is no legal same-sex marriage in the

United States. Yet at the very least, heterosexual marriage is a recognized possibility, while homosexual marriage is not. Whereas an unmarried heterosexual relationship is one that could involve marriage, an unmarried homosexual relationship can not. But should we recognize same-sex marriage as a legal possibility?

For us, one question that may lie behind issues of same-sex marriage is whether or not homosexuality is immoral. If it is, then it is hard to see why society should support same-sex marriage. Many arguments do aim to show that homosexuality is indeed immoral, but this is much more difficult to demonstrate than many people suppose. Part of the problem is that heterosexuals often know very little about homosexuality and rely upon stereotypical thinking or feelings rather than on logic and facts. But if a successful argument could be made here, then any ground for same-sex marriage would be destroyed.

One argument that is sometimes made does not directly address the morality of homosexuality; instead, it focuses on the precedent that would be set with same-sex marriage. The idea here is a kind of "slippery slope" argument to the effect that if same-sex marriage is allowed, then there is nothing to keep us from sliding farther down this slippery slope and allowing such things as polygamous marriage, incestuous marriage, and so on—at least if this is what the parties to the marriage want. But this argument depends on just how slippery the slope is. Here, one must face the question: Is it really true that there will be no principled place to stop and draw the line?

In the following selection, Jonathan Rauch first argues for the acceptability of same-sex marriage. Indeed, he argues that it fosters some of the same goals that society already has. Then Jeff Jordan presents a case against same-sex marriage from a purely secular point of view. This issue can generate much negativity on both sides, but Rauch and Jordan argue logically and respectfully.

How Straights Will Benefit

All tragedies are finished by a death," Lord Byron writes in *Don Juan*, "All comedies are ended by a marriage." ("The future states of both," he adds wryly, "are left to faith.") From Shakespeare's day to our own, it has been a given that a wedding is a grand and happy event, a cause for rejoicing, not just for the bride and groom and their immediate families but for the whole town (and, for Shakespeare, the audience). As Byron's dry aside reminds us, marriages do not necessarily work out. Some are a triumph of hope over wisdom. And yet we rejoice nonetheless. It seems obvious, and indeed it is obvious, that, other things being equal, the union of a pair in matrimony is good news.

Obvious, at least, if the pair consists of a man and a woman. What if Bill and Bob got married? Mary and Monica? Should the community rejoice? Should it panic? Should it care?

That gay lives might improve with legal marriage seems clear enough, but that, too often, is where the plus-side accounting ends (if it happens at all). The potential costs of same-sex marriage are hashed out endlessly, sometimes in apocalyptic terms. Marriage will be wrecked, children will be devastated, polygamy will prevail across the land, and so on. Even many gay advocates of same-sex marriage tend sometimes to view the issue as purely one of gay civil rights or equality, overlooking or underappreciating the benefits to society as a whole. . . . [Here,] I propose to redress the imbalance, at least partially. Where the nongay world is concerned, allowing gay couples to seal their bonds in law is not just a lesser of evils: it is a positive good.

In his book *The Moral Sense*, James Q. Wilson observes, "A family is not an association of independent people; it is a human commitment designed to make possible the rearing of moral and healthy children. Governments care—or ought to care—about families for this reason, and scarcely for any other." Wilson here speaks of "family" rather than "marriage" as such, but I think one can read him as speaking of marriage without doing an injustice to his meaning. The resulting proposition—governments should care about marriage because of children, and scarcely for any other reason—will strike some readers as reasonable. They will conclude that governments and, by implication, societies have no compelling interest in same-sex marriage. If gay people want to cohabit, hold a ceremony, and act like a married couple, well and good. If they prefer to lead a life of solitude or celibacy, okay. If they prefer promiscuity or dissipation, that is not desirable, but it is their business.

For many years, in the United States, such was the prevalent attitude. One group of people wanted to persecute homosexuals and viewed them as a threat to the social order. A larger group, however, preferred to leave them alone and, ideally, out of sight. Society had nothing to gain by legitimizing gay relationships, and it had nothing to lose by ignoring them. Homosexuality, then, was best left as a personal and private matter. Sometimes same-sex couples (especially lesbians) would live together for years, go everywhere together, do everything together, and yet somehow their acquaintances and neighbors managed to pretend to see nothing but "inseparable friends." Isn't friendship a lovely thing?

Today, I think, someone like Wilson (I haven't asked the actual Wilson) would probably be more than willing to acknowledge a gay couple for who they are and to have the couple over for dinner. In the view of many people, the culture should accept the fact of same-sex coupledom, if only because, in today's out-and-proud world, the old pretenses have become absurd. But formal government recognition, they feel, crosses a new line and is neither necessary nor wise. No one would even be talking about it if not for the determined activism of the gay lobby. So some people maintain.

Is it true that society has no stake in same-sex marriage? I don't see how it could be.

To begin with, nowadays many gay households contain children, whether by adoption, insemination, or a previous marriage. Of the 594,000 same-sex couples counted by the Census Bureau in its 2000 survey of American households, 28 percent—just over a third of lesbian couples and just over a fifth of male couples—had children. (For married couples, the comparable figure was 46 percent.) The census doesn't say how many children lived in these households, but one or two kids per couple would translate into at least 166,000 children and possibly well over 300,000. Because gay households are rare and reticent, many demographers assume that the census figures are probably an undercount: a minimum. Other estimates put the number of gay-couple households with children at up to 2 million, and the number of children in such households at up to 3 million. Personally, I think the answer is somewhere in between, but closer to the census findings—still a large enough number to mean that, even if society cares about marriage only for the sake of children, it ought to care about the many thousands of children in gay households.

If you were the child of a same-sex couple, would you feel more secure with legally married parents, or less secure? Probably the former. If, at your tender age, you read through the social-science literature, you would certainly prefer married parents. Everything we know about children suggests they do best in stable homes, and everything we know about homes suggests that marriage makes them more stable.

You might protest that a married gay couple, particularly if male, will not be as stable as a married straight couple and so won't be as good for children.

Because we have no experience with married gay couples, we have no way to know if this is true. It may or may not be. Either way, however, same-sex couples with children do not have the option of becoming opposite-sex couples with children. Moreover, forbidding gay people to raise children is neither humane nor practical (especially since many gay couples are raising one partner's *natural* children). Given the reality of children in gay households, and given the many ways in which marriage supports and sustains unions, the relevant point is that children will be more secure and happy with married gay couples than with unmarried gay couples.

If, therefore, the presence of children is what makes a relationship matter in the eyes of society, then same-sex relationships can certainly pass the test; and if the welfare of children in those relationships matters, then marriage seems the best bet. Still, we need to consider the welfare of that large majority of children in nongay households; the welfare of the many may outweigh the welfare of the few. . . .

◦◦◦◦

Should society care if childless people get married? Should governments care? According to Wilson, no; or in any event they should not care very much. Many people today agree—or think they agree. For instance, some argue that getting divorced should be easier for people without minor children. Isn't it their own business? But folk wisdom and wise people like Shakespeare have always known better. Society's stake in marriage may begin with children, but it hardly ends there.

An aging widow takes a second husband. She is long past child-bearing age. Her children are grown and have kids of their own. But her family and friends are not dismissive or nonchalant. Unless the new husband is a scoundrel, they are happy and relieved. The wedding is an occasion for joy—more modest than many a first wedding, perhaps, but possibly more touching, too. The community receives the new couple with warm blessings. Why? No one wants to live in dotage alone, to die alone, to depend on children or, God forbid, on strangers. No one wants to be the child or stranger who is depended upon. Children or no, a marriage means one less person living on the frontier of vulnerability.

The town delinquent takes a wife. For the last few years, since he dropped out of school, he has been getting high and drunk, starting fights, having trouble holding jobs, running arrears on his rent, flitting between girlfriends, and shuttling in and out of court for minor offenses which threaten someday to become major crimes. He is not prime marriage material. One almost hopes he does not have children, at least not for a while. Yet the town breathes a sigh of relief at the news of his wedding. Why? A few farsighted people may be thinking, "When he has children, they'll be legitimate." But most people just think: "Thank goodness. Maybe he's settling down."

In both cases, the conventional wisdom is right. We all know in our gut that children are far from the only reason to care about marriage, important as children are. [Previously,] I argued that marriage serves three essential social needs: providing a healthy environment for children (one's own and other people's), helping the young (especially men) settle down and make a home, and providing as many people as possible with caregivers. The first rationale applies only to a minority of homosexuals, namely those who are raising kids. The latter two rationales, though, apply at least as strongly to gays as to straights. Marriage will help gay people settle down, and it will help provide them with care and comfort in their hour of need—and so society will have reason to feel relieved and happy when gay couples take the vows.

Some people argue that women and children, more than just the fact of marriage, socialize and settle men. That may be true, up to a point. But that hardly means that the settling effect of marriage on gay men would be negligible. To the contrary, being tied into a committed relationship plainly helps stabilize gay men. Even without marriage, coupled gay men have steady sex partners and relationships which they value, and those things act as anchors. In American gay-male life, it's a cliché that men in relationships vanish from the clubs and the parties. "Haven't seen you out in ages," people say. "You must have found someone." Because of the realities of stitching two lives together, couples simply do not have as much time or energy for getting around, or as much desire to do so. I may have met a few gay men who prefer constant imper sonal sex to a steady partner and a warm bed, but if so, I can't remember any of them. I do know some gay men—mostly of the 1960s generation—who celebrate the sexual and social libertinism of the decade before AIDS, but many of those men are now in relationships themselves. If you ask yourself whether a man in a relationship will be more wanton or less wanton than a man on his own, the answer will seem pretty obvious. Relationships are stabilizing.

And marriage stabilizes relationships. Add it to the mix, and you get the binding power of legal entitlements and entanglements, of caterers and in-laws, of the publicly acknowledged fact that the two partners are a couple. Even without kids or women, abandoning a marriage is much harder than abandoning a relationship. Gay divorce will look very much like childless straight divorce: complicated, wrenching, and a real deterrent to breaking up. (Which is one reason some gay activists of the "party on!" school are ambivalent about marriage.)

Controversy swirls around the question of the extent to which gay-male married couples will act like opposite-sex couples. . . . [The] only honest answer is that we don't know, because there are no gay-male married couples. It seems beyond dispute, however, that marriage will make male-male couples more settled and durable than will nonmarriage. (No one bothers to dispute that lesbian couples can and do bond durably.) The only question is: Somewhat more settled and durable, or a lot more settled and durable? As social scientists say, we may not know the magnitude of the change, but we know that the direction is positive.

Over time, as a new generation of gay children and nongay parents learn to expect and accept marriage, the cultural residue of the Long Dark Age will wash away. It is not just that today's homosexuals will become more relationship-oriented; it is that homosexual culture will become more relationship-oriented. That, too, will militate for domesticity among gay people.

Domesticity may be less of an issue for older people, but caregiving is always an issue. One of the first things many people worry about when coming to terms with their homosexuality is: Who will take care of me when I'm old? When I'm sick?

If it is true that marriage creates kin, then surely society's interest in kin creation is strongest of all for people who are less likely to have children of their own to rely on in old age and who may be rejected or even evicted—it is still not all that uncommon—by their own parents in youth. If the AIDS crisis showed anything, it was that homosexuals can and will take care of each other, sometimes with breathtaking devotion—and that no institution or government program can begin to match the love of a devoted partner.

It may seem a bit odd to mention the benefits of domesticity and caregiving here, under the heading of benefits for straights, rather than benefits for gays. Obviously, it is very good for homosexuals to have the security of a home and a partner. It is good for men and good for women and good for the horny young and good for the infirm old and good, period. But what may not be obvious is the stake straight society has in helping homosexuals establish settled lives. One way to see that stake is to reflect on the AIDS crisis and its enormous social cost (to say nothing of the horrific cost in gay lives). A culture of marriage might not have stopped the virus altogether, but it certainly would have slowed the virus down, and saved who knows how many lives and who knows how much money and agony. A sexual underworld is inevitable in every society, but in a marriageless society its extent is greater and its allure stronger. And, of course, its cost is higher. Syphilis, gonorrhea, and all the rest have haunted sexual underworlds since long before AIDS appeared. Beyond disease, there is a moral cost. In the context of heterosexual life, conservatives take for granted that a culture in which marriage is the norm is a healthier culture for children. It has always struck me as peculiar that so many conservatives have denounced the "homosexual lifestyle"—meaning, to a large extent, the gay sexual underworld—while fighting tooth and nail against letting gays participate in the institution which would do the most to change that lifestyle. And this, purportedly, in the name of protecting children!

What children, all children, need is protection from the bleak allure of a culture without commitment and a future without marriage. They need to grow up taking for granted that love, sex, and marriage go together—for everybody. They need to live among friends and neighbors, including gay friends and neighbors, who are married, not shacked up. No matter how you look at things, it is hard to see how a marriageless homosexual culture sends a good message for children or improves their social environment.

Some parents have gay children. That probably isn't their first choice. (Our genes want grandchildren.) Even if they understand and accept the phenomenon of homosexuality, their first thought is likely to be: "What sort of future awaits my child? How hard will his life be? What about the discrimination? What about the loneliness?" Their child may have come out to them as a teenager or a young adult. Every parent knows all too well how hard it is to get through that stage of life without making serious mistakes. Most parents would greet the prospect that their gay son or daughter could look forward to marriage with deep relief. The availability of marriage would give their child a path through the jungle. I doubt any parent would say, on learning a child is gay, "Well, thank goodness he can't marry."

The rest of us are parents of gay children, only a few steps removed. We live next door or down the block. We know instinctively that the neighborhood will be more solid if a large share of its residents are married couples. A moment's reflection suggests that the neighborhood will likewise be more solid if a large share of its homosexual residents are married couples, for all the same reasons. To say a neighborhood would be better off with fewer married gay couples and more gay singles or "domestic partners" seems perverse. Or suppose your children have a gay aunt or uncle. Suppose the neighbors' children have a gay aunt or uncle. What example would you like Uncle Jack or Aunt Janet to set?

⋘❦⋙

As you may have noticed, all these arguments I'm making are variations on a theme. For eons, human communities have favored more marriage over less. They have believed that marriage is a powerful stabilizing force: that it disciplines and channels crazy-making love and troublemaking libido; that stability and discipline are socially beneficial, even precious. Communities everywhere believe this, and everywhere they have been right. Their belief is a deeply conservative one, based on the age-old wisdom that love and sex and marriage go together and are severed at society's peril. The question, then, boils down to this: Why should homosexuals be the one exception? Why, in fact, should the precise opposite of history's tried-and-true wisdom apply to them?

A few answers are possible. One is that homosexuality is bad and legitimizing homosexuality will produce more of it. That view misunderstands homosexuality. A small fraction of the population is homosexual and cannot reasonably do anything about it and will fall in love and form couples and do so openly. The question is whether society is better off with homosexuals doing those things inside or outside the confines of marriage. What does society gain by excluding them?

A second answer is that marriage will not have the same effects on gays as on straights. . . . Here let me just say again that it is very hard to see how legal marriage could make gay relationships *less* successful or enduring. The question is only how much it would help.

A third answer is that homosexuals will simply not get married. They will view matrimony as a minority taste, and so society won't get much out of the deal. After all, only a minority of gay people in Vermont seem to be signing up for civil unions.

I confess this last possibility worries me. If it is good for society to have people durably attached, then it is not enough just to make marriage available. Marriage should also be *expected*. That is as true for gays as for straights. So, if homosexuals are justified in expecting access to marriage, society is equally justifed in expecting them to use it. If marriage is to work, it cannot be merely a "lifestyle option." It must be privileged. That is, it must be understood to be better than other ways of living. Not mandatory, not good where everything else is bad, but better: a general norm, rather than a personal taste. Gay neglect of marriage would not greatly erode the bonding power of heterosexual marriage; homosexuals are, after all, only a small fraction of the population. But it would certainly not help. In any case, the benefits to gay people and to society obviously materialize only to the extent that gay people actually get married. Heterosexual society would rightly feel betrayed if, after legalization, homosexuals treated marriage as a minority taste rather than as a core institution of life.

No one knows how homosexuals will respond to legal marriage. My guess is that only a minority will marry at the beginning, after legalization. But then? Here it becomes important to say a word about the element of time.

ꞏ⟨◉⟩ꞏ

Russians and East Europeans suffered under Communist rule for seventy years. Even before Communism they had not known freedom, and then Communism plunged them into a world of utter repression. Told that they could not do what they must do and that they must do what they could not do, people and societies bent to the point of dysfunction. Individuals learned to mistrust one another, to game the system, to regard personal initiative as a fool's errand. Logic itself, the daily logic of living, became warped. "The Soviet system is basically senseless," wrote the Russian dissident Andrei Amalrik. "Like a paranoiac, it *behaves* logically; but since its premises are senseless, the same is true of the results."

Then one day it ended. Down came the wall, down came the regime. Many Westerners expected a rapid flowering of democracy and capitalism in the former Soviet Union and its satellites. Just watch as the miracle of capitalism unfolds! Instead, we saw only halting progress. After a while, disappointment set in. But the disappointment was as unrealistic as the earlier optimism. Adjusting a culture to the twin shocks of freedom and responsibility takes time, probably a few generations. People need to relearn who they are. They need to build trust and a new social compact. Nowadays, most Western observers have come to see the transition out of Communism as a work in progress. Yes, it could be going faster, and in some places it isn't really going at all. But the wonder is that it is going so well.

Homosexuals have suffered under a Long Dark Age of not seventy years but seven hundred or more. Until as recently as the 1960s, there was no place, not anywhere, where gay people were at liberty to be themselves. As with the coming of capitalism to the Soviet empire, so with the coming of marriage to gay culture. Freedom and responsibility take time to learn.

The wonder is not how slowly gay culture is maturing but how quickly. Recently I had coffee with my friend Dale, who, at forty-one, was in a relationship with a man of twenty-four. We had a conversation which is becoming something of a staple among gay men in their forties. Dale marveled at how naturally his partner, Bill, had settled into the relationship. Bill just seemed to assume that domesticity was his birthright. I asked if faithfulness wasn't a problem for a twenty-four-year-old man with a forty-one-year-old partner. No, Dale replied. At the ripe age of twenty-four, Bill had already had his fill of one-night stands. Then we indulged in the obligatory moment of wistful head shaking. Gay men our age sound like geezers: "Why, these young people today—they have no idea how lucky they are!" Many a gay man of twenty-four thinks nothing, now, of leaving behind the sexual adolescence that his elders spent much of their lives floundering in.

Gay culture is changing, in large part because society has come to tolerate and, increasingly, even accept same-sex relationships. But the event that signaled the start of gay liberation, the Stonewall riot, occurred as recently as 1969, and the biggest change of all, the entitlement of gay couples to marriage, has yet to be introduced. If and when gay marriage is introduced, expect progress, not miracles. Expect a few decades between the legalization of same-sex marriage and its full integration into gay lives and culture.

Remember, not one same-sex couple has ever married, expected to marry, or even hoped to marry. Having built their relationships and lives outside marriage, often in the face not only of legal indifference but of social hostility, many gay adults will see marriage as an optional but hardly necessary government imprimatur. Others will be ideologically opposed. Marriage? That's for straights! Still others, viewing marriage as a way to get health insurance, will marry for the benefits, as heterosexuals sometimes marry for money. Yet others will hesitate to marry because parents or close family don't know they are gay or want to keep pretending not to know. At first, in other words, many gays will not marry, and some will marry for the wrong reasons or too casually. And, of course, some will head straight to the courthouse and do matrimony proud.

How the numbers will shake out is impossible to say. The question, though, is not primarily one of speed but of direction. Marriage, with the prestige and prerogatives and security and expectations it brings, has a way of putting down roots even in rocky soil. My guess is that there is a tipping point out there somewhere. As personal and legal and communal expectations reinforce each other—as gay people get used to asking themselves, "Could this relationship lead to marriage?"—a time will come when same-sex marriage crosses from new and exotic to established and expected. Then the Long Dark Age will really be over.

Is it possible that, even several decades after legalization, gay marriage will turn out to be a minority choice, an adornment rather than an institution? Yes. Anything is possible. But I would bet on marriage as the choice of the masses, just as I would bet on democracy and capitalism, because marriage, like democracy and capitalism, meets the personal and social needs of human beings as nothing else can.

To the skeptics I would say: I can't prove you wrong. But do you really want to bet *against* marriage? Do you want to put your money on quasi-marriage or semimarriage or nonmarriage? That would not be a particularly conservative bet. Indeed, it would be a radical one.

Jeff Jordan

Contra Same-Sex Marriage

Three models concerning the nature of marriage are discernable in the debate over same-sex marriage.[1] While not exhaustive of possible models of marriage, the three are relevant because they represent the understandings of marriage that inform many of the disputants in the same-sex debate.[2] The first is what we might call the "Sacramental" model of marriage. The characteristic propositions of this model include:

1. God instituted marriage as a lifelong relationship between one man and one woman.
2. Marriage is the proper environment for sexuality, procreation, and the rearing of children.
3. Marriage and the family are basic units of society, and are necessary for social stability.

Clearly enough, the Sacramental model sees marriage as essentially heterosexual and monogamous. Also, clearly enough, the Sacramental model, since it entails that God exists, and that there are certain natural laws built into the fabric of creation, is, we might say, "ontologically thick."[3] ["Ontologically thick": involving the existence of numerous things—such as, in this case, God and certain natural laws. —Ed] Propositions (2) and (3) provide the legal rationale for state recognition and support of marriage. Since marriage is necessary for the good of society, the state has ample justification to accord marriage a prominent legal status, which it denies to other relationships that persons may form or join. The social meaning of marriage—the set of expectations generally shared by the members of the society about the sort of relationship that the couple has[4]—is also shaped by (2) and (3) and includes an expectation of sexual intimacy, cooperation in economic matters, and a subordination of one's individual interests for the interests of the children and the good of the relationship.

The second model is what we might call the "Communional" model. The characteristic propositions of this model include propositions (2) and (3) and:

4. There is a natural or biological teleology apparent between the male and the female—"a two-in-one-flesh Communion of persons that is consummated and actualized by acts that are reproductive in type, whether or not they are reproductive in effect. . . ."[5]

112

Germain Grisez describes the "two-in-one-flesh" idea:

> Each animal is incomplete, for a male or a female individual is only a potential part of the mated pair, which is the complete organism that is capable of reproducing sexually. This is true also of men and women: as mates who engage in sexual intercourse suited to initiate new life, they complete each other, and become an organic unit. In doing so, it is literally true that "they become one flesh."[6]

The Communional model sees individuals as being, in an important respect, biologically incomplete. Marriage is the civil recognition of the social importance of this two-in-one biological completion. This is reminiscent of Aristophanes' "myth of the hermaphrodite" recounted in Plato's *Symposium*: "and so, gentlemen, we are all like pieces of the coins that children break in half for keepsakes—making two out of one, like the flatfish—and each of us is forever seeking the half that will tally with himself."[7]

The Communional model, unlike the Sacramental model, does not entail the existence of God. While the Communional model fits easily within a theological context, it neither entails nor depends upon theology. One might say that biology replaces theology in this model. Since this model can survive in either a naturalistic or theistic setting, it is "ontologically thin." ["Ontologically thin": not necessarily involving the existence of numerous things. —Ed] While many proponents of this model are theists, some are not. David Hume, for instance, can be seen as a proponent of the Communional model since he characterizes marriage as "an engagement entered into by mutual consent, and has for its end the propagation of the species, it is evident, that it must be susceptible of all the variety of conditions, which consent establishes, provided they be not contrary to this end."[8] Hume's variety of conditions, by the way, excludes polygamy and divorce as harmful of the teleology of marriage. Like the Sacramental model, the Communional model is essentially heterosexual and monogamous. And like the first model, this model entails that marriage merits a privileged legal status, in good part because marriage provides benefits to society as a whole. These social benefits include providing the best setting for the rearing of the next generation, and the "civilizing" or taming of young males. Marriage is typically an incentive to maturity.

The third model is what we might call the "Transactional" model of marriage. The essential features posited by this model are social in nature, since it sees marriage as a kind of transaction, recognized and regulated by the state, in much the same way as contractual relationships are treated. Marriage is seen as a legal arrangement akin to a contract, though this model need not see marriage as a contract. As Ralph Wedgwood points out, "Marriage need not strictly speaking be a contract, however. Under US law, for example, the rights and obligations of marriage can be changed by new legislation even without the consent of the spouses themselves."[9] The characteristic propositions of this model include:

5. Marriage is beneficial to the persons involved.
6. Marriage is a transaction regulated by the state.

The benefits flowing from marriage to the spouses include legal benefits such as preferential spousal immigration treatment, inheritance rights, and spousal health insurance benefits; and emotional benefits such as long-term commitment and sexual intimacy. Importantly, the Transactional model does not entail that marriage is essentially heterosexual and monogamous. Indeed, as persons explore and desire relationships different from those currently available, marriage law, according to this model, should change to accommodate the desires of the prospective spouses. The first two models understand marriage as a static relationship the parameters of which are determined by theology or biology, with procreation accorded a central place in the social meaning of marriage. Procreation is almost an afterthought in the Transactional model. It sees marriage as a largely plastic arrangement that flexes to social innovation, the basic rationale of which is the benefit of the spouses and not to any children involved. This dismissal of procreation as central to the meaning of marriage is seen in the majority opinion of the Massachusetts Supreme Judicial Court in *Goodridge v. Department of Public Health*, when the majority, in paragraph 48, asserted:

> While it is certainly true that many, perhaps most, married couples have children together (assisted or unassisted), it is the exclusive and permanent commitment of the marriage partners to one another, not the begetting of children, that is the sine qua non of civil marriage.[10]

Much of the current debate over the propriety of same-sex marriage involves a clash of these models. Defenders of traditional marriage typically hold to one or the other of first two models, while those supporting the propriety of same-sex marriage hold to a version of the third model.

In what follows I argue that there is good reason to deny legal marital status to same-sex relationships. In particular, I argue that extending legal marital status to same-sex unions is illiberal. This is a surprising argument but, as we'll see, state recognition of same-sex unions violates two fundamental principles of liberalism. By liberalism I mean the tradition associated historically with Hobbes, Locke, Hume, Kant, and Jefferson, and in our day, with Rawls, Dworkin, and Nagel. Roughly, liberalism regards individuals of a state as free and equal citizens, and requires a constitutional democratic polity, with policies and laws the legitimacy of which require the consent of its citizens.

The argument proceeds via two steps. The first step consists in showing that the most promising argument in support of same-sex marriage, the Equality argument, which contends that equality is violated when the state denies legal status to same-sex marriage, fails.[11] This failure is due to two problems. First, the Equality argument has a false premise. The falsity of this premise will be obvious once we highlight a basic principle of liberalism, "that the state should not promote or justify its actions by appeal to controversial conceptions of the good."[12] And second, even if the soundness of the Equality argument were conceded, it has the absurd result of justifying not only same-sex marriage, but also polygyny, polyandry, and polygynandry.[13] That is, the Equality argument, if successful, disconnects marriage from the traditional requirement of different sexes. But once that uncoupling is done, there's no principled way to maintain the traditional requirements that marriage is limited to a couple. In short, anything goes.

The second step consists in an argument that the case for same-sex marriage requires the state to adopt a controversial model of the nature and value of marriage. In brief, the case for same-sex marriage requires the Transactional model. But the Communional model is just as compatible with liberalism as is the Transactional model. Thus, the extension of legal status to same-sex marriages requires that the state adopt a controversial model of the nature and value of marriage as the correct model of marriage. Once again, the case for same-sex marriage is exposed as illiberal.

Along the way, I also examine two common objections to the denial of legal status to same-sex marriage. One is the claim that homosexuals are uniquely harmed by traditional marriage. The other is the claim that the prohibition contra same-sex marriage is strictly analogous to racist prohibitions against mixed-race marriages. Both objections, as we'll see, come apart under scrutiny.

The Equality Argument: Part I

In its most careful version the Equality argument asserts that the essential rationale for marriage is found in homosexual couples as well as heterosexual couples. What is this essential rationale? It is simply, argues Ralph Wedgwood, "that many people *want* to be married, where this desire to marry is typically a serious desire that deserves to be respected."[14] A desire is serious just in case it is a desire "of a certain kind, such that there is widespread agreement there are good reasons for the state to support and assist people's attempts to fulfill such desires, and strong reasons for the state not to impede or hinder people's attempts to fulfill such desires."[15] Moreover, "it is strong evidence that a desire is of this kind if the desire is widely and strongly held, and if few people sincerely resent those who succeed in fulfilling the desire."[16] Further, Wedgwood contends, the desire of homosexual couples to wed is every bit as real as that of heterosexual couples, "many same-sex couples have exactly the same desire, to make a mutual commitment of this kind, as opposite-sex couples."[17]

If the essential rationale of marriage is simply the serious desire to wed, the Equality argument looks like this:

7. The state should support certain serious desires—call the set of serious desires deserving state support, α. And,
8. the desire to marry is an element of α. So,
9. the state should support marriage. And,
10. same-sex desire to wed and opposite-sex desire to wed are such that any public policy toward the one is morally permissible if and only if that same policy toward the other is morally permissible. So,
11. the state should support same-sex marriages.

The Equality argument provides a rationale for state support of marriage as such, and a rationale for state support of same-sex marriages. Again, as Wedgwood puts it:

So legal marriage really is indispensable for enabling these couples to fulfill this serious desire. If marriage also imposes no serious burdens on anyone else, and violates no principle of justice, then this fact would justify
the institution of marriage.[18]

Wedgwood's provision that marriage is justified, given the desire to wed, if it
also imposes no serious burdens on anyone else is infelicitously stated. The
legal status of marriage may impose a serious burden as long as that burden is
morally justified. Eminent domain imposes serious burdens, but some times it
is fully justified.

Let's state the obvious: marriage provides legal benefits to those married.
Many of the legal benefits involved in marriage are subsidies provided by the
state to the spouses, done at the expense of the public. Such public subsidies
are not cost free. For example, to expand the class of persons eligible for spousal health insurance increases the cost of the program, or to expand the class
of persons eligible for family-leave benefits increases the costs of that program. Or consider taxes: for every tax advantage provided married couples
(say the marriage exemption to the federal estate tax), the tax burden of
unmarried persons or corporations increases, since this kind of tax relief is
not likely to spur economic expansion.[19] For the state to subsidize one group
by decreasing its tax burden typically requires an increase of the burden
borne by some other group. And this is true also with public subsidies that are
not directly financial. Consider legal quotas for immigration. To provide preferential treatment to spouses means that spouses "jump to the head of the
line," which implies that another citizen's relative or friend is lower on the
queue than she otherwise would have been in the absence of that benefit.

Public subsidies are burdensome. As such they should be carefully
rationed to both maximize the good of society at large, and minimize the
increased burden on those not receiving the subsidy. Indeed, the liberal principle of distributing public subsidies would require that the practice or arrangement subsidized provide a vital good to society as a whole, including those
who bear an increased burden because of the subsidy. More fully, the Legitimacy Principle for Public Subsidies would be:

> A public subsidy of a practice or institution is legitimate if and only if sub-
> sidizing that practice or institution is necessary for producing a vital good
> for society, which good cannot be produced or secured in a less burden-
> some way.

That the subsidy is beneficial to those who receive it is not sufficient to justify it
if someone else, who is not subsidized, is subjected to increased burdens or costs
without comparable benefits in return. There must be a benefit flowing to society generally if the state is justified in providing a public subsidy. . . . Proposition (8) seems obvious enough since two vital benefits flowing to society from
marriage are that of procreation and rearing of the next generation within a
two-parent family, and the protection of children.[20] . . .

Homosexual relationships do not, indeed cannot, provide the vital goods
to society that heterosexual ones provide. Apart from artificial insemination

homosexual couples cannot procreate, and thereby generate the next generation. Moreover, consisting of the same sex, it is far from clear that homosexual
couples can provide gender-differentiated parenting important for human
development.[21] Marriage of a man and a woman, however, provides a father and
a mother for any child produced or adopted.[22] Even an aged heterosexual couple can provide a father and mother for any child adopted. In addition, same-sex
marriage would not provide the protection of children associated with traditional marriage. Heterosexuals present a high risk of producing out-of-wedlock
children. This risk can be dramatically lowered if fidelity is maintained among
married heterosexuals. Even infertile married heterosexual couples probably
provide this protection, since it is rare that an infertile couple consists of both
spouses being infertile. As long as the fertile spouse remains faithful, there is no
risk of an out-of-wedlock child.[23] Homosexuals, however, whether faithful or
not, present almost no risk of producing out-of-wedlock children. So, again,
there is no comparable social good gained from same-sex marriages. . . .

. . . [H]eterosexual marriages provide vital social goods not provided by
homosexual relationships, ... It is not true that there is a moral equivalence
between state recognition of homosexual and heterosexual desires to marry.
The latter provides vital social goods that the former does not. Hence, state
subsidy of the one but not the other accords with the liberal principle governing public subsidies. For a state to extend legal marital status to same-sex couples, would be illiberal, since the state would be granting a burdensome
public subsidy without receiving any compensating social benefit.

The Equality Argument: Part II

The second problem with the Equality argument is that, if sound, we find ourselves with an embarrassment of matrimonial riches, since the reasoning
involved in the Equality argument supports a parallel argument justifying
poly-marriages, whether polygyny, polyandry, or polygynandry. Groups of
people can enter into transactions just as couples do. Indeed, if the essential
rationale of marriage is simply the serious desire to wed, it seems arbitrary to
hold that two people can have that serious desire, but three could not. In
other words, of the two primary restrictions imposed on traditional marriage—
heterosexuality and monogamy—the Equality argument seeks to lift the former
restriction, but, if successful, a parallel argument can be used equally well to
lift the latter. This embarrassment of matrimonial riches is what we might call
the "Anything Goes" problem. In short, if the Equality argument is sound,
then anything goes. Since the concern of this paper is the propriety of same-
sex marriage and not poly-marriage, I assume without argument that the latter
is problematic.[24]

The proponent of the Equality argument has to produce a stopper to
prevent the Anything Goes problem. Wedgwood, to his credit, admits there's
a problem:

> It would be presumptuous to deny that anyone could have a serious desire
> to have more than one marriage at the same time. It seems perfectly possible

for someone to have the most serious religious or personal reasons for wanting this. So, offhand, my version of the fundamental argument for same-sex marriage seems to support a parallel argument for polygamy.[25]

Wedgwood's stopper consists of two claims: there is little demand for polygamy, and "there is a serious concern that polygamy would have uncontroversial harmful effects, especially for women."[26] Wedgwood's stopper is remarkably porous. First, it is very likely that were matrimonial law revised to accommodate same-sex marriage, fundamentalist Mormons and Muslims will seek to have their desires for polygamous marriages accommodated by matrimonial law as well. Second, consider the concern that polygamy (or more narrowly, polygyny) may be harmful to women, keeping in mind that marriage is a voluntary arrangement among consenting adults. Even if it were the case that polygamy is a net harm to the consenting participants, it is far from clear that that is a good reason to deny legal status. Paternalism does not sit well with liberalism. Moreover, whatever historical evidence there may be that polygamy has been harmful to the participants is irrelevant. There are no cases of legal polygamous marriage in a liberal state, with all the protections of modern property laws, so there is no relevant historical evidence that polygamy is a net harm to the participants. Wedgwood's stopper stops nothing.

What's needed is a reason to think that the lifting of the quantity restriction would either harm society, or that the public subsidy involved in legal recognition is not warranted because poly-marriages provide no vital good to society. Jonathan Rauch, in his 2004 book, *Gay Marriage*, takes on the Anything Goes problem.[27] Rauch argues that polygny would harm society, since it would violate an important legal concern. Rauch first asserts "as a mathematical necessity (given that polyandry is extremely rare), for one man to have two wives means that some other man will have none. Moreover, the higher the man's status, the more wives he gets."[28] This would result in a shortage of available women, and in a population of low-status unmarried men. Polygyny would result in a skewed market in which the supply of available women is diminished. A high sex ratio—when there are many more men than women—is a recipe, Rauch claims, for social problems. So, the state has a good reason to deny legal status to poly-marriages: "The law's interest is only in making sure that, in a world full of romantic disappointment, we can all find plenty of other candidates if our first choice falls through."[29] "Everyone," Rauch claims, "should have a reasonable chance of marrying somebody, as opposed to nobody, or everybody, or anybody."[30]

This is a remarkable assertion; so let's dub it "Rauch's principle":

The state has a legitimate role in ensuring that everyone has an opportunity of marriage.

Rauch's principle is the foundation upon which he erects his contention that legal poly-marriages would be harmful to society. But how plausible is Rauch's principle?

It is just about as implausible as it could be. For one thing, is it at all plausible that the force of law should be employed to advance the matrimonial prospects of individuals? For another, it erroneously assumes that the pool of marriage candidates is constituted only by the subject's preferences. It neglects that the preferences of others also play a crucial role in whether one has any real opportunity of marriage. That is, Jones may be attracted to Smith, but Smith may not be attracted to Jones. It's conceivable that no one finds Jones an attractive marriage partner. Hence his pool is empty. And there is nothing that the state could or should do to remedy this misfortune.

Indeed Rauch's principle may inadvertently support poly-marriages. Imagine a society with twenty adult females, and twenty-one adult males, all of whom are heterosexual and desire to marry. Clearly, if Rauch's principle was true, polyandry or polygynandry would be legally necessitated in our imagined society, otherwise the odd man out would have no marriage prospects at all.

Moreover, Rauch's claim that a high sex ratio is a ready recipe for social problems is dubious. There's good evidence that with a high sex ratio—many more men than women—marriage is commonplace and cohabitation is rare, divorce is infrequent, and children are more often raised in two-parent homes, with women playing the more traditional roles.[31] With a high sex ratio "women have a lot of bargaining power and so find it easier to get men to marry and stay with them. . . ."[32] In the absence of evidence that the social ills produced by a high sex ratio outweigh the social benefits associated with it, Rauch's claim is best rejected.

Although I have provided no proof that there is no stopper to the Anything Goes problem, I have provided good reason to think that two prominent attempts to blunt the problem are abject failures. It is safe to conclude that the Equality argument, if sound, has the absurd result of justifying poly-marriages as well as same-sex ones. The Anything Goes problem is a bane to the Equality argument.

Condemned to Loneliness?

Rauch presents a clever wrinkle to the appeal to equality that's worth considering. Gays are uniquely harmed, he contends, by limiting legal marriage to unions that are heterosexual and monogamous:

> If, therefore, the rule is that the law should give everyone a realistic hope of marrying somebody he loves—not zero people, not two people, not three people, but one person—there is no other group in the country whose situation is comparable to homosexuals', because only homosexuals are barred, by law, from marrying anybody they love. The gay situation is unique. It is not that gays have to settle for their second or third choice. It is that gay people's set of choices is the null set.[33]

Hence equality requires that gays be treated as everyone else and not exposed to a singular harm. David Boonin makes a similar point when he claims:

> A law forbidding same-sex marriage . . . says that a heterosexual man can marry any member of the sex he is attracted to while a homosexual man can marry any member of the sex he is *not* attracted to, and that a heterosexual

man is forbidden to marry any member of the sex he is not attracted to while a homosexual man is forbidden to marry any member of the sex that he is attracted to.[34]

I suspect that Boonin does not really mean what he says. No law anywhere has ever granted anyone a license to marry "any member of the sex he is attracted to." Marriages under such a legal regime would be "nasty, brutish, and short." Boonin's point, like Rauch's, is that limiting legal marriage to heterosexual unions singularly harms gays.

Does limiting legal marriage to unions that are monogamous and heterosexual uniquely harm gays? There's reason to think not. Since the claim that it does presupposes Rauch's principle, it suffers from "implausibility by association." More important, someone desiring a poly-marriage is not settling for his second or third choice if he is legally allowed to marry only one wife. The poly person's desires are frustrated by the monogamy restriction every bit as much as the gay person's desires are by the heterosexual restriction. Does this mean that marital nonconformists—whether gay or poly—are condemned to loneliness? No. In a society in which cohabitation is legally possible, same-sex cohabitation is possible, as is group cohabitation. Persons with no desire to marry have other options.

The Basic Principle of Liberalism and Models of Marriage

Liberalism's basic raison d'être is the principle that the state should not promote or justify its actions by appeal to controversial conceptions of the good. Expressed a bit differently, the state should be neutral between competing conceptions of the good. Now, of course, this principle, the Basic Principle, we might call it, is itself a moral principle, and is itself controversial. Still, a subscription to liberalism implies an acceptance of the Basic Principle. What follows for state recognition of marriage, given a commitment to liberalism? Clearly enough, the state ought to be neutral regarding the nature of marriage. The Basic Principle requires that the state forswear ontologically thick models and restrict itself to models that are ontologically thin. For this reason, the Sacramental model is a nonstarter for the liberal as a justification for state action, since the Sacramental model implies that God exists. While the Communional model and the Transactional model present competing views of the nature of marriage, they are both ontologically thin. Hence, the Basic Principle of liberalism requires the state to be neutral between the Communional model and the Transactional model of marriage.

Notice however that legal recognition of same-sex marriage is compatible with the Transactional model (but not required by it), while it is incompatible with the Communional model. Proposition (4) presents an insurmountable obstacle to same-sex marriage. Proposition (4) implies that a union is a valid marriage only if it is a member of the kind whose characteristic actions are reproductive in type, even if not in effect. Hence (4) is compatible with infertile heterosexual unions, but not with same-sex unions. The latter is not a kind of union that can in principle be procreative, while infertile heterosexual marriages are a kind of union that in principle could be procreative. Proposition (4) accommodates the one but not the other.

The case for same-sex marriage is at home only within the Transactional model. For the state to recognize same-sex marriage, then, requires an appeal to a controversial view of marriage as a justification for that state action. By recognizing same-sex marriage the state would, in effect, declare that the Transactional model is correct, and that the Communional model is incorrect. In this way the state would be violating its desirable neutrality regarding controversial views of the nature of marriage. Once again, the push for same-sex marriage is exposed as illiberal. . . .

As Bad as Antimiscegenation?

A common objection to the refusal to extend legal status to same-sex marriage is that it is morally equivalent to laws precluding mixed-race marriages:

> People today forget how the language now being used against same-sex couples' equal marriage rights not so long ago was used against interracial couples—denying people's equal human dignity and freedom to share in the rights and responsibilities of marriage.[35]

The idea here is that arguments contra same-sex marriage are in the same boat as the laws and arguments contra mixed-race marriage that were prevalent in the United States decades ago. Since the latter were morally reprehensible, so too are the former.

This is serious indictment, if true. Is it? There's conclusive reason to think not. For one thing, it's a breathtaking claim that ignores the historical context of antimiscegenation laws. Antimiscegenation laws were just one part of a regime designed to oppress blacks. Whether education, or employment, or public accommodations, or housing, or politics, a society-wide system was in place that violated the civil rights of blacks. This violation was punctuated by legally tolerated violence as a way of ensuring compliance. To claim that the denial of legal recognition of same-sex marriage is akin to the reign of Jim Crow is astonishingly inaccurate, and belittles the sacrifices made in the long struggle against racial injustice.

Every argument supporting antimiscegenation was in historical fact either motivated by racist attitudes or intended to harm blacks.[36] The reasons for supporting antimiscegenation were inextricably linked to racism. But there is nothing like this with reasons or arguments contra same-sex marriage. Arguments contra same-sex marriage need not be motivated by animus toward gays, nor intended to harm gays. Let me briefly sketch six arguments contra same-sex marriage, any one of which are acceptable without moral blemish. By sketching these arguments I suggest nothing about their soundness or cogency, only that one could endorse any of them, without having done anything immoral.

A. The argument from the Communional model. If one believes that this model best represents marriage, then she will naturally favor public policies that exclude same-sex marriage and poly-marriages.
B. The argument from analyticity. One might hold that it is analytically true that a marriage consists of a husband and a wife, and that, necessarily, husbands are male, while wives are female. If one accepts the analyticity of these terms, then one will favoring reserving the term "marriage" for heterosexual unions.
C. The argument from religious doctrine. Traditional Catholicism, many denominations of Protestantism, the Orthodox branch of Judaism, and traditional or Orthodox Islam all assert that homosexual activity is immoral. Hence a "marriage" predicated on that activity is sinful according to the doctrines of these religions. So, a proponent of one of these religious traditions will favor public policies that exclude same-sex marriage.
D. The argument from the freedom of the conscience. Understanding the argument from religious doctrine, and knowing that there are many sincere adherents of religious traditions that assert that homosexual behavior is immoral, one could hold that state endorsement of same-sex marriage unduly tramples the freedom of conscience and religious liberty of those religious believers. Since state recognition is a de facto endorsement, the state, by extending legal recognition, would be declaring that a certain theology was incorrect. While there are theological disputes in which the state cannot in principle avoid involvement, this is one dispute in which it can and should avoid involvement.
E. The argument from public disagreement. One could hold that deep social controversies should generally be settled in a liberal society via legislation, and not by judicial intervention. The latter is permissible only when fundamental rights are at issue, and one could hold that there is no fundamental right to same-sex marriage. Both polls and referendums (witness the popular referendums in two of the more politically progressive American states—Hawaii in 1998, California in 2000—both of which passed by substantial majorities laws precluding same-sex marriage) provide sufficient evidence that a substantial majority of Americans disagree with same-sex marriage, and hence should be excluded. Knowing this, one would naturally favor public policies that exclude same-sex marriage, as this respects and reflects the majority will.
F. The cumulative case argument. One could adopt any combination of (A) through (E). . . .

Arguments and reasons employed in support of antimiscegenation policies were always morally problematic or factually misguided, since it is hard to imagine such an argument or reason that was neither motivated by animus toward blacks, nor intended to harm blacks. Arguments or reasons employed in support of traditional marriage are crucially and relevantly different. It is obvious that such arguments and reasons can be advanced without any antigay motivation or intent to harm gays. This is a significant disanalogy, which demonstrates that the common charge that arguments in support of traditional marriage are close relatives to racist arguments is false. Why then is it commonly leveled? Probably because it is an attempt to piggyback on the moral stature of the civil rights movement in the United States, thereby gaining the moral high ground in the public debate over same-sex marriage. It is always advantageous in combat to control the high ground, and one way to gain an advantage in a debate over public policy is to cast your opponents and their proposals as hopelessly immoral. If this diagnosis is correct, then it is likely that the charge is nothing more than overheated rhetoric masking the lack of argumentative support, and obscuring the relevant issues.

Liberalism and Same-Sex Marriage

Liberalism does not require legal recognition of same-sex marriage.[37] In fact, it cannot, since legal recognition is incompatible with at least two principles of liberalism—the Legitimacy Principle for Public Subsidies and the Basic Principle of liberalism. The push for legal recognition of same-sex marriage, though often packaged as being motivated or required by liberal reasons, is in fact illiberal. As has been so often the case with the illiberal, the push for legal recognition is also Orwellian in its means, as the ballot box is disregarded in favor of judicial fiat. Litigation replaces legislation. In any case, it is now clear that even if marriage is seen as nothing but a transaction, same-sex marriages are not justified within a liberal society.[38]

Notes

1. By marriage I mean the civil arrangement found in England, and other Western countries, since at least the thirteenth century. This arrangement, recognized by the state, is formed by mutual consent and, traditionally, restricted to monogamous and heterosexual unions. See James Q. Wilson, *The Marriage Problem: How Our Culture Weakens Families* (New York: HarperCollins, 2002), pp. 65–105. All three of the models I discuss see marriage as satisfying this minimal characterization.

2. James Witte examines five prominent models of marriage, from the Catholic model of the mid-twelfth century to the contemporary contractual model, in western Europe and the United States. See his *From Sacrament to Contract: Marriage, Religion, and Law in the Western Tradition* (Louisville, KY: Westminster John Knox Press, 1997).

3. Typically proponents of the Sacramental model hold that God has created humans with certain psychological traits and propensities, such that conforming to the divine design facilitates human well-being.

4. On the notion of the social meaning of marriage see Ralph Wedgwood, "The Fundamental Argument for Same-Sex Marriage," *Journal of Political Philosophy* 7, no. 3 (1999): 229.

5. Robert P. George, "'Same-Sex' Marriage and 'Moral Neutrality,'" in *The Clash of Orthodoxies: Law, Religion, and Morality in Crisis* (Wilmington, DE: ISI Books, 2001), p. 77, and see his *In Defense of Natural Law* (Oxford: Clarendon Press, 1999), pp. 139–83, 213–18. See also Gerard Bradley, "Same-Sex Marriage: Our Final Answer?" *Notre Dame Journal of Law, Ethics & Public Policy* 14, no. 2 (2000): 729–52.

6.   Germain Grisez, *The Way of the Lord Jesus*, vol. 2, *Living a Christian Life* (Quincy, IL: Franciscan Press, 1993), p. 570.

7.   Plato, *Symposium*, trans. Michael Joyce (London: Everyman's Library, 1935), p. 191d.

8.   David Hume, "Of Polygamy and Divorce," in *Essays: Moral, Political, and Literary* (1742; reprint, London: Longmans, Green, 1882), p. 231. By "propagation of the species" I take Hume to mean procreation.

9.   Wedgwood, "The Fundamental Argument for Same-Sex Marriage," p. 231.

10. *Goodridge v. Department of Public Health*, 440 Mass. 309 (2003).

11. I take Wedgwood's 1999 article, "The Fundamental Argument for Same-Sex Marriage," as a guide to the Equality argument.

12. Wedgwood, "The Fundamental Argument for Same-Sex Marriage," p. 225.

13. I understand polygyny as one husband with several wives, polyandry as one wife with several husbands, polygynandry as group marriage, whether same-sex or opposite-sex, and polygamy as marriages taking the form of either polygyny or polygynandry. I will use the term "poly-marriages" as a general term for either polygamous marriages or polygynandry.

14. Wedgwood, "The Fundamental Argument for Same-Sex Marriage," p. 235.

15. Ibid.

16. Ibid.

17. Ibid., p. 240.

18. Ibid., p. 236.

19. Notoriously, under the US income tax code married couples often face higher rates of taxation than they would if single. This "marriage penalty" has of late been reduced.

20. See, for instance, David Popenoe, *Life without Father: Compelling New Evidence That Fatherhood and Marriage Are Indispensable for the Good of Children and Society* (New York: Free Press, 1996); Judith Wallerstein, Julia Lewis, and Sandra Blakeslee, *The Unexpected Legacy of Divorce: A 25-Year Landmark Study* (New York: Hyperion, 2000); and Barbara Dafoe Whitehead, "Dan Quayle Was Right: The Social-Science Evidence Is In—Though It May Benefit the Adults Involved. The Dissolution of Intact Two-Parent Families Is Harmful to Large Numbers of Children," *Atlantic Monthly* (April 1993), and her *The Divorce Culture* (New York: Alfred A. Knopf, 1997). Each of these works presents strong evidence that an intact, two-parent home is generally the best environment for the rearing of children.

21. Even if a homosexual couple provides gender-differentiated parenting, via a kind of role-playing, it is questionable whether that's sufficient for full human development. See Popenoe, *Life without Father*, p. 146.

22. I owe this point to Maggie Gallagher, "What Marriage Is For: Children Need Mothers and Fathers" *Weekly Standard* 8, no. 45 (2003): 25.

23. Ibid.

24. For an argument against poly-marriages, one might begin with Hume, "Of Polygamy and Divorce."

25. Wedgwood, "The Fundamental Argument for Same-Sex Marriage," p. 242.

26. Ibid.

27. Jonathan Rauch, *Gay Marriage: Why It Is Good for Gays, Good for Straights, and Good for America* (New York: Times Books, 2004), pp. 123–37.

28. Ibid., p. 129.

29. Ibid., pp. 126–27.

30.   Ibid., p. 136.

31.   Marcia Guttentag and Paul F. Secord, *Too Many Women? The Sex Ratio Question* (Newbury Park, CA: Sage Publications, 1983), pp. 19–33, 43–49, 153–71.

32.   Wilson, *The Marriage Problem*, p. 47.

33.   Rauch, *Gay Marriage*, p. 127.

34.   David Boonin, "Same-Sex Marriage and the Argument from Public Disagreement," *Journal of Social Philosophy* 30, no. 2 (1999): 256.

35.   Evan Wolfson, "Why We Should Fight for the Freedom to Marry," in *Same-Sex Marriage: Pro and Con*, ed. Andrew Sullivan (New York: Vintage Books, 1997), p. 131.

36.   Were there arguments in support of antimiscegenation that were not predicated on racism? Perhaps some supporters of antimiscegenation based their views on arguments gleaned from science or theology. But these arguments were factually misguided, and the propensity to entertain them was, I suspect, largely facilitated by racism.

37.   A note on Federalism: Some proponents of same-sex marriage in the United States suggest that the states should be used as social laboratories, with some legalizing it and others precluding it, and we can then observe whether same-sex marriage is socially pernicious, beneficial, or benign. The problem with this proposal is illustrated by a similar "experiment" done with "no-fault" divorce laws, which are now generally seen as socially pernicious, but were adopted by nearly all the states less than twenty years after adoption by one state. The effects of a social policy can take decades to reveal themselves, but once the proverbial camel has its nose under the tent, it may be too late to keep it out.

38.   I thank Robin Andreasen, Bob Baird, Joel Pust, Mike Rea, Kate Rogers, and David Silver for their generous comments. Problems that remain are mine alone.

POSTSCRIPT

Should Same-Sex Marriage Be Allowed?

Marriage has rather surprisingly changed over time. For example, both now and in the past (as recorded in the Old Testament, for example), there are cases of men with several wives—indeed, King Solomon is said to have had 700 wives and 300 concubines! More recently, interracial marriages have been banned, and then later allowed, in several states. Currently, civil unions for homosexuals are available in Vermont, and several American and Canadian jurisdictions are considering, or have already performed, gay marriages. Meanwhile, there is much heated discussion among both elected lawmakers and the public at large.

Generally, we want to live in a society that is not tied to a specific religion—for we want to recognize diversity and to grant freedom of religion— but we don't want to live in a society that has no specific values; nor do we want to live in a society that allows people to do whatever they want. (We can't allow absolute freedom because we want to maintain some rights against people who are not allowed to transgress those rights.) Hence, we need to draw some lines. The question is whether we should include same-sex marriage inside the line or not.

One general approach that is often recognized by both proponents and opponents of gay marriage is what might be called *liberalism* (in the classical sense): liberalism recognizes that individuals have rights, and that those rights should extend as far as possible until they start to interfere with the rights of other individuals. Classical liberalism is also committed to refraining from endorsing controversial conceptions of the good—it is neutral in this respect. For example, if some people prefer to spend their time reading literary classics (and this is part of *their* conception of "the good"), while other people spend their time playing video games (and this is part of *their* conception of "the good"), the government is not to say that one group of people has the correct conception of the good—it is to remain neutral and let the different parties pursue happiness along the paths that they themselves determine (as long as no rights are violated).

It might seem that classical liberalism must automatically support same-sex marriage. After all, the parties to the marriage are acting according to their own conception of the good, and they are not violating anyone else's rights. But Jeff Jordan has argued that there are several different models of marriage, and that a state endorsement of same-sex marriage *would* endorse one of these as right. So in recognizing same-sex marriage, the state wouldn't be neutral. It would be illiberal. Jonathan Rauch, on the other hand, has argued that the institution of marriage exerts a powerful stabilizing force and contributes to the well-being of society, and is something that *should* be recognized.

This issue is not only about gay rights and the social acceptance of gays, but also about our idea of marriage. It is worthwhile examining Jordan's models and his argumentation to see exactly what he views and acceptable and what he views as not acceptable.

Relevant literature here includes David Moats, *Civil War: A Battle for Gay Marriage* (Harcourt, 2004); George Chauncey, *Why Marriage? The History Shaping Today's Debate Over Gay Equality* (Basic Books, 2004); Evan Wolfson, *Why Marriage Matters: America, Equality, and Gay People's Right to Marry* (Simon & Schuster, 2004); and the TFP Committee on American Issues, *Defending a Higher Law: Why We Must Resist Same-Sex "Marriage" and the Homosexual Movement* (The American Society for the Defense of Tradition, Family and Property, 2004).

ISSUE 7

Should Human Cloning Be Banned?

YES: George J. Annas, from "Why We Should Ban Human Cloning," *The New England Journal of Medicine* (July 9, 1998)

NO: John A. Robertson, from "Human Cloning and the Challenge of Regulation," *The New England Journal of Medicine* (July 9, 1998)

ISSUE SUMMARY

YES: Law professor George J. Annas argues that human cloning devalues people by depriving them of their uniqueness and that it would radically alter the idea of what it is to be human.

NO: Law professor John A. Robertson maintains that there should not be a complete ban on human cloning but that regulatory policy should be focused on ensuring that it is performed in a responsible manner.

The issue of human cloning requires careful consideration. Each person is believed to be uniquely valuable. Also, many prefer to differentiate humans from animals. If it is proven that the same technology that allows for the cloning of sheep can also be applied to the cloning of humans, both of these ideas are brought into question. In light of animal cloning, the existence of humans seems to be based on the very same biological processes that exist in sheep and other animals. And if there can be such a thing as human cloning, what happens to the idea that we are all unique? What happens to the idea that we all have our individual lives to lead, and that each person is responsible for his or her own choices?

Moreover, cloning can change ideas about reproduction. In cloning, no male is required. Consider the case of Dolly, the sheep cloned from the cell of an adult ewe. An egg cell, taken from a female sheep, had its nucleus removed; this was replaced with the nucleus of a cell taken from another female sheep. Then the result was implanted and grew in the uterus of a third female sheep, who eventually gave birth to Dolly. Normally, a newborn has genetic input from both the father's side and the mother's side. The original egg cell that was used in Dolly's case contributed almost nothing in this regard. The nucleus from the cell of the second sheep contained virtually all of the genetic input for Dolly.

Identical twins are familiar cases of human beings who, like clones, share a common genetic input. When environmental factors connected with identical twins are closely the same, and when they have similar clothes, haircut, etc., they can be difficult to tell apart. But when the environmental factors that impinge on their lives are quite different—as in the case of twins separated at birth—the twins can be quite different in obvious physical ways.

Physical aspects such as height have both genetic and environmental inputs; two people with the same genes can easily have different heights if environmental conditions (e.g., their diets) are different.

In some ways, clones are like identical twins, but in many cases there would be far less resemblance between clones than between identical twins, since they would be subject to very different environmental factors. Being conceived and born at different times—perhaps years or even decades apart from each other—they may have radically different environmental input.

Human cloning can be seen as beneficial. Cloning may provide another way for people to utilize technological assistance in reproduction. For example, a couple who could not have children naturally might consider a range of options, including cloning. Some maintain that is a relatively innocent use of human cloning, and can benefit those who are infertile.

Some object to cloning by citing other possible scenarios. Suppose a person wanted numerous clones of himself or herself. Suppose a sports star desires a clone who would then be expected to achieve greatness in sports. Suppose parents want a replacement for a child that they had lost, or want a child who could serve as a bone marrow or organ donor. These cases give some pause, since the motivation for cloning appears to be questionable.

To counter this argument, it is stated that proper regulation would prevent these types of scenarios from occurring. Instead, cloning would be performed only under the correct circumstances, and would promote scientific progress.

In the following selections, George J. Annas argues that human cloning radically undermines our beliefs in human uniqueness and self-identity. John A. Robertson counters that human cloning, if properly regulated, should be allowed to occur.

YES

George J. Annas

Why We Should Ban Human Cloning

In February [1998] the U.S. Senate voted 54 to 42 against bringing an anti-cloning bill directly to the floor for a vote.[1] During the debate, more than 16 scientific and medical organizations, including the American Society of Reproductive Medicine and the Federation of American Societies for Experimental Biology, and 27 Nobel prize–winning scientists, agreed that there should be a moratorium on the creation of a human being by somatic nuclear transplants. What the groups objected to was legislation that went beyond this prohibition to include cloning human cells, genes, and tissues. An alternative proposal was introduced by Senator Edward M. Kennedy (D-Mass.) and Senator Dianne Feinstein (D-Calif.) and modeled on a 1997 proposal by President Bill Clinton and his National Bioethics Advisory Commission. It would, in line with the views of all of these scientific groups, outlaw attempts to produce a child but permit all other forms of cloning research.[2, 3] Because the issue is intimately involved with research with embryos and abortion politics, in many ways the congressional debates over human cloning are a replay of past debates on fetal-tissue transplants[4] and research using human embryos.[5] Nonetheless, the virtually unanimous scientific consensus on the advisability of a legislative ban or voluntary moratorium on the attempt to create a human child by cloning justifies deeper discussion of the issue than it has received so far.

It has been more than a year since embryologist Ian Wilmut and his colleagues announced to the world that they had cloned a sheep.[6] No one has yet duplicated their work, raising serious questions about whether Dolly the sheep was cloned from a stem cell or a fetal cell, rather than a fully differentiated cell.[7] For my purpose, the success or failure of Wilmut's experiment is not the issue. Public attention to somatic-cell nuclear cloning presents an opportunity to consider the broader issues of public regulation of human research and the meaning of human reproduction.

Cloning and Imagination

In the 1970s, human cloning was a centerpiece issue in bioethical debates in the United States.[8, 9] In 1978, a House committee held a hearing on human cloning in response to the publication of David Rorvik's *In His Image: The Cloning of a Man*.[10] All the scientists who testified assured the committee that

From *New England Journal of Medicine*, vol. 339, no. 2, July 9, 1998, pp. 122–125. Copyright © 1998 by Massachusetts Medical Society. All rights reserved. Reprinted by permission.

the supposed account of the cloning of a human being was fictional and that the techniques described in the book could not work. The chief point the scientists wanted to make, however, was that they did not want any laws enacted that might affect their research. In the words of one, "there is no need for any form of regulation, and it could only in the long run have a harmful effect."[11] The book was an elaborate fable, but it presented a valuable opportunity to discuss the ethical implications of cloning. The failure to see it as a fable was a failure of imagination. We normally do not look to novels for scientific knowledge, but they provide more: insights into life itself.[12]

This failure of imagination has been witnessed repeatedly, most recently in 1997, when President Clinton asked the National Bioethics Advisory Commission to make recommendations about human cloning. Although acknowledging in their report that human cloning has always seemed the stuff of science fiction rather than science, the group did not commission any background papers on how fiction informs the debate. Even a cursory reading of books like Aldous Huxley's *Brave New World,* Ira Levin's *The Boys from Brazil,* and Fay Weldon's *The Cloning of Joanna May,* for example, would have saved much time and needless debate. Literary treatments of cloning inform us that cloning is an evolutionary dead end that can only replicate what already exists but cannot improve it; that exact replication of a human is not possible; that cloning is not inherently about infertile couples or twins, but about a technique that can produce an indefinite number of genetic duplicates; that clones must be accorded the same human rights as persons that we grant any other human; and that personal identity, human dignity, and parental responsibility are at the core of the debate about human cloning.

We might also have gained a better appreciation of our responsibilities to our children had we examined fiction more closely. The reporter who described Wilmut as "Dolly's laboratory father,"[13] for example, probably could not have done a better job of conjuring up images of Mary Shelley's *Frankenstein* if he had tried. Frankenstein was also his creature's father and god; the creature told him, "I ought to be thy Adam." As in the case of Dolly, the "spark of life" was infused into the creature by an electric current. Shelley's great novel explores virtually all the noncommercial elements of today's debate.

The naming of the world's first cloned mammal also has great significance. The sole survivor of 277 cloned embryos (or "fused couplets"), the clone could have been named after its sequence in this group (for example, C-137), but this would only have emphasized its character as a laboratory product. In stark contrast, the name Dolly (provided for the public and not used in the scientific report in *Nature,* in which she is identified as 6LL3) suggests a unique individual. Victor Frankenstein, of course, never named his creature, thereby repudiating any parental responsibility. The creature himself evolved into a monster when he was rejected not only by Frankenstein, but by society as well. Naming the world's first mammal clone Dolly was meant to distance her from the Frankenstein myth both by making her something she is not (a doll) and by accepting "parental" responsibility for her.

Unlike Shelley's world, the future envisioned in Huxley's *Brave New World,* in which all humans are created by cloning through embryo splitting and conditioned to join a specified worker group, was always unlikely. There are much more efficient ways of creating killers or terrorists (or even soldiers and workers) than through cloning. Physical and psychological conditioning can turn teenagers into terrorists in a matter of months, so there is no need to wait 18 to 20 years for the clones to grow up and be trained themselves. Cloning has no real military or paramilitary uses. Even clones of Adolf Hitler would have been very different people because they would have grown up in a radically altered world environment.

Cloning and Reproduction

Even though virtually all scientists oppose it, a minority of free-marketers and bioethicists have suggested that there might nonetheless be some good reasons to clone a human. But virtually all these suggestions themselves expose the central problem of cloning: the devaluing of persons by depriving them of their uniqueness. One common example suggested is cloning a dying or recently deceased child if this is what the grieving parents want. A fictional cover story in the March 1998 issue of *Wired*, for example, tells the story of the world's first clone.[14] She is cloned from the DNA of a dead two-week-old infant, who died from a mitochondrial defect that is later "cured" by cloning with an enucleated donor egg. The closer one gets to the embryo stage, the more cloning a child looks like the much less problematic method of cloning by "twinning" or embryo splitting. And proponents of cloning tend to want to "naturalize" and "normalize" asexual replication by arguing that it is just like having "natural" twins.

Embryo splitting might be justified if only a few embryos could be produced by an infertile couple and all were implanted at the same time (since this does not involve replicating an existing and known genome). But scenarios of cloning by nuclear transfer have involved older children, and the only reason to clone an existing human is to create a genetic replica. Using the bodies of children to replicate them encourages all of us to devalue children and treat them as interchangeable commodities. For example, thanks to cloning, the death of a child need no longer be a singular human tragedy but, rather, can be an opportunity to try to replicate the no longer priceless (or irreplaceable) dead child. No one should have such dominion over a child (even a dead or dying child) as to use his or her genes to create the child's child.

Cloning would also radically alter what it means to be human by replicating a living or dead human being asexually to produce a person with a single genetic parent. The danger is that through human cloning we will lose something vital to our humanity, the uniqueness (and therefore the value and dignity) of every human. Cloning represents the height of genetic reductionism and genetic determinism.

Population geneticist R. C. Lewontin has challenged my position that the first human clone would also be the first human with a single genetic parent by arguing that, instead, "a child by cloning has a full set of chromosomes like anyone else, half of which were derived from a mother and half from a father. It happens that these chromosomes were passed through another individual, the cloning donor, on the way to the child. That donor is certainly not the child's 'parent' in any biological sense, but simply an earlier offspring of the original parents."[15] Lewontin takes genetic reductionism to perhaps its logical extreme. People become no more than containers of their parents' genes, and their parents have the right to treat them not as individual human beings, but rather as human embryos—entities that can be split and replicated at their whim without any consideration of the child's choice or welfare. Children (even adult children), according to Lewontin's view, have no say in whether they are replicated or not, because it is their parents, not they, who are reproducing. This radical redefinition of reproduction and parenthood, and the denial of the choice to procreate or not, turns out to be an even stronger argument against cloning children than its biologic novelty. Of course, we could require the consent of adults to be cloned—but why should we, if they are not becoming parents?

Related human rights and human dignity would also prohibit using cloned children as organ sources for their father or mother original. Nor is there any constitutional right to be cloned in the United States that is triggered by marriage to someone with whom an adult cannot reproduce sexually, because there is no tradition of asexual replication and because permitting asexual replication is not necessary to safeguard any existing concept of ordered liberty (rights fundamental to ordered liberty are the rights the Supreme Court sees as essential to individual liberty in our society).

Although it is possible to imagine some scenarios in which cloning could be used for the treatment of infertility, the use of cloning simply provides parents another choice for choice's sake, not out of necessity. Moreover, in a fundamental sense, cloning cannot be a treatment for infertility. This replication technique changes the very concept of infertility itself, since all humans have somatic cells that could be used for asexual replication and therefore no one would be unable to replicate himself or herself asexually. In vitro fertilization, on the other hand, simply provides a technological way for otherwise infertile humans to reproduce sexually.

John Robertson argues that adults have a right to procreate in any way they can, and that the interests of the children cannot be taken into account because the resulting children cannot be harmed (since without cloning the children would not exist at all).[16] But this argument amounts to a tautology. It applies equally to everyone alive; none of us would exist had it not been for the precise and unpredictable time when the father's sperm and the mother's egg met. This biologic fact, however, does not justify a conclusion that our parents had no obligations to us as their future children. If it did, it would be equally acceptable, from the child's perspective, to be gestated in a great ape, or even a cow, or to be composed of a mixture of ape genes and human genes.

The primary reason for banning the cloning of living or dead humans was articulated by the philosopher Hans Jonas in the early 1970s. He correctly noted that it does not matter that creating an exact duplicate of an existing person is impossible. What matters is that the person is chosen to be cloned because of some characteristic or characteristics he or she possesses (which, it is hoped, would also be possessed by the genetic copy or clone). Jonas argued that cloning is always a crime against the clone, the crime of depriving the clone of his or her "existential right to certain subjective terms of being"— particularly, the "right to ignorance" of facts about his or her origin that are likely to be "paralyzing for the spontaneity of becoming himself" or herself.[17] This advance knowledge of what another has or has not accomplished with the clone's genome destroys the clone's "condition for authentic growth" in seeking to answer the fundamental question of all beings, "Who am I?" Jonas continues: "The ethical command here entering the enlarged stage of our powers is: never to violate the right to that ignorance which is a condition of authentic action; or: to respect the right of each human life to find its own way and be a surprise to itself."[17]

Jonas is correct. His rationale, of course, applies only to a "delayed genetic twin" or "serial twin" created from an existing human, not to genetically identical twins born at the same time, including those created by cloning with use of embryo splitting. Even if one does not agree with him, however, it is hypocritical to argue that a cloning technique that limits the liberty and choices of the resulting child or children can be justified on the grounds that cloning expands the liberty and choices of would-be cloners. [18]

Moratoriums and Bans on Human Cloning

Members of the National Bioethics Advisory Commission could not agree on much, but they did conclude that any current attempt to clone a human being should be prohibited by basic ethical principles that ban putting human subjects at substantial risk without their informed consent. But danger itself will not prevent scientists and physicians from performing first-of-their-kind experiments—from implanting a baboon's heart in a human baby to using a permanent artificial heart in an adult—and cloning techniques may be both safer and more efficient in the future. We must identify a mechanism that can both prevent premature experimentation and permit reasonable experimentation when the facts change.

The mechanism I favor is a broad-based regulatory agency to oversee human experimentation in the areas of genetic engineering, research with human embryos, xenografts, artificial organs, and other potentially dangerous boundary-crossing experiments.[19] Any such national regulatory agency must be composed almost exclusively of nonresearchers and nonphysicians so it can reflect public values, not parochial concerns. Currently, the operative American ethic seems to be that if any possible case can be imagined in which a new technology might be useful, it should not be prohibited, no matter what harm might result. One of the most important procedural steps Congress should take in setting up a federal agency to regulate human experimentation would be to put the burden of proof on those who propose to undertake novel experiments (including cloning) that risk harm and call deeply held social values into question.

This shift in the burden of proof is critical if society is to have an influence over science.[20] Without it, social control is not possible. This model applies the precautionary principle of international environmental law to cloning and other potentially harmful biomedical experiments involving humans. The principle requires governments to protect the public health and the environment from realistic threats of irreversible harm or catastrophic consequences even in the absence of clear evidence of harm.[21] Under this principle, proponents of human cloning would have the burden of proving that there was some compelling contravailing need to benefit either current or future generations before such an experiment was permitted (for example, if the entire species were to become sterile). Thus, regulators would not have the burden of proving that there was some compelling reason not to approve it. This regulatory scheme would depend on at least a de facto, if not a de jure, ban or moratorium on such experiments and a mechanism such as my proposed regulatory agency that could lift the ban. The suggestion that the Food and Drug Administration (FDA) can substitute for such an agency is fanciful. The FDA has no jurisdiction over either the practice of medicine or human replication and is far too narrowly constituted to represent the public in this area. Some see human cloning as inevitable and uncontrollable.[22, 23] Control will be difficult, and it will ultimately require close international cooperation. But this is no reason not to try—any more than a recognition that controlling terrorism or biologic weapons is difficult and uncertain justifies making no attempt at control.

On the recommendation of the National Bioethics Advisory Commission, the White House sent proposed anti-cloning legislation to Congress in June 1997. The Clinton proposal receded into obscurity until early 1998, when a Chicago physicist, Richard Seed, made national news by announcing that he intended to raise funds to clone a human. Because Seed acted like a prototypical "mad scientist," his proposal was greeted with almost universal condemnation.[24] Like the 1978 Rorvik hoax, however, it provided another opportunity for public discussion of cloning and prompted a more refined version of the Clinton proposal: the Feinstein-Kennedy bill. We can (and should) take advantage of this opportunity to distinguish the cloning of cells and tissues from the cloning of human beings by somatic nuclear transplantation[25] and to permit the former while prohibiting the latter. We should also take the opportunity to fill in the regulatory lacuna that permits any individual scientist to act first and consider the human consequences later, and we should use the controversy over cloning as an opportunity to begin an international dialogue on human experimentation.

References

1. U.S. Senate. 144 Cong. Rec. S561–S580, S607–S608 (1998).

2. S. 1611 (Feinstein-Kennedy Prohibition on Cloning of Human Beings Act of 1998).

3. Cloning human beings: report and recommendations of the National Bioethics Advisory Commission. Rockville, Md.: National Bioethics Advisory Commission, June 1997.

4. Annas GJ, Elias S. The politics of transplantation of human fetal tissue. N Engl J Med 1989;320:1079–82.

5. Annas GJ, Caplan A, Elias S. The politics of human embryo research—avoiding ethical gridlock. N Engl J Med 1996;334:1329–32.

6. Wilmut I, Schnieke AE, McWhir J, Kind AJ, Campbell KH. Viable offspring derived from fetal and adult mammalian cells. Nature 1997; 385:810–3.

7. Butler D. Dolly researcher plans further experiments after challenges. Nature 1998;391:825–6.

8. Lederberg J. Experimental genetics and human evolution. Am Naturalist 1966;100:519–31

9. Watson JD. Moving toward the clonal man. Atlantic Monthly. May 1971:50–3.

10. Rorvik DM. In his image: the cloning of a man. Philadelphia: J.B. Lippincott, 1978.

11. Development in cell biology and genetics, cloning. Hearings before the Subcommittee on Health and the Environment of the Committee on Interstate and Foreign Commerce of the U.S. House of Representatives, 95th Congress, 2d Session, May 31, 1978.

12. Chomsky N. Language and problems of knowledge: the Managua lectures. Cambridge, Mass.: MIT Press, 1988.

13. Montalbano W. Cloned sheep is star, but not sole project, at institute. Los Angeles Times. February 25, 1997:A7.

14. Kadrey R. Carbon copy: meet the first human clone. Wired. March 1998:146–50.

15. Lewontin RC. Confusion over cloning. New York Review of Books. October 23, 1997:20–3.

16. Robertson JA. Children of choice: freedom and the new reproductive technologies. Princeton, N.J.: Princeton University Press, 1994:169.

17. Jonas H. Philosophical essays: From ancient creed to technological man. Englewood Cliffs, N.J.: Prentice-Hall, 1974:162–3.

18. Annas GJ. Some choice: law, medicine and the market. New York: Oxford University Press, 1998:14–5.

19. Annas GJ. Regulatory models for human embryo cloning: the free market, professional guidelines, and government restrictions. Kennedy Inst Ethics J 1994;4:235–49.

20. Hearings before the U.S. Senate Subcommittee on Public Health and Safety, 105th Congress, 1st Session, March 12, 1997. . . .

21. Cross FB. Paradoxical perils of the precautionary principle. Washington Lee Law Rev 1996;53:851–925.

22. Kolata GB. Clone: the road to Dolly, and the path ahead. New York: W. Morrow, 1998.

23. Silver LM. Remaking Eden: cloning and beyond in a brave new world. New York: Avon Books, 1997.

24. Knox RA. A Chicagoan plans to offer cloning of humans. Boston Globe. January 7, 1998:A3.

25. Kassirer JP, Rosenthal NA. Should human cloning research be off limits? N Engl J Med 1998;338:905–6

John A. Robertson  **NO**

Human Cloning and the Challenge of Regulation

T he birth of Dolly, the sheep cloned from a mammary cell of an adult ewe, has initiated a public debate about human cloning. Although cloning of humans may never be clinically feasible, discussion of the ethical, legal, and social issues raised is important. Cloning is just one of several techniques potentially available to select, control, or alter the genome of offspring.[1-3] The development of such technology poses an important social challenge: how to ensure that the technology is used to enhance, rather than limit, individual freedom and welfare.

A key ethical question is whether a responsible couple, interested in rearing healthy offspring biologically related to them, might ethically choose to use cloning (or other genetic-selection techniques) for that purpose. The answer should take into account the benefits sought through the use of the techniques and any potential harm to offspring or to other interests.

The most likely uses of cloning would be far removed from the bizarre or horrific scenarios that initially dominated media coverage.[4] Theoretically, cloning would enable rich or powerful persons to clone themselves several times over, and commercial entrepreneurs might hire women to bear clones of sports or entertainment celebrities to be sold to others to rear. But current reproductive techniques can also be abused, and existing laws against selling children would apply to those created by cloning.

There is no reason to think that the ability to clone humans will cause many people to turn to cloning when other methods of reproduction would enable them to have healthy children. Cloning a human being by somatic cell nuclear transfer, for example, would require a consenting person as a source of DNA, eggs to be enucleated and then fused with the DNA, a woman who would carry and deliver the child, and a person or couple to raise the child. Given this reality, cloning is most likely to be sought by couples who, because of infertility, a high risk of severe genetic disease, or other factors, cannot or do not wish to conceive a child.

Several plausible scenarios can be imagined. Rather than use sperm, egg, or embryo from anonymous donors, couples who are infertile as a result of gametic insufficiency might choose to clone one of the partners. If the husband were the source of the DNA and the wife provided the egg that received

From *New England Journal of Medicine*, vol. 339, no. 2, July 9, 1998, pp. 119–121. Copyright © 1998 as conveyed via the Copyright Clearance Center. Reprinted by permission.

the nuclear transfer and then gestated the fetus, they would have a child biologically related to each of them and would not need to rely on anonymous gamete or embryo donation. Of course, many infertile couples might still prefer gamete or embryo donation or adoption. But there is nothing inherently wrong in wishing to be biologically related to one's children, even when this goal cannot be achieved through sexual reproduction.

A second plausible application would be for a couple at high risk of having offspring with a genetic disease.[5] Couples in this situation must now choose whether to risk the birth of an affected child, to undergo prenatal or preimplantation diagnosis and abortion or the discarding of embryos, to accept gamete donation, to seek adoption, or to remain childless. If cloning were available, however, some couples, in line with prevailing concepts of kinship, family, and parenting, might strongly prefer to clone one of themselves or another family member. Alternatively, if they already had a healthy child, they might choose to use cloning to create a later-born twin of that child. In the more distant future, it is even possible that the child whose DNA was replicated would not have been born healthy but would have been made healthy by gene therapy after birth.

A third application relates to obtaining tissue or organs for transplantation. A child who needed an organ or tissue transplant might lack a medically suitable donor. Couples in this situation have sometimes conceived a child coitally in the hope that he or she would have the correct tissue type to serve, for example, as a bone marrow donor for an older sibling.[6, 7] If the child's disease was not genetic, a couple might prefer to clone the affected child to be sure that the tissue would match.

It might eventually be possible to procure suitable tissue or organs by cloning the source DNA only to the point at which stem cells or other material might be obtained for transplantation, thus avoiding the need to bring a child into the world for the sake of obtaining tissue.[8] Cloning a person's cells up to the embryo stage might provide a source of stem cells or tissue for the person cloned. Cloning might also be used to enable a couple to clone a dead or dying child so as to have that child live on in some closely related form, to obtain sufficient numbers of embryos for transfer and pregnancy, or to eliminate mitochondrial disease.[5]

Most, if not all, of the potential uses of cloning are controversial, usually because of the explicit copying of the genome. As the National Bioethics Advisory Commission noted, in addition to concern about physical safety and eugenics, somatic-cell cloning raises issues of the individuality, autonomy, objectification, and kinship of the resulting children.[5] In other instances, such as the production of embryos to serve as tissue banks, the ethical issue is the sacrifice of embryos created solely for that purpose.

Given the wide leeway now granted couples to use assisted reproduction and prenatal genetic selection in forming families, cloning should not be rejected in all circumstances as unethical or illegitimate. The manipulation of embryos and the use of gamete donors and surrogates are increasingly common. Most fetuses conceived in the United States and Western Europe are now screened for genetic or chromosomal anomalies. Before conception, screening to identify carriers of genetic diseases is widespread.[9] Such practices also deviate from conventional notions of reproduction, kinship, and medical treatment of infertility, yet they are widely accepted.

Despite the similarity of cloning to current practices, however, the dissimilarities should not be overlooked. The aim of most other forms of assisted reproduction is the birth of a child who is a descendant of at least one member of the couple, not an identical twin. Most genetic selection acts negatively to identify and screen out unwanted traits such as genetic disease, not positively to choose or replicate the genome as in somatic-cell cloning.[3] It is not clear, however, why a child's relation to his or her rearing parents must always be that of sexually reproduced descendant when such a relationship is not possible because of infertility or other factors. Indeed, in gamete donation and adoption, although sexual reproduction is involved, a full descendant relation between the child and both rearing parents is lacking. Nor should the difference between negative and positive means of selecting children determine the ethical or social acceptability of cloning or other techniques. In both situations, a deliberate choice is made so that a child is born with one genome rather than another or is not born at all.

Is cloning sufficiently similar to current assisted-reproduction and genetic-selection practices to be treated similarly as a presumptively protected exercise of family or reproductive liberty?[10] Couples who request cloning in the situations I have described are seeking to rear healthy children with whom they will have a genetic or biologic tie, just as couples who conceive their children sexually do. Whether described as "replication" or as "reproduction," the resort to cloning is similar enough in purpose and effects to other reproduction and genetic-selection practices that it should be treated similarly. Therefore, a couple should be free to choose cloning unless there are compelling reasons for thinking that this would create harm that the other procedures would not cause.[10]

The concern of the National Bioethics Advisory Commission about the welfare of the clone reflects two types of fear. The first is that a child with the same nuclear DNA as another person, who is thus that person's later-born identical twin, will be so severely harmed by the identity of nuclear DNA between them that it is morally preferable, if not obligatory, that the child not be born at all.[5] In this case the fear is that the later-born twin will lack individuality or the freedom to create his or her own identity because of confusion or expectations caused by having the same DNA as another person.[5, 11]

This claim does not withstand the close scrutiny that should precede interference with a couple's freedom to bear and rear biologically related children.[10] Having the same genome as another person is not in itself harmful, as widespread experience with monozygotic twins shows. Being a twin does not deny either twin his or her individuality or freedom, and twins often have a special intimacy or closeness that few non-twin siblings can experience.[12] There is no reason to think that being a later-born identical twin resulting from cloning would change the overall assessment of being a twin.

Differences in mitochondria and the uterine and childhood environment will undercut problems of similarity and minimize the risk of overidentification with the first twin. A clone of Smith may look like Smith, but he or she will not be Smith and will lack many of Smith's phenotypic characteristics. The effects of having similar DNA will also depend on the length of time before the second twin is born, on whether the twins are raised together, on whether they are informed that they are genetic twins, on whether other people are so informed, on the beliefs that the rearing parents have about genetic influence on behavior, and on other factors. Having a previously born twin might in some circumstances also prove to be a source of support or intimacy for the later-born child.

The risk that parents or the child will overly identify the child with the DNA source also seems surmountable. Would the child invariably be expected to match the phenotypic characteristics of the DNA source, thus denying the second twin an "open future" and the freedom to develop his or her own identity?[5, 11, 13] In response to this question, one must ask whether couples who choose to clone offspring are more likely to want a child who is a mere replica of the DNA source or a child who is unique and valued for more than his or her genes. Couples may use cloning in order to ensure that the biologic child they rear is healthy, to maintain a family connection in the face of gametic infertility, or to obtain matched tissue for transplantation and yet still be responsibly committed to the welfare of their child, including his or her separate identity and interests and right to develop as he or she chooses.

The second type of fear is that parents who choose their child's genome through somatic-cell cloning will view the child as a commodity or an object to serve their own ends.[5] We do not view children born through coital or assisted reproduction as "mere means" just because people reproduce in order to have company in old age, to fulfill what they see as God's will, to prove their virility, to have heirs, to save a relationship, or to serve other selfish purposes.[14] What counts is how a child is treated after birth. Self-interested motives for having children do not prevent parents from loving children for themselves once they are born.

The use of cloning to form families in the situations I have described, though closely related to current assisted-reproduction and genetic-selection practices, does offer unique variations. The novelty of the relation—cloning in lieu of sperm donation, for example, produces a later-born identical twin raised by the older twin and his spouse—will create special psychological and social challenges. Can these challenges be successfully met, so that cloning produces net good for families and society? Given the largely positive experience with assisted-reproduction techniques that initially appeared frightening, cautious optimism is justified. We should be able to develop procedures and guidelines for cloning that will allow us to obtain its benefits while minimizing its problems and dangers.

In the light of these considerations, I would argue that a ban on privately funded cloning research is unjustified and likely to hamper important types of research.[8] A permanent ban on the cloning of human beings, as advocated by the Council of Europe and proposed in Congress, is also unjustified.[15, 16] A more limited ban—whether for 5 years, as proposed by the National Bioethics Advisory Commission and enacted in California, or for 10 years, as in the bill of

Senator Dianne Feinstein (D-Calif.) and Senator Edward M. Kennedy (D-Mass.) that is now before Congress—is also open to question.[5, 17, 18] Given the early state of cloning science and the widely shared view that the transfer of cloned embryos to the uterus before the safety and efficacy of the procedure has been established is unethical, few responsible physicians are likely to offer human cloning in the near future.[5] Nor are profit-motivated entrepreneurs, such as Richard Seed, likely to have many customers for their cloning services until the safety of the procedure is demonstrated.[19] A ban on human cloning for a limited period would thus serve largely symbolic purposes. Symbolic legislation, however, often has substantial costs.[20, 21] A government-imposed prohibition on privately funded cloning, even for a limited period, should not be enacted unless there is a compelling need. Such a need has not been demonstrated.

Rather than seek to prohibit all uses of human cloning, we should focus our attention on ensuring that cloning is done well. No physician or couple should embark on cloning without careful thought about the novel relational issues and child-rearing responsibilities that will ensue. We need regulations or guidelines to ensure safety and efficacy, fully informed consent and counseling for the couple, the consent of any person who may provide DNA, guarantees of parental rights and duties, and a limit on the number of clones from any single source.[10] It may also be important to restrict cloning to situations where there is a strong likelihood that the couple or individual initiating the procedure will also rear the resulting child. This principle will encourage a stable parenting situation and minimize the chance that cloning entrepreneurs will create clones to be sold to others.[22] As our experience grows, some restrictions on who may serve as a source of DNA for cloning (for example, a ban on cloning one's parents) may also be defensible.[10]

Cloning is important because it is the first of several positive means of genetic selection that may be sought by families seeking to have and rear healthy, biologically related offspring. In the future, mitochondrial transplantation, germ-line gene therapy, genetic enhancement, and other forms of prenatal genetic alteration may be possible.[3, 23, 24] With each new technique, as with cloning, the key question will be whether it serves important health, reproductive, or family needs and whether its benefits outweigh any likely harm. Cloning illustrates the principle that when legitimate uses of a technique are likely, regulatory policy should avoid prohibition and focus on ensuring that the technique is used responsibly for the good of those directly involved. As genetic knowledge continues to grow, the challenge of regulation will occupy us for some time to come.

References

1. Silver LM. Remaking Eden: cloning and beyond in a brave new world. New York: Avon Books, 1997.
2. Walters L, Palmer JG. The ethics of human gene therapy. New York: Oxford University Press, 1997.
3. Robertson JA. Genetic selection of offspring characteristics. Boston Univ Law Rev 1996;76:421–82.
4. Begley S. Can we clone humans? Newsweek. March 10, 1997:53–60.

5. Cloning human beings: report and recommendations of the National Bioethics Advisory Commission. Rockville, Md.: National Bioethics Advisory Commission, June 1997.

6. Robertson JA. Children of choice: freedom and the new reproductive technologies. Princeton, N.J.: Princeton University Press, 1994.

7. Kearney W, Caplan AL. Parity for the donation of bone marrow: ethical and policy considerations. In: Blank RH, Bonnicksen AL, eds. Emerging issues in biomedical policy: an annual review. Vol. 1 New York: Columbia University Press, 1992:262–85.

8. Kassirer JP, Rosenthal NA. Should human cloning research be off limits? N Engl J Med 1998;338:905–6.

9. Holtzman NA. Proceed with caution: predicting genetic risks in the recombinant DNA era. Baltimore: Johns Hopkins University Press, 1989.

10. Robertson JA. Liberty, identity, and human cloning. Texas Law Rev 1998; 77:1371–456.

11. Davis DS. What's wrong with cloning? Jurimetrics 1997;38:83–9.

12. Segal NL. Behavioral aspects of intergenerational human cloning: what twins tell us. Jurimetrics 1997;38:57–68.

13. Jonas H. Philosophical essays: from ancient creed to technological man. Englewood Cliffs, N.J.: Prentice-Hall, 1974:161.

14. Heyd D. Genethics: moral issues in the creation of people. Berkeley: University of California Press, 1992.

15. Council of Europe. Draft additional protocol to the Convention on Human Rights and Biomedicine on the prohibition of cloning human beings with explanatory report and Parliamentary Assembly opinion (adopted September 22, 1997). XXXVI International Legal Materials 1415 (1997).

16. Human Cloning Prohibition Act, H.R. 923, S. 1601 (March 5, 1997).

17. Act of Oct. 4, 1997, ch. 688, 1997 Cal. Legis. Serv 3790 (West, WESTLAW through 1997 Sess.).

18. Prohibition on Cloning of Human Beings Act, S. 1602, 105th Cong. (1998).

19. Stolberg SG. A small spark ignites debate on laws on cloning humans. New York Times. January 19, 1998:A1.

20. Gusfield J. Symbolic crusade: status politics and the American temperance movement. Urbana: University of Illinois Press, 1963.

21. Wolf SM. Ban cloning? Why NBAC is wrong. Hastings Cent Rep 1997;27(5):12.

22. Wilson JQ. The paradox of cloning. The Weekly Standard. May 26, 1997:23–7.

23. Zhang J, Grifo J, Blaszczyk A, et al. In vitro maturation of human preovulatory oocytes reconstructed by germinal vesicle transfer. Fertil Steril 1997; 68:Suppl:S1. abstract.

24. Bonnicksen AL. Transplanting nuclei between human eggs: implications for germ-line genetics. Politics and the Life Sciences. March 1998:3–10.

POSTSCRIPT

Should Human Cloning Be Banned?

The social and legal debates about cloning are appropriate because the technology is so fundamentally groundbreaking. Note that, as much as Annas and Robertson disagree in the preceding readings, neither would think it advisable for human cloning to proceed in a totally unregulated way.

One problem that might seem small at first but is quite serious is that we do not have a good way of assimilating the new ideas of cloning into our vocabulary and thought. For example, we think of a baby as having both a father and a mother. But a clone would be made from a single person. The clone and the single original person would both have the same set of genes. This set of genes comes from the parents of the original person, who are also the parents, as viewed from a biological standpoint, of the clone. So, this creates a situation in which people can have children when they are very old or even after death. Moreover, if the original person and the clone share genes, then they seem like identical twins. But they could be of vastly different ages; in fact, one of the "twins" could be an adoptive parent of the other.

Some say that the fact that cloning doesn't fit into our normal system for making sense of family relationships is due to the fact that cloning upsets the system in a fundamental way. This view holds that human cloning causes people to be viewed as objects instead of being viewed as unique individuals. But others will say that the fact that our traditional vocabulary is inadequate to the situation only shows that we are unprepared for this new situation, not that human cloning should be totally banned.

For the original bioethics report discussed by both Annas and Robertson, see *Cloning Human Beings: Report and Recommendations of the National Bioethics Advisory Commission* (Gem Publications, 1998). A variety of views about cloning can be found in Gregory E. Pence, *Who's Afraid of Human Cloning?* (Rowman & Littlefield, 1998); Glenn McGee, ed., *The Human Cloning Debate* (Berkeley Hills Books, 1998); James C. Hefley and Lane P. Lester, *Human Cloning: Playing God or Scientific Progress?* (Fleming H. Revell, 1998); Gregory E. Pence, ed., *Flesh of My Flesh: The Ethics of Cloning Humans: A Reader* (Rowman & Littlefield, 1998); Martha Nussbaum and Cass R. Sunstein eds., *Clones and Clones: Facts and Fantasies About Human Cloning* (W. W. Norton, 1998); M. L. Rantala and Arthur J. Milgram, eds., *Cloning: For and Against* (Open Court, 1999); Lori B. Andrews, *The Clone Age: Adventures in the New World of Reproductive Technology* (Henry Holt, 1999); Michael C. Brannigan, ed., *Ethical Issues in Human Cloning: Cross-Disciplinary Perspectives* (Seven Bridges Press, 2000); and Leon R. Kass, *Human Cloning and Human Dignity: The Report of the President's Council on Bioethics* (Public Affairs, 2002).

Internet References . . .

Drugs

The Drug Reform Coordination Network (DRCN) sponsors this site of links to drug policy organizations and studies.

http://druglibrary.org

The Drug Enforcement Administration's Web site contains numerous useful links.

http://www.dea.gov/

Affirmative Action

A collection of sites dealing with affirmative action has been posted by Yahoo! at:

**http://dir.yahoo.com/society_and_culture/
issues_and_causes/affirmative_action/**

Punishment and the Death Penalty

This *Ethics Updates* site contains discussion forums, court decisions, statistical resources, and Internet resources on the death penalty.

http://ethics.sandiego.edu/Applied/DeathPenalty/index.asp

Gun Control and Gun Rights

Numerous links regarding gun control and gun rites are on the following sites:

**http://www.guncite.com/
http://jurist.law.pitt.edu/gunlaw.htm**

Euthanasia and End-of-Life Decisions

This *Ethics Updates* site contains discussion questions, court decisions, statistical resources, and Internet resources on euthanasia and physician-assisted suicide.

http://ethics.sandiego.edu/Applied/Euthanasia/index.asp

Law and Society

*L*iving in groups is part of the social nature of human beings. And this requires that we have laws or rules that govern our behavior and interpersonal interactions. Morality and shared values can be positive tools for social living. One presupposition in a democratic society is that social differences must be settled by open discussion, argument, and persuasion—not by force. The issues in this section include some that have strongly divided our own society and some that currently challenge existing social institutions and practices.

- Is Cloning Pets Ethically Justified?

- Should Congress Allow the Buying and Selling of Human Organs?

- Should Drugs Be Legalized?

- Is Gambling Immoral?

- Is Affirmative Action Fair?

- Should Handguns Be Banned?

- Should the Death Penalty Be Abolished?

- Is Torture Ever Justified?

- Is Physician-Assisted Suicide Wrong?

ISSUE 8

Is Cloning Pets Ethically Justified?

YES: **Autumn Fiester**, from "Creating Fido's Twin," *Hastings Center Report* (July/August 2005)

NO: **Hilary Bok**, from "Cloning Companion Animals Is Wrong," *Journal of Applied Animal Welfare Science* (vol. 5, no. 3, 2002)

ISSUE SUMMARY

YES: Autumn Fiester argues in support of cloning animals (in particular, people's pets). She emphasizes the point that pet owners really care about their pets. One result of this is that they spend large amounts of money on veterinary care for their pets. Cloning their pets could serve as a useful extension of this idea—and also serve as a positive demonstration of society in general that individual pets have intrinsic value and cannot simply be replaced by new pets.

NO: Hilary Bok argues that cloning pets is immoral first of all because it causes great harm to animals. The animal that results from cloning, for example, is much more likely to have physical defects than the animal from which it was cloned. Moreover, the process of cloning itself necessarily involves harm to other animals (e.g., the animal that will carry the new pet to term). Finally, the end result simply does not provide pet owners with what they were looking for.

The idea of cloning pets rather than human beings raises some interesting questions for both issues. If there is virtually nothing different between human beings and pets, then the answers to the questions in the issues should be the same. If there is a difference in the answers, then some further explanation should be given in order to show that two different answers are required.

But even if we just consider cloning pets, many questions are raised. For one thing, there are factual (empirical, often scientific) questions about what exactly a clone of a pet is. So, for example, we might wonder about the extent, if any, that it is true to think that having a clone of your beloved pet dog Fido is a way of having Fido live on—or, admitting that he died, but bringing him back to life—or having Fido as a puppy all over again—or an exercise in nostalgia perhaps, harkening back to days when Fido was your faithful companion. But further, if it is true (as I think we can all agree) that cloning Fido does not bring him back to life, suppose that a certain percentage of pet owners think that this is indeed the case and want to have the cloning done. In general, even if we can establish the actual truth with respect to factual and scientific matters, does it make a difference that pet owners might not be aware of the truth—or might be in a state of denial? Then there are further questions associated with the fact that some people have more money and resources than others, and might stand to benefit by the use of this cloning, while others, whose relationship with their pets is no different from that in the first group, are nevertheless unable to take advantage of this technology. Moreover, we might wonder whether the newly cloned pets (for example, Fido II) would be done a disservice since their owners might expect them to be just like the original Fido.

Note that the idea of cloning pets seems to be a special case, different from cloning other sorts of animals. We might think that the idea of cloning cows, for example, doesn't give us much pause, because of all the milk (and possibly meat) that they can provide, the benefits are widespread and clear. Anyway, that's the reason most people raise cows in the first place. The situation is similar in the case of animals (such as rats) cloned for scientific or medical research. If cloning animals in this context can provide researchers with important data or even cures for cancer, heart disease, etc., then again the benefit is widespread and clear. Of course, people who support the idea of animal rights might say that the benefits to us are clear—but the animals suffer. I think we should put this thought aside, at least for the moment, although it may arise again in the course of the argument about cloning pets. The key point for us right now is that these animals (both the agricultural kind and the laboratory kind) can contribute to human welfare as a whole, whereas the cloning of pets seems to benefit pet owners exclusively. So, whereas we can point to a general benefit (even if it is a benefit *for us*) that we derive from agricultural and laboratory animals, the point here is that these benefits are based on the animals' inpact on human beings in general, while cloning pets seems to benefit only private certain individuals.

Many of these issues arose in the case of the Missyplicity Project, for example. Here, wealthy owners of a dog named Missy spent millions of dollars in an attempt to clone her. Various scientific breakthroughs in the Missyplicity Project allowed the formation of a commercial enterprise, Genetic Savings and Clone, which aimed to clone pets. The following essays discuss these points, both in general, and with specific reference to the Missyplicity Project and the commercial enterprise that grew from it. First, Autumn Fiester argues that pet cloning is indeed ethically justified; Hilary Bok argues that it is wrong.

YES

Autumn Fiester

Creating Fido's Twin: Can Pet Cloning Be Ethically Justified?

Commercial pet cloning—currently cats only—is now available from the firm Genetic Savings and Clone for the small price of $30,000. In December 2004, a nine-week-old cat clone was delivered to its owner, the first of six customers waiting for the identical twin of a beloved pet.[1] "Little Nicky," as he's known, has stirred up a great deal of ethical controversy, with more to come as the firm expands to dog cloning. . . .

For many, the cloning of companion animals seems morally suspect in a way that the cloning of animals for agricultural purposes or for biomedical research does not. In judging the ethics of cloning animals that will be healthier to eat or will advance science or medicine, there is a natural argument to be made that the technique will serve the greater human good. But in the case of pet cloning, there is really no analogous argument, however wonderful the original "Missy," the mixed-breed dog whose owner funded the now-famous Missyplicity Project at Texas A&M to make pet cloning possible. Cloned companion animals will not significantly enhance general human well-being. In balancing the cost to animals against the possible benefit to humans, the ethics of pet cloning seems to be a simple equation: a concern for animal welfare equals an anti-cloning stance.

But what if there were benefits to animals, and what if these benefits outweighed the pain and suffering they endure from cloning research and procedures? Then there would be an argument in favor of pet cloning at least as strong as those offered for cloning conducted for agriculture or medical research. The idea of animals suffering for *animal* benefit makes a tidy moral case that just might justify the practice.

Of course, making this case will be a challenge given the serious anti-cloning objections raised by animal advocacy organizations and cloning critics. But the benefit to animals that I will consider is this: the practice of pet cloning—like advanced veterinary care such as transplants, neurosurgery, orthopedics, and psychopharmaceuticals—might improve the public's perception of the moral status of companion animals because it puts animals in the category of being worthy of a very high level of expense and concern. Something that warrants this level of commitment and investment seems valuable intrinsically,

Fiester: © The Hastings Center. Reprinted by permission. This article originally appeared in the Hastings Center Report, vol. 35, no. 4 (2005).

not merely instrumentally, and this change in the public's perception could have far-reaching benefits for all animals.

Of course, even if this controversial claim is true—that pet cloning might contribute to an increase in the public's esteem for companion animals—it can justify pet cloning only for those who already find some forms of animal cloning morally acceptable. My case rests on the premise that some types of cloning are morally justified by the benefits that will result from them. People opposed in principle to all forms of animal cloning—for example, because this type of biotechnology is "playing God" or because animals should never be used in research—will not accept this consequentialist starting point. The most straightforward way to make the point is this: we can talk about justifying pet cloning only on the assumption that animal cloning for clearly important ends—like medical or pharmaceutical advances—is morally permissible. If one rejects those types of cloning, the argument about pet cloning cannot get off the ground.

The Anti-Cloning Case

Critics of pet cloning typically offer three objections: (1) the cloning process causes animals to suffer; (2) widely available pet cloning could have bad consequences for the overwhelming numbers of unwanted companion animals; and, (3) companies that offer pet cloning are deceiving and exploiting grieving pet owners.

Animal Suffering   Animal welfare advocates have been quick to point out the cost of animal cloning to the animals involved in the procedures. [2] A large body of literature documents high rates of miscarriage, stillbirth, early death, genetic abnormalities, and chronic diseases among the first cloned animals. These problems occur against a backdrop of what in cloning science is called "efficiency," the percentage of live offspring from the number of transferred embryos. The efficiency of animal cloning has typically been about 1 to 2 percent, meaning that of every one hundred embryos implanted in surrogate animals, ninety-eight or ninety-nine fail to produce live offspring.[3] Given the invasive techniques used to implant the embryos in the surrogate, these numbers represent a certain amount of suffering on the part of the donor animals: for every one or two live animals, one hundred eggs must be harvested and one hundred embryos implanted. In the experiments conducted to clone "CC" the calico cat, one hundred and eighty-eight eggs were harvested, eighty-seven cloned embryos were transferred into eight female cats, two of the females became pregnant, and one live kitten was born.[4]

Further, of the live clones born, many have experienced compromised health status or early death. In one study of cloned pigs, researchers reported a 50% mortality rate for the live offspring, with five out of ten dying between three and one hundred and thirty days of age from ailments including chronic diarrhea, congestive heart failure, and decreased growth rate.[5] A study published last year showed that cloned mice experience early death due to liver failure and lung problems.[6] Another study showed that cloned mice had a high tendency to morbid obesity.[7]

Cloning scientists respond that both efficiency rates and health outcomes are radically improving, and that we can reasonably expect in the very near future to see fewer animals involved in the cloning process and better health status for the clones that are born.[8] Although the process that produced "CC" was inefficient, there were no kittens born with compromised health status. Research on cloned cattle published last year showed that once the animals survived infancy, they had no health problems when compared with non-clones.[9] Genetics Savings and Clone claims that it has pioneered a new cloning technique that not only improves the health status of clones but greatly increases cloning efficiency, achieving pregnancy loss rates on par with those of breeders.[10] Although information is limited, the company claims that six healthy kittens have been born with no deformities. If this proves to be true, then the animal suffering caused by the process is limited to that of the surrogate mothers. There aren't even any donor animals involved, since the company uses eggs harvested from ovaries purchased from spay clinics. And the suffering of the surrogates is surely not greater than that of cats who "donate" kidneys for feline kidney transplants, a practice that has not received widespread criticism on grounds of inordinate feline suffering.[11]

Unwanted Pets   A second objection to pet cloning is that there are millions of unwanted pets in the United States. How can we justify the creation of designer companion animals when so many wonderful animals languish in shelters? This is the main argument behind the Humane Society's anticloning position. Says Senior Vice President Wayne Pacelle, "The Humane Society of the United States opposes pet cloning because it is dangerous for the animals involved, it serves no compelling social purpose, and it threatens to add to the pet overpopulation problem. It doesn't sit well with us to create animals through such extreme and experimental means when there are so many animals desperate for homes."[12] To be sure, the data on the number of companion animals euthanized in American shelters are sobering. The 2001 Human Society report on the state of animals in the United States found that four to six million dogs and cats were euthanized in shelters in 2001.[13] These figures do not include the millions of stray animals in the country: the ASPCA estimates that 70 million stray dogs and cats live in the United States.[14]

But what is the connection between the sorry state of unwanted companion animals in this country and the anti-pet-cloning stance? Surely one cannot hold that no new animals ought to be intentionally created until all shelter animals are adopted. Anticloners would then have bigger fish to fry than pet cloning—namely, the breeders and puppy farms that produce millions of dogs and cats each year. By comparison, pet cloning, even if it becomes a viable industry, will produce only trivial numbers of animals.

Critics of pet cloning say that pet owners who are so devoted to their animal companions that they would spend thousands of dollars to clone one are precisely the type of adoptive parents who could save an already-existing animal's life through pet adoption, sparing one more dog or cat from euthanasia.[15] But why should a person devoted to a particular animal be more obligated than anyone else to save others of that same species? Being a parent doesn't obligate me more than childless folks to help parentless children. Critics will say this comparison is outrageous. We can't compare animals and children. But for the pet owner willing to clone a deceased pet, there *is* one analogy between a child and a companion animal: you can't substitute or exchange one for another. Pet owners grieving a lost animal see their animal as unique and irreplaceable, so they can't just go to a shelter and get any old animal as a replacement pet. Naturally, this invites the third criticism, which we will discuss below, that this clone *isn't* actually the original pet. But the point is that what these pet owners are after cannot be found in a shelter or purchased from a breeder.

What about the money involved? Isn't there something wrong with spending $30,000 on an animal? Perhaps so, but the problem certainly isn't limited to pet cloning—think of race horses, for example. And if the charge is really that pet cloning is a frivolous use of money that could be better spent on noble causes, then this is just a universal attack on all luxury goods. It doesn't make pet cloning any morally worse than boat-buying.

Exploitation and Deception   But what about the concern that pet owners are being tricked into believing that they are getting Fido back, when in truth, Fido and the clone could be as different as any identical twins? There are two separate charges here: one is about false advertising or exploitation on the part of the cloning firm; the other is about the pet owner's self-deception.

Take the cloning firm first. Opponents argue that grieving pet owners are deceived by companies like Genetic Savings and Clone into believing that cloning is a way of resurrecting a deceased and beloved pet. They argue that the business of pet cloning assumes genetic determinism—that genes alone determine all physical and behavioral characteristics—which is false. For example, criticizing the practice of companion animal cloning, bioethicist David Magnus argues, "The people who want this are spending huge sums of money to get their pet immortalized or to guarantee they're getting a pet exactly like the one they had before—and it's simply not possible."[16] If pet cloning firms are contributing to this false belief, then they are engaging in a type of fraud and are certainly exploiting the grief of the devoted pet owner. Genetic Savings and Clone argues that they have an informed consent process that educates clients about the environmental and in utero factors that influence personality and behavior—maybe even physical characteristics. But whatever policies need to be put in place to make sure the owner has realistic expectations, how cloning firms market pet cloning and educate potential customers does not bear on the moral legitimacy of pet cloning itself. There is a clear need to regulate this emerging industry to ensure truth in advertising, but that could be achieved without eliminating the product.

As for the self-deception of the pet owner, this is a psychological, not an ethical concern. Again, Magnus:

> I can completely sympathize with people who become so attached to their pet that they want to bring it back at any cost, but there is nothing that can bring that animal back. Attempting to do so is unhealthy. It's trying to

pretend that death doesn't exist, which speaks to a larger symptom in our culture of not dealing with death. It's better to just move on.[17]

There are two responses here. First, if the customers don't feel betrayed or deceived (and indeed, they do not) and are satisfied with their investment and comforted by the clone's existence, then it is hard to get this psychological concern going. Second, this argument assumes that there is no good reason to clone a pet unless one *were* deceived[18]—and this is false. The bereft pet owner might know full well that the clone will be nothing more than a genetic twin, and the decision to clone might be merely an attempt to preserve something important from the original animal, rather than *resurrect* it. In the human context, we think of offspring this way. We say things like, "I am so glad my son had children before he died." For animals that were neutered at an early age, who have no offspring, it is perfectly rational to desire the genetic "starting blocks" Fido had, even under complete comprehension that this animal will not be Fido. Wanting to get as close as possible to the original animal is not irrational. In the absence of immortality, genetic identity is the next best thing.

Pet Cloning and "Rising Status"

Now consider an argument in favor of pet cloning: pet cloning may change common views of what in philosophy is called the "moral status" of animals. The fact that companion animals are deemed worthy recipients of this level of effort and expense might encourage people to view animals as having intrinsic value and uniqueness.

The public's perception of the value of animals is not fixed. In fact, the public's estimation of animals' status is arguably rising fast. Getting at perceptions of animal status is difficult, but consider some of the following facts: a 2001 ABC News poll found that 41 percent of Americans believe that animals go to heaven,[19] and a May 2003 Gallup poll found that a full 33 percent of Americans are at least somewhat supportive of an all-out ban on medical research involving laboratory animals.[20] Attitudes among pet owners are even more interesting. For example, a 1999 survey by the American Animal Hospital Association found that 84 percent of pet owners refer to themselves as their pet's "mommy" or "daddy," 63 percent celebrate the pet's birthday, and 72 percent of married respondents greet their pet first when they return home.[21] There are also more pet owners now than ever before; 62 percent of households in the United States own pets in 2005,[22] up from 50 percent in 1975.[23]

The dramatic shift in the status of American pets can also be seen in the resources devoted to them. Americans spent over $30 billion on small animal companions in 2003,[24] a 10 percent increase over 2002 spending,[25] and two and a half times the spending levels of 1978 (in adjusted dollars, Americans spent $11 billion in 1978 vs. $30 billion today).[26] A large part of this figure represents a surge in veterinary service spending: Americans are spending more not only on routine care for companion animals, but on specialty care as well, reflecting a change in priorities and values. For example, pain management expenditures have increased 275 percent in the last six years.[27] Pet owners are now investing in pain control medicines for animals that would have been euthanized a decade ago.

These figures represent what has been called the "pet as family" trend.[28] While it is difficult to empirically document that these figures correspond to an increase in status of companion animals, experts in the field believe they do. Robert Gilbert, associate dean for clinical programs at Cornell Hospital for Animals, describes pet owners' attitudes toward pets as somewhat like parents' attitudes toward children; when he started practicing veterinary medicine in 1977, "a pet was a pet."[29] Thomas Cusick, president of the American Animal Hospital Association, declares, "Pets are clearly becoming an integral part of the American family, enjoying much of the same attention, care, and treatment that is given to a child or spouse."[30]

There is also anecdotal evidence that those who don't own pets are beginning to acknowledge and adopt the changing attitudes of their pet-owning friends and relatives. It is no longer appropriate, for example, to say to a grieving pet owner, "What's the fuss about? Just get another pet." News of an ill pet now engenders concern and sympathy.

The argument I want to advance is that the treatment of companion animals by their caretakers alters what the public in general thinks about them. Attitudes toward companion animals are heavily influenced by the dominant view and mainstream practice (indeed it is the majority of Americans who currently have pets).

More specifically, I want to offer a hypothesis about one mechanism by which this kind of cultural change takes place, namely, that the routinization of certain practices and expenses on the part of pet owners normalizes that behavior, which affects the general view of what care animals deserve; and this in turn enhances the public's estimation of the value of companion animals because it encourages the public to view animals as entities worthy enough to merit this attention and care. One of the most significant influences on the public's perceptions is the effort expended to improve the health and extend the lives of companion animals. Pet cloning is just the extreme form of pet owners' attempts to extend the life (in this case, in the form of the genome) of a beloved animal.

Advanced veterinary care is the paradigm case. Veterinary services are the fastest-growing segment of the companion animal industry, increasing at an annual rate of 4.7 percent, with current expenditures pegged at close to $8 billion.[31] As noted earlier, much of the spending increase is directed at services unheard of a few decades ago. Veterinary medicine has specialized into surgery, dermatology, ophthalmology, orthopedics, neurology, oncology, and even transplant surgery. At a price estimated to be between $5,000 and $15,000 (plus $50–$150 per month in immunosuppressant drugs for life), one's dog or cat can receive a renal transplant at one of the country's new transplant centers.[32] Kidney transplants are still rare, but many other specialty services are not, including x-rays, psychopharmaceuticals, and insulin therapy.

As each new procedure or service is incorporated into veterinary care, pet owners' acceptance of the new standard of care alters the overall public's attitude toward those procedures. No longer seen as a bizarre or exorbitant waste of money and resources, the new procedure starts to seem entirely war-ranted. Think of the public's attitude toward now commonplace treatments, such as daily shots of insulin, arthritis medicines, corrective surgery for orthopedic problems, or antianxiety medicines. These expenses easily exceed the original price of the animal, but few people would now tell a pet owner to cut her losses and buy a new pet. What is happening to the public's attitude toward companion animals if these advance treatments seem like reasonable measures and expenses to protect animal lives and well-being? At a minimum, the normalization of advanced veterinary care indicates the public's recogni-tion of the "irreplaceability" for the pet owner of one animal with some other. We no longer think of companion animals as disposable or interchangeable, despite the ready supply of homeless animals.

Of course, this argument may suffer from the classic "chicken or the egg" question: is the attention given to animals raising public perceptions of animals' status, or is the perception of animals' status rising independently of the actions of pet owners? In fact, it can go both ways. To the pet owner, the intrinsic value of the companion animal is already recognized, which is why she expends the resources and energy to treat the animal. To someone observ-ing that practice, the effect is to affirm or alter the perception of value that companion animals have—or ought to have. So while only a handful of people may value their pets enough to go through the expense of an organ transplant, the effect of employing "pet organ transplants" is much more widespread. As this type of practice becomes reasonable, it becomes a statement about the intrinsic value and worth of its recipients.

It is plausible that pet cloning will have a parallel effect. Pet cloning makes the statement that one's companion animal is so important that it is worth trying to come as close as possible to preserving it by investing in a genetic twin. The hypothesis is that when pet cloning is seen as a rational, jus-tifiable activity for pet owners as a response to the (impending) death of an animal, the societal effect—as with advanced veterinary care—will be to enhance the companion animal's position on the moral map through the public's recognition that these entities have high value.

One possible rejoinder is that the dignity and uniqueness of the original pet is degraded by an attempt to obtain a clone. Believing that we can replace a companion animal with its clone demonstrates that animals are, in fact, mere objects, not at all like children, and the effect of widespread use of pet cloning will be to downgrade animals' status, not raise it. But whether pet cloning will have this effect will depend on how society interprets it. A pet-cloning-as-mass-production view will undoubtedly reinforce the idea that companion animals are replaceable consumer goods, and this will have a deleterious effect on perceptions of their status. In the cloning-as-solace view as I have described above, however, companion animal cloning will be seen as a tribute to the value of the original animal. There are parents who desperately want to clone their lost children.[33] Pet owners, mirroring their feelings, are making a statement about both the animal's immeasurable value and the level of loss and grief they feel at its death. Whatever one thinks of human cloning, no one argues that the parents who request it don't assign the highest possible worth to the deceased child; the sentiment to clone is a testimony to the parents' belief in the infinite value of that unique person. If this becomes widely understood, the cloning-as-solace interpretation may indeed win out.

If pet cloning bolsters even slightly a perception that companion animals have intrinsic value, then the positive consequences for companion animals will far outweigh the minimal suffering the animals undergo through the cloning process. The rising status of companion animals has already begun to translate into laws that offer more protection for them, including changes in the designation of pet owners to "animal guardians" in some areas.[34] If companion animals' status continues to rise, and if pet cloning contributes at all to that trend, then there is an argument for the moral legitimacy of pet cloning.

References

1. P. Fimrite, "Cat Has 10 Lives, Thanks to $50,000 Cloning," *San Francisco Chronicle,* December 23, 2004.

2. See H. Bok, "Cloning Animals Is Wrong," *Journal of Applied Animal Welfare Science* 5, no. 3 (2002), 233–38.

3. A. Coleman, "Somatic Cell Nuclear Transfer in Mammals: Progress and Application," *Cloning* 1 (1999), 185–200. See also L. Paterson, "Somatic Cell Nuclear Transfer (Cloning) Efficiency,". . . .

4. T. Shin et al., "Cell Biology: A Cat Cloned by Nuclear Transplantation," *Nature* 415 (2002): 859.

5. A.B. Carter, "Phenotyping of Transgenic Cloned Pigs," *Cloning and Stem Cells* 4 (2002): 131–45.

6. N. Ogonuki et al., "Early Death of Mice Cloned from Somatic Cells," *Nature Genetics* 30 (2002): 253–54.

7. K. Tamashiro, "Cloned Mice Have an Obese Phenotype Not Transmitted to Their Offspring," *Nature Genetics* 8 (2002): 262–67.

8. *Nature Biotechnology* recently published a metareview of the health status of clones from prior studies, and it reports that 77 percent of cloned animals showed no developmental abnormalities throughout the period of follow-up, although the percentage of healthy clones ranged from 20 percent to 100 percent across the studies. J.B. Cibelli et al. "The Health Profile of Cloned Animals," *Nature Biotechnology* 20 (2002), 13–14.

9. C. Yang, X.C. Tian, and X. Yang, "Serial Bull Cloning by Somatic Cell Nuclear Transfer," *Nature Biotechnology* 22 (2004), 693–94.

10. M. Fox, "Company Says It Cloned Copy Cats," Reuters, August 5, 2004; Fimrite, "Cat Has 10 Lives."

11. Of course, the obvious objection to this comparison is that the kidneys are harvested to save the life of another cat, whereas the animals who suffer through egg harvesting and embryo implantation are not saving an existing cat but creating an entirely new (unneeded) one. But what is in question here is the amount of suffering—not the justification for it.

12. Humane Society of the United States, "Cat Cloning Is Wrong-Headed," February 14, 2002. . . .

13. P.G. Irwin, "Overview: The State of Animals in 2001," in *The State of Animals 2001,* ed. D.J. Salem and A.N. Rowan, (Washington, D.C.: Humane Society Press, 2001).

14. American Society for the Prevention of Cruelty to Animals, "Annual Shelter Statistics". . . .

15. The pet owners most likely to request a clone of a deceased pet are those who originally adopted pets from shelters, because these animals are often mixed-breed animals whose personality traits or other features cannot be generated by conventional breeding. It was the owner of a mixed-breed dog, "Missy," that funded the now-famous Missyplicity Project at Texas A&M, which resulted in the cloning of "CC" the cat. But the owner of Missy chose to invest $3.7 million in trying to create Missy's twin; he did not invest the $3.7 million in improving the lives of shelter animals, the original source of Missy herself. . . .

16. M. Shiels, "Carbon Kitty's $50,000 Price Tag," *BBC News,* April 27, 2004.

17. Fimrite, "Cat Has 10 Lives."

18. Magnus reaches this conclusion: "There is no good reason why anybody would do this." Fimrite, "Cat Has 10 Lives."

19. The Roper Center For Public Opinion Research, "Do You Think Animals Go to Heaven When They Die or Only People Go to Heaven?" ABC News/BeliefNet Poll (June 2001). . . .

20. The Roper Center For Public Opinion Research, "Banning All Medical Research on Laboratory Animals," Gallup Poll (May, 2003). . . .

21. American Animal Hospital Association, Pet Owner Survey, 1999. . . .

22. American Pet Products Manufacturers Association, "APPMA Survey Finds Pet Ownership Continues Growth Trend in U.S.". . . .

23. C.W. Schwabe et al., *Veterinary Medicine and Human Health,* third ed. (Baltimore, Md.: Williams & Wilkins Co, 1976).

24. DVM News Magazine, "Pet Spending to Top $37 Billion by '08". . . .

25. S. Aschoff, "Pet RX," *Floridian,* June 10, 2003.

26. Schwabe et al., *Veterinary Medicine and Human Health.*

27. Aschoff, "Pet RX."

28. J.E. Brody. "V.I.P. Medical Treatment Adds Meaning to Dog's (or Cat's) Life." *New York Times,* August 14, 2001: Section F; Page 4; Column 2.

29. J.E. Brody. "V.I.P. Medical Treatment Adds Meaning to Dog's (or Cat's) Life," *New York Times,* August 14, 2001.

30. American Veterinary Medical Association, "Survey Says: Owners Taking Good Care of Their Pets," *Journal of the American Veterinary Medical Association.* . . .

31. *DVM News Magazine,* "Pet Spending to Top $37 Billion by '08". . . .

32. L. Copeland. "Transplant Offers Hope for a Tabby; With Kidney Comes 2nd Chance at 9 Lives," *Washington Post,* March 14, 1999. Also B. Bilger, "The Last Meow," *New Yorker,* September 8, 2003, at 46. Donor cats are taken from local shelters and research labs, and the owners of the transplantee must agree to adopt the donor (p. 49).

33. Offering a pro-pet cloning argument in no way commits me to a pro-human cloning argument, although I can understand the powerful sentiments that would drive a parent to desire the ability to clone a beloved child. The difference is that we can accept a sacrifice in animal lives (we euthanize them, we experiment on them, and we eat them) that we cannot accept in human lives. But if human cloning could be guaranteed never to result in a birth defect, stillbirth, or compromised health status of a child, the debate about human cloning would be quite different.

34. *CBS Evening News,* "Legal Relationship Between Pets and Their Owners," CBS News Transcripts, Aug. 7, 2000; B. Pool, "In West Hollywood, Pets are Part of the Family," *Los Angeles Times,* February 22, 2001; "Pet Owners in San Francisco become 'Pet Guardians,'" *The San Diego Union Tribune,* March 1, 2001; and "Students Make History by Helping to Draft & Pass Animal Rights Legislation," *News from General Assembly,* September 26, 2001. . . .

Hilary Bok  **NO**

Cloning Companion
Animals Is Wrong

In principle, I have nothing against cloning either nonhuman animals or humans. If cloning were as safe as natural procreation and if those who chose to clone themselves or others completely understood cloning (in particular, how clones are related to their originals), I would not worry about cloning being tantamount to, in Hawthorne's words, "playing God" or "cheating death" (Hawthorne, 2002 . . .). I would view it simply as a complicated and expensive way of producing an identical twin born at a different time and from a different mother than the original. In fact, however, neither of these things is true. Cloning is not safe, and it is not widely understood. Nonetheless, I suppose that some extremely compelling reason might justify our cloning animals. However, there is no such justification for the Missyplicity Project.

Suffering and Complications

Cloning causes animals to suffer. Egg donors must have their ovaries artificially stimulated with hormone treatments and their eggs surgically harvested. Given the unusually high rates of late-term miscarriages and high birth weights among clones, the surrogate mothers are at greater risk of dying or suffering serious complications than animals who become pregnant naturally. The clones, themselves, however, suffer the most serious problems: They are much more likely than other animals to be miscarried, have birth defects, develop serious illnesses, and die prematurely.

Hawthorne (2002 . . .) acknowledges that this is "the ethical issue of greatest concern" (p. 229) raised by animal cloning. However, he greatly understates its seriousness. He claims, for instance, that 20% of cattle clones detectable in utero experience some sort of physical problem resulting in miscarriages, early deaths, or later health problems. In fact, to go by the published reports of cloning surveyed by the National Academy of Sciences (2002) in its recent report on cloning, the numbers are much higher: Of at least 242 pregnancies from cloned adult cattle cells, at least 174 were miscarried. Of the 68 calves born alive, only 42 were still alive at the time of publication, and investigators reported that 5 of those had significant health problems other

From *Journal of Applied Animal Welfare Science*, vol. 5, no. 3, 2002, pp. 233–238. Copyright © 2002 by Lawrence Erlbaum Associates. Reprinted by permission.

than high birth weight. This means that the number of cattle clones detectable in utero who go on to experience serious health problems is not 20% but at least 85%.

In a recent study, Ogonuki et al. (2002) compared the lifespan of 12 cloned mice, 7 genetically matched, naturally conceived mice, and 6 mice produced by a process of spermatid injection performed under the same laboratory conditions as the cloning but resulting in natural conception. Eight hundred days after their birth, 10 of 12 cloned mice had died, compared with 1 of the 7 mice conceived naturally and 2 of the 6 produced by spermatid injection. Autopsies performed on 6 of the cloned mice revealed that all had severe pneumonia, 4 had necrotic livers, and 2 had tumors. In addition, the cloned mice had reduced immune system function, which the researchers believed might account for their pneumonia. Here again, the number of clones with serious health problems is much higher than Hawthorne (2002 . . .) suggests: In Ogonuki et al.'s study, two thirds of the animals who were born alive died prematurely as a result of physical problems associated with their being clones.

Real Problems, Unknown Solutions

Hawthorne (2002 . . .) suggests that these problems may be species specific and that researchers do not know whether dogs and cats will exhibit them. This is disingenuous. It is true that researchers do not yet know what problems cloned dogs and cats might have. No one has yet cloned a dog, and it is too early to tell whether the one cloned cat in existence will develop the kinds of health problems seen in other species. We do know, however, that these problems have turned up in every other species cloned, including goats. Therefore, there is every reason to expect that they will turn up in cats and dogs as well.

Hawthorne also suggests that some test yet to be developed might detect abnormalities prior to implantation. It seems extremely unlikely that in the foreseeable future someone will develop a reliable preimplantation test for problems with gene expression comprehensive enough to ensure that the clones we produce will be healthy. The number of genes whose expression would have to be tested is enormous, and researchers do not now understand the effects of various possible differences in their expression on an animal's subsequent development. In addition, many of these genes are not active before implantation; therefore, it is unclear how one could test their expression at that stage. For these reasons, it is unlikely that such a test will be developed in the near future.

In the meantime, cloned animals will continue to suffer serious health problems at much higher rates than other animals of the same species. Some will be suffocated when their lungs do not inflate, some will be poisoned because of liver or kidney failure, and some will be eaten away by cancer. Some will die from heart failure, and some will have only such "minor" problems as gross obesity or premature arthritis. Almost all clones will suffer and die, and they will do so, not because of some natural illness or misfortune but because researchers have chosen to bring them into existence using a process that is not understood well enough to use safely.

Of course, the only way researchers can learn enough about cloning cats and dogs to do it safely is by trying and learning from their mistakes. This, however, does not justify conducting this process of trial and error on the bodies of dogs and cats, absent some reason to think that learning how to clone dogs and cats is worth the cost in animal suffering. One must ask whether enabling humans to clone their pets is important enough to justify the considerable suffering involved in learning how to do so.

Why Clone Pets?

As the caregiver for two cats, I can easily understand why persons who do not understand what cloning involves might be tempted to clone their pets. Pet owners love their pets. When an animal one loves dies, the most natural thing in the world is to want that animal back. Just as a parent whose child has died is unlikely to be comforted by the thought that there are plenty of other children waiting for adoption, most grieving pet owners are not consoled by the thought that they can always adopt another dog or cat. This is not because pet owners are unduly sentimental or confused about the differences between pets and children. It is because, like parents, they love individuals, and adopting another dog or cat will not replace the individual they have loved and lost.

Cloning is not a way of bringing back the animal one loves. That is the point of loving an individual: Not even an exact replica can be the particular being one loves. Still, to a grieving pet owner an exact replica might seem to be the next best thing, and some pet owners might think that cloning could produce one. This misconception is easy to remove: One need only point out that clones will not have the same memories as their originals and that because their upbringing and environment will differ, their behavior and temperament will differ as well.

However, even after this mistake is corrected, one might still think that cloned animals will be identical to their originals in all respects except those that depend on environment and upbringing. One might, that is, think that although a clone of one's dog will not be a copy of that dog as an adult, the clone, when born, will be identical to the newborn puppy who grew up to be that dog. This is, I think, what many of those who are interested in cloning their pets believe. Unfortunately, they are wrong. Cloning produces animals who are genetically identical to their originals. However, genetic identity is not, and does not ensure, physical identity; the difference between the two is extremely significant.

The genes in an adult animal's somatic cells are programmed not for directing embryonic development but for directing the activities of skin cells, liver cells, and so forth. If researchers tried to clone a cat by inducing one skin cell to divide without reprogramming its DNA, they would end up not with a kitten but with, at best, a kitten-sized mass of skin cells. That mass would be genetically identical to the original cat but, presumably, would not be what the owners had in mind when they asked to clone the cat. To produce not a mass of skin cells but a kitten, the skin cell's DNA needs to be reprogrammed.

To produce a kitten largely, although not entirely, similar to the kitten the cat once was, researchers would have to reprogram the cat's DNA to exactly the state it was in when that cat was a fertilized egg.

In practice, it is extraordinarily unlikely that any animal's DNA can be reprogrammed perfectly. Tens of thousands of genes might need reprogramming, and researchers do not know what they all are, let alone what would count as their correct expression. Nor is it known in most cases, what contribution they make to an animal's subsequent development. Moreover, although the word *reprogramming* might suggest the existence of easily manipulable switches that could be reset one by one, in practice reprogramming is a messy and haphazard process that is neither understood nor controllable.

For these reasons, the likelihood that every gene will be reset correctly is minute. Some problems with reprogramming might be benign. Others might be so serious that any fetus who has them will be miscarried. There is, however, a middle group: problems serious enough to create significant physical differences between clones and their originals but not serious enough to prevent those clones from being born at all. Given the number of such mistakes that it is possible to make and the impossibility in practice of screening for any appreciable number of them, clones probably will differ in unpredictable and potentially significant respects from their originals.

Consider in this light that 85% of cattle clones detected in utero are miscarried, die prematurely, or suffer serious health problems. As far as is known, these cattle were cloned from healthy adults whose lungs, livers, and kidneys did not malfunction; who were born without serious cardiac problems or joint irregularities: and who did not have juvenile diabetes or severe anemia. All these problems appeared among their clones. This indicates three things. First, that clones are genetically identical to their originals does not mean that they will be physically identical to them. Second, the differences between clones and their originals will involve not only relatively unimportant things like coat coloring but also crucial ones like whether their hearts work. Third, these differences are not rare or anomalous: They are the norm.

Cloning, then, is not a way for a pet owner to acquire, say, a puppy just like the puppy who grew up to be his or her dog. It is a way of acquiring a dog who is genetically identical to that dog, but who is much more likely to have major physical defects that cause real suffering and require serious medical care. Moreover, even if that dog is lucky enough not to have serious health problems, he or she is likely to differ from his or her original in subtler ways. In particular, there is no reason to think that the genes that underlie a dog's temperament are less likely than other genes to be reprogrammed incorrectly and, therefore, no reason to think that cloned dogs will necessarily share their originals' temperament and disposition. If pet owners want to get dogs similar to ones who have died, they are much more likely to succeed by adopting puppies of the same breed with similar dispositions than by cloning their pets.

The one goal pet owners might accomplish by cloning their pets is to make it possible for the genes of spayed, neutered, or otherwise infertile pets to be passed on to another generation. Although many clones have serious physical defects because these defects result mostly from problems with gene expression rather than with the genes themselves, clones are unlikely to pass these defects on to their offspring (Tamashiro et al., 2002). Cloning might make sense, then, as a very complicated way of reversing a spaying or neutering operation one had come to regret.

Although a pet owner might achieve this goal through cloning, it is clearly immoral. To clone a dog for this reason is to subject other dogs to hormonal treatments to stimulate their ovaries; surgically harvest their eggs; create hundreds of fetuses; implant them in dogs who will risk unusually dangerous pregnancies; and finally, bring into existence a clone who probably will suffer serious health problems, just to make it possible for this dog to have puppies genetically related to one's original pet. This would display great callousness toward the suffering of animals and a willingness to sacrifice their interests to one's whims.

If the arguments above are sound, then people who want to clone their pets must be either mistaken about what cloning is or immoral. In the first case, it would be wrong of the Missyplicity Project to take advantage of their misconceptions, especially at the expense of other animals. In the second, it would be wrong for the Missyplicity Project to collude in their wrongdoing. In no case is it morally justifiable either to clone one's pet or to enable others to clone theirs.

References

Hawthorne, L. (2002). A project to clone companion animals. *Journal of Applied Animal Welfare Science, 5,* 227–229.

National Academy of Sciences: Committee on Science, Engineering, and Public Policy, (2002). *Scientific and medical aspects of human reproductive cloning* (Appendix B). Washington, DC: National Academy Press.

Ogonuki, N., Inove, K., Yamamoto, Y., Noguchi, Y., Tanemura, K., Suzuki, O., et al. (2002, February 11). Early death of mice cloned from somatic cells. *Nature Genetics* [Advance on-line publication]. . . .

Tamashiro, K. L. K., Wakayama, T., Akutsu, H., Yamazaki, Y., Lachey, J. L., Wortman, M. D., et al. (2002). Cloned mice have an obese phenotype not transmitted to their offspring. *Nature Medicine, 8,* 262–267.

POSTSCRIPT

Is Cloning Pets Ethically Justified?

The Missyplicity Project (and the related commercial enterprise called Genetic Savings and Clone) can be a fascinating case study in animal cloning. See the online sources at http://www.the-scientist.com, http://en.wikipedia.org, http://www.mindfully.org, and http://www.pamperedpuppy.com.

As for the idea of cloning pets in general, it is remarkable that some people have immediate reactions that are highly positive, while others have immediate reactions that are highly negative. This suggests that emotions play a great role in the way we think about this. To some extent, we can transcend emotional reactions and try to gain a rational view of the matter. Yet, this raises some additional questions because we wonder whether, if emotion is totally removed, this issue can still be appreciated for what it is. Indeed, pet owners can feel such strong emotional bonds with their pets. Nevertheless, even if emotions are allowed a place here, it is undeniable that it is also worthwhile to attend to scientific and factual matters about cloning. Some relevant sources here are http://www.ornl.gov and http://en.wikipedia.org.

A couple of factors still remain though. First, even though cloning is sometimes discussed in the abstract—as if all the kinks with the procedure had been worked out—there are several severe problems with cloning: It is highly inefficient, often requiring hundreds of implantations in order to generate even one live birth, and even if the clone is successfully born, clones are often subject to serious disease and a shorter-than-normal lifespan. The trouble with discussion that ignores these problems and proceeds as if everything were fine is that these problems may never be solved. There is often a great optimism surrounding discussions of cloning yet problems remain.

Another source of unease is that there is a gap between the two kinds of people who are (or would be) most closely involved with pet cloning: the scientists and the pet owners. Scientists may have accurate ideas about what cloning is, but it is far from clear that pet owners have accurate ideas. For example, pet owners might think that the newly cloned animals will be guaranteed to have the same dispositions and behavioral traits (and perhaps even the same memories) as the original pet. Pet owners may have established emotional bonds here that prevent them from seeing (or acknowledging) the truth. "Idealized" discussion of pet cloning often overlooks this fact, since in the ideal case, everyone knows (and fully acknowledges) the facts.

For further reading, see "Pet cloning misses point," *The Register-Guard*, Eugene, Oregon (February 20, 2002). Pet cloning is also discussed by John Kilner, *Basic Questions in Genetics, Stem Cell Research and Cloning* (Kregel, 2003) and Hwa A. Lim, *Multiplicity Yours* (World Scientific, 2006).

ISSUE 9

Should Congress Allow the Buying and Selling of Human Organs?

YES: Robert J. Cihak and Michael A. Glueck, from "Should Congress Allow the Buying and Selling of Human Organs? Yes," *Insight on the News* (May 7, 2001)

NO: James F. Childress, from "Should Congress Allow the Buying and Selling of Human Organs? No," *Insight on the News* (May 7, 2001)

ISSUE SUMMARY

YES: Robert J. Cihak and Michael A. Glueck—both physicians—argue that a free market in human kidneys would be much more beneficial than the current arrangement. Those in need of a kidney would be able to acquire it, and those in financial need would be able to sell one of their kidneys.

NO: James F. Childress, professor of ethics and professor of medical education, argues that a free market would cause the loss of important altruistic motivations and would turn organs into commodities; moreover, such an untried market might make fewer—not more—organs available.

Some facts are important for the proper appreciation of this issue. First, the supply of organs—particularly kidneys, on which Robert J. Cihak and Michael A. Glueck focus—is vastly lower than the demand. This is so not only in the United States, but on a worldwide basis. In America, people who need a new kidney have to be put on a waiting list. In the meantime, they may be able to use a dialysis machine. Receiving dialysis is a noncurative procedure, which must be performed on a regular basis—often three times a week for several hours. Unless people who need new kidneys receive them, the dialysis machine must become a regular part of their lives—forever. Secondly, when an organ such as a kidney is transplanted into someone selected for transplantation, numerous parties receive compensation for the services they render. Thousands of dollars are paid to physicians and hospitals and the nonprofit organizations that procure the organs. But donors must be *donors*:

they must *give* the organ and must not receive any compensation of any kind, except perhaps a small amount for their time or for their own expenses. (Since 1984 and the passage of the National Organ Transplant Act, it has been a federal offense to buy or sell organs.) Finally, Cihak and Glueck concentrate their discussion on kidneys. Human beings normally have two kidneys but can easily live with one, as long as it is a functioning kidney.

Many people think that there is something wrong, perhaps something distasteful, with buying or selling an organ. By contrast, *donating* an organ is often regarded as an extremely worthy—perhaps heroic—act. But also, to *receive* an organ through transplantation is thought to be extremely beneficial, not distasteful or shameful at all. A donor can give a kidney to a recipient, and both of them will be thought well of. But we tend to look askance at a situation in which money changes hands.

And yet, from one point of view, it seems only fair for the person who gives up a kidney to be compensated for doing so. Everyone else involved in the transplant situation seems to be benefited or compensated. But the donor is supposed to be motivated by pure altruism and not at all by money. This works well when the donor and the recipient are close relations. It is not infrequent for transplantations to occur between family members. (What parent would not give a kidney to a son or daughter who desperately needed one?) But there remains the problem of the general societal lack of organs for transplantation.

In the first of the two selections below, Robert J. Cihak and Michael A. Glueck argue that there should indeed be a market for kidneys. This, they claim, would greatly increase the supply. Then, on the other side of the issue, James F. Childress argues against all forms of buying and selling organs; he emphasizes the values that would be lost if there were to be such a market, and he casts doubt on the idea that a market in human organs really would increase the supply. According to Childress, instead of establishing a market in organs—which would likely put a damper on donations—donations and the altruistic motivation that generally lies behind them should be actively encouraged.

YES

Robert J. Cihak and
Michael A. Glueck

Should Congress Allow the Buying and Selling of Human Organs?

Let the Free Market Multiply the Number of Critically Needed Transplant Organs

"Kidney desperately needed. Will pay market rate." Can we expect this as a routine classified ad of the future? Will entire Websites be dedicated to such transactions? While many of us find the idea of buying and selling human organs a little creepy at best, it is one potential solution to the critical shortage of transplant organs in the United States. And, there are many other possible incentives in addition to cash.

We have one liver, heart and pancreas, yet most of us are born with two kidneys. We only require one kidney to live a normal life. Therefore, in the United States, with a population of 280 million persons, there should be enough extra kidneys to go around.

More than 1,000 Americans die of kidney failure every year while waiting for a kidney transplant. Under the current system, only about 12,000 kidneys will be available [by 2001]. But as of March 10, there were 48,200 people who needed kidney transplants registered on waiting lists, more than twice as many as in 1992. That's almost four times as many people as available kidneys for the year.

The median waiting time before transplant increased significantly from 1990 to 1997—from 427 days to 1,196 days for females, more than an 18-month increase; and from 353 days to 1,033 days for males, a 22-month increase.

Probably because of these increasing delays in receiving a transplanted kidney, the death rate of people on the waiting lists has increased from 63 patients out of 1,000 in 1990 to 79 in 1999. Ironically, better technology has increased the death rate of those waiting for a kidney.

More patients are eligible for transplantation because of improvements in management of medical problems for patients with failing organs and better prevention of organ rejection. Surgical procedures for both donors and recipients have become simpler and safer than when the first operations were performed in the 1960s.

Life expectancy for voluntary donors is not lessened, and health problems don't increase. Only one out of 50 life-insurance companies surveyed charges higher life-insurance premiums if you're a kidney donor.

According to the current United Network for Organ Sharing (UNOS) report, kidneys from living donors have about half the failure rate of kidneys from dead donors. Only a few percent of kidneys from living donors failed to survive the first year after transplant, compared with a 10.6 percent failure rate for kidneys from dead donors. The one-year survival rate for patients who received a kidney from a living donor was 98 percent. After five years, 21.6 percent of kidney transplants from living donors had failed, compared with a 35.3 percent failure rate for kidneys from dead donors. Of the 12,488 kidney-only transplant patients treated in 1999, a total of 4,457 kidneys (36 percent) were from living donors.

Kidney failure can be managed for a limited time with dialysis, a time-consuming procedure often requiring hours of treatment every other day. But dialysis is second-best to kidney transplantation.

As well as being more satisfactory medically, kidney transplantation also is financially more effective. UNOS is the private, nonprofit agency that maintains the nation's organ-transplant waiting lists under contract to the U.S. Department of Health and Human Services (HHS). According to its 1994 report, "the government's cost of dialysis averages $40,000 annually, and its cost for a kidney transplant averages $87,000 during the first year. Costs during each year thereafter total about $12,000." In other words, over time, successful kidney transplants cost less than dialysis.

So what's the problem? Well-intentioned government intervention may have done more harm than good. HHS Secretary Tommy Thompson, who recognizes the problem, recently announced that he will launch new national efforts to encourage organ donation as one of his first initiatives. Unfortunately, not even the most ardent government-inspired voluntarism can meet the need.

The National Organ Transplant Act of 1984 (42 U.S.C. §274e) bans privately acquiring, receiving or transferring kidneys and other organs in the United States under penalty of as much as $50,000 in fines and five years in prison. This virtually ensures a shortage of kidneys, as well as other organs.

The current system requires willing American buyers to travel overseas to acquire a kidney. According to news stories, about 400 people per year purchased a kidney in India in the early 1990s before the Indian government outlawed the practice. We don't know how many Americans might have taken this route, if any. If any Americans did buy kidneys overseas, they freed up a place on the waiting list for another patient who stayed in the United States.

The lawmakers and regulators who created the current system apparently believe that a mandated system both works better and is more ethical than allowing choice for individual patients and potential donors. But just look at the current Medicare system to see a government monopoly at work.

So, what can be done to provide incentives to donors and allow additional choices for both patients and donors?

The answer is a free market in kidneys, with more options for everyone. Writing in the winter 2001 issue of *The Independent Review*, Loyola University economists William Barnett, Michael Saliba and Deborah Walker argue that a free market would improve both the quantity and the quality of kidneys available for transplant.

A. Frank Adams III, A. H. Barnett and David L. Kaserman, writing in *Contemporary Economic Policy* in April 1999, estimate that an adequate supply of living kidneys could be recruited at a price of about $1,000 per kidney. Even if this $1,000 estimate were 1,000 percent too low, many people would consider $10,000 a very reasonable price to obtain freedom from the dialysis machine. Of course, compensation can take many forms, such as services or goods, as well as cash.

Since kidneys, not financial resources, are in short supply, allowing compensation for living donors would give many more people incentives to donate a kidney. No one who needed a kidney transplant would go without one. The poor aren't shut out because the federal government actually functions as the payer of last resort. Current law provides that Medicaid and Medicare programs cover medical expenses not covered by private insurance.

Others point out that it is only the organ donor, out of all the people involved in the transplantation process, who cannot receive compensation for helping save another person's life. Hospitals, doctors, technicians and government officials receive compensation for their participation in the transplantation process.

Some people opposed to compensation for donors claim that the donor individual or family wouldn't have as much "emotional gain." However, compensation would not be forced on donors or their families, so those seeking pure "emotional gain" could still have it. We anticipate that many family members or close friends of transplant recipients would not want any additional compensation. Everyone would thus have more choices available.

Another objection is the paternalistic argument that the poor would be exploited and enticed into risky surgery, and that they need protection against the rich. The current prohibition prevents poor people from taking one avenue for improving their family's condition in life by acquiring needed services or goods or paying debts.

Making more kidneys available would help solve the rationing and allocation problems brought on by the current rationing system. People needing transplants would get them on a much more timely basis. Nettlesome questions, such as whether sicker or healthier patients should receive transplants, would be moot, as every patient would be able to receive a kidney. Medically, better tissue matches would more likely be available. As noted above, kidney transplants from living donors are more successful in people with kidney failure than kidneys from dead donors.

Current federal law allows "reasonable payments associated with the removal, transportation, implantation, processing, preservation, quality control and storage of a human organ, or the expenses of travel, housing and lost wages incurred by the donor of a human organ in connection with the donation of the organ" (42 U.S.C. §274e(c)).

"It is the current system of kidney procurement that is immoral, not the proposed free market for kidneys," according to the Loyola economists cited above.

There also are options for those who do not want to buy or sell a kidney. One way to allow some incentives for such donors would be to allow an in-kind market for organs. Robert M. Sade, a heart surgeon and professor at the Medical University of South Carolina, proposed an in-kind market for organs several years ago. Adults could sign an organ-donor card as a precondition for priority in receiving a transplant should they need one in the future.

Alex Tabarrok, research director of the Independent Institute in Oakland, Calif., has further developed this idea. Children automatically would be eligible to receive transplants. At age 16, they would have the option of signing their own donor card. Organ-donor cards could be available each time we renew our driver's licenses. The current waiting-list protocols for transplants already includes status as a prior organ donor as one of the criteria in the calculation of a patient's priority for a needed organ.

Other forms of compensation could be created in a freer market. Living donors or donors' surviving families might have hospital, health insurance or other expenses paid. People who do not want to trade kidneys on an open free market would not be forced to do so. Currently, people willing to engage in a mutually beneficial exchange of an organ for compensation are prohibited from doing so.

HHS Secretary Tommy Thompson says, "American generosity is unparalleled. Let's use that generosity to increase organ donation and make miracles happen through transplantation." We applaud his focus on this issue but hope he will explore some changes in organ-procurement policy that would give donors more choice and incentives. The result would be fewer families, parents and patients waiting in quiet desperation for a call from the transplant team that never comes.

James F. Childress

NO

Should Congress Allow the Buying and Selling of Human Organs?

A Free Market Would Reduce Donations and Would Commodify the Human Body

The number of patients awaiting an organ transplant exceeded 75,000 in late March [2001]. Yet in 1999, the last year for which there are complete figures, there only were 21,655 transplants with organs from 4,717 living donors and 5,859 from cadavers (many of which provided more than one organ). Organ donation continues to fall further and further behind the demand for organs, and new initiatives have failed to reduce the gap. In this situation, why shouldn't we turn to the free market to increase the supply of transplantable organs, which can save lives and improve the quality of life?

Buying or selling an organ isn't always morally wrong. We don't, and shouldn't, always condemn those who sell or purchase an organ. We can understand why someone might do so. But should we change our laws to permit sales of organs and even enforce contracts to sell organs? Should we turn away from a system of gifts to a market in organs?

Our society has very strong reasons not to allow the transfer of organs from the living or the dead for money. In presenting these reasons, it is useful to separate the acquisition of organs from their distribution. Normally, acquisition and distribution go together. However, if those who need organs had to purchase them directly, then the poor would end up selling organs to the rich—a distribution that would strike many as unfair. Thus, let's assume that the government or a private organization under government regulation will purchase organs and then distribute them in a fair and equitable way. I'll call this an "organ-procurement market."

Such a market could target living donors or cadaveric sources of organs. I use the term "sources" because those who sell their organs are not donors, they are sellers or vendors. Let's begin with cadaveric organs removed after an individual's death.

The main argument for rescinding the federal prohibition on the sale of organs is based on utility—allowing the sale of organs would increase their supply. But would a market actually increase the number of cadaveric organs for transplantation? Despite the claims of market fundamentalists, we simply do not know whether a market would reduce the scarcity of organs, in contrast to many other goods. And we have good reasons to be skeptical.

Indeed, I will argue, we shouldn't legalize a market in organ procurement because it probably would be ineffective, perhaps counterproductive (in reducing donations and possibly even the overall number of organs available for transplantation) and likely change our attitudes and practices by commodifying the human body and its parts. Furthermore, it is unnecessary to take this route, with all its problems, because we can make the system of donation effective without such ethical risks.

It would be unwise to move away from a system of donation unless we have good evidence that a market actually would increase the supply of organs. After all, organ donations provide a substantial (though insufficient) number of organs. Some evidence against a potential market's effectiveness in cadaveric organ procurement comes from the reasons people now give for not signing donor cards. One proponent of the market contends that people now fail to donate "because of inertia, mild doubts about their preferences, a slight distaste for considering the subject or the inconvenience involved in completing or carrying a donor card." If these reasons for nondonation were the only ones, a market in cadaveric organ procurement probably would work. In fact, however, opinion polls indicate that fears of being declared dead prematurely or having one's death hastened in order to provide organs seriously inhibit many from signing donor cards.

The fears and distrust that limit organ donation would render utterly ineffective a system of organ procurement based on sales. A futures market—whereby individuals contract now for delivery of organs upon their deaths—is the most defensible because people sell their own, not others', organs. However, if people at present are reluctant to sign donor cards because they fear they may not receive proper care in the hospital, imagine their fears about accepting money for the delivery of usable organs upon their deaths. Once they have signed the contract, all that remains for its fulfillment is their death. And a regulated market would not eliminate their fears. After all, such fears persist in our regulated system of organ donation.

Critics often contend that allowing sales of organs would turn bodies and parts into commodities. Such commodification could lead us to think about and treat dead bodies in merely instrumental terms, thereby damaging important social values. In addition, many claim, commodification could damage and even reduce altruism. A market in organs would drive out, or very substantially reduce, organ donations, in part because it would redefine acts of donating organs. No longer would donors provide the "gift of life"—they instead would donate the equivalent of the market value of the organs provided.

In short, market defenders have not proposed an effective system to obtain additional cadaveric organs. Not only would a procurement market probably be ineffective, it could be counterproductive and have other social costs. Its financial costs would not be negligible. Furthermore, the system of donation has features, including its connection with altruism, that make it ethically preferable, other things being equal. And we can make our system of express donation more effective.

It works fairly well now. For example, according to some estimates, the acts of cadaveric-organ donation in 1999 represented close to half of the patients who died in circumstances where their organs could be salvaged for transplantation (usually following brain death). It might be possible, and desirable, to expand the categories of potential donors to include many who die according to cardiopulmonary standards. Beyond expanding the criteria of donor eligibility, we need to work to make effective the recently adopted policy of required referral. This policy mandates referral to an organ-procurement organization that can then ask the family about organ donation.

Programs to educate the public about organ donation must attend to attitudes of distrust and mistrust, not merely to the tremendous need for organs. It is difficult to alter those attitudes, but increasing the public's understanding of brain death certainly is one way to proceed.

The public's willingness to donate cadaveric organs generally presupposes trust not only in the society's criteria and procedures for determining death, but in its criteria for fairly and effectively distributing donated organs as well. In addition, the provision of access to basic health care for everyone would create a sense of solidarity that dramatically could increase organ donation, but that vision is a distant one.

I salute the decisions in some states to give the decedent's signed donor card priority over family objections, but it is even more important to educate individuals as members of families. They need to share their decisions with their families and consider their roles as potential donors of a family member's organs. Donor cards may be a useful mechanism to stimulate such conversations, but in and of themselves they are too individualistic, legalistic and formalistic. The process of intrafamilial communication is more important.

Society also provides various incentives for organ donation, such as by recognizing and honoring donors in various ways. Would it be possible to offer some financial incentives without crossing over into a market for organ procurement? Consider the following: As a regular expression of its gratitude for organ donation, society could cover the decedent's funeral expenses up to a certain amount, perhaps $1,000 or more. In this way, the community would recognize with gratitude the decedent's and/or the family's act of donation and also pay respects to the donor or source of the organs by sharing in the disposition of his/her final remains.

Any proposal for such "rewarded gifting" will require careful scrutiny, in part because organ donation is such a highly sensitive area, marked by complex beliefs, symbols, attitudes, sentiments and practices, some of them religious in nature. But a carefully conceived pilot experiment, such as providing death benefits—as Pennsylvania has discussed—may be justifiable. However, it may infringe current laws. In any event, it requires the utmost caution because of its risks. One risk is that it will be perceived as purchasing organs rather than as expressing gratitude and providing incentives for donation.

I have focused on cadaveric organs, but what about a market in organ procurement from living individuals? Such a market probably would be more effective than a futures market in cadaveric organs—more individuals probably would be willing to part with a kidney, especially with reduced risks from kidney removal and with generous compensation. However, the social risk of commodification—of treating living human bodies and their parts as commodities—is very troubling. In addition, the risks of coercion and exploitation, especially of poor people, are substantial. The assertion of a moral right to sell a kidney against the legal prohibition of such a sale is not persuasive; we have good reasons, based on concerns about commodification, coercion and exploitation, to reject such sales as incompatible with our moral vision of the kind of society to which we aspire.

Vigorous efforts along the paths I have indicated should obviate the need to adopt a market in organ procurement, whether from living or cadaveric sources. We have little reason to believe that a futures market will be effective in obtaining cadaveric organs and considerable reason to worry about the risks and social costs of such a market, as well as a market for living organ procurement. We should just say "no" to both markets.

POSTSCRIPT

Should Congress Allow the Buying and Selling of Human Organs?

This is a difficult issue to discuss. One of the difficulties is fairly straight-forward. We need to know the medical facts about kidneys because both of the parties in this debate talk specifically about kidneys. The facts are, we're born with two kidneys, but we need only one to survive. (And the form of survival here is not just marginal or borderline. As Cihak and Glueck report, 98 percent of the life insurance companies they surveyed did not charge a higher premium for people with only one kidney.) If your kidneys don't function properly, and you are unable to receive a transplanted kidney, it may be possible to survive through the use of a kidney dialysis machine—but this requires attachment to a machine for several hours, several times a week. The use of the machine does not *cure* or solve the problem; it merely "puri-fies" your blood, removing some of the unwanted products and chemicals, while saving what's useful. However, the problem is never cured this way, and you must return to the machine in about two days for several hours' more purification—and the process never ends. But if you could have a kidney transplant, and your body didn't reject it, then the kidney could do the blood purifying, and you wouldn't have to use the dialysis machine anymore. Hence, the great need for a functioning kidney.

But at this point, we encounter another problem in dealing with this issue. There is a certain feeling of ghoulishness associated with the buying and selling of human organs. It might be nice, we think, for a good friend or family member to *donate* a kidney—and perhaps it is even somewhat noble— but the buying and selling of human organs threatens to turn them into mere commodities. Childress even suggests that if kidneys can be bought and sold, and have a market value, then there will be less donation. This would occur because what used to be *donations* of kidneys would simply be superseded by the market; under a market system, if the good friend or relative wanted to help the person on the dialysis machine, all that would be required is money or a loan. Childress wants to encourage donation, not a market. But as Cihak and Glueck point out, the supply of donated kidneys falls far short of the demand. And these are the conditions that most favor a market solution.

Recent publications that address this issue are Patrick Waldron, "You Gave Me a New Life: St. Charles Gymnastics Coach Receives Kidney Donation from Her Co-Worker," *Daily Herald* [Arlington Heights, IL] (July 2, 2004); James Stacey Taylor, *Stakes and Kidneys: Why Markets in Human Body Parts Are Morally Imperative* (Ashgate, 2005); Mark J. Cherry, *Kidney for Sale by Owner: Human Organs, Transplantation, and the Market* (Georgetown University Press, 2005).

ISSUE 10

Should Drugs Be Legalized?

YES: David Boaz, from "A Drug-Free America—or a Free America?" *U.C. Davis Law Review* (Spring 1991)

NO: Drug Enforcement Administration, from "Speaking Out Against Drug Legalization," http://www.DEA.gov (May 2003)

ISSUE SUMMARY

YES: Political analyst David Boaz argues that in a free country, people have the right to ingest whatever substances they choose without governmental interference. Moreover, as our national experience with Prohibition shows, attempts at restricting substances create more problems than they solve.

NO: The Drug Enforcement Administration presents the case that drugs are illegal for good reason—they are harmful. If the legalization proponents were heeded, we as a society would be much worse off. We should be concentrating harder on fighting drug use and drug trafficking, where there is significant progress.

No one can deny that the use of psychoactive substances has a great impact on society today—from the health effects of cigarettes to the criminal activity of street-corner crack dealers. In many ways, the greatest impact is from the smuggling, trafficking, and consumption of illegal drugs. These practices inevitably lead to bribery, inner-city crime, babies born addicted to drugs such as crack, and a host of other social ills.

In recent years, there has been a "war on drugs" that is supposed to address (if not solve) these problems. Since the problems still exist, and the war on drugs has been going on now for some time, critics might wonder how effective the war is. Severe critics would say that the so-called war on drugs isn't working at all and that it's time to try another approach.

Some have called for the legalization of drugs. If drugs were legal, proponents say, their sale and use could be regulated and controlled. The government would be able to raise revenue through taxation (instead of having huge drug profits go to organized crime), the quality and quantity of the drugs could be officially monitored, and much inner-city street crime could be eliminated. On the other hand, even after legalization, there would still be many drug addicts (and perhaps even more of them), "crack babies," and other victims of drug use.

Proponents of drug legalization must offer a realistic plan for the legal market they propose. At least two elements should be addressed. First, what exactly is meant by *legalization*? Substances that are legal are not necessarily available at all times to everyone. Alcohol, for example, is a legal substance, but when and where and to whom it may be sold are all regulated by federal and local authorities. And some currently legal drugs are available only by prescription. Second, some further clarification is needed about what is meant by *drugs*. Talk about drugs can be very vague. Caffeine and nicotine are common drugs, but since they are already legal, we might say that we are considering here only illegal drugs. But why are some drugs legal and some illegal?

Twentieth-century (alcohol) Prohibition is one of the useful test cases that people on both sides of this issue can appeal to—while we obviously cannot experiment with changing the legal status of a drug for a limited time to see what would happen, Prohibition is a historical reality. Prohibition became effective on January 16, 1920, and was repealed December 5, 1933. During this time, the Constitution was amended to outlaw "the manufacture, sale, or the transportation of intoxicating liquors within . . . the United States." Also outlawed were all import and export of these items. During Prohibition, many of the problems that we now associate with the modern drug world existed: smuggling, official corruption, murder, large amounts of money being made by violent criminals, and organized criminal networks. Members of the public could, with a little effort—and in some cases with very little effort—buy and consume the very products that were against the law. And what was bought on the black market had no guarantees with respect to health or safety.

In the following selections, David Boaz and the Drug Enforcement Agency present radically different cases. Boaz argues that the government does not have the right to prohibit people from using the substances that they wish to use. He argues that governmental programs that are meant to control the use of certain substances are misguided; these efforts are themselves responsible for much drug-related crime. Moreover, they do not (and cannot) succeed in keeping the substances out of the hands of people who want them. On the other hand, the Drug Enforcement Administration argues that it is the drugs themselves that are harmful, and that much progress and success have been achieved by fighting drug use. Drug legalization, they say, would be much more problematic than legalization proponents admit and would certainly lead to an increase in drug abuse and drug addiction. Social ills would follow in the wake of drug legalization.

YES

David Boaz

A Drug-Free America—or a Free America?

Introduction: The Drug Problem

Human beings have used mind-altering substances throughout recorded history. Why? . . . Perhaps because we fail to love one another as we should. Perhaps because of the social pressure for success. Perhaps because and this is what really irks the prohibitionists—we enjoy drugs' mind-altering effects.

Though the reasons for drug use are numerous, the governmental response has been singular: almost as long as humans have used drugs, governments have tried to stop them. In the sixteenth century the Egyptian government banned coffee. In the seventeenth century the Czar of Russia and the Sultan of the Ottoman Empire executed tobacco smokers. In the eighteenth century England tried to halt gin consumption and China penalized opium sellers with strangulation.

The drug prohibition experiment most familiar to Americans is the prohibition of alcohol in the 1920s. The period has become notorious for the widespread illegal consumption of alcohol and the resultant crime. Movies such as *Some Like It Hot* typify the popular legend of the era. The failure of Prohibition, however, is not just legendary. Consumption of alcohol probably fell slightly at the beginning of Prohibition but then rose steadily throughout the period. Alcohol became more potent, and there were reportedly more illegal speakeasies than there had been legal saloons. More serious for nondrinkers, the per capita murder rate and the assault-by-firearm rate both rose throughout Prohibition.

Most of the same phenomena are occurring with today's prohibition of marijuana, cocaine, and heroin. Use of these drugs has risen and fallen during the seventy-seven years since Congress passed the Harrison Narcotics Act [designed to curb opium trafficking], with little relationship to the level of enforcement. In the past decade, the decade of the "War on Drugs," use of these drugs seems to have declined, but no faster than the decline in the use of the legal drugs alcohol and tobacco. In the 1980s Americans became more health- and fitness-conscious, and use of all drugs seems to have correspondingly decreased. Drug prohibition, however, has not stopped thirty million people from trying cocaine and sixty million people from trying marijuana. Prohibition also has not stopped the number of heroin users from increasing by one hundred fifty percent and the number of cocaine users from increasing by ten thousand percent. Moreover, prohibition has not kept drugs out of the hands of children: in 1988 fifty-four percent of high school seniors admitted to having tried illicit drugs; eighty-eight percent said it was fairly easy or very easy to obtain marijuana; and fifty-four percent said the same about cocaine.

Although drug prohibition has not curtailed drug use, it has severely limited some fundamental American liberties. Programs such as "Zero Tolerance," which advocates seizing a car or boat on the mere allegation of a law enforcement official that the vehicle contains drugs, ignore the constitutional principle that a person is innocent until proven guilty.

In attempting to fashion a solution to "the drug problem," one first needs to define the problem society is trying to solve. If the problem is the age-old human instinct to use mind-altering substances, then the solution might be God, or evolution, or stronger families, or Alcoholics Anonymous. History suggests, however, that the solution is unlikely to be found in the halls of Congress. If, on the other hand, the problem is the soaring murder rate, the destruction of inner-city communities, the creation of a criminal subculture, and the fear millions of Americans experience on their own streets, then a solution may well be found in Congress—not in the creation of laws but in their repeal.

This Article proposes that the repeal of certain laws will force individuals to take responsibility for their actions; the repeal of other laws will provide individuals the right to make important decisions in their lives free from outside interference. Together these changes will create the society in which drugs can, and must, be legalized. Legalization of drugs, in turn, will end the need for the government to make the intrusions into our fundamental rights as it does so often in its War on Drugs.

The Futility of Prohibition

A. The War on Drugs

Prohibition of drugs is not the solution to the drug problem. [Since 1981] the United States has waged a "War on Drugs." The goals of this War were simple: prohibit the cultivation or manufacture of drugs, prohibit the import of drugs, and prohibit the use of drugs. As the aforementioned statistics demonstrate, the War has not achieved its goals.

Prohibitionists, however, sometimes claim that the United States has not yet "really fought a drug war." The prohibitionists argue that a "true drug war" would sharply lower drug use. They feel that the government has not fully committed itself to winning this battle. One need only look at the War on Drug's record, however, to see the commitment.

- Congress passed stricter anti-drug laws in 1984, 1986, and 1988. Congress and state legislators steadily increased penalties for drug law violations, mandating jail time even for first offenders, imposing large civil fines, seizing property, denying federal benefits to drug law violators, and evicting tenants from public housing.

- Federal drug war outlays tripled between 1980 and 1988, and the federal government spent more than $20 billion on anti-drug activities during the decade. Adjusted for inflation, the federal government spends ten times as much on drug-law enforcement every year as it spent on Prohibition enforcement throughout the Roaring Twenties.
- Police officers made more than one million drug law arrests in 1989, more than two-thirds of them for drug possession.
- The number of drug busts tripled during the 1980s, and the number of convictions doubled.
- America's prison population more than doubled between 1981 and 1990, from 344,283 to 755,425. Prisons in thirty-five states and the District of Columbia are under court orders because of overcrowding or poor conditions. An increasing percentage of these prisoners are in jail for nonviolent drug law violations.
- The armed services, Coast Guard, and Civil Air Patrol became more active in the drug fight, providing search and pursuit planes, helicopters, ocean interdiction, and radar. Defense Department spending on the War on Drugs rose from $200 million in 1988 to $800 million in 1990.
- The Central Intelligence Agency (CIA) and National Security Agency began using spy satellites and communications listening technology as part of the drug war. The CIA also designed a special Counter Narcotics Center.
- The federal government forced drug testing upon public employees and required contractors to establish "drug-free" workplaces. Drug testing has also expanded among private companies.
- Seizures of cocaine rose from 2,000 kilograms in 1981 to 57,000 kilograms in 1988.

Despite this enormous effort, drugs are more readily available than ever before. The War on Drugs has failed to achieve its primary goal of diminishing the availability and use of drugs.

B. Prohibition Creates Financial Incentives

One reason for the failure of the War on Drugs is that it ignores the fact that prohibition sets up tremendous financial incentives for drug dealers to supply the demand. Prohibition, at least initially, reduces the supply of the prohibited substance and thus raises the price. In addition, a large risk premium is added onto the price. One has to pay a painter more to paint the Golden Gate Bridge than to paint a house because of the added danger. Similarly, drug dealers demand more money to sell cocaine than to sell alcohol. Those who are willing to accept the risk of arrest or murder will be handsomely—sometimes unbelievably—rewarded.

Drug dealers, therefore, whatever one may think of them morally, are actually profit-seeking entrepreneurs. Drug researcher James Ostrowski points out that "[t]he public has the false impression that drug enforcers are highly innovative, continually devising new schemes to catch drug dealers. Actually, the reverse is true. The dealers, like successful businessmen, are usually one step ahead of the 'competition.'"[1]

New examples of the drug dealers' entrepreneurial skills appear every day. For example, partly because the Supreme Court upheld surveillance flights over private property to look for marijuana fields, marijuana growers have been moving indoors and underground. The Drug Enforcement Administration seized about 130 indoor marijuana gardens in California in 1989; by November the figure for 1990 was 259.

Overseas exporters have also been showing off their entrepreneurial skills. Some have been sending drugs into the United States in the luggage of children traveling alone, on the assumption that authorities will not suspect children and will go easy on them if they are caught. Others have concealed drugs in anchovy cans, bean-sprout washing machines, fuel tanks, and T-shirts. At least one man surgically implanted a pound of cocaine in his thighs. Some smugglers swallow drugs before getting on international flights. Professor Ethan Nadelmann has explained the spread of overseas exporters as the "pushdown/ pop-up factor": push down drug production in one country, and it will pop up in another.[2] For example, Nadelmann notes that "Colombian marijuana growers rapidly expanded production following successful eradication efforts in Mexico during the mid-1970s. Today, Mexican growers are rapidly taking advantage of recent Colombian government successes in eradicating marijuana."

Prohibition of drugs creates tremendous profit incentives. In turn, the profit incentives induce drug manufacturers and dealers to creatively stay one step ahead of the drug enforcement officials. The profit incentives show the futility of eradication, interdiction, and enforcement and make one question whether prohibition will ever be successful. . . .

Individual Rights

Many of the drug enforcement ideas the prohibitionists suggest trample upon numerous constitutional and natural rights. In any discussion of government policies, it is necessary to examine the effect on natural rights for one simple reason: Individuals have rights that governments may not violate. In the Declaration of Independence, Thomas Jefferson defined these rights as life, liberty, and the pursuit of happiness. I argue that these inviolable rights can actually be classified as one fundamental right: Individuals have the right to live their lives in any way they choose so long as they do not violate the equal rights of others. To put this idea in the drug context, what right could be more basic, more inherent in human nature, than the right to choose what substances to put in one's own body? Whether it is alcohol, tobacco, laetrile, AZT, saturated fat, or cocaine, this is a decision that the individual should make, not the government. This point seems so obvious to me that it is, to borrow Jefferson's words, self-evident.

The prohibitionists, however, fail to recognize this fundamental freedom. They advance several arguments in an effort to rebut the presumption in favor of liberty. First, they argue, drug users are responsible for the violence of the drug trade and the resulting damage to innocent people. The erstwhile Drug Czar, William Bennett, when asked how his nicotine addiction differed from a drug addiction, responded, "I didn't do any drive-by shootings."[3] Similarly former First Lady Nancy Reagan said, "The casual user may think when he takes a line of cocaine or smokes a joint in the privacy of his nice condo, listening to his expensive stereo, that he's somehow not bothering anyone. But there is a trail of death and destruction that leads directly to his door. I'm saying that if you're a casual drug user, you are an accomplice to murder."[4]

The comments of both Mr. Bennett and Mrs. Reagan, however, display a remarkable ignorance about the illegal-drug business. Drug use does not cause violence. Alcohol did not cause the violence of the 1920s, Prohibition did. Similarly drugs do not cause today's soaring murder rates, drug prohibition does. The chain of events is obvious: drug laws reduce the supply and raise the price of drugs. The high price causes addicts to commit crimes to pay for a habit that would be easily affordable if obtaining drugs was legal. The illegality of the business means that business disputes—between customers and suppliers or between rival suppliers—can be settled only through violence, not through the courts. The violence of the business then draws in those who have a propensity—or what economists call a comparative advantage—for violence. When Congress repealed Prohibition, the violence went out of the liquor business. Similarly, when Congress repeals drug prohibition, the heroin and cocaine trade will cease to be violent. As columnist Stephen Chapman put it, "the real accomplices to murder" are those responsible for the laws that make the drug business violent.[5]

Another prohibitionist argument against the right to take drugs is that drug use affects others, such as automobile accident victims and crack babies. With regard to the former, certainly good reasons exist to strictly penalize driving (as well as flying or operating machinery) while under the influence of drugs. It hardly seems appropriate, however, to penalize those who use drugs safely in an attempt to stop the unsafe usage. As for harm to babies, this is a heart-rending problem (though perhaps not as large a problem as is sometimes believed). Again, however, it seems unnecessary and unfair to ban a recreational drug just because it should not be used during pregnancy. Moreover, drug-affected babies have one point in common with driving under the influence: misuse of legal drugs (alcohol, tobacco, codeine, caffeine) as well as illegal drugs, contribute to both problems. Thus, if society wants to ban cocaine and marijuana because of these drugs' potential for misuse, society should logically also ban alcohol, tobacco, and similar legal drugs.

The question of an individual right to use drugs comes down to this: If the government can tell us what we can put into our own bodies, what can it not tell us? What limits on government action are there? We would do well to remember Jefferson's advice: "Was the government to prescribe to us our medicine and diet, our bodies would be in such keeping as our souls are now."[6]

The Solution: Re-establish Individual Responsibility

For the past several decades a flight from individual responsibility has taken place in the United States. Intellectuals, often government funded, have concocted a whole array of explanations as to why nothing that happens to us is our own fault. These intellectuals tell us that the poor are not responsible for their poverty, the fat are not responsible for their overeating, the alcoholics are not responsible for their drinking. Any attempt to suggest that people are sometimes responsible for their own failures is denounced as "blaming the victim."

These nonresponsibility attitudes are particularly common in discussions of alcohol, tobacco, and other drugs. Development of these attitudes probably began in the 1930s with the formulation of the classic disease theory of alcoholism. The disease theory holds that alcoholism is a disease that the alcoholic cannot control. People have found it easy to apply the theory of addiction to tobacco, cocaine, heroin, even marijuana. In each case, according to the theory, people get "hooked" and simply cannot control their use. Author Herbert Fingarette, however, stated that "*no* leading research authorities accept the classic disease concept [for alcoholism]."[7] Many scientists, though, believe it is appropriate to mislead the public about the nature of alcoholism in order to induce what they see as the right behavior with regard to alcohol.

In the popular press the addiction theory has spread rapidly. Popular magazines declare everything from sex to shopping to video games an addiction that the addicted person has no power to control. As William Wilbanks said, the phrase "I can't help myself" has become the all-purpose excuse of our time.[8]

The addiction theory has also gained prominence in discussions of illegal drugs. Both prohibitionists and legalizers tend to be enamored of the classic notion of addiction. Prohibitionists say that because people cannot help themselves with respect to addictive drugs, society must threaten them with criminal sanctions to protect them from their own failings. Legalizers offer instead a "medical model": treat drug use as a disease, not a crime. The legalizers urge that the billions of dollars currently spent on drug enforcement be transferred to treatment programs so that government can supply "treatment on demand" for drug addicts.

Despite the popular affection for the addiction theory, numerous commentators denounce the theory. For example, addiction researcher Stanton Peele deplores the effects of telling people that addictive behavior is uncontrollable:

> [O]ne of the best antidotes to addiction is to teach children responsibility and respect for others and to insist on ethical standards for everyone—children, adults, addicts. Crosscultural data indicate, for instance, that when an experience is defined as uncontrollable, many people experience such loss of control and use it to justify their transgressions against society. For example, studies find that the "uncontrollable" consequences of alcohol consumption vary from one society to another, depending upon cultural expectations.[9]

. . . The United States requires . . . more reforms—in addition to drug legalization—to create the kind of society in which people accept responsibility for their actions. . . .

Americans might take . . . steps to restore traditional notions of individual responsibility. Laws regarding drugs should only punish persons who violate the rights of others; private actions should go unpunished. Thus, laws should strictly punish those who drive while under the influence of alcohol or other drugs. Intoxication, moreover, should not be a legal defense against

charges of theft, violence, or other rights violations, nor should a claim of "shopping addiction" excuse people from having to pay their debts. Physicians, intellectuals, and religious leaders should recognize that the denial of responsibility has gone too far, and they should begin to stress the moral value of individual responsibility, the self-respect such responsibility brings, and the utilitarian benefits of living in a society in which all persons are held responsible for the consequences of their actions.

Conclusion

Society cannot really make war on drugs, which are just chemical substances. Society can only wage wars against people, in this case people who use and sell drugs. Before America continues a war that has cost many billions of dollars and many thousands of lives—more than eight thousand lives per year even before the skyrocketing murder rates of the past few years—Americans should be sure that the benefits exceed the costs. Remarkably, all of the high-ranking officer in the Reagan administration's drug war reported in 1988 that they knew of n studies showing that the benefits of prohibition exceeded the costs.

There is a good reason for the lack of such a study. Prohibition is futi We cannot win the War on Drugs. We cannot even keep drugs out of our pr ons. Thus, we could turn the United States into a police state, and we still wou not win the War on Drugs. The costs of prohibition, however, are very real: te of billions of dollars a year, corruption of law enforcement officials, civil lib ties abuses, the destruction of inner-city communities, black-market murde murders incident to street crime by addicts seeking to pay for their habit, a the growing sense that our major cities are places of uncontrollable violence.

Hundreds, perhaps thousands, of years of history teach us that we i never make our society drug-free. In the futile attempt to do so, however, may well make our society unfree.

Notes

1. Ostrowski, *Thinking About Drug Legalization*, 121 POL'Y ANALYSIS, May 1989, at 34. . . .

2. Nadelmann, *The Case for Legalization*, 92 PUB. INTEREST 3, 9 (1988). . . .

3. Isikoff, *Bennett Rebuts Drug Legalization Ideas*, Washington Post, Dec. 12, 1 at A10, col. 1.

4. Chapman, *Nancy Reagan and the Real Villains in the Drug War*, Chicago Trib Mar. 6, 1988, §4, at 3, col. 1. . . .

5. Chapman, *supra* note 4.

6. T. Jefferson, *Notes on Virginia*, in THE LIFE AND SELECTED WRITING: THOMAS JEFFERSON 187, 275 (1944).

7. H. Fingarette, HEAVY DRINKING at 3 (1988) (emphasis in original). . . .

8. Wilbanks, *The New Obscenity*, 54 VITAL SPEECHES OF THE DAY 658, 6! (1988).

9. *See generally* S. Peele, *Control Yourself*, REASON, Feb. 1990, at 25.

 **NO**

Speaking Out Against Drug Legalization

A Message from the Drug Enforcement Administration

In many circles, U.S. drug policy is under attack. It is being criticized primarily by those who favor a legalization agenda. It is also being challenged by those who encourage certain trends in European drug policy, like decriminalization of drug use, "harm reduction" programs, and distinctions between hard and soft drugs.

Proponents of legalization are spending huge amounts of money to encourage a greater tolerance for drug use. A number of states have passed referendums to permit their residents to use drugs for a variety of reasons. The citizens who vote in these referendums too often have to rely on the information or rather, misinformation—being presented by the sponsors of these expensive campaigns to legalize drugs.

This [publication], *Speaking Out Against Drug Legalization*, is designed to cut through the fog of misinformation with hard facts. The ten factual assertions, taken together, present an accurate picture of America's experience with drug use, the current state of the drug problem, and what might happen if America chooses to adopt a more permissive policy on drug abuse. . . .

Summary of the Top Ten Facts on Legalization

Fact 1: We have made significant progress in fighting drug use and drug trafficking in America. Now is not the time to abandon our efforts.
The Legalization Lobby claims that the fight against drugs cannot be won. However, overall drug use is down by more than a third in the last twenty years, while cocaine use has dropped by an astounding 70 percent. Ninety-five percent of Americans do not use drugs. This is success by any standards.

Fact 2: A balanced approach of prevention, enforcement, and treatment is the key in the fight against drugs.
A successful drug policy must apply a balanced approach of prevention, enforcement and treatment. All three aspects are crucial. For those who end up hooked on drugs, there are innovative programs, like Drug Treatment Courts,

From U.S Department of Justice, Drug Enforcement Administration, January 2000.

that offer non-violent users the option of seeking treatment. Drug Treatment Courts provide court supervision, unlike voluntary treatment centers.

Fact 3: Illegal drugs are illegal because they are harmful.

There is a growing misconception that some illegal drugs can be taken safely. For example, savvy drug dealers have learned how to market drugs like Ecstasy to youth. Some in the Legalization Lobby even claim such drugs have medical value, despite the lack of conclusive scientific evidence.

Fact 4: Smoked marijuana is not scientifically approved medicine.
Marinol, the legal version of medical marijuana, is approved by science.

According to the Institute of Medicine, there is no future in smoked marijuana as medicine. However, the prescription drug Marinol—a legal and safe version of medical marijuana which isolates the active ingredient of THC—has been studied and approved by the Food & Drug Administration as safe medicine. The difference is that you have to get a prescription for Marinol from a licensed physician. You can't buy it on a street corner, and you don't smoke it.

Fact 5: Drug control spending is a minor portion of the U.S. budget.
Compared to the social costs of drug abuse and addiction, government spending on drug control is minimal.

The Legalization Lobby claims that the United States has wasted billions of dollars in its anti-drug efforts. But for those kids saved from drug addiction, this is hardly wasted dollars. Moreover, our fight against drug abuse and addiction is an ongoing struggle that should be treated like any other social problem. Would we give up on education or poverty simply because we haven't eliminated all problems? Compared to the social costs of drug abuse and addiction—whether in taxpayer dollars or in pain and suffering—government spending on drug control is minimal.

Fact 6: Legalization of drugs will lead to increased use and increased levels of addiction. Legalization has been tried before, and failed miserably.

Legalization has been tried before—and failed miserably. Alaska's experiment with Legalization in the 1970s led to the state's teens using marijuana at more than twice the rate of other youths nationally. This led Alaska's residents to vote to re-criminalize marijuana in 1990.

Fact 7: Crime, violence, and drug use go hand-in-hand.

Crime, violence and drug use go hand in hand. Six times as many homicides are committed by people under the influence of drugs, as by those who are looking for money to buy drugs. Most drug crimes aren't committed by people trying to pay for drugs; they're committed by people on drugs.

Fact 8: Alcohol has caused significant health, social, and crime problems in this country, and legalized drugs would only make the situation worse.

The Legalization Lobby claims drugs are no more dangerous than alcohol. But drunk driving is one of the primary killers of Americans. Do we want our bus drivers, nurses, and airline pilots to be able to take drugs one evening, and operate freely at work the next day? Do we want to add to the destruction by making drugged driving another primary killer?

Fact 9: Europe's more liberal drug policies are not the right model for America.
The Legalization Lobby claims that the "European Model" of the drug problem is successful. However, since legalization of marijuana in Holland, heroin addiction levels have tripled. And Needle Park seems like a poor model for America.

Fact 10: Most non-violent drug users get treatment, not jail time.
The Legalization Lobby claims that America's prisons are filling up with users. Truth is, only about 5 percent of inmates in federal prison are there because of simple possession. Most drug criminals are in jail—even on possession charges—because they have plea-bargained down from major trafficking offences or more violent drug crimes.

Fact 1: We have made significant progress in fighting drug use and drug trafficking in America. Now is not the time to abandon our efforts.

- Legalization advocates claim that the fight against drugs has not been won and is, in fact, unconquerable. They frequently state that people still take drugs, drugs are widely available, and that efforts to change this are futile. They contend that legalization is the only workable alternative.
- The facts are to the contrary to such pessimism. On the demand side, the U.S. has reduced casual use, chronic use and addiction, and prevented others from even starting using drugs. Overall drug use in the United States is down by *more than a third* since the late 1970s. That's 9.5 million people fewer using illegal drugs. We've reduced cocaine use by an astounding 70% during the last 15 years. That's 4.1 million fewer people using cocaine.
- Almost two-thirds of teens say their schools are drugfree, according to a new survey of teen drug use conducted by The National Center on Addiction and Substance Abuse (CASA) at Columbia University. This is the first time in the seven-year history of the study that a majority of public school students report drug-free schools. . . .
- There is still much progress to make. There are still far too many people using cocaine, heroin and other illegal drugs. In addition, there are emerging drug threats like **Ecstasy** and **methamphetamine**. But the fact is that our current policies balancing prevention, enforcement, and treatment have kept drug usage outside the scope of acceptable behavior in the U.S.
- To put things in perspective, less than 5 percent of the population uses illegal drugs of any kind. Think about that: More than 95 percent of Americans do not use drugs. How could anyone but the most hardened pessimist call this a losing struggle? . . .

- Progress does not come overnight. America has had a long, dark struggle with drugs. It's not a war we've been fighting for 20 years. We've been fighting it for 120 years. In 1880, many drugs, including opium and cocaine, were legal. We didn't know their harms, but we soon learned. We saw the highest level of drug use ever in our nation, per capita. There were over 400,000 opium addicts in our nation. That's twice as many per capita as there are today. And like today, we saw rising crime with that drug abuse. But we fought those problems by passing and enforcing tough laws and by educating the public about the dangers of these drugs. And this vigilance worked—by World War II, drug use was reduced to the very margins of society. And that's just where we want to keep it. With a 95 percent success rate—bolstered by an effective, three-pronged strategy combining education/prevention, enforcement, and treatment—we shouldn't give up now.

Fact 2: A balanced approach of prevention, enforcement, and treatment is the key in the fight against drugs.

- Over the years, some people have advocated a policy that focuses narrowly on controlling the supply of drugs. Others have said that society should rely on treatment alone. Still others say that prevention is the only viable solution. As the 2002 National Drug Strategy observes, "What the nation needs is an honest effort to integrate these strategies."
- Drug treatment courts are a good example of this new balanced approach to fighting drug abuse and addiction in this country. These courts are given a special responsibility to handle cases involving drug-addicted offenders through an extensive supervision and treatment program. Drug court programs use the varied experience and skills of a wide variety of law enforcement and treatment professionals: judges, prosecutors, defense counsels, substance abuse treatment specialists, probation officers, law enforcement and correctional personnel, educational and vocational experts, community leaders and others—all focused on one goal: to help cure addicts of their addiction, and to keep them cured. . . .

Fact 3: Illegal drugs are illegal because they are harmful.

- There is a growing misconception that some illegal drugs can be taken safely—with many advocates of legalization going so far as to suggest it can serve as medicine to heal anything from headaches to bipolar diseases. Today's drug dealers are savvy businessmen. They know how to market to kids. They imprint Ecstasy pills with cartoon characters and designer logos. They promote parties as safe and alcohol-free. Meanwhile, the drugs can flow easier than water. Many young people believe the new "club drugs," such as Ecstasy, are safe, and tablet testing at raves has only fueled this misconception.
- Because of the new marketing tactics of drug promoters, and because of a major decline in drug use in the 1990s, there is a growing perception

among young people today that drugs are harmless. A decade ago, for example, 79 percent of 12th graders thought regular marijuana use was harmful; only 58 percent do so today. Because peer pressure is so important in inducing kids to experiment with drugs, the way kids perceive the risks of drug use is critical. There always have been, and there continues to be, real health risks in using illicit drugs. . . .

Marijuana

- Drug legalization advocates in the United States single out marijuana as a different kind of drug, unlike cocaine, heroin, and methamphetamine. They say it's less dangerous. . . . However, as many people are realizing, marijuana is not as harmless as some would have them believe. Marijuana is far more powerful than it used to be. In 2000, there were six times as many emergency room mentions of marijuana use as there were in 1990, despite the fact that the number of people using marijuana is roughly the same. In 1999, a record 225,000 Americans entered substance abuse treatment primarily for marijuana dependence, second only to heroin—and not by much.
- At a time of great public pressure to curtail tobacco because of its effects on health, advocates of legalization are promoting the use of marijuana. Yet, according to the National Institute on Drug Abuse, "Studies show that someone who smokes five joints per week may be taking in as many cancer-causing chemicals as someone who smokes a full pack of cigarettes every day." Marijuana contains more than 400 chemicals, including the most harmful substances found in tobacco smoke. For example, smoking one marijuana cigarette deposits about four times more tar into the lungs than a filtered tobacco cigarette.
- Those are the long-term effects of marijuana. The short-term effects are also harmful. They include: memory loss, distorted perception, trouble with thinking and problem solving, loss of motor skills, decrease in muscle strength, increased heart rate, and anxiety. Marijuana impacts young people's mental development, their ability to concentrate in school, and their motivation and initiative to reach goals. And marijuana affects people of all ages: Harvard University researchers report that the risk of a heart attack is five times higher than usual in the hour after smoking marijuana.

Fact 4: Smoked marijuana is not scientifically approved medicine. Marinol, the legal version of medical marijuana, *is* approved by science.

- Medical marijuana already exists. It's called Marinol.
- A pharmaceutical product, Marinol, is widely available through prescription. It comes in the form of a pill and is also being studied by researchers for suitability via other delivery methods, such as an inhaler or patch. The active ingredient of Marinol is synthetic THC, which has been found to relieve the nausea and vomiting associated with chemotherapy for cancer patients and to assist with loss of appetite with AIDS patients.

- Unlike smoked marijuana—which contains more than 400 different chemicals, including most of the hazardous chemicals found in tobacco smoke—Marinol has been studied and approved by the medical community and the Food and Drug Administration (FDA), the nation's watchdog over unsafe and harmful food and drug products. Since the passage of the 1906 Pure Food and Drug Act, any drug that is marketed in the United States must undergo rigorous scientific testing. The approval process mandated by this act ensures that claims of safety and therapeutic value are supported by clinical evidence and keeps unsafe, ineffective, and dangerous drugs off the market. . . .

Fact 5: Drug control spending is a minor portion of the U.S. budget. Compared to the social costs of drug abuse and addiction, government spending on drug control is minimal.

- Legalization advocates claim that the United States has spent billions of dollars to control drug production, trafficking, and use, with few, if any, positive results. As shown in previous [sections], the results of the American drug strategy have been positive indeed—with a 95 percent rate of Americans who do *not* use drugs. If the number of drug abusers doubled or tripled, the social costs would be enormous.

Social Costs

- Legalization would result in skyrocketing costs that would be paid by American taxpayers and consumers. Legalization would significantly increase drug use and addiction—and all the social costs that go with it. With the removal of the social and legal sanctions against drugs, many experts estimate the user population would at least double. For example, a 1994 article in the *New England Journal of Medicine* stated that it was probable, that if cocaine were legalized, the number of cocaine addicts in America would increase from 2 million to at least 20 million.
- Drug abuse drives some of America's most costly social problems—including domestic violence, child abuse, chronic mental illness, the spread of AIDS, and homelessness. Drug treatment costs, hospitalization for long-term drug-related disease, and treatment of the consequences of family violence burden our already strapped health care system. In 2000, there were more than 600,000 hospital emergency department drug episodes in the United States. Health care costs for drug abuse alone were about $15 billion. . . .
- Legalizers fail to mention the hidden consequences of legalization. . . .
- Advocates also argue that legalization will lower prices. But that raises a dilemma: If the price of drugs is low, many more people will be able to afford them and the demand for drugs will explode. For example, the cost of cocaine production is now as low as $3 per gram. At a market price of, say, $10 a gram, cocaine could retail for as little as ten cents a hit. That means a young person could buy six hits of cocaine for the price of a candy bar. On the other hand, if legal drugs are

priced too high, through excise taxes, for example, illegal traffickers will be able to undercut it.

- Advocates of legalization also argue that the legal market could be limited to those above a certain age level, as it is for alcohol and cigarettes. . . . But teenagers today have found many ways to circumvent the age restrictions, whether by using false identification or by buying liquor and cigarettes from older friends. According to the 2001 National Household Survey on Drug Abuse, approximately 10.1 million young people aged 12–20 reported past month alcohol use (28.5 percent of this age group). Of these, nearly 6.8 million (19 percent) were binge drinkers. With drugs, teenagers would have an additional outlet: the highly organized illegal trafficking networks that exist today and that would undoubtedly concentrate their marketing efforts on young people to make up for the business they lost to legal outlets.

Costs to the Taxpayer

- . . . Legalization advocates fail to note the skyrocketing social and welfare costs, not to mention the misery and addiction, that would accompany outright legalization of drugs.
- Legalizers also fail to mention that, unless drugs are made available to children, law enforcement will still be needed to deal with the sale of drugs to minors. In other words, a vast black market will still exist. Since young people are often the primary target of pushers, many of the criminal organizations that now profit from illegal drugs would continue to do so.
- Furthermore, it is reasonable to assume that the health and societal costs of drug legalization would also increase exponentially. Drug treatment costs, hospitalization for long-term drug-related diseases, and treatment of family violence would also place additional demands on our already overburdened health system. More taxes would have to be raised to pay for an American health care system already bursting at the seams. . . .

Fact 6: Legalization of drugs will lead to increased use and increased levels of addiction. Legalization has been tried before, and failed miserably.

- Legalization proponents claim, absurdly, that making illegal drugs legal would not cause more of these substances to be consumed, nor would addiction increase. They claim that many people can use drugs in moderation and that many would choose not to use drugs, just as many abstain from alcohol and tobacco now. Yet how much misery can already be attributed to alcoholism and smoking? Is the answer to just add more misery and addiction? . . .

The Alaska Experiment and Other Failed Legalization Ventures

- The consequences of legalization became evident when the Alaska Supreme Court ruled in 1975 that the state could not interfere with an adult's possession of marijuana for personal consumption in the home.

The court's ruling became a green light for marijuana use. Although the ruling was limited to persons 19 and over, teens were among those increasingly using marijuana. According to a 1988 University of Alaska study, the state's 12- to 17-year-olds used marijuana at more than twice the national average for their age group. Alaska's residents voted in 1990 to recriminalize possession of marijuana, demonstrating their belief that increased use was too high a price to pay.

- By 1979, after 11 states decriminalized marijuana and the Carter administration had considered federal decriminalization, marijuana use shot up among teenagers. That year, almost 51 percent of 12th graders reported they used marijuana in the last 12 months. By 1992, with tougher laws and increased attention to the risks of drug abuse, that figure had been reduced to 22 percent, *a 57 percent decline.* . . .

- When legalizers suggest that easy access to drugs *won't* contribute to greater levels of addiction, they aren't being candid. The question isn't whether legalization will increase addiction levels—it will—it's whether we care or not. The compassionate response is to do everything possible to prevent the destruction of addiction, not make it easier.

Fact 7: Crime, violence, and drug use go hand-in-hand.

- Proponents of legalization have many theories regarding the connection between drugs and violence. Some dispute the connection between drugs and violence, claiming that drug use is a *victimless crime* and users are putting only themselves in harm's way and therefore have the right to use drugs. Other proponents of legalization contend that if drugs were legalized, crime and violence would decrease, believing that it is the illegal nature of drug production, trafficking, and use that fuels crime and violence, rather than the violent and irrational behavior that drugs themselves prompt.

- Yet, under a legalization scenario, a black market for drugs would still exist. And it would be a vast black market. If drugs were legal for those over 18 or 21, there would be a market for everyone under that age. People under the age of 21 consume the majority of illegal drugs, and so an illegal market and organized crime to supply it would remain—along with the organized crime that profits from it. After Prohibition ended, did the organized crime in our country go down? No. It continues today in a variety of other criminal enterprises. Legalization would not put the cartels out of business; cartels would simply look to other illegal endeavors. . . .

- The greatest weakness in the logic of legalizers is that the violence associated with drugs is simply a product of drug trafficking. That is, if drugs were legal, then most drug crime would end. But most violent crime is committed not because people want to buy drugs, but because people are on drugs. Drug use changes behavior and exacerbates criminal activity, and there is ample scientific evidence that demonstrates the links between drugs, violence, and crime. Drugs often cause people to do things they wouldn't do if they were rational and free of the influence of drugs. . . .

- For experts in the field of crime, violence, and drug abuse, there is no doubt that there is a connection between drug use and violence. As Joseph A. Califano, Jr., of the National Center on Addiction and Substance Abuse at Columbia University stated, "Drugs like marijuana, heroin and cocaine are not dangerous because they are illegal; they are illegal because they are dangerous." . . .

Fact 8: Alcohol has caused significant health, social, and crime problems in this country, and legalized drugs would only make the situation worse.

- Drugs are far more addictive than alcohol. According to Dr. Mitchell Rosenthal, director of Phoenix House, only 10 percent of drinkers become alcoholics, while up to 75 percent of regular illicit drug users become addicted. . . .

Fact 9: Europe's more liberal drug policies are not the right model for America.

- Over the past decade, European drug policy has gone through some dramatic changes toward greater liberalization. The Netherlands, considered to have led the way in the liberalization of drug policy, is only one of a number of West European countries to relax penalties for marijuana possession. Now several European nations are looking to relax penalties on all drugs—including cocaine and heroin—as Portugal did in July 2001, when minor possession of all drugs was decriminalized.. . . .
- The Netherlands has led Europe in the liberalization of drug policy. "Coffee shops" began to emerge throughout the Netherlands in 1976, offering marijuana products for sale. Possession and sale of marijuana are not legal, but coffee shops are permitted to operate and sell marijuana under certain restrictions, including a limit of no more than 5 grams sold to a person at any one time, no alcohol or hard drugs, no minors, and no advertising. In the Netherlands, it is illegal to sell or possess marijuana products. So coffee shop operators must purchase their marijuana products from illegal drug trafficking organizations.
- Apparently, there has been some public dissatisfaction with the government's policy. Recently the Dutch government began considering scaling back the quantity of marijuana available in coffee shops from 5 to 3 grams.
- Furthermore, drug abuse has increased in the Netherlands. From 1984 to 1996, marijuana use among 18–25 year olds in Holland increased twofold. Since legalization of marijuana, heroin addiction levels in Holland have tripled and perhaps even quadrupled by some estimates.
- The increasing use of marijuana is responsible for more than increased crime. It has widespread social implications as well. The head of Holland's best-known drug abuse rehabilitation center has described what the new drug culture has created: The strong form of marijuana that most of the young people smoke, he says, produces "a chronically passive individual—someone who is lazy, who doesn't want to

take initiatives, doesn't want to be active—the kid who'd prefer to lie in bed with a joint in the morning rather than getting up and doing something.". . .

- The United Kingdom has also experimented with the relaxation of drug laws. Until the mid-1960s, British physicians were allowed to prescribe heroin to certain classes of addicts. . . . Many addicts chose to boycott the program and continued to get their heroin from illicit drug distributors. The British Government's experiment with controlled heroin distribution . . . resulted in, at a minimum, a 30-fold increase in the number of addicts in ten years.

- Switzerland has some of the most liberal drug policies in Europe. In [the] late 1980s, Zurich experimented with what became known as Needle Park, where addicts could openly purchase drugs and inject heroin without police intervention. Zurich became the hub for drug addicts across Europe, until the experiment was ended, and "Needle Park" was shut down.

- Many proponents of drug legalization or decriminalization claim that drug use will be reduced if drugs were legalized. However, history has not shown this assertion to be true. According to an October 2000 CNN report, marijuana, the illegal drug most often decriminalized, is "continuing to spread in the European Union, with one in five people across the 15-state bloc having tried it at least once."

- It's not just marijuana use that is increasing in Europe. According to the *2001 Annual Report on the State of the Drugs Problem in the European Union,* there is a Europe-wide increase in cocaine use. . . .

- Drug policy also has an impact on general crime. In a 2001 study, the British Home Office found violent crime and property crime increased in the late 1990s in every wealthy country except the United States.

Fact 10: Most non-violent drug users get treatment, not just jail time.

- There is a myth in this country that U.S. prisons are filled with drug users. This assertion is simply *not* true. Actually, only 5 percent of inmates in *federal* prison on drug charges are incarcerated for drug possession. In our *state* prisons, it's somewhat higher—about 27% of drug offenders. In New York, which has received criticism from some because of its tough Rockefeller drug laws, it is estimated that 97% of drug felons sentenced to prison were charged with sale or intent to sell, not simply possession. In fact, first time drug offenders, even sellers, typically do not go to prison. . . .

Policy Shift to Treatment

- There has been a shift in the U.S. criminal justice system to provide treatment for non-violent drug users with addiction problems, rather than incarceration. The criminal justice system actually serves as the largest referral source for drug treatment programs.

- Any successful treatment program must also require accountability from its participants. Drug treatment courts are a good example of combining treatment with such accountability. These courts are given a special responsibility to handle cases involving drug-addicted offenders through an extensive supervision and treatment program. Drug treatment court programs use the varied experience and skills of a wide variety of law enforcement and treatment professionals: judges, prosecutors, defense counsels, substance abuse treatment specialists, probation officers, law enforcement and correctional personnel, educational and vocational experts, community leaders and others—all focused on one goal: to help cure addicts of their addiction, and to keep them cured.

- Drug treatment courts are working. Researchers estimate that more than 50 percent of defendants convicted of drug possession will return to criminal behavior within two to three years. Those who graduate from drug treatment courts have far lower rates of recidivism, ranging from 2 to 20 percent. . . .

POSTSCRIPT

Should Drugs Be Legalized?

Boaz states that governmental efforts to control drug use will create serious social problems, and in the end fail to keep the forbidden substances out of the hands of people who want to use them. A strong governmental effort—like the current war on drugs—threatens people's civil liberties and provides criminals with incentive to engage in illegal drug trafficking. Boaz asserts that the tendency of the government to attempt to control its citizens' lives is wrong. An individual should be able to take personal responsibility for his or her actions and choose what substances he or she consumes.

The Drug Enforcement Administration (DEA) opposes Boaz at almost every turn. Moreover, the DEA's position, as outlined here, is not just a simple restatement of the law, but an articulate series of arguments that directly respond to the claims and arguments of legalization supporters such as Boaz. The DEA begins from a point that supporters of legalization must face. If, under legalization, there would be increased availability of drugs, and little or no social sanction against using them, then there would be an increase in use and in drug abuse, and the consequences that follow from that (for example, more drug addicts).

Boaz criticizes the War on Drugs and says that the solution to the current situation is to re-establish personal responsibility. "Personal responsibility" seems to mean two different things, though. One meaning is that an individual has the choice to use drugs or not. Another meaning is that people who have personal responsibility will actually *be* responsible (i.e., not only will they have the choice, but they will select appropriate options). Somehow, Boaz seems to want to take advantage of both of these meanings. His first intention is probably the first meaning, where people have choices (instead of the government deciding what we can and cannot put into our bodies). But proponents of the War on Drugs may see this as merely begging the question. How can Boaz be so sure that this really will be a solution? Is he assuming—in line with the second meaning of "personal responsibility"—that people will actually make appropriate choices?

And now I can return to the idea of drug addiction. If some people do develop a drug habit (or addiction), Boaz seems to suggest these people have the ability to just change their minds about their usage. Yet we know from our experience with legal substances, such as tobacco, that it is extremely difficult for smokers to stop. And "difficult" may not even be the right word, for it suggests that we have to really try, and then we'll do it. But consider the case of smokers who can't stop. Maybe they've tried the patch, they've tried the gum, and they've even tried to go cold turkey. They're really trying, but they are addicted. And that is what can happen with addictive drugs.

Both Boaz and the DEA seem at times to go too far. But that is just the challenge of this issue: maintaining a reasonable position when it is very easy to slide off into extremes.

For further reading on this issue, see James A. Inciardi, *The War on Drugs III: The Continuing Saga of the Mysteries and Miseries of Intoxication, Addiction, Crime, and Public Policy* (Allyn & Bacon, 2001); Robert J. MacCoun and Peter Reuter, *Drug War Heresies: Learning from Other Vices, Times, and Places* (Cambridge University Press, 2001); Douglas Husak, *Drugs and Rights* (Cambridge University Press, 2002); and Jeffrey A. Miron, *Drug War Crimes: The Consequences of Prohibition* (Independent Institute, 2004).

ISSUE 11

Is Gambling Immoral?

YES: Lisa Newton, from "Gambling: A Preliminary Inquiry," *Business Ethics Quarterly* (vol. 3, no. 4, 1993)

NO: Peter Collins, from "Is Gambling Immoral? A Virtue Ethics Approach," in Mark Timmons, ed., *Disputed Moral Issues* (Oxford University Press, 2007)

ISSUE SUMMARY

YES: Lisa Newton, a philosopher at Fairfield University, argues that gambling is immoral on the grounds that it violates stewardship (and not on the grounds that it violates anyone's rights or that it leads to negative results). Most of the paper examines the concept of stewardship and how it relates to gambling. Stewardship, which is an old concept that is known to us primarily through religious tradition, can also be given a modern secular form.

NO: Peter Collins, a British philosopher, argues that gambling is not immoral. He addresses gambling from both traditional utilitarian (or consequentialist) and Kantian perspectives—and finds the critiques from these perspectives lacking. He then specifically considers the more recent criticism that is based on the idea of stewardship—this too he finds lacking. Collins concludes with the idea of true happiness, and expresses the judgment that although gambling is not necessarily a part of a truly happy life, it is morally trivial.

Gambling has traditionally been considered a vice. It has traditionally been considered immoral. But it may be difficult to specify what exactly is wrong with it. For example, it is not difficult to realize that theft and lying are wrong. But with the case of gambling, determining if it's wrong become somewhat more difficult. It is not hard to realize that theft and lying violate people's rights, but while some cases of gambling violate people's rights, some do not. For example, if I take the rent money and gamble it away, then I have trespassed against the rights of those who are depending on me to take care of the rent. You could say that I have wrongfully deprived them of what

197

was theirs—just as in the case of theft. But that would be the case if I just spent the rent money on books—and no one says that reading is immoral. But if there is something wrong with gambling in particular, we still haven't managed to say exactly what that is. Now, it's sometimes the case that gamblers will waste their time and that others have a claim on that time. This point can be granted, but people can waste time on a variety of things without those things having to be thought immoral. What is it, we ask, that is immoral about gambling?

One way of looking at this issue invites us to step away from "rights-talk" and think not in terms of rights but—to use a rather old-fashioned word—virtues. The language of rights encourages us to look for the absolute minimum that one person owes another. But the language of virtues encourages us to look higher than the minimum. Thus, for example, if I do not steal from someone, at least I am not violating that person's rights—but this a minimum. People don't think that they are good people on the grounds that they don't steal. That is, it's hardly a claim to moral goodness that one isn't a thief. Of course, being a thief is a *disqualification* from being a good person. But is that all that people should do in order to be good? Avoid the disqualifications?

One non-rights approach to gambling (and to ethics in general) suggests that we use the language of *virtues*. "Responsible," for example, is a virtue word. (I'm thinking of the sense of the term in which a person you can count on is said to be a *responsible* person, not the sense in which the thief who took the money is said to be *responsible* for its disappearance.) One difference between this sort of word and a rights-word, is that different people can have various *degrees* of the virtue. One person may be highly responsible, for example—far more responsible than another responsible individual.

Lisa Newton, in her article below on gambling, speaks of *stewardship*. Here again, we can see that this old-fashioned-sounding term suggests degrees: There is the idea of being a good steward, or an even better steward, or possibly a poor steward, while rights-talk encourages an all-or-nothing approach. (If you violate someone's rights, that action is wrong; there are no "low-level" violations that gradually shade off into non-violations. But if you are a poor steward of some resources, then this could gradually shade off into higher and higher levels of stewardship, including—at some distance—even good stewardship.)

The author of the answering article, Peter Collins, not only examines gambling from a variety of viewpoints, but includes specific criticism of the ideas of stewardship. His conclusion is that gambling is "morally trivial."

YES

Lisa Newton

Gambling: A Preliminary Inquiry

Abstract: In all the criticisms that have shadowed the financial industry in recent years, the burden seems to be, that the reckless (as opposed to malicious) bankers too often took money of which they were the appointed stewards, and used it for speculation, especially in junk bonds. As Shaheen Borna and James Lowry argue in their "Gambling and Speculation" (the only article on gambling that I was able to raise on my computer[1]) business speculation is probably wrong, since it is very like gambling, which everyone knows is wrong. But why is gambling wrong? If we, as the ethicists of business, are to adopt an uncharacteristically judgmental posture toward the most venerable American institutions, occupying the tallest and closest of American buildings, by calling their residents "gamblers," then surely we ought to be able to provide an account of the blameworthiness of gambling itself.[2] That, at any rate, is the challenge I set myself for this paper.

Why Is Gambling Wrong?

Not because it injures others than the gambler. Others are surely injured, and every chronicle of gambling details the miseries of the gamblers' families and friends as they struggle to survive themselves, cover for the gambler and pay the debts. But the injury is not a violation of their rights, and whether or not they "accept" the gambling, they accept the situation overall and voluntarily remain in it [to one who is willing no injury is done]. Nor is the injury one that the law punishes whether or not the victim accepts it: whatever the peculiar mental anguish of the gambler's family, the only material damage they suffer is impoverishment, and they might suffer that from any number of causes (if the family breadwinner is laid off from work, for instance), without anyone thinking an injury has been done.

Not because it injures the gambler. When the gambler voluntarily engages in the activity, he or she accepts the possibility of loss of as much money as is wagered—that is the definition of gambling, is it not?—so the results of the gamble are apparently acceptable. The gambler may claim that they are not, but from the fact that he or she repeatedly engages in the activity we have reason to doubt the sincerity of the claim. In any case, the loss suffered is no different from that imposed on the family—loss of money—which

From *Business Ethics Quarterly*, vol. 3, issue 4, 1993, pp. 405–413. Copyright © 1993 by Business Ethics Quarterly. Reprinted by permission.

can result from any number of misguided voluntary actions (making a bad investment in the stock market, for instance) without any claim of injury arising. The literature that grounds our societal commitment to individual rights is eloquent in its defense of the right to make mistakes without thereby inviting social intervention; after all, what other right makes any sense without that one?

The origin of the moral condemnation of gambling (as opposed to the literature of regret for the social consequences) seems to lie in the duty of *stewardship,* and the egregious violation of that duty constituted by gambling, at an individual and societal level. Since the term has not been common in recent literature, especially in the literature of business ethics, a few words of review might be in order.

Stewardship has essentially to do with property not your own, and is governed more by what we now call "agency theory" than any other set of moral principles. It designates simultaneously the occupancy of a position (the position of "steward," one hired by a property owner to watch out for his property in his absence), and the duties associated with that position. If you are a steward, you have property that has been entrusted to you to take care of by the owner, and it is your duty to make sure that it is well maintained, well used by those who use it, improved as appropriate, self-sustaining and profitable. The duties extend to whatever new property may arise out of the entrusted property; if the cows calve, the calves must be taken care of, and if the property yields a substantial income, the money must be appropriately invested. The investments must be "safe," as opposed to "risky," unless the owner has given specific instructions to take risks (and specified the risks), for the duty to keep the property safe and whole outweighs any duty to make it profitable. At no time is the steward free to use, or use up, the property at will.

Yes, but what has this to do with the gambler's gambling with the gambler's own money? Three lines of reasoning lead from that duty to the gambler's risk. First, stewardship actually derives from ownership: the primary command for the steward, or agent, is to treat the property of the master, or principal, as if it were one's own. But at the time the concept was cemented into the moral tradition, "ownership" was understood to carry an enormous baggage of duties with it, duties less familiar in this century. The property the human race has known for 99% of its settled existence has been the land we farmed and the animals we kept for food, milk and wool. Land and animals are uncompromising: you will take care of them, or you will get no good of them, either for yourself (in immediate use for food or cloth) or for trade, in exchange for other things you might need. Your living depends upon judicious investment in the future of your property, digging wells, buying new rams, or purchasing new seed or machines; above all you must maintain the property in good condition. You could assume new positions only by liquidating (selling or otherwise consuming) part of your property in order to enhance others; that was the element of capitalistic flexibility that made our ancestors good businessmen and businesswomen.

Of course there was always the theoretical possibility of liquidating *all* your property—selling off all your sheep, seed, acreage and buildings, for cash—but then, of course (the story of the Prodigal Son), you would have nothing left after the cash was spent. Life depended on a very careful balance between investment (saving) and liquidation (spending), with the balance always tipped to saving. Let the balance tip the other way, and that particular community was destined for bankruptcy, and extinction. That is the way we lived from neolithic times through the last century, in which the habits cultivated over millennia were transferred without remainder to the factories and industrial empires of the burgeoning industries of iron and steel, rail transportation and petroleum. Communities that did not understand the duties of ownership presumably died out in hard times, vanished without a trace, and are not available for comparison. So the necessities of sheer survival created, not exactly a duty (for we cannot get an ought from an is), but a fact situation in which those who did not adopt certain hypothetical imperatives as duties failed to transmit their culture to descendants—making such duty part, I suppose, of what H. L. A. Hart would call the "minimum natural law."[3]

So the gambler, first, in ignoring the duties of ownership to property, violates a taboo of great antiquity. Second, and perhaps more immediately for our Calvinist ancestors, there is a question whether property can be "owned" by humans at all. For the earth, come to that, is the Lord's, as is the yield thereof—the world, and they that dwell therein; for He founded it upon the seas, and established it upon the floods. To the extent that we "own" property, under the secular laws of our land at this time, we actually hold it in trust for God, we are His stewards, and (to put a finer point on it) we can be called from this life at any moment to render an account to God of our stewardship of that which was never really ours. It would not be pleasant to have that moment arrive as we sat at the green felt gaming tables.

Third, there is a secular version of the argument above, to the effect that there is a strong social interest in the care and conservation of all property in the commonwealth, that gives the public a justified and lively concern with the way people dispose of wealth that by law is their private property. The law and its regulations, after all, are never far from the exercise of property rights: I am compelled to spend my money on things I may not want (casualty insurance); I am prohibited from spending my money on things I may want (controlled substances, including non-approved medications); I must maintain my land, especially if it contains salt marshes, in accordance with zoning and other regulations. Only diehard libertarians seriously oppose such regulation, which amounts to a strong state interest in the management of property as a whole. (In passing, we may note that if the gambler ends in poverty, the taxpayers end up footing the welfare bills.) Our duty of "stewardship" of the nation's property in general, then, can entail that putting that property at risk at the gaming tables is seriously wrong.

The conclusion that gambling is wrong, because it is a violation of our duty of stewardship of property, is consistent with several otherwise anomalous facts in the checkered career of the activity in this country: that gambling is illegal or severely restricted in most jurisdictions, although no basis can be found for opposition to gambling in rights theory, which is elsewhere our first (and usually last) court of appeal; that gambling has been publicly prohibited or carefully controlled through much of our history by most of our legislatures even though (see next section) there is no utilitarian warrant for public prohibition of gambling; and that the Protestant churches that most controlled the country's moral life until this century consistently condemned gambling, in the absence of any Biblical warrant for such condemnation. As a preliminary suggestion for further research, we might want to follow up the notion of "stewardship" for other applications at the border of private behavior and business enterprise.

If Gambling Is Wrong, Should It Be Against the Law?

Probably not. Very powerful arguments have been advanced, that the criminalization of gambling and other consensual transactions creates a whole new class of "crimes without victims," and does much more harm than good.[4] We need not rehearse these familiar arguments in any detail. In brief, it has been observed that where the "crime" consists of a transaction between consenting adults, its commission is extremely difficult to detect; information is very difficult to gather, involving the police in distasteful recruitment of spies and informants; the police find it impossible to resist corruption of their own number in protection rackets for the activity in question; the participants in the activity are driven underground and isolated from the help and community support that might draw them into healthier lines of work and recreation; blackmail, loansharking, and organized crime in general rapidly take over the conduct of the activity and corrupt the community as a whole. As long as there is a willing market for gambling, prostitution, and narcotics purchases (older accounts include abortion and homosexual encounters), and as long as there is money available to pay for them, they will take place, and their criminalization will have no effect but to degrade participants and law enforcement alike.

Then Should the Society Encourage Gambling?

This is the question of the hour. The costs and benefits of two forms of societal encouragement of gambling—the state lotteries, for one, and the legalization of casino gambling, for the other—are debated as we speak in legislatures across the country, including my home state of Connecticut. Benefits and costs are simple enough to discover; the problem is one of weighting. Let us run through the exercise, very briefly.

The benefits of legalized gambling are public revenue and jobs. Any legal income can be taxed, and that includes gambling income; any legal enterprise is subject to business taxes, Federal, state and local. A casino or other gambling establishment is a new source of revenue for the state, politically palatable (unlike new taxes) and endlessly profitable. Because the casino is so sure to make money, entrepreneurs (and the banks that back them) gladly venture the capital to construct them, without government subsidy or tax breaks, and even in locations that have found it difficult to attract other sorts of business (the crumbling downtown districts of the older cities, for instance). The building alone cleans out the slums, cleans up the streets, and provides construction jobs at union wages. Once the casinos begin operating, they provide more jobs immediately suitable for the unskilled inner-city unemployed—work in the restaurants, maintenance, maid service. (We may assume that the executive-level and skilled jobs—croupiers and the like—will come from outside.) And they pay taxes: real estate taxes to cities long unused to successful industry, state taxes for public education, and federal taxes, to fund new programs for the inner cities.

And the beauty of it all is, that the whole profitable deal is entirely voluntary and without limit. No one loses money at the tables who has not asked to do so. The gambler is probably aware that the house skims a percent off the top of every transaction; and is also probably aware that the state does too; but the gambling continues. There is no apparent natural limit on the amount of money the enterprise will yield: the more casinos, and the more hours they are open, the higher the state revenue from casino gambling. What could be the objections to this goose of endless golden eggs?

The state lottery, a different form of state encouragement of gambling, is a lower budget version of the same argument. Here the state takes all the profit, but incurs all the expenses. Its moral status, whatever that turns out to be, is the same as that of the collection of revenue from casino gambling, and the decision to emphasize one or the other is a simple business decision. Again, since all play is voluntary, no effort is required to collect the revenue, and no political consequences follow from advocating an expansion.

The drawbacks of legalized gambling are also reasonably well known. First, there is the sleaze factor. There is little evidence that, legalized, these activities suddenly become clean and harmless ways for the citizenry to spend their time. Another literature surveys the communities that make their living on gambling, notably Las Vegas and Atlantic City, and concludes that most of the evils of illegal gambling followed the law into the legal casino, where they continue to hold sway.[5] Nor is it clear that the proposed benefits to the inner cities actually took place. The picture given of the life of the casinos, and of the pockets of poverty in the cities that harbor them, is of human associations severely unbalanced, engines to produce human misery behind the shield of "voluntary participation." Given the experience of Las Vegas and especially Atlantic City (since the decision to permit casino gambling there was more recent and self-conscious), communities should think long and hard about the decision to cash in on the easy revenues.

The second objection, the objection from Rawlsian justice, is harder to calculate. John Rawls has asked us to evaluate each scheme for the betterment of the society by one simple test: does it improve the lot of the least advantaged?[6] Gambling does not, except maybe it does. First, if we look only to the objective, material, effects, gambling (legal or illegal) takes from the poor, who gamble, and gives to the rich. If the only one to profit is the policy banker, the injustice is clear; but even if the take from gambling is distributed through the state education system, it remains the case that the least well off of society have contributed their money for the benefit of an aggregate on average richer than the contributors. In effect, gambling is worse than a regressive tax, which takes from all equally; gambling takes disproportionately from the poor and almost none from the successful professional class. This is clearly unjust.

The injustice is compounded by deception, or arguable deception, in the advertising of the state lotteries or other legal opportunities to gamble. The odds of winning—*against* winning—are well known, by cognoscenti—but how many of the poor fall into that category? Meanwhile, the percent of the take distributed to *actual* winners may be much less than that, since the state gets to keep an extra percentage of every pot that is not won. Should it not be wrong to add to the temptation to gamble by the slick advertising campaigns now in use?

On the other hand, there is evidence that suggests that not only are the disadvantaged themselves much happier for having the opportunity to gamble, but that it is indeed rational for them to do so. In districts where hope is in short supply, the numbers chit or lottery ticket is hope, and that alone is worth the price of the ticket. Second, the hope is not irrational: if your goal is to achieve the material American Dream, you should know that saving your pennies, including the extra two dollars a week that you spend on the lottery, from a minimum wage job in the inner city, will never get you there; a hit on the numbers, or the lottery, will do that. Never mind that the chances are miniscule; without the ticket, they are nonexistent. Finally, the very fact that the lowest of the rackets, the numbers game, is confined to the ghetto, renders it a special area of activity and expertise, a social event with its own gratifying rituals and non-material rewards.[7]

Do I have the right to enslave an unsuspecting tribe of masochists that plead with me to enslave them? Do I have the right to profit from the hopes of the poor, when the society that has treated me so well has created the conditions that make the gambling, from which I profit, their only hope?

The third objection, from the teaching responsibility of the State, is related to the second, but more amorphous yet. What is our responsibility for creating the conditions for a good life for all citizens—not necessarily a materially good life, but a life in which they can be good? Suppose it should turn out, and I suspect it might, that it is easier to resist temptation and develop justice and kindness as traits of character in settings where the encouragement of virtue and the condemnation (and punishment) of vice is part of public commitment—in short, where virtue is publicly rewarded, and vice is against the law (one remembers Sparta)? What is the responsibility of the political association to form its citizens into virtuous people? We cannot pursue this objection in this paper, but the classical conservative political tradition takes it very seriously.[8]

Can Gambling Be Good Business?

If by "good business" all we mean is "profitable," the question is not worth asking. Las Vegas continues to build casinos, Atlantic City processes enormous amounts of cash on a daily basis, the Pequot Indians of Connecticut know more prosperity than they have had since the White Man first landed on their shores. Of course it can be, and is, profitable. (But then, have you ever known organized crime to get into a line of work that was *not* profitable?)

But if we mean to determine the moral status of the enterprise, the question is more interesting, and again, surprisingly unasked, in any literature with which I am familiar. This is no time for any attempt at detailed evaluation of the ethical dimensions of Las Vegas and its relatives; the following preliminary sketch of the issues may be enough to get us started:

1. Is there any way that gambling can be useful, or at least entertaining and harmless? (Does it have, we may ask, any redeeming social value?) If so, then the ethical casino would make good faith attempts to ensure that gambling happened there only in that way. The analogy that suggests itself is the manufacture and sale of alcoholic beverages. We know that if the product is misused, terrible injury can result (from violence, drunken operation of machinery or automobiles, or alcohol-related disease); we know that there are an indefinitely large number of people who will, by reason of their physical or psychological predispositions, misuse it; and we suspect that non-alcohol-related aspects of our society are being compromised by it (50% of hospital admissions are alcohol related, entailing a large but incalculable effect of alcohol consumption on our national health care bill). But alcohol can be consumed affordably, harmlessly, and enjoyably, so it is possible to run a manufactury, tavern, or wine and liquor emporium, to cater to that trade alone. On the other hand, it would be difficult to conceive of an ethical trade in cocaine, as it is becoming harder to imagine an ethical trade in cigarettes. Along the spectrum from the harmless entertainment (subject to misuse by some) to the obnoxious product with no redeeming features, where does gambling fall?

2. Is it possible to run the industry in such a way as to extract it from organized crime? If not, is there an ethical way to include, and deal with, the Mob? If we can free the industry from organized crime, who would run it? Could we justify keeping gambling as a government monopoly, as a source of revenue for the states, especially if it turns out that private operators cannot stay clear of criminal associations? If it turns out that it is impractical to have the government run it, that private operators are inevitably part of the Mafia or rapidly become captured by it, is that reason enough, in the absence of other reasons, to criminalize gambling?

3. What, if any, responsibility does the industry bear for the compulsive gambler? Is there something wrong with placing the means of one more addiction in front of people already addicted? The liquor industry takes no responsibility for the alcoholic *per se,* but the bartender is responsible for refusing to serve someone obviously drunk. Should the casino take responsibility for ascertaining the financial means of each patron, and barring from play any who go over a preset limit?

These are not easy questions to answer. It is no real help to flesh out the analogy of the ethical tavern with the analogy of Prohibition, to point out that, as above, gambling will take place illegally if not legally, so we might as well try to run ethical casinos as at least a small improvement. Prohibition of the manufacture and sale of alcohol clearly "did not work"—it was a disaster for law enforcement and demoralized (and criminalized) the middle class, never something a lawgiver wants to do. But while it was in effect, alcohol-caused disease dropped significantly, especially among the poor. By reverse projection, we may expect that if casino gambling is legalized, the take from illegal gambling will drop, and the middle class will no longer gamble illegally. And we may also expect that gambling losses over the whole population will increase significantly, especially among the poor. Is it worth it?

To conclude, at very long last, what do we, as a people, expect of ourselves? There is an ironic justice in the fact that our eagerness to legalize casino gambling for the sake of the revenues follows directly from our unwillingness to assess ourselves a fair and adequate amount in taxes. The problems with our public character dovetail with the problems in our private character. There is a good possibility that we will make progress on neither until we are willing to address both.

Notes

1. *Journal of Business Ethics* 6(3):219–224 (April, 1987). That isn't quite true, actually. The computer search showed a fascinating literature, now over ten years old, on John Harris' proposal (in the spirit of Jonathan Swift) for a mandatory "survival lottery"—requiring an unlucky "donor" to be sacrificed if two or more persons with otherwise terminal diseases could be saved by the use of his organs. The proposal can be shown to maximize survival if not happiness, and to accord with certain rules of justice, but the thought of it makes some of us a little queasy. See Harris, John, "The Survival Lottery," *Philosophy* 50(191):81–87 (January 1975); Hanink, J. G. "On the Survival Lottery," *Philosophy* 51:223–225 (April 1976); Morillo, Carolyn R. "As Sure As Shooting," *Philosophy* 51:80–89 (January 1976); Singer, Peter, "Utility and the Survival Lottery," *Philosophy* 52:218–222 (April 1977); Green, Michael B., "Harris's Modest Proposal," *Philosophy* 54:400–406 (July 1979); Trammell, Richard L. and Wren, Thomas E., "Fairness, Utility and Survival," *Philosophy* 52:331–337 (July 1977); Harris, John, "Hanink on the Survival Lottery," *Philosophy* 53:100–101 (January 1978). All of which brings us back to the original question: since the profession seems to have no problem tackling the issues of games of chance when they are far-fetched and imaginary, why the avoidance of games of chance real, actual, and grossing a billion dollars a day all around us?

2. We may note in passing that the industry under consideration here, the industry that provides and draws its profits from the slot machines and card games of Las Vegas and Atlantic City, prefers to call itself the "gaming" industry, not "gambling." "Gaming" certainly sounds better, conjuring up visions of children playing games for amusement. We take the two activities to be conceptually distinct: "Gaming" means playing games, no more or less; "gambling" means placing property at risk, as described below in the paper. We are concerned with the ethical implications of the latter, not the former, so we retain the term "gambling" to describe our subject.

3. H. L. A. Hart, *The Concept of Law,* Oxford: Oxford University Press, 1961.

4. See the report by the American Friends Service Committee, *Struggle For Justice: A Report on Crime and Punishment in America,* New York: Hill and Wang, 1971; also Troy Duster, *The Legislation of Morality,* New York: The Free Press, 1970; Gilbert Geis, *Not the Law's Business? An Examination of Homosexuality, Abortion, Prostitution, Narcotics, and Gambling in the United States,* National Institute of

Mental Health, Crime and Delinquency Monograph Series, Washington, DC: U.S. Government Printing Office, 1972; *The Knapp Commission Report on Police Corruption,* New York: George Braziller, 1972;

Herbert L. Packer, *The Limits of the Criminal Sanction,* Stanford: Stanford University Press, 1968; Edwin M. Schur, *Crimes Without Victims,* Englewood Cliffs, NJ: Prentice-Hall, Inc. 1965; Schur, *Labeling Deviant Behavior,* New York: Harper and Row, 1971; Schur, "The Case for Abolition," in *Victimless Crimes: Two Sides of a Controversy,* by Edwin Schur and Hugo Adam Bedau, Englewood Cliffs, NJ: Prentice-Hall, Inc., 1974. All of these have something to do with gambling; other literature on publicly condemned consensual transactions (for instance, the *Report* of the Wolfenden Committee on Homosexual Offences and Prostitution, Home Office, London, 1972) base their conclusions on similar observation and argument.

5. See Wallace Turner, *Gamblers' Money: The New Force in American Life,* Cambridge, MA: The Riverside Press, 1965; Ed Reid and Ovid Demaris, *The Green Felt Jungle,* New York: Trident Press, 1963; Ovid Demaris, *(How Greed, Corruption and the Mafia Turned Atlantic City into) The Boardwalk Jungle,* New York: Bantam Books, 1986. See also, for a gamblers' eye view of gambling, Stuart Winston and Harriet Harris, M.D. *Nation of Gamblers: America's Billion Dollar A Day Habit,* Englewood Cliffs, NJ: Prentice-Hall, 1984.

6. John Rawls, *A Theory of Justice,* Cambridge, MA: Harvard University Press, 1971.

7. Or so Gilbert Geis argues, citing abundant sources. Geis, *op.cit* pp. 225 ff.

8. See George F. Will, *Statecraft as Soulcraft: What Government Does,* New York: Simon and Schuster, 1983

Peter Collins  **NO**

Is Gambling Immoral?
A Virtue Ethics Approach

1. Introduction

The question of whether gambling should be prohibited or legalised and, if legalised, how it should be regulated has received considerable attention from people who think about public policy. It is no part of my purpose here to try to contribute to answering those questions. Clearly, in as far as these questions raise moral issues, they are issues of public rather than private morality. That is, they are about what governments should or should not use their coercive powers to do rather than about how we individually should conduct our lives in conformity with what morality requires.

Historically, gambling along with other activities deemed to constitute vices has been legally proscribed because two beliefs were widely held: first that gambling is immoral and second, that it is the business of government to try to stamp out activities which are immoral. The second of these beliefs, however, has for better or for worse been largely discredited in pluralist societies committed to the principles of liberal democracy, on the grounds that it is neither morally defensible nor politically practicable. As a consequence, advocates of banning or limiting legal gambling tend to avoid invoking the claim that gambling is intrinsically immoral even though this is a belief which many of them hold. Instead they focus on trying to show that prohibition or legal restriction is justified on the basis of the illegitimate harm that legalised gambling does to gamblers themselves, to third parties and to society as a whole.

But is gambling immoral? Suppose it were agreed, on the purest libertarian grounds, that the State should do absolutely nothing to try to prevent or discourage people from gambling as much as they like; would there still be any good reasons why you and I should nevertheless decide on moral grounds that gambling ought to play little or no part in the way we conduct our daily lives?

I want to anchor this discussion by identifying [two] reasons why this question deserves substantial attention from moral philosophers and certainly more attention than it has recently received.[1] . . .

First, the role which pleasure and pleasures should play in our lives is a fundamental issue in moral philosophy to the extent that it addresses the question of how ordinary people ought to conduct their everyday lives. Gambling

From *2005 Collection of Papers on Self Study and Institutional Improvement*, April 2005. Copyright © 2005 by the Higher Learning Commission of the North Central Association of Colleges and Schools. Reprinted by permission of the Higher Learning Commission and the Peter Collins. ncahlc.org furnishes a particularly good case study for this kind of philosophising since it not only tends to consume considerable time and money which could arguably be better spent but also has a propensity to become addictive. For reasons which may be largely self-serving we tend to avoid reflection on this kind of question when it applies to our own pleasures or those of our friends. But it becomes inescapable when we think about the need to offer rational guidance to children about how they should conduct themselves in relation to different kinds of pleasure. And as soon as we ask: "What should we teach children about gambling?" we confront the question of the morality or otherwise of gambling.

Secondly, it is clear that gambling provides an interesting case against which to test different types of ethical theory. As we shall see, some people argue that gambling violates the principle of utility. Others claim on Kantian grounds that it is inconsistent with conduct of a rational and autonomous person. Gambling has also, of course, been condemned by those who espouse a puritan ethic whether based on religious convictions or on secular considerations.

Finally we need to consider the claim that gambling is incompatible with living the best or most fulfilling kind of life of which human beings are capable. . . .

2. What Is Gambling?

Before we can properly address questions about the morality of gambling we need to make some conceptual points about the nature of the activity we are discussing.

The standard definition of gambling is that it involves three components:

- Something valuable is placed at risk (staked).
- With the prospect of winning something more valuable if one set of events occurs and of losing one's stake if another set of events occurs.
- Where the outcome is wholly or partly unpredictable by the gambler.

This definition, however, seems to leave some important questions unanswered amongst which I wish to single out two because of their relevance to the moral issues.

First there is the question of whether buying stocks and shares is gambling. The thought here is that a pro-gambling argument might be developed along the following lines. If there is no difference between speculating on the stock market and gambling in a casino, the latter activity can only be morally culpable if the former is too. But it would obviously be absurd to condemn investing on the stock exchange as immoral. Therefore it is absurd to condemn gambling in casinos as immoral.

In order to refute this argument it is not necessary to rebut the full (and considerable) force of Marx's arguments to the effect that those who make money out of the mere ownership of capital in the form of shares are robbing workers of the private property which is rightfully theirs because it was created by their labour. All that is necessary is to point out that the stock exchange is not in its essence a provider of gambling services but rather of opportunities for genuine investment. The stock exchange thus differs from a casino or lottery in at least two crucial ways. First, success on the stock exchange depends primarily on the exercise of rational judgment. Second, investing in the stock market is not a zero sum game. That is, making profits on the stock exchange does not necessitate the making of losses by others: in the normal case it depends on the creation of new wealth. It is true that some investing on the stock exchange is, from the point of view of the investor, exactly like gambling— for example, if they pick their investments using a pin. Similarly, some gambling is indeed like investing on the stock exchange: the professional poker player or the bettor on horse races who is an expert on form is trying to make money out of superior knowledge and judgment. But the essence of investing in the stock market does not consist in people literally "trying their luck" in circumstances where one person's gain is always another's loss. The essence of gambling—or at least of the most widespread forms of gambling with whose morality this essay is mainly concerned—consists in just this.

This is why some of the most telling arguments against gambling are that, unlike investing, it is an irrational activity which is unproductive, at best, and destructive of wealth, at worst.

The second distinction which needs to be added to the standard definition of gambling is that between social gambling and commercial gambling. In the heyday of temperance movements, opponents of gambling argued that playing low-stakes social bridge was no less to be condemned on moral grounds than betting on horses, playing roulette or going to a gambling den. For the purposes of the present discussion, however, I shall assume that there could be a great deal of difference from a moral point of view between:

- games of skill engaged in as a social pastime and spiced up with wagers which all participants have a formally equal chance of winning, and
- gambling on games where the outcome is unavoidably and mainly dependent on luck, in commercial contexts where the games are set up so as to make it certain that the players will in the long run lose.

Thus the morality of gambling on slot machines, as opposed to having a bet on a game of golf, may be significantly affected by the fact that anyone who plays gaming machines ought to know that over time they are bound to lose. This may, for example, strengthen the claim that such gambling must be irrational and as such morally wrong. Note also that such an argument would not be affected by whether the amount wagered was large or small.

A very important question for conceptual analysis which underlies the question of what principles we should adopt in shaping both personal conduct and public policy in regard to gambling is: "To what extent is gambling like and unlike other pleasures which have historically been banned on the grounds that they are immoral?" At one extreme some would claim that gambling is like taking hard drugs and should be eschewed on the grounds that it is immoral and banned on the grounds that it is highly dangerous. At the other extreme, people argue that gambling is no more vicious or dangerous than going to the theatre or cinema which was also once much disapproved of by puritans. Rather than discussing these questions fully here, I simply note that to the extent that gambling is both similar to and different from other pleasurable activities to which we devote time and money we will benefit in our thinking about both public and private morality if we accept the demands of consistency in this area, i.e., if we accept that we should take the same position with respect to all pleasures except to the extent that we can demonstrate relevant differences between them. The discussion which follows, therefore, is implicitly though not explicitly concerned that a satisfactory answer can be given to the question: "What are the morally relevant differences, if any, between gambling and, say, dancing, playing golf (on the Sabbath), watching sexually exciting movies or consuming psychotropic drugs for pleasure?"

To summarise these considerations, then, I shall be here predominantly concerned with the morality of individuals' playing games of chance in commercial contexts where the odds are systematically stacked against them. The paradigm will be games like roulette or slot machine gambling. I shall also be concerned with table games played in casinos such as poker or blackjack where the opportunities to exercise skill are rendered systematically nugatory, as well as with lotteries and other number games like keno and bingo. With respect to most sports- and other event-betting I take it that ignorance of the relevant facts for most punters is sufficient to make the outcome the equivalent to one which is predominantly determined by luck. By contrast, I shall not concern myself with the morality of either professional gamblers who rely on superior knowledge and skill in order to make money or of the suppliers of gambling services who earn their money by offering only games in which the odds always favour the House.

I shall proceed by considering what light may be shed on the first question I identify above, namely how does gambling relate to a general moral theory of pleasure, by considering what light may be shed on this question by the four types of ethical theory alluded to above. Not only does applying these theories illuminate the ethics of gambling but we also learn something about the power of the theories by testing them against the case of gambling.

In general, I shall argue that a strong puritan position—it is always good to deny oneself pleasure—is indefensible. I shall also argue against a weaker puritan position which says that it is wrong to engage in any wasteful and addictive activities of which gambling is clearly one. On the other hand, I do not take the view—though I do take it seriously—that gambling is unconditionally good for one's moral health. Perhaps rather tamely, I conclude by adopting what I take to be an Aristotelian view of the morality of gambling and I hope that this position is sustainable with respect to all those pleasures which have been and continue to be deemed by some to be "vices."

3. Mill, Utilitarianism and Vice

A good place to begin considering whether we ought to refrain from or restrict our indulgence in gambling even if the law does not oblige us to do so is with John Stuart Mill's extraordinarily rich, subtle and sensible Chapter 5 of *On Liberty*. Here he treats of each of fornicating, gambling, drunkenness and drugs.

Under the title "Applications," Mill addresses the question of what would happen in terms of actual policy and legislation if his two great principles were adopted by government. The principles are that:

- "That the individual is not accountable to society for his actions, in so far as these concern the interests of no person but himself"
- "That for such actions as are prejudicial to the interests of others, the individual is accountable and may be subjected either to social or to legal punishment if society is of the opinion that the one or the other is requisite for its protection".[2]

Clearly on Mill's view, we cannot outlaw consensual fornication, gambling or self-intoxication. Nor, according to Mill can we subject people who engage in such activities to social sanctions such as ostracism. This is because in an ideal libertarian society, the State makes no attempt to stop people enjoying themselves in whatever way they choose provided only that they do not illegitimately harm others. In such a state anyone may do as they please within the limits of the harm proviso; and in particular, there are no restrictions on indulgence in all manner of pleasures deemed to be vices, no matter how widespread and deeply ingrained the conviction may be that these activities are immoral. But this does not mean, according to Mill, that there are no good moral grounds for refraining from indulgence in vicious pleasures. His felicific ethics as expounded in *Utilitarianism* allow him at least two arguments.

The first is that vicious self-indulgence may be contrary to the principle of utility to the extent that it is self-damaging and conducive for the individual to a preponderance of misery over pleasure in the long run. The second is that fornication, gambling and drunkenness are "lower pleasures" which ought to be abstained from in favour of higher pleasures such as enjoying works of great art.

Neither of these reasons is very convincing as they stand. The first turns on matters of empirical fact: for example, will my indulgence in drugs or gambling ultimately lead to the madness and misery of addiction? The answer in at least many cases is "No" and as Mill himself says, "no-one but the person himself can judge of the motive which may prompt him to incur the risk."[3] Consequently, the most others may legitimately do is to ensure that "he be warned of the danger."[4]

With regard to the argument from higher pleasures, apart from the well-known difficulty which this notion creates for the utilitarian calculus generally, it is also far from clear that the vices would always fail Mill's own test. This test consists in asking moral or hedonic experts who have experience of both higher pleasures such as reading poetry and lower pleasures such as playing pushpin, which of the two activities afford them the greater pleasure. Unfortunately for puritans, however, plenty of people who thoroughly appreciate Picasso's paintings, nevertheless rate the pleasures of fornication even more highly. (Perhaps Picasso himself did.)

On the other hand, I think both kinds of argument have some force in relation to at least the commonest forms of gambling, namely wagering on mechanical devices like roulette wheels or slot machines. Even non-pathological gambling consumes significant amounts of time and money on an activity which arguably affords no significant intellectual or physical stimulation, which, in other words is literally mechanical and mindless. On a purely utilitarian calculus of maximising personal pleasure it is probably easy for most people to get a bigger bang for their leisure buck. I also think that gambling fares poorly in relation to the question of higher pleasures and that it ought to be possible for most people to get a better as well as a bigger bang for their buck.

However, as far as Mill is concerned, the truth is, I believe, that the logic of his position really supports the hedonistic, "whatever-turns-you-on" permissivism. However, Mill didn't embrace such an ethic himself partly because he was concerned to defend utilitarianism against criticism from high-minded Victorian moralists but more because he was himself largely in sympathy with their puritanism, at least in relation to traditional vices. He would almost certainly have regarded modern permissivism as decadent.

However, even if Mill's arguments against vices in general are inadequate to shore up a general defence of puritanism against permissivism, there may be some other and better arguments against unrestrained self-indulgence at least in relation to gambling even though these arguments do not support stronger forms of puritanism or a moral requirement for teetotalism in respect of gambling. Kantian moral reasoning might furnish such arguments.

4. Kantian Arguments and Gambling

The general form of Kantian arguments vetoing particular practices is that one could not rationally desire the world to be a place in which everyone acted in accordance with the principle of conduct which informs the particular practice under discussion. Thus, one could not rationally want the world to be a place where everyone told lies or broke promises whenever it suited them. This seems plausible to the extent that there does seem to be something very like a piece of self-contradiction in asserting: "It would be a good thing if people always told lies when they felt like it" or "Everyone ought to break their promises if they think they will gain thereby." It also seems plausible to claim that there would be something not just bad but mad about someone who asserted without any further explanation that it is just or right for blue-eyed people to be paid much more than brown-eyed people for doing the same job.

The most plausible way in which Kantian reasoning has been used against gambling is by focussing on the fact the whole point of gambling is to distribute property randomly: to make some people richer who have done nothing to deserve it and others poorer simply as a consequence of chance. Allied to this is the thought that gamblers are people who want something for nothing. A Kantian might then argue that one could not rationally desire a world in which what people possess bears no relation to what they deserve in terms of their natural endowments, the talents they cultivate and deploy, theft industry and/or their general contribution to the welfare of society.

One objection to this line of reasoning would be a sort of socialist argument which pointed out that, as a matter of fact, property in society mostly has been and mostly still is distributed according to accidents of birth. It might then be further urged that it would be much fairer and perhaps less divisive if, instead of allowing people to inherit wealth (and otherwise benefit materially from fortunate accidents of birth), differences in at least unearned wealth should be entirely determined by a literal lottery rather than the so-called "lottery of life."

This is perhaps fanciful. A more down-to-earth objection to the Kantian anti-gambling argument is to deny that gambling is all about wanting something for nothing. On the contrary, it may plausibly be urged, gambling is merely a pastime in which some people take pleasure and for which they are willing to pay in the form of the losses which they incur as a result of the fact that the odds are set, to a modest degree, against the player and in favour of the House. Surely, there is nothing irrational about the principle that people should be able to spend their own time and money on entertainments of their own choosing. . . .

There may, however, be a more persuasive and subtle argument against at least the forms of gambling whose paradigm is the gambling machine. This argument is usually couched in Kantian terms and suggests that gambling is an anti-rational activity which runs counter to our character as autonomous agents and, in some sense, requires us to surrender our freedom of will, something which it can no more be rationally right to do than to choose to submit to a condition of slavery. It can, however, also be articulated in utilitarian terms, employing Bentham's notion of the importance of the fecundity of pleasures and pains in doing the felicific calculus as well as noting the role of the principle of diminishing returns. On this view, we should judge pleasures and pains in respect of their propensity to spawn other pleasures and pains, as well as in the tendency of pleasures to grow stale on us the more we indulge in them.

Thus, the kinds of reason that one is intuitively most disposed to urge against regularly gambling on slot machines is that it is a vapid, pointless and mindless activity. As such, it may actually undermine or degrade the intelligence, given that there is no skill involved and that perhaps one becomes inveigled into deceiving oneself into believing that one may actually win in the long run. From a Kantian point of view, this may be thought to be inconsistent with living as a fully rational and autonomous human being. From a utilitarian point of view, it is at least a waste of time and money which could be more usefully employed. It may also actually blunt one's capacity for more profound pleasures.

The difficulty with this line of reasoning is partly that so are many of the other activities—playing solitaire, watching soap operas, etc.—which human beings divert themselves in their moments of leisure in the interval between birth and death. It is not obvious that it is more *rational* to spend time listening to Beethoven rather than playing roulette. On the other hand for many people who enjoy gambling, Beethoven's music sadly remains mere noise no matter how sincerely they attempt to appreciate it. What is obviously true as a matter of fact is that lots of people actually do get a lot of pleasure from gambling, that it does them no harm, and that they get as much benefit from it as others (such as Wittgenstein) get from other forms of recreation such as reading thrillers.

Of course, any time or money whatsoever which we spend on enjoying ourselves could in principle be used to improve ourselves or the lot of our fellow human beings, often in a manner that would be required of a fairly narrowly construed felicific calculus. Perhaps this means that we should regard gambling as indeed but one among many available diversions. However, in this case we might say, with Pascal, that any diversion which serves to distract us from the business of contemplating our ultimate destiny and thereby learning the truths which are necessary for the salvation of our immortal souls is *eo ipso* sinful. This brings us directly to a consideration of the religious case against gambling and secular versions of the same case.

5. Puritan Arguments and Gambling

The view that all indulgence in worldly pleasures is immoral is associated with the more fundamentalist and ascetic strands of all religions. It has a secular counterpart in the views of people who ascribe to political commitment the same importance as others ascribe to religious faith: the pursuit of private pleasure distracts from the work of establishing the political kingdom of heaven. An interesting, if eccentric, puritan view about gambling is to be found in Freud's claim that gambling is really a substitute for masturbation and, as such, an impediment to achieving the ideal of full genitality.

It is perhaps also worth mentioning that some people are puritanical about some pleasures on grounds that are more akin to aesthetic than moral ones. Very obviously people have objections of this kind to all sorts of sexual practices probably preferring to describe those who engage in them as disgusting rather than wicked. It is certainly true that many people who disapprove of Las Vegas would now be inclined to describe it as a monument to crassness and vulgarity rather than as a den of iniquity.

It must be conceded that by far the most common objections to gambling come from people who are in principle opposed to it on religious grounds which they take to possess the self-evidence of revealed truth. Typically they feel the same about sexual activity outside marriage as well as about getting drunk or high. Since, in the nature of the case, puritans tend to appeal either to contested authority or to faith or to taste, it is not clear what arguments could effectively be urged against them. Clearly, they would be right if in fact it turns out that those who indulge themselves in certain kinds of pleasure are going to suffer greatly after they are dead while those who abstain receive great blessings. But this seems equally clearly to be in the realm of the publicly unshowable even if it is not strictly unknowable.

Against puritanism one can urge but not demonstrate that pleasure is always a good and, as such, always a good prima facie reason for action. Thus, if there is anything morally wrong about indulging in any alleged vice, this cannot be a function of the character of the pleasure it offers, let alone of the fact that it offers pleasure at all. It is difficult to see how gambling could be rationally adjudged immoral merely on the grounds that people enjoy it. Like any other activity in which people take pleasure, if it is immoral this must be because of its propensity for corrupting character or otherwise doing damage to those who engage in it or to others. This must be to a significant extent an empirical issue and on this the evidence seems to be that in most cases gambling does not do any harm including harm to people's character.

A much more persuasive basis for arguments against dissipation of all sorts derives from the idea of stewardship. Here the religious version claims that our minds and bodies, our time and our talents, are all gifts of God. We are the stewards of our lives and our nature is such that we can only find true fulfillment and happiness by living in a manner befitting the creatures of God. We do this by attending to the workings of divine grace within us and engaging in works which are pleasing in the sight of our Creator. At all events we should not squander our lives in trivialities and we should acknowledge that a life given over to self-indulgence is an ultimately unsatisfying one.

The secular version of the stewardship argument sometimes appeals to the general economic well-being of society which allegedly requires a good deal of self-denial. More generally it appeals to our alleged obligations to future generations. In its simplest and, I think, strongest form it asserts that this life is all we have. Consequently, we should do everything in our power to ensure that we live it as well as we can and do not waste the only chance at living which we shall ever get.

Thinking in either of these ways enables us to make sense of what people have been getting at in their hostility to drugs, gambling and promiscuity. In each case a plausible argument can be made for the view that loveless sex is not a right use of the body, that consigning one's property to chance is improper stewardship of one's possessions, and that altering one's state of mind with chemicals is an abuse of one's mind. Arguments of this kind will never be decisive but that does not mean they are without rational force. And the force of these stewardship arguments is to alert us in what may be a very salutary way to the dangers of squandering our lives. It does not, however, support the view, nor is it usually taken as supporting the view, that any particular pleasures are in themselves wrong, including gambling.

6. Eudaimonic Ethics and the Place of Pleasure in the Good Life

At this point I think the stewardship argument becomes part of what I take to be the most convincing of all ethical theories, namely what I call eudaimonic ethical theory which most explicitly characterises Greek ethical thought but which is also at the basis of all moral systems which derive from religious creeds or secular belief systems such as Marxism or Psychoanalysis. The fundamental tenet of this kind of theory is that the answers to ethical questions are to be found by discovering what is the best kind of life that a human being can lead. Here the best kind of life is understood as the one which is most conducive to true inner well-being or happiness. This may be thought to have a different answer for different people or a general answer which is true for everyone. It is also clear that there are many different views about what constitutes the summum bonum or supreme good for human beings.

The great strength of such theories is that they make all ethical judgments ultimately a matter of enlightened self-interest and thus render the facts about human nature and human experience crucial for determining how we ought to live. In technical terms, it is analytic that one ought to live the best possible life of which one is capable and it is also analytic that the best possible life is the one which most conduces to eudaimonia or true happiness.

If this line of reasoning is to be helpful in answering the question: "Is gambling immoral?" we need to ask the question which is asked by the Greeks in a self-consciously philosophical way and to which all religions and secular ideologies offer (usually dogmatic) answers, namely: "What is the role of pleasure generally and of individual pleasures specifically in the life of a truly happy man?"

At this point I want to claim that, in general, the view of Aristotle is superior to that, not only of later religious puritans, but also to that of other secular philosophers in both the ancient and the modern worlds. For Aristotle, pleasure is indeed an important part of the best kind of life which a human being can lead, as is wealth. A life in which there is no fun can no more be accounted a happy life than a life of grinding poverty.

But pleasure, like money, is not the only ingredient in a truly happy human life nor is it the most important ingredient. And indeed a life which is exclusively devoted to the pursuit of either pleasure or money will not be a happy one. Hence the famous doctrine of the golden mean which in this case would require finding the right median course between the opposing vices of an excessive asceticism, on the one hand, and of hedonistic over-indulgence on the other.

Obviously for many people gambling will not be an important source of pleasure in their lives. But for those who do derive significant pleasure from gambling, what Aristotle defends in respect of pleasure generally seems to be a sensible view to take in respect of gambling. This is the Delphic injunction: "Nothing in excess."

The virtue of temperance which this maxim recommends is one which it is highly plausible to see as an essential ingredient in living the best kind of life of which we are capable, especially in respect of the commonest sources of pleasurable recreation. Not only does temperance obviously avoid the dangers of addiction but it is not unreasonable to suppose that it issues in a life which is better than one of total abstinence. Thus it may in fact be the case that more people who drink in moderation, have temperate sex lives, and even enjoy the occasional game of chance have lives which are not only more enviable but also more admirable than those who eschew all such pleasures. Their obvious advantages over both the hedonist and the ascetic is that their wants are tempered to their ability to satisfy them. Moreover, they do not find themselves in the condition of permanent tantalization which Schopenhauer believed to be our natural lot.

At least this is a way I can imagine we might talk to our children about "adult pleasures" with honesty and helpfulness.

7. Conclusion

I want to conclude by first trying to express as forcefully as I can what I take to be a synthesis of all the anti-gambling views we have considered from all philosophical standpoints and then to say some things which seem to me to be relevant to a defence of gambling against these charges.

The worst that can be said about the sort of gambling which is typified by repetitively inserting money into gambling machines is that as a way of spending time and money it is mindless, anti-social, boring, dehumanizing, vulgar, ugly, degrading, depraving, cretinising, soul-destroying, feckless and stupid.

Against this need to be set a number of considerations which relate to why people actually engage in this activity and what the actual effect on their character may be supposed to be.

In the first place people who spend money on gambling are buying three distinct kinds of product. The first is the pleasure of play. People play slot machines and table games pretty much as they play pinball machines or games of patience. Precisely because it is not intellectually or physically taxing, some people find this an especially relaxing form of amusement. It is hard to make a serious moral case against indulging in the pleasures of playing games for recreation or entertainment. Secondly, people who gamble on machines which offer large jackpots, who buy lottery tickets or do the pools are really buying (through theft losses) fuel for their fantasies of getting suddenly and fabulously rich beyond the dreams of avarice. In itself this puts gambling in the same morally trivial category as other forms of innocuous escapism such as watching soap operas or reading sex-and-shopping novels. From one point of view, indeed, buying a lottery ticket may not only be a harmless form of escapism but also a rational investment. For the poor who have no other prospect of ever becoming really rich no matter how hard they work, it is better to have a very remote chance of attaining great wealth than no chance at all. Thirdly, people pay for the ancillary pleasures they associate with gambling—the conviviality of the bingo hall or the betting shop, the glamour of the casino or the racetrack, and in all cases the defence against loneliness. This seems to be not just harmless but positively benign.

We should perhaps also consider the view that gambling may actually be good for the character. Perhaps gambling accustoms us to sit more loosely than we otherwise would towards money and material possessions and this may be morally desirable. Perhaps, too, gambling inculcates the virtues of courage, equanimity, and graciousness in adversity and good fortune alike. . . .

In some ways it would be nice to conclude with the suggestion that not only is gambling generally good for the moral character but that gambling for very high stakes is particularly likely to develop moral heroism. The truth of the matter, however, is almost certainly much duller. This is that for the vast majority of people who engage in it gambling has no significant impact on their moral character at all. Moreover, when it appears to, it is more likely to be an expression of character traits which for better or worse are already established rather than being the cause of the emergence of new vices or virtues which otherwise would not have developed.

If this is so, then it looks as if the truth about gambling is that, despite all the passion which continues to inform the attacks of opponents of gambling, it is in fact for the most part a morally trivial issue. What is of course not morally trivial is that no one ought to devote too much of their time, their talents, their energies and their resources to activities which are morally trivial, and that includes gambling.

Notes

1. Amongst the articles which have addressed recently this issue, the following deserve mention: Barrett, Will: "Gambling and Public Policy" *Public Affairs Quarterly.* Vol. 14. No 1, January 2000; Lorenz, Valerie C: "Gambling" in *Encyclopaedia of Applied Ethics.* San Diego Academic Press. 1998; Newton, Lisa: "Gambling, A Preliminary Inquiry." *Business Ethics Quarterly.* Vol. 3. Issue 4. 1993. Murphy, Jeffrie. "Indian Casinos and the Morality of Gambling." *Public Affairs Quarterly,* Vol. 12. Jan 1998. Versions of all the anti-gambling arguments discussed here can also be found in a form which repays philosophical analysis in MacKenzie, W. Douglas: *The Ethics of Gambling.* (4th Edition). The Sunday School Union. London 1899.

2. J.S. Mill: *On Liberty.* (1859) Everyman's Library Edition Edited by H.B. Acton. 1910. New Edition 1972. pp. 162–3.

3. Ibid., p. 165.

4. Ibid.

POSTSCRIPT

Is Gambling Immoral?

Gambling is an unusual issue in this respect: Whereas many social issues have both proponents and opponents, gambling seems to have opponents but no real proponents. (Even libertarians and other who support the right to do with one's money as one pleases, as long as it doesn't infringe on anyone else's rights, do not argue that one of the good things about their view is that we will be free to gamble. Freedom to gamble may well be a result, or implication, of that view. But they do not taut it as one of things that makes their viewpoint appealing.) They too might agree with Collins that gambling itself is "morally trivial"—it's just another way of disposing of one's money. Almost no one thinks that gambling is a positively good thing. Thus, for example, we generally do not find gambling clubs alongside sports clubs, coin-collecting clubs, cycling clubs, photography clubs, etc. In fact, the only gambling group one is likely to find is something like Gamblers Anonymous.

In this way, gambling is somewhat like drinking alcohol. Some people say drinking is wrong—in fact, whole religions forbid it, and at one time the U.S. Constitution did so too. But many people regard it as "morally trivial." In both cases, of course, some individuals become "over-involved" and indulge in problematic compulsive behavior (or addiction), as evidenced by the very existence of such groups as Alcoholics Anonymous and Gamblers Anonymous. But these are dismissed as "not the usual case."

We generally apply the language of *rights* to behavior. And we find that individuals are within their rights when they engage in gambling. But the focus of such "rights-talk" is on the individual and the isolated act. What some people find problematic in gambling is not that rights are violated, or even that there is some problem about an isolated act, but that the individual who regularly gambles is irresponsible. So in some ways, Peter Collins is correct that gambling (on a one-time basis) is morally trivial. So is daydreaming (on a one-time basis). But a person who habitually gambles (or habitually daydreams) is not a responsible human being. Yet we can't press the analogy between gambling and daydreaming too far—after all, there are no compulsive daydreamers.

The views of Peter Collins are further elaborated in his book, *Gambling and the Public Interest* (Praeger, 2003). For a detailed history of gambling, see David G. Schwartz, *Roll the Bones: The History of Gambling* (Gotham, 2006). For an interesting account of gambling, written by a man who is both a gambler himself and a therapist who works with compulsive gamblers, see Neil Isaacs, *You Bet Your Life: The Burdens of Gambling* (University Press of Kentucky, 2001). See also Mike W. Martin, *From Morality to Mental Health: Virtue and Vice in a Therapeutic Culture* (Oxford University Press, 2006).

ISSUE 12

Is Affirmative Action Fair?

YES: Albert G. Mosley, from "Affirmative Action: Pro," in Albert G. Mosley and Nicholas Capaldi, eds., *Affirmative Action: Social Justice or Unfair Preference?* (Rowman & Littlefield, 1996)

NO: Louis P. Pojman, from "The Case Against Affirmative Action," *International Journal of Applied Philosophy* (Spring 1998)

ISSUE SUMMARY

YES: Professor of philosophy Albert G. Mosley argues that affirmative action is a continuation of the history of black progress since the *Brown v. Board of Education* desegregation decision of 1954 and the Civil Rights Act of 1964. He defends affirmative action as a "benign use of race."

NO: Professor of philosophy Louis P. Pojman contends that affirmative action violates the moral principle that maintains that each person is to be treated as an individual, not as representative of a group. He stresses that individual merit needs to be appreciated and that respect should be given to each person on an individual basis.

Throughout history, women and minority groups have been discriminated against in the United States. However, it might be difficult for many of us today to appreciate the extent of past discrimination and the ways in which social, legal, and political institutions were discriminatory.

Slavery is probably the most blatant form of past racism. We know that people were bought and sold, but the words are so familiar that the realities they stand for may never rise to consciousness. Many particular events and experiences lie behind a simple word like *slavery*. For example, the importation of slaves to this country was illegal before slaveholding itself became so. When ships at sea bringing African slaves to America found themselves in danger of being confronted by the law, it was easy to do what smugglers on the high seas always do with their contraband: the blacks, chained together and weighted down, were dropped overboard. Even after the Civil War, blacks were denied the right to vote, to testify in court, to own land, or to make contracts. In many states, laws restricted blacks in every conceivable aspect of their lives, including education, employment, and housing.

221

With respect to discrimination against women, consider the following, written by U.S. Supreme Court justice Joseph Bradley in concurring with the Court's decision in *Bradwell v. Illinois* (1873) that the state of Illinois was justified in denying Myra Bradwell a license to practice law on the grounds that she was a woman:

> [T]he civil law, as well as nature herself, has always recognized a wide difference in the respective spheres and destinies of man and woman. Man is, or should be, woman's protector and defender. The natural and proper timidity and delicacy which belongs to the female sex evidently unfits it for many of the occupations of civil life. The constitution of the family organization, which is founded in the divine ordinance, as well as in the nature of things, indicates the domestic sphere as that which properly belongs to the domain and functions of womanhood. The harmony . . . of interests and views which belong . . . to the family institution is repugnant to the idea of a woman adopting a distinct and independent career from that of her husband. . . . The paramount destiny and mission of woman are to fulfill the noble and benign offices of wife and mother.

Such thoughts are rarely openly expressed these days, and segregation and discrimination do not have legal support. One wonders, though, how much attitudes have actually changed. The law can change, but old attitudes can persist, and they can even be preserved and passed down from generation to generation. Moreover, the results of past social injustices are with us today.

Some of the consequences of past discrimination are systemic rather than individual-based. However much *individuals* might reject certain attitudes and practices of the past, there will usually be some *systemic* problems that are not so easily eliminated. There are systemic consequences of racist and sexist practices in the professions, in housing, in education, in the distribution of wealth, etc. For example, even if previously "white only" schools take down their "white only" signs, and the individuals involved agree to accept applicants of any race, the school system itself would be left virtually unchanged from its segregationist days. The situation of white-only schools would systematically perpetuate itself. This is where many feel that affirmative action can step in and change the system.

Albert G. Mosley places controversies surrounding affirmative action in a historical context and considers the justification of affirmative action both from the "backward-looking" perspective of corrective justice and from the "forward-looking" perspective of the social distribution of harms and benefits. Louis P. Pojman explains what he means by the term *affirmative action*. He maintains that affirmative action requires us to practice *reverse discrimination*, to fail to treat people as individuals, and to undervalue merit.

YES

Albert G. Mosley

Affirmative Action: Pro

Legislative and Judicial Background

In 1941, Franklin Roosevelt issued Executive Order 8802 banning discrimination in employment by the federal government and defense contractors. Subsequently, many bills were introduced in Congress mandating equal employment opportunity but none were passed until the Civil Rights Act of 1964. The penalty for discrimination in Executive Order 8802 and the bills subsequently proposed was that the specific victim of discrimination be "made whole," that is, put in the position he or she would have held were it not for the discriminatory act, including damages for lost pay and legal expenses.

The contemporary debate concerning affirmative action can be traced to the landmark decision of *Brown v. Board of Education* (1954), whereby local, state, and federal ordinances enforcing segregation by race were ruled unconstitutional. In subsequent opinions, the Court ruled that state-mandated segregation in libraries, swimming pools, and other publicly funded facilities was also unconstitutional. In *Swann v. Charlotte-Mecklenburg* (1971), the Court declared that "in order to prepare students to live in a pluralistic society" school authorities might implement their desegregation order by deciding that "each school should have a prescribed ratio of Negro to White students reflecting the proportion for the district as a whole."[1] The ratio was not to be an inflexible one, but should reflect local variations in the ratio of Whites to Blacks. But any predominantly one-race school in a district with a mixed population and a history of segregation was subject to "close scrutiny." This requirement was attacked by conservatives as imposing a "racial quota," a charge that reverberates in the contemporary debate concerning affirmative action.

With the Montgomery bus boycotts of the mid-1950s, Blacks initiated an era of nonviolent direct action to publicly protest unjust laws and practices that supported racial discrimination. The graphic portrayals of repression and violence produced by the civil rights movement precipitated a national revulsion against the unequal treatment of African Americans. Blacks demanded their constitutional right to participate in the political process and share equal access to public accommodations, government-supported programs, and employment opportunities. But as John F. Kennedy stated in an address to Congress: "There is little value in a Negro's obtaining the right to be admitted to hotels and restaurants if he has no cash in his pocket and no job."[2]

Kennedy stressed that the issue was not merely eliminating discrimination, but eliminating as well the oppressive economic and social burdens imposed on Blacks by racial discrimination.[3] To this end, he advocated a weak form of affirmative action, involving eliminating discrimination and expanding educational and employment opportunities (including apprenticeships and on-the-job training). The liberal vision was that, given such opportunities, Blacks would move up the economic ladder to a degree relative o their own merit. Thus, a principal aim of the Civil Rights Act of 1964 was to effect a redistribution of social, political, and economic benefits and to provide legal remedies for the denial of individual rights.

The Civil Rights Act of 1964

The first use of the phrase "affirmative action" is found in Executive Order 10952, issued by President John F. Kennedy in 1961. This order established the Equal Employment Opportunity Commission (EEOC) and directed that contractors on projects funded, in whole or in part, with federal funds "take affirmative action to ensure that applicants are employed, and employees are treated during their employment, without regard to the race, creed, color, or national origin."

As a result of continuing public outrage at the level of violence and animosity shown toward Blacks, a stronger version of the Civil Rights Bill was presented to the Congress than Kennedy had originally recommended. Advocates pointed out that Blacks suffered an unemployment rate that was twice that of Whites and that Black employment was concentrated in semiskilled and unskilled jobs. They emphasized that national prosperity would be improved by eliminating discrimination and integrating Black talent into its skilled and professional workforce.[4]

Fewer Blacks were employed in professional positions than had the requisite skills, and those Blacks who did occupy positions commensurate with their skill level had half the lifetime earnings of Whites. Such facts were introduced during legislative hearings to show the need to more fully utilize and reward qualified Blacks throughout the labor force, and not merely in the unskilled and semiskilled sectors. . . .

Conceptual Issues

There are many interests that governments pursue—maximization of social production; equitable distribution of rights, opportunities, and services; social safety and cohesion; restitution—and those interests may conflict in various situations. In particular, governments as well as their constituents have a prima facie obligation to satisfy the liabilities they incur. One such liability derives from past and present unjust exclusionary acts depriving minorities and women of opportunities and amenities made available to other groups.

"*Backward looking*" arguments defend affirmative action as a matter of *corrective justice*, where paradigmatically the harmdoer is to make restitution to the harmed so as to put the harmed in the position the harmed most likely would have occupied had the harm not occurred. An important part of making restitution is the acknowledgment it provides that the actions causing injury were unjust and such actions will be curtailed and corrected. In this regard Bernard Boxill writes:

> Without the acknowledgement of error, the injurer implies that the injured has been treated in a manner that befits him. . . . In such a case, even if the unjust party repairs the damage he has caused . . . nothing can be demanded on legal or moral grounds, and the repairs made are gratuitous. . . . justice requires that we acknowledge that this treatment of others can be required of us; thus, where an unjust injury has occurred, the injurer reaffirms his belief in the other's equality by conceding that repair can be demanded of him, and the injured rejects the allegation of his inferiority . . . by demanding reparation.[5]

This view is based on the idea that restitution is a basic moral principle that creates obligations that are just as strong as the obligations to maximize wealth and distribute it fairly.[6] If x has deprived y of opportunities y had a right not to be deprived of in this manner, then x is obligated to return y to the position y would have occupied had x not intervened; x has this obligation irrespective of other obligations x may have. . . .

|An| application of this principle involves the case where x is not a person but an entity, like a government or a business. If y was unjustly deprived of employment when firm F hired z instead of y because z was White and y Black, then y has a right to be made whole, that is, brought to the position he/she would have achieved had that deprivation not occurred. Typically, this involves giving y a position at least as good as the one he/she would have acquired originally and issuing back pay in the amount that y would have received had he/she been hired at the time of the initial attempt.

Most critics of preferential treatment acknowledge the applicability of principles of restitution to individuals in specific instances of discrimination. The strongest case is where y was as or more qualified than z in the initial competition, but the position was given to z because y was Black and z was White.[7] Subsequently, y may not be as qualified for an equivalent position as some new candidate z', but is given preference because of the past act of discrimination by F that deprived y of the position he or she otherwise would have received.

Some critics have suggested that, in such cases, z' is being treated unfairly. For z', as the most qualified applicant, has a right not to be excluded from the position in question purely on the basis of race; and y has a right to restitution for having unjustly been denied the position in the past. But the dilemma is one in appearance only. For having unjustly excluded y in the past, the current position that z' has applied for is not one that F is free to offer to the public. It is a position that is already owed to y, and is not available for open competition. Judith Jarvis Thomson makes a similar point:

> suppose two candidates [A and B] for a civil service job have equally good test scores, but there is only one job available. We could decide between

them by coin-tossing. But in fact we do allow for declaring for A straightway, where A is a veteran, and B is not. It may be that B is a non-veteran through no fault of his own . . . Yet the fact is that B is not a veteran and A is. On the assumption that the veteran has served his country, the country owes him something. And it is plain that giving him preference is not an unjust way in which part of that debt of gratitude can be paid.[8]

In a similar way, individual Blacks who have suffered from acts of unjust discrimination are owed something by the perpetrator(s) of such acts, and this debt takes precedence over the perpetrator's right to use his or her options to hire the most qualified person for the position in question.

Many White males have developed expectations about the likelihood of their being selected for educational, employment, and entrepreneurial opportunities that are realistic only because of the general exclusion of women and non-Whites as competitors for such positions. Individuals enjoying inflated odds of obtaining such opportunities because of racist and sexist practices are recipients of an "unjust enrichment."

Redistributing opportunities would clearly curtail benefits that many have come to expect. And given the frustration of their traditional expectations, it is understandable that they would feel resentment. But blocking traditional expectations is not unjust if those expectations conflict with the equally important moral duties of restitution and just distribution. It is a question, not of "is," but of "ought": not "Do those with decreased opportunities as a result of affirmative action feel resentment?" but "Should those with decreased opportunities as a result of affirmative action feel resentment?". . .

Since Title VII [of the Civil Rights Act of 1964] protects bona fide seniority plans, it forces the burden of rectification to be borne by Whites who are entering the labor force rather than Whites who are the direct beneficiaries of past discriminatory practices. Given this limitation placed on affirmative action remedies, the burden of social restitution may, in many cases, be borne by those who were not directly involved in past discriminatory practices. But it is generally not true that those burdened have not benefited at all from past discriminatory practices. For the latent effects of acts of invidious racial discrimination have plausibly bolstered and encouraged the efforts of Whites in roughly the same proportion as it inhibited and discouraged the efforts of Blacks. Such considerations are also applicable to cases where F discriminated against y in favor of z, but the make-whole remedy involves providing compensation to y′ rather than y. This suggests that y′ is an *undeserving beneficiary* of the preferential treatment meant to compensate for the unjust discrimination against y, just as z′ above appeared to be the innocent victim forced to bear the burden that z benefited from. Many critics have argued that this misappropriation of benefits and burdens demonstrates the unfairness of compensation to groups rather than individuals. But it is important that the context and rationale for such remedies be appreciated.

In cases of "egregious" racial discrimination, not only is it true that F discriminated against a particular Black person y, but F's discrimination advertised a general disposition to discriminate against any other Black person who might seek such positions. The specific effect of F's unjust discrimination was that y was refused a position he or she would otherwise have received. The latent (or dispositional) effect of F's unjust discrimination was that many Blacks who otherwise would have sought such positions were discouraged from doing so. Thus, even if the specific y actually discriminated against can no longer be compensated, F has an obligation to take affirmative action to communicate to Blacks as a group that such positions are indeed open to them. After being found in violation of laws prohibiting racial discrimination, many agencies have disclaimed further discrimination while in fact continuing to do so.[9] In such cases, the courts have required the discriminating agencies to actually hire and/or promote Blacks who may not be as qualified as some current White applicants until Blacks approach the proportion in F's labor force they in all likelihood would have achieved had F's unjust discriminatory acts not deterred them.

Of course, what this proportion would have been is a matter of speculation. It may have been less than the proportion of Blacks available in the relevant labor pool from which applicants are drawn if factors other than racial discrimination act to depress the merit of such applicants. This point is made again and again by critics. Some, such as Thomas Sowell, argue that cultural factors often mitigate against Blacks meriting representation in a particular labor force in proportion to their presence in the pool of candidates looking for jobs or seeking promotions.[10] Others, such as Michael Levin, argue that cognitive deficits limit Blacks from being hired and promoted at a rate proportionate to their presence in the relevant labor pool.[11] What such critics reject is the assumption that, were it not for pervasive discrimination and overexploitation, Blacks would be equally represented in the positions in question. What is scarcely considered is the possibility that, were it not for racist exclusions, Blacks might be over rather than under represented in competitive positions.

Establishing Blacks' presence at a level commensurate with their proportion in the relevant labor market need not be seen as an attempt to actualize some valid prediction. Rather, given the impossibility of determining what level of representation Blacks would have achieved were it not for racist discrimination, the assumption of proportional representation is the only *fair* assumption to make. This is not to argue that Blacks should be maintained in such positions, but their contrived exclusion merits an equally contrived rectification.[12]

Racist acts excluding Blacks affected particular individuals, but were directed at affecting the behavior of the group of all those similar to the victim. Likewise, the benefits of affirmative action policies should not be conceived as limited in their effects to the specific individuals receiving them. Rather, those benefits should be conceived as extending to all those identified with the recipient, sending the message that opportunities are indeed available to qualified Black candidates who would have been excluded in the past. . . .

Forward-Looking Justifications of Affirmative Action

. . . [Some] have defended preferential treatment but denied that it should be viewed as a form of reparation. This latter group rejects "backward looking" justifications of affirmative action and defends it instead on "forward-looking" grounds that include distributive justice, minimizing subordination, and maximizing social utility.

Thus, Ronald Fiscus argues that backward-looking arguments have distorted the proper justification for affirmative action policies.[13] Backward-looking arguments depend on the paradigm of traditional tort cases, where a specific individual x has deprived another individual y of a specific good t through an identifiable act a, and x is required to restore y to the position y would have had, had a not occurred. But typically, preferential treatment requires that x′ (rather than x) restore y′ (instead of y) with a good t′ that y′ supposedly would have achieved had y not been deprived of t by x. The displacement of perpetrator (x′ for x) and victim (y′ for y) gives rise to the problem of (1) White males who are innocent of acts having caused harm nonetheless being forced to provide restitution for such acts; and (2) Blacks who were not directly harmed by those acts nonetheless becoming the principal beneficiaries of restitution for those acts. . . .

Fiscus argues that the backward-looking argument reinforces the perception that preferential treatment is unfair to innocent White males, and so long as this is the case, both the courts and the public are likely to oppose strong affirmative action policies such as quotas, set-asides, and other preferential treatment policies.

In contrast, Fiscus recommends that preferential treatment be justified in terms of distributive justice, which as a matter of equal protection, "requires that individuals be awarded the positions, advantages, or benefits they would have been awarded under fair conditions," that is, conditions under which racist exclusion would not have precluded Blacks from attaining "their deserved proportion of the society's important benefits." Conversely, "distributive justice also holds that individuals or groups may not claim positions, advantages, or benefits that they would not have been awarded under fair conditions."[14] These conditions jointly prohibit White males from claiming an unreasonable share of social benefits and protects White males from having to bear an unreasonable share of the redistributive burden.

Fiscus takes the position that any deviation between Blacks and Whites from strict proportionality in the distribution of current goods is evidence of racism. Thus, if Blacks were 20 percent of a particular population but held no positions in the police or fire departments, that is indicative of past and present racial discrimination. . . .

Because the Equal Protection Clause of the Fourteenth Amendment protects citizens from statistical discrimination on the basis of race, the use of race as the principal reason for excluding certain citizens from benefits made available to other citizens is a violation of that person's constitutional rights. This was one basis for [Alan] Bakke's suit against the UC-Davis medical school's 16 percent minority set-aside for medical school admission. There were eighty-four seats out of the one hundred admission slots that he was eligible to fill, and he was excluded from competing for the other sixteen slots because of his race. On the basis of the standard criteria (GPA, MCAT scores, etc.), Bakke argued that he would have been admitted before any of the Black applicants admitted under the minority set-aside. He therefore claimed that he was being excluded from the additional places available because he was White.

Currently, Blacks have approximately 3.25 times fewer physicians than would be expected given their numbers in the population. Native Americans have 7 times fewer physicians than what would have been expected if intelligent, well-trained, and motivated Native Americans had tried to become physicians at the same rate as did European Americans.

For Fiscus, the underrepresentation of African and Native Americans among physicians and the maldistribution of medical resources to minority communities is clearly the effect of generations of racist exclusions. . . . Not only are qualified members of the oppressed group harmed by . . . prejudice, but even more harmed are the many who would have been qualified but for injuries induced by racial prejudice.

For Fiscus, individuals of different races would have been as equally distributed in the social body as the molecules of a gas in a container and he identifies the belief in the inherent equality of races with the Equal Protection Clause of the Fourteenth Amendment.[15] In a world without racism, minorities would be represented among the top one hundred medical school applicants at UC-Davis in the same proportion as they were in the general population. Accordingly, because Bakke did not score among the top eighty-four Whites, he would not have qualified for admission. Thus, he had no right to the position he was contesting, and indeed if he were given such a position in lieu of awarding it to a minority, Bakke would be much like a person who had received stolen goods. "Individuals who have not personally harmed minorities may nevertheless be prevented from reaping the benefits of the harm inflicted by the society at large."[16]

Justice O'Connor has voiced skepticism toward the assumption that members of different races would "gravitate with mathematical exactitude to each employer or union absent unlawful discrimination."[17] She considers it sheer speculation as to "how many minority students would have been admitted to the medical school at Davis absent past discrimination in educational opportunities."[18] I likewise consider it speculative to assume that races would be represented in every area in proportion to their proportion of the general population. But because it is impossible to reasonably predict what that distribution would have been absent racial discrimination, it is not mere speculation but morally fair practice to assume that it would have been the same as the proportion in the general population. Given the fact of legally sanctioned invidious racism against Blacks in U.S. history, the burden of proof should not be on the oppressed group to prove that it would be represented at a level proportionate to its presence in the general population. Rather, the burden of proof should be on the majority to show why its overrepresentation among the most well off is not the result of unfair competition imposed by racism. We are morally obligated to assume proportional representation until there are more plausible reasons than racism for assuming otherwise. . . .

Thus, it should be the responsibility of the Alabama Department of Public Safety to show why no Blacks were members of its highway patrol as of 1970, even though Blacks were 25 percent of the relevant workforce in Alabama. It should be the responsibility of the company and the union to explain why there were no Blacks with seniority in the union at the Kaiser plant in Louisiana, although Blacks made up 39 percent of the surrounding population. Likewise, it should be the responsibility of the union to explain why no Blacks had been admitted to the Sheet Metal Workers' Union in New York City although minorities were 29 percent of the available workforce. If no alternative explanations are more plausible, then the assumption that the disparity in representation is the result of racism should stand.

The question should not be whether White males are innocent or guilty of racism or sexism, but whether they have a right to inflated odds of obtaining benefits relative to minorities and women. A White male is innocent only up to the point where he takes advantage of "a benefit he would not qualify for without the accumulated effects of racism. At that point he becomes an accomplice in, and a beneficiary of, society's racism. He becomes the recipient of stolen goods."[19]. . .

Cass Sunstein also argues that the traditional compensation model based on the model of a discrete injury caused by one individual (the tort-feasor or defendant) and suffered by another individual (the plaintiff) is inadequate to capture the situation arising from racial and sexual discrimination.[20] With the traditional tortlike model, the situation existing prior to the injury is assumed to be noncontestable, and the purpose of restitution is to restore the injured party to the position that party would have occupied if the injury had not occurred. But in cases where the injury is not well defined, where neither defendant nor plaintiff are individuals connected by a discrete event, and where the position the injured party would have occupied but for the injury is unspecifiable, then in such cases dependence on the traditional model of compensatory justice is questionable.[21]

In contrast to the position taken by Fiscus, Sunstein argues that the claim that affirmative action and preferential treatment is meant to put individuals in the position they would have occupied had their groups not been subject to racial and sexual discrimination is nonsensical: "What would the world look like if it had been unaffected by past discrimination on the basis of race and sex? . . . the question is unanswerable, not because of the absence of good social science, but because of the obscure epistemological status of the question itself."[22]

Affirmative action must be justified in terms of alternative conceptions of the purpose of legal intervention, and Sunstein recommends instead the notion of "risk management" (intended to offset increased risks faced by a group rather than compensate the injuries suffered by a particular individual) and the "principle of nonsubordination" (whereby measures are taken to reverse a situation in which an irrelevant difference has been transformed by legally sanctioned acts of the state into a social disadvantage). The notion of risk management is meant to apply to cases where injuries are "individually small but collectively large" so that pursuing each case individually would be too costly both in terms of time and effort.[23] In such cases, those harmed may be unable to establish a direct causal link between their injuries and the plaintiff's actions. Thus, a person who develops a certain type of cancer associated with a toxin produced by a particular company might have developed that condition even in the absence of the company's negligent behavior. At most, they can argue that the company's actions caused an increased risk of injury, rather than any specific instance of that injury.

Harms suffered in this way systematically affect certain groups with higher frequency than other groups, without it being possible to establish causal links between the injuries of specific plaintiffs and the actions of the defendant. Regulatory agencies should be designed to address harms that are the result of increased risks rather than of a discrete action.[24] One of their principle aims should be not to compensate each injured party (and only injured parties), "but instead to deter and punish the risk-creating behavior" by redistributing social goods.[25] . . .

The principle of nonsubordination is meant to apply to cases where the existing distribution of wealth and opportunities between groups are the result of law rather than natural attributes.[26] The purpose of affirmative action from a forward-looking perspective should be to end social subordination and reverse the situation in which irrelevant differences have been, through social and legal structures, turned into systematic disadvantages operative in multiple spheres that diminish participation in democratic forms of life.[27] . . .

> affirmative action does not appear an impermissible 'taking' of an antecedent entitlement. Because the existing distribution of benefits and burdens between Blacks and Whites and men and women is not natural . . . and because it is in part a product of current laws and practices having discriminatory effects, it is not decisive if some Whites and men are disadvantaged as a result.[28]

A central question in the debate over affirmative action is the extent to which racial classifications are important in accomplishing the goal of relieving the subordinate status of minorities and women. Given the aim of improving safety in transportation, classifying people in terms of their race is rationally irrelevant, while classifying them in terms of their driving competency, visual acuity, and maturity is essential. On the other hand, given the aim of improving health care in Black neighborhoods, classifying applicants for medical school in terms of their race is, in addition to their academic and clinical abilities, a very relevant factor.

To illustrate, African Americans, Hispanics, and Native Americans make up 22 percent of the population but represent only 10 percent of entering medical students and 7 percent of practicing physicians. A number of studies have shown that underrepresented minority physicians are more likely than their majority counterparts to care for poor patients and patients of similar ethnicity. Indeed, "each ethnic group of patients was more likely to be cared for by a physician of their own ethnic background than by a physician of another ethnic background."[29] This suggests that sociocultural factors such as language, physical identity, personal background, and experiences are relevant factors in determining the kinds of communities in which a physician will establish a practice. If this is the case, then the race of a medical school applicant would be an important factor in providing medical services to certain underrepresented communities. Thus, while there might be some purposes for which race is irrelevant, there might be other purposes in which race is important (though perhaps not necessary) for achieving the end in view.[30] The remedy targets Blacks as a group because racially discriminatory practices were directed against Blacks as a group.[31]

. . . Preferential treatment programs are meant to offset the disadvantages imposed by racism so that Blacks are not forced to bear the principal costs of that error.

. . . To condemn polices meant to correct for racial barriers as themselves erecting barriers is to ignore the difference between action and reaction, cause and effect, aggression and self-defense. . . .

Conclusion

Racism was directed against Blacks whether they were talented, average, or mediocre, and attenuating the effects of racism requires distributing remedies similarly. Affirmative action policies compensate for the harms of racism (overt and institutional) through antidiscrimination laws and preferential policies. Prohibiting the benign use of race as a factor in the award of educational, employment and business opportunities would eliminate compensation for past and present racism and reinforce the moral validity of the status quo, with Blacks overrepresented among the least well off and underrepresented among the most well off.

It has become popular to use affirmative action as a scapegoat for the increased vulnerability of the White working class. But it should be recognized that the civil rights revolution (in general) and affirmative action (in particular) has been beneficial, not just to Blacks, but also to Whites (e.g., women, the disabled, the elderly) who otherwise would be substantially more vulnerable than they are now.

Affirmative action is directed toward empowering those groups that have been adversely affected by past and present exclusionary practices. Initiatives to abolish preferential treatment would inflict a grave injustice on African Americans, for they signal a reluctance to acknowledge that the plight of African Americans is the result of institutional practices that require institutional responses.

Notes

1. Kent Greenawalt, *Discrimination and Reverse Discrimination* (New York: Alfred A. Knopf, 1983), 129 ff.
2. Kathanne W. Greene, *Affirmative Action and Principles of Justice* (New York: Greenwood Press, 1989), 22.
3. Kennedy stated: "Even the complete elimination of racial discrimination in employment—a goal toward which this nation must strive—will not put a single unemployed Negro to work unless he has the skills required." Greene, *Affirmative Action*, 23.
4. Greene, *Affirmative Action*, 31.
5. Bernard Boxill, "The Morality of Reparation" in *Social Theory and Practice*, 2, no. 1, Spring 1972: 118–119. It is for such reasons that welfare programs are

not sufficient to satisfy the claims of Blacks for restitution. Welfare programs contain no admission of the unjust violation of rights and seek merely to provide the basic means for all to pursue opportunities in the future.

6. I am presuming that most of us would recognize certain primae facie duties such as truth telling, promise keeping, restitution, benevolence, justice, non-malficience as generally obligatory. See W. D. Ross, *The Right and the Good* (Oxford: Clarendon Press, 1930).

7. Even in the case where y was only as qualified as z, a fair method of choice between candidates should produce an equitable distribution of such positions between Blacks and Whites in the long run if not in the short.

8. Judith Jarvis Thompson, *Philosophy and Public Affairs* 2 (Summer 1973): 379–380.

9. *Sheet Metal Workers v. EEOC* (1986); *United States v. Paradise* (1987).

10. Thomas Sowell, *Ethnic America* (New York: Basic Books, 1981); *Preferential Policies: An International Perspective* (New York: William Morrow, 1990); For a recent critique of Sowell's position, see Christopher Jencks, *Rethinking Social Policy: Race, Poverty, and the Underclass* (New York: Harper, 1993) chap. 1.

11. Michael Levin, "Race, Biology, and Justice" in *Public Affairs Quarterly*, 8, no. 3 (July 1994). There are many good reasons for skepticism regarding the validity of using IQ as a measure of cognitive ability. See *The Bell Curve Wars* ed. Steven Fraser (New York: Basic Books, 1995); *The Bell Curve Debate* ed. by Russell Jacoby and Naomi Glauberman (New York: Times Books, 1995); Allan Chase, *The Legacy of Malthus* (Urbana: University of Illinois Press, 1980); Steven J. Gould, *The Mismeasure of Man* (New York: Norton, 1981); R. C. Lewontin, S. Rose, L. J. Kamin, *Not In Our Genes* (New York: Pantheon Books, 1984).

12. See Robert Fullinwider, *The Reverse Discrimination Controversy: A Moral and Legal Analysis* (Totowa, N.J.: Rowman & Littlefield, 1980), 117. Ronald Fiscus, *The Constitutional Logic of Affirmative Action* (Durham, N.C.: Duke University Press, 1992).

13. Ronald J. Fiscus, *The Constitutional Logic of Affirmative Action* (Durham, N.C.: Duke University Press, 1992).

14. Fiscus, *Constitutional Logic*, 13.

15. Fiscus, *Constitutional Logic*, 20–26.

16. Fiscus, *Constitutional Logic*, 38.

17. *Sheet Metal Workers v. EEOC*, 478 US 421, 494 (1986); Fiscus, *Constitutional Logic*, 42.

18. *City of Richmond v. J. A. Croson Co.*, 109 S.Ct. at 724 (1989); Fiscus, *Constitutional Logic*, 42.

19. Fiscus, *Constitutional Logic*, 47. With regard to the problem of so-called "undeserving beneficiaries" of affirmative action Fiscus writes: "When the rightful owner of stolen goods cannot be found, the law . . . may or may not award possession to the original but wrongful claimant; but if it does not, if it awards possession to a third party whose claim is arguable, the original claimant cannot justifiably feel morally harmed. And the government's action cannot be said to be arbitrary unless it awards the goods to an individual whose claim is even less plausible than that of the original claimant." (49).

20. Cass Sunstein, "Limits of Compensatory Justice" in *Nomos* 33, *Compensatory Justice*, ed. John Chapman (New York: New York University Press, 1991), 281–310.

21. "It is not controlling and perhaps not even relevant that the harms that affirmative action attempts to redress cannot be understood in the usual compensatory terms. . . . the nature of the problem guarantees that the legal response cannot take the form of discrete remedies for discrete harms" (Sunstein, "Limits," 297).

22. Sunstein, "Limits," 303.

23. The orientation of the EEOC toward investigating individual cases of alleged discrimination is one explanation of its extraordinary backlog of over 80,000 cases. This orientation precludes it from focusing on systemic practices that affect many individuals, and instead forces it to expend resources dealing with particular instances. See "The EEOC: Pattern and Practice Imperfect" by Maurice Munroe in *Yale Law and Policy Review*, 13, no. 2, (1995): 219–80.

24. Sunstein, "Limits," 292.

25. Sunstein, "Limits," 289.

26. "The current distribution of benefits and burdens as between blacks and whites and women and men is not part of the state of nature but a consequence of past and present social practices" (Sunstein, "Limits," 294).

27. See also Thomas H. Simon, *Democracy and Social Justice* (Lanham, Md.: Rowman & Littlefield, 1995), chap. 5.

28. Sunstein, "Limits," 306.

29. Gang Xu, Sylvia Fields, et al., "The Relationship between the Ethnicity of Generalist Physicians and Their Care for Underserved Populations," Ohio University College of Osteopathic Medicine, Athens, Ohio, 10.

30. Of course, we may ask whether the use of race is necessary for the achievement of the end in view or whether it is one among alternative ways of achieving that end. For instance, it might be possible to induce doctors to practice in Black neighborhoods by providing doctors, irrespective of their race, with suitable monetary incentives. But given the importance of nonmonetary factors in physician-patient relationships, it is doubtful that purely monetary rewards would be sufficient to meet the needs of underserved populations.

31. Remedial action based on the imbalance between blacks in the available work force and their presence in skilled jobs categories presumes that imbalance is caused by racial discrimination. This assumption has been challenged by many who cite cultural and cognitive factors that might equally be the cause of such imbalances. See Thomas Sowell, *Markets and Minorities* (New York: Basic Books, 1981); Richard Herrenstein and Charles Murray, *The Bell Curve* (New York: The Free Press, 1994). This literature has itself been subject to critique: for Sowell, see Christopher Jencks, *Rethinking Social Policy* (New York: Harper, 1993); for Herrenstein and Murray, see *The Bell Curve Wars*, ed. Steven Fraser (New York: Basic Books, 1995).

Louis P. Pojman

The Case Against Affirmative Action

Let us agree that despite the evidences of a booming economy, the poor are suffering grievously, with children being born into desperate material and psychological poverty; for them the ideal of "equal opportunity for all" is a cruel joke. Many feel that the federal government has abandoned its guarantee to provide the minimum necessities for each American, so that the pace of this tragedy seems to be worsening daily. In addition to this, African-Americans have a legacy of slavery and unjust discrimination to contend with, and other minorities have also suffered from injustice. Women have their own peculiar history of being treated unequally in relevant ways. What is the answer to this national problem? Is it increased welfare? More job training? More support for education? Required licensing of parents to have children? Negative income tax? More support for families or for mothers with small children? All of these have merit and should be part of the national debate. But, my thesis is, however tragic the situation may be (and we may disagree on just how tragic it is), one policy is *not* a legitimate part of the solution and that is *reverse, unjust discrimination* against young white males. Strong Affirmative Action, which implicitly advocates reverse discrimination, while no doubt well intentioned, is morally heinous, asserting, by implication, that *two wrongs make a right*.

The *Two Wrongs Make a Right* Thesis goes like this: Because *some* Whites once enslaved some Blacks, the descendants of those slaves (some of whom now may enjoy high incomes and social status) have a right to opportunities and offices over better qualified Whites who had nothing to do with either slavery or the oppression of Blacks (and who may even have suffered hardship comparable to that of poor Blacks). In addition, Strong Affirmative Action creates a new Hierarchy of the Oppressed: Blacks get primary preferential treatment, women second, Native Americans third, Hispanics fourth, Handicapped fifth, and Asians sixth and so on until White males, no matter how needy or well qualified, must accept the leftovers. . . .

Before analyzing arguments concerning Affirmative Action, I must define my terms.

By *Weak Affirmative Action* I mean policies that will increase the opportunities of disadvantaged people to attain social goods and offices. It includes such things as dismantling of segregated institutions, widespread advertisement to groups not previously represented in certain privileged positions,

From *International Journal of Applied Philosophy*, Prentice Hall 2007. Copyright © 1998 by International Journal of Applied Philosophy. Reprinted by permission.

special scholarships for the disadvantaged classes (e.g., the poor, regardless of race or gender), and even using diversity or under-representation of groups with a history of past discrimination as a tie breaker when candidates for these goods and offices are relatively equal. The goal of *Weak Affirmative Action* is equal opportunity to compete, not equal results. We seek to provide each citizen regardless of race or gender a fair chance to the most favored positions in society. . . .

By *Strong Affirmative Action* I mean preferential treatment on the basis of race, ethnicity or gender (or some other morally irrelevant criterion), discriminating in favor of underrepresented groups against overrepresented groups, aiming at roughly equal results. *Strong Affirmative Action* is *reverse discrimination*. It says it is right to do wrong to correct a wrong. This is the policy currently being promoted under the name of *Affirmative Action*, so I will use that term or "AA" for short throughout this essay to stand for this version of affirmative action. I will not argue for or against the principle of *Weak Affirmative Action*. Indeed, I think it has some moral weight. *Strong Affirmative Action* has none, or so I will argue.

This essay concentrates on AA policies with regard to race, but the arguments can be extended to cover ethnicity and gender. I think that if a case for Affirmative Action can be made it will be as a corrective to racial oppression. I will examine eight arguments regarding AA. The first six will be *negative*, attempting to show that the best arguments for Affirmative Action fail. The last [two] will be *positive* arguments for policies opposing Affirmative Action:

A Critique of Arguments for Affirmative Action

The Need for Role Models

This argument is straightforward. We all have need of role models, and it helps to know that others like us can be successful. We learn and are encouraged to strive for excellence by emulating our heroes and "our kind of people" who have succeeded.

In the first place it's not clear that role models of one's own racial or sexual type are necessary (let alone sufficient) for success. One of my heroes was Gandhi, an Indian Hindu, another was my grade school science teacher, Miss DeVoe, and another Martin Luther King, behind whom I marched in Civil Rights demonstrations. More important than having role models of one's "own type" is having genuinely good people, of whatever race or gender, to emulate. Our common humanity should be a sufficient basis for us to see the possibility of success in people of virtue and merit. To yield to the demand, however tempting it may be, for "role-models-just-like-us" is to treat people like means not ends. . . .

The Compensation Argument

The argument goes like this: blacks have been wronged and severely harmed by whites. Therefore white society should compensate blacks for the injury caused them. Reverse discrimination in terms of preferential hiring, contracts, and scholarships is a fitting way to compensate for the past wrongs.[1]

This argument actually involves a distorted notion of compensation. Normally, we think of compensation as owed by a specific person A to another person B whom A has wronged in a specific way C. For Example, if I have stolen your car and used it for a period of time to make business profits that would have gone to you, it is not enough that I return your car. I must pay you an amount reflecting your loss and my ability to pay. If I have made $5,000 and only have $10,000 in assets, it would not be possible for you to collect $20,000 in damages—even though that is the amount of loss you have incurred. . . .

On the face of it, demands by blacks for compensation do not fit the usual pattern. Southern States with Jim Crow laws could be accused of unjustly harming blacks, but it is hard to see that the United States government was involved in doing so. Much of the harm done to blacks was the result of private discrimination, not state action. . . . Furthermore, it is not clear that all blacks were harmed in the same way or whether some were *unjustly* harmed or harmed more than poor whites and others (e.g., short people). Finally, even if identifiable blacks were harmed by identifiable social practices, it is not clear that most forms of Affirmative Action are appropriate to restore the situation. The usual practice of a financial payment seems more appropriate than giving a high level job to someone unqualified or only minimally qualified. . . .

Still, there may be something intuitively compelling about compensating members of an oppressed group who are minimally qualified. Suppose that the Hatfields and the McCoys are enemy clans and some youths from the Hatfields go over and steal diamonds and gold from the McCoys, distributing it within the Hatfield economy. Even though we do not know which Hatfield youths did the stealing, we would want to restore the wealth, as far as possible, to the McCoys. One way might be to tax the Hatfields, but another might be to give preferential treatment in terms of scholarships and training programs and hiring to the McCoys.

This is perhaps the strongest argument for Affirmative Action, and it may well justify some weaker versions of AA, but it is doubtful whether it is sufficient to justify strong versions with quotas and goals and time tables in skilled positions. There are at least two reasons for this. First, we have no way of knowing how many people of any given group would have achieved some given level of competence had the world been different. . . . Secondly, the normal criterion of competence is a strong prima facie consideration when the most important positions are at stake. There are three reasons for this: (1) treating people according to their merits respects them as persons, as ends in themselves, rather than as means to social ends (if we believe that individuals possess a dignity which deserves to be respected, then we ought to treat that individual on the basis of his or her merits, not as a mere instrument for social policy); (2) society has given people expectations that if they attain certain levels of excellence they will be awarded appropriately; and (3) filling the most important positions with the best qualified is the best way to ensure efficiency in job-related areas and in society in general. These reasons are not absolutes.

They can be overridden.[2] But there is a strong presumption in their favor, so that a burden of proof rests with those who would overrride them. . . .

The Argument for Compensation From Those Who Innocently Benefitted From Past Injustice

Young White males as innocent beneficiaries of unjust discrimination against blacks and women have no grounds for complaint when society seeks to level the tilted field. They may be innocent of oppressing blacks, other minorities, and women, but they have unjustly benefitted from that oppression or discrimination. So it is perfectly proper that less qualified women and blacks be hired before them.

The operative principle is: He who knowingly and willingly benefits from a wrong must help pay for the wrong. Judith Jarvis Thomson puts it this way. "Many [white males] have been direct beneficiaries of policies which have downgraded blacks and women . . . and even those who did not directly benefit . . . had, at any rate, the advantage in the competition which comes of the confidence in one's full membership [in the community] and of one's right being recognized as a matter of course."[3] That is, white males obtain advantages in self respect and self-confidence deriving from a racist/sexist system which denies these to blacks and women.

Here is my response to this argument: As I noted in the previous section, compensation is normally individual and specific. If A harms B regarding x, B has a right to compensation from A in regards to x. If A steals B's car and wrecks it, A has an obligation to compensate B for the stolen car, but A's son has no obligation to compensate B. Furthermore, if A dies or disappears, B has no moral right to claim that society compensate him for the stolen car—though if he has insurance, he can make such a claim to the insurance company. Sometimes a wrong cannot be compensated, and we just have to make the best of an imperfect world. . . .

The Diversity Argument

It is important that we learn to live in a pluralistic world, learning to get along with those of other races, conditions, and cultures, so we should have schools and employment situations as fully integrated as possible. . . . Diversity is an important symbol and educative device. Thus, proponents of AA argue, preferential treatment is warranted to perform this role in society.

Once again, there is some truth in these concerns. Diversity of ideas challenges us to scrutinize our own values and beliefs. . . . Diversity may expand our moral horizons. But, again, while we can admit the value of diversity, it hardly seems adequate to override the moral requirement to treat each person with equal respect. *Diversity for diversity's sake is moral promiscuity*, since it obfuscates rational distinctions, undermines treating individuals as ends, treating them, instead as mere means (to the goals of social engineering), and, furthermore, unless those hired are highly qualified, the diversity factor threatens to become a fetish. . . .

There may be times when diversity may seem to be "crucial" to the well-being of a diverse community, such as for a police force. Suppose that White policemen tend to overreact to young Black males and the latter group distrusts White policemen. Hiring more less qualified Black policemen, who would relate better to these youth, may have overall utilitarian value. But such a move, while we might make it as a lesser evil, could have serious consequences in allowing the demographic prejudices to dictate social policy. A better strategy would be to hire the best police, that is, those who can perform in [a] disciplined, intelligent manner, regardless of their race. A White policeman must be able to arrest a Black burglar, even as a Black policeman must be able to arrest a White rapist. The quality of the police man or woman, not their race or gender, is what counts.

On the other hand, if a Black policeman, though lacking some of the formal skills of the White policeman, really is able to do a better job in the Black community, this might constitute a case of merit, not Affirmative Action. As Stephen Kershnar points out, this is similar to the legitimacy of hiring Chinese men to act as undercover agents in Chinatown.[4]

The Equal Results Argument

Some philosophers and social scientists hold that human nature is roughly identical, so that on a fair playing field the same proportion from every race and ethnic group and both genders would attain to the highest positions in every area of endeavor. It would follow that any inequality of results itself is evidence for inequality of opportunity.

> History is important when considering governmental rules like Test 21 because low scores by blacks can be traced in large measure to the legacy of slavery and racism: segregation, poor schooling, exclusion from trade unions, malnutrition, and poverty have all played their roles. Unless one assumes that blacks are naturally less able to pass the test, the conclusion must be that the results are themselves socially and legally constructed, not a mere given for which law and society can claim no responsibility.
>
> The conclusion seems to be that genuine equality eventually requires equal results. Obviously blacks have been treated unequally throughout U.S. history, and just as obviously the economic and psychological effects of that inequality linger to this day, showing up in lower income and poorer performance in school and on tests than whites achieve. Since we have no reason to believe that differences in performance can be explained by factors other than history, equal results are a good benchmark by which to measure progress made toward genuine equality (John Arthur, *The Unfinished Constitution* [Belmont, CA: Wadsworth Publishing Co, 1990], p. 238)

. . . Albert G. Mosley develops a similar argument. "Establishing Blacks' presence at a level commensurate with their proportion in the relevant labor market need not be seen as an attempt to actualize some valid prediction. Rather, given the impossibility of determining what level of representation Blacks would have achieved were it not for racial discrimination, the assumption of proportional representation is the only *fair* assumption to make. This is not to argue that Blacks should be maintained in such positions, but their contrived exclusion merits equally contrived rectification."[5]. . . However, Arthur [and] Mosley . . . fail even to consider studies that suggest that there are innate differences between races, sexes, and groups. If there are genetic differences in intelligence, temperament, and other qualities within families, why should we not expect such differences between racial groups and the two genders? Why should the evidence for this be completely discounted?

Mosley's reasoning is as follows: Since we don't know for certain whether groups proportionately differ in talent, we should presume that they are equal in every respect. So we should presume that if we were living in a just society, there would be roughly proportionate representation in every field (e.g., equal representation of doctors, lawyers, professors, carpenters, airplane pilots, basketball players, and criminals). Hence, it is only fair—productive of justice—to aim at proportionate representation in these fields.

But the logic is flawed. Under a situation of ignorance we should not presume equality or inequality of representation—but conclude that we *don't know* what the results would be in a just society. Ignorance doesn't favor equal group representation any more than it favors unequal group representation. It is neutral between them . . .

The "No One Deserves His Talents" Argument Against Meritocracy

According to this argument, the competent do not deserve their intelligence, their superior character, their industriousness, or their discipline; therefore they have no right to the best positions in society; therefore it is not unjust to give these positions to less (but still minimally) qualified blacks and women. In one form this argument holds that since no one deserves anything, society may use any criteria it pleases to distribute goods. The criterion most often designated is social utility. Versions of this argument are found in the writings of John Arthur, John Rawls, Bernard Boxill, Michael Kinsley, Ronald Dworkin, and Richard Wasserstrom. Rawls writes, "No one deserves his place in the distribution of native endowments, any more than one deserves one's initial starting place in society. The assertion that a man deserves the superior character that enables him to make the effort to cultivate his abilities is equally problematic; for his character depends in large part upon fortunate family and social circumstances for which he can claim no credit. The notion of desert seems not to apply to these cases."[6] Michael Kinsley is even more adamant:

> Opponents of affirmative action are hung up on a distinction that seems more profoundly irrelevant: treating individuals versus treating groups. What is the moral difference between dispensing favors to people on their "merits" as individuals and passing out society's benefits on the basis of group identification?
>
> Group identifications like race and sex are, of course, immutable. They have nothing to do with a person's moral worth. But the same is true of most of what comes under the label "merit." The tools you need for getting ahead in a meritocratic society—not all of them but most: talent,

education, instilled cultural values such as ambition—are distributed just as arbitrarily as skin color. They are fate. The notion that people somehow "deserve" the advantages of these characteristics in a way they don't "deserve" the advantage of their race is powerful, but illogical.[7]

It will help to put the argument in outline form.

1. Society may award jobs and positions as it sees fit as long as individuals have no claim to these positions.
2. To have a claim to something means that one has earned it or deserves it.
3. But no one has earned or deserves his intelligence, talent, education or cultural values which produce superior qualifications.
4. If a person does not deserve what produces something, he does not deserve its products.
5. Therefore better qualified people do not deserve their qualifications.
6. Therefore, society may override their qualifications in awarding jobs and positions as it sees fit (for social utility or to compensate for previous wrongs).

So it is permissible if a minimally qualified black or woman is admitted to law or medical school ahead of a white male with excellent credentials or if a less qualified person from an "underutilized" group gets a professorship ahead of an eminently better qualified white male. Sufficiency and underutilization together outweigh excellence.

My response: Premise 4 is false. To see this, reflect that just because I do not deserve the money that I have been given as a gift (for instance) does not mean that I am not entitled to what I get with that money. If you and I both get a gift of $100 and I bury mine in the sand for 5 years while you invest yours wisely and double its value at the end of five years, I cannot complain that you should split the increase 50/50 since neither of us deserved the original gift. . . .

But there is no good reason to accept the argument against [moral] desert. We do act freely and, as such, we are responsible for our actions. We deserve the fruits of our labor, reward for our noble feats and punishment for our misbehavior.[8]

We have considered six arguments for Affirmative Action and have found no compelling case for Strong AA and only one plausible argument (a version of the compensation argument) for Weak AA. We must now turn to the arguments against Affirmative Action to see whether they fare any better.

Arguments Against Affirmative Action

Affirmative Action Requires Discrimination Against a Different Group

Weak AA weakly discriminates against new minorities, mostly innocent young white males, and Strong Affirmative Action strongly discriminates against these new minorities. . . . [T]his discrimination is unwarranted, since, even if some compensation to blacks were indicated, it would be unfair to make innocent white males bear the whole brunt of the payments. . . . [I]t is poor white youth who become the new pariahs on the job market. The children of the wealthy have little trouble getting into the best private grammar schools and, on the basis of superior early education, into the best universities, graduate schools, managerial and professional positions. Affirmative Action simply shifts injustice, setting Blacks, Hispanics, Native Americans, Asians and women against young white males, especially ethnic and poor white males. It makes no more sense to discriminate in favor of a rich Black or female who had the opportunity of the best family and education available against a poor White, than it does to discriminate in favor of White males against Blacks or women. It does little to rectify the goal of providing equal opportunity to all. . . .

Respect for persons entails that we treat each person as an end in him or herself, not simply as a means to be used for social purposes. What is wrong about discrimination against Blacks is that it fails to treat Black people as individuals, judging them instead by their skin color not their merit. What is wrong about discrimination against women is that it fails to treat them as individuals, judging them by their gender, not their merit. What is equally wrong about *Affirmative Action* is that it fails to treat White males with dignity as individuals, judging them by *both their race and gender*, instead of their merit. *Current Strong Affirmative Action* is both racist and sexist. . . .

An Argument From the Principle of Merit

Traditionally, we have believed that the highest positions in society should be awarded to those who are best qualified. Rewarding excellence both seems just to the individuals in the competition and makes for efficiency. Note that one of the most successful acts of racial integration, the Brooklyn Dodgers's recruitment of Jackie Robinson in the late 40s, was done in just this way, according to merit. If Robinson had been brought into the major league as a mediocre player or had batted .200 he would have been scorned and sent back to the minors where he belonged.

As mentioned earlier, merit is not an absolute value, but there are strong *prima facie* reasons for awarding positions on that basis, and it should enjoy a weighty presumption in our social practices.

. . . We generally want the best to have the best positions. . . . Only when little is at stake do we weaken the standards and content ourselves with sufficiency (rather than excellence)—there are plenty of jobs where "sufficiency" rather than excellence is required. Perhaps we have even come to feel that medicine or law or university professorships are so routine that they can be performed by minimally qualified people—in which case AA has a place.

Note! no one is calling for quotas or proportional representation of *underutilized* groups in the National Basketball Association where blacks make up 80% of the players. But, surely, if merit and merit alone reigns in sports, should it not be valued at least as much in education and industry?

The case for meritocracy has two pillars. One pillar is a deontological argument which holds that we ought to treat people as ends and not merely means.

By giving people what they deserve as *individuals*, rather than as members of *groups*, we show respect for their inherent worth. . . .

The second pillar for meritocracy is utilitarian. In the end, we will be better off by honoring excellence. We want the best leaders, teachers, policemen, physicians, generals, lawyers, and airplane pilots that we can possibly produce in society. So our program should be to promote equal opportunity, as much as is feasible in a free market economy, and reward people according to their individual merit.[9]

Conclusion

Let me sum up my discussion. The goal of the Civil Rights movement and of moral people everywhere has been justice for all, including equal opportunity. The question is: how best to get there. Civil Rights legislation removed the unjust legal barriers, opening the way towards equal opportunity, but it did not tackle the deeper causes that produce differential results. Weak Affirmative Action aims at encouraging minorities to strive for excellence in all areas of life, without unduly jeopardizing the rights of majorities. The problem of Weak Affirmative Action is that it easily slides into Strong Affirmative Action where quotas, "goals and timetables," "equal results"—in a word—*reverse discrimination*—prevail and are forced onto groups, thus promoting mediocrity, inefficiency, and resentment. Furthermore, AA aims at the higher levels of society—universities and skilled jobs, but if we want to improve our society, the best way to do it is to concentrate on families, children, early education, and the like, so all are prepared to avail themselves of opportunity. Affirmative Action, on the one hand, is too much, too soon and on the other hand, too little, too late. . . .

Martin Luther said that humanity is like a man mounting a horse who always tends to fall off on the other side of the horse. This seems to be the case with Affirmative Action. Attempting to redress the discriminatory iniquities of our history, our well-intentioned social engineers now engage in new forms of discriminatory iniquity and thereby think that they have successfully mounted the horse of racial harmony. They have only fallen off on the other side of the issue.[10]

Notes

1. For a good discussion of this argument see B. Boxill, "The Morality of Reparation," in *Social Theory and Practice* 2:1 (1972) and Albert G. Mosley in his and Nicholas Capaldi, *Affirmative Action; Social Justice or Unfair Preference?* (Rowman and Littlefield, 1996), pp. 23-27.

2. Merit sometimes may be justifiably overridden by need, as when parents choose to spend extra earnings on special education for their disabled child rather than for their gifted child. Sometimes we may override merit for utilitarian purposes. E.g., suppose you are the best shortstop on a baseball team but are also the best catcher. You'd rather play shortstop, but the manager decides to put you at catcher because, while your friend can do an adequate job at [shortstop], no one else is adequate at catcher. It's permissible for you to

be assigned the job of catcher. Probably, some expression of appreciation would be due you.

3. Judith Jarvis Thomson, "Preferential Hiring," in Marshall Cohen, Thomas Nagel and Thomas Scanlon, eds., *Equality and Preferential Treatment* (Princeton: Princeton University Press, 1977).

4. Stephen Kershnar pointed this out in written comments (December 22, 1997).

5. See Mosley, op cit., p. 28, and Bernard Boxill, *Blacks and Social Justice* (Rowman & Littlefield, 1984), whom Mosley quotes in his article, also defends this position.

6. John Rawls, *A Theory of Justice* (Harvard University Press, 1971), p. 104. See Bernard Boxill, "The Morality of Preferential Hiring," *Philosophy and Public Affairs* 7:3 (1983).

7. Michael Kinsley, "Equal Lack of Opportunity," *Harper's* (June 1983).

8. My point does not depend on any particular theory of free will. One is reminded of Nozick's point that Rawls' professed aim of articulating the enormous worth of each individual seems contrary to the reductive determinism in his natural lottery argument.

9. For further discussion of this point see my "Equality and Desert," *Philosophy* 72 (1997).

10. Some of the material in this essay appeared in "The Moral Status of Affirmative Action," *Public Affairs Quarterly* 6:2 (1992). I have not had space to consider all the objections to my position or discuss the issue of freedom of association which, I think, should be given much scope in private but not in public institutions. Barbara Bergmann (*In Defense of Affirmative Action* [New York: Basic Books, 1996], pp. 122–25) and others argue that we already offer preferential treatment for athletes and veterans, especially in university admissions, so being consistent, we should provide it for women and minorities. My answer is that I am against giving athletic scholarships, and I regard scholarships to veterans as a part of a contractual relationship, a reward for service to one's country. But I distinguish entrance programs from actual employment. I don't think that veterans should be afforded special privilege in hiring practice, unless it be as a tiebreaker.

I should also mention that my arguments from merit and respect apply more specifically to public institutions than private ones, where issues of property rights and freedom of association carry more weight.

POSTSCRIPT

Is Affirmative Action Fair?

That racial discrimination and sexual discrimination have existed in the United States is a matter of historical record and beyond dispute. But the question remains, What follows for us here and now?

Opponents of affirmative action say that nothing at all follows, except perhaps that we might be more careful and vigilant about allowing any form of discrimination, including modern forms of reverse discrimination.

Proponents of strong affirmative action say that although these views might *look* fair and aim to *be* fair, they are not fair. Just preventing discrimination without taking positive action to improve minorities' positions in society would simply freeze an unfairly established status quo. As American society is now, blacks are not represented in professions, in graduate schools, in business boardrooms, or in positions of social and political leadership in a way that is consistent with their numbers in the population. This is not for lack of interest or ability; it is a legacy of social injustice. To insist that we now freeze this status quo and proceed "fairly," on a case-by-case basis, will guarantee that the white-biased social momentum will continue for at least the foreseeable future. Advocates of affirmative action want to eradicate the effects of past discrimination and to put an end to the bias in momentum as soon as possible. They call for active measures to achieve this.

Sources that are relevant to this issue include Gertrude Ezorsky, *Racism and Justice: The Case for Affirmative Action* (Cornell University Press, 1991); Andrew Kull, *The Colorblind Constitution* (Harvard University Press, 1992); Bernard R. Boxhill, *Blacks and Social Justice*, rev. ed. (Rowman & Littlefield, 1992); Andrew Hacker, *Two Nations: Black and White, Separate, Hostile, Unequal* (Scribner, 1992); Stanley Fish, "Reverse Racism, or How the Pot Got to Call the Kettle Black," *The Atlantic Monthly* (November 1993); Steven M. Cahn, ed., *Affirmative Action and the University* (Temple University Press, 1993); Carl Cohen, *Naked Racial Preference: The Case Against Affirmative Action* (Madison Books, 1995); Ralph R. Reiland, "Affirmative Action or Equal Opportunity?" *Regulation* (vol. 18, 1995), pp. 19–23; and Steven M. Cahn, ed., *The Affirmative Action Debates*, 2d ed. (Routledge, 2002).

Other sources on this controversial policy are George E. Curry, ed., *The Affirmative Action Debate* (Addison-Wesley, 1996); Richard F. Thomasson, Faye J. Crosby, and Sharon D. Herzberger, *Affirmative Action: The Pros and Cons of Policy and Practice* (University Press of America, 1996); John David Skrentny, *The Ironies of Affirmative Action: Politics, Culture, and Justice in America* (University of Chicago Press, 1996); Robert Emmett Long, ed. , *Affirmative Action* (H. W. Wilson, 1996); Barbara Bergmann, *In Defense of Affirmative Action* (Basic Books, 1996); Terry Eastland, *Ending Affirmative Action: The Case* for *Colorblind Justice* (Basic Books, 1996); Jewelle Taylor Gibbs, *Color of Justice: Rodney King, O. J. Simpson, and Race in America* (Jossey-Bass, 1996); K. Anthony Appiah and Amy Gutmann, *Color Conscious: The Political Morality of Race* (Princeton University Press, 1996); David Theo Goldberg, *Racial Subjects: Writing on Race in America* (Routledge, 1997); Michael Levin, *Why Race Matters: Race Differences and What They Mean* (Greenwood Publishing Group, 1997); Abigail Thernstrom and Stephen Thernstrom, *America in Black and White: One Nation, Indivisible* (Simon & Schuster, 1997); Peter Skerry, "The Strange Politics of Affirmative Action," *Wilson Quarterly* (Winter 1997); Francis J. Beckwith, Todd E. Jones, eds., *Affirmative Action: Social Justice or Reverse Discrimination?* (Prometheus Books, 1997); Glenn C. Loury, "How to Mend Affirmative Action," *The Public Interest* (Spring 1997); Charles R. Lawrence III and Mari Matsuda, *We Won't Go Back: Making the Case for Affirmative Action* (Houghton Mifflin, 1997); David K. Shipler, *A Country of Strangers: Blacks and Whites in America* (Alfred A. Knopf, 1997); Lincoln Caplan, *Up Against the Law: Affirmative Action and the Supreme Court* (Century Foundation, 1997); Jim Sleeper, *Liberal Racism* (Viking Penguin, 1997); "Racism and the Law: The Legacy and Lessons of Plessy," a special issue of *Law and Philosophy* (May 1997); "The Affirmative Action Debate," a special issue of *Report From the Institute for Philosophy and Public Policy* (Winter-Spring 1997); Bryan K. Fair, *Notes of a Racial Caste Baby: Color Blindness and the End of Affirmative Action* (New York University Press, 1997); John Davis Skrentny, "Affirmative Action: Some Advice for the Pundits," *American Behavioral Scientist* (April 1998); *Focus on Law Studies* (Spring 1998) (this entire issue concerns affirmative action); Matt Cavanagh, *Against Equality of Opportunity* (Clarendon Press, 2002); Samuel Leiter and William M. Leiter, *Affirmative Action in Antidiscrimination Law and Policy: An Overview and Synthesis* (State University of New York Press, 2002); Charles V. Dale, *Affirmative Action Revisited* (Nova Science Publishers, 2002); and Fred L. Pincus, *Reverse Discrimination: Dismantling the Myth* (Lynne Rienner Publishers, 2003).

A concise account of civil rights history (including the birth of the phrase "affirmative action") is Hugh Davis Graham, *Civil Rights and the Presidency: Race and Gender in American Politics, 1960-1972* (Oxford University Press, 1992). Another useful historical account is Paul D. Moreno, *From Direct Action to Affirmative Action: Fair Employment Law and Policy in America, 1933–1972* (Louisiana State University Press, 1999). The position that affirmative action policies are necessary for women is defended by Susan D. Clayton and Faye J. Crosby, *Justice, Gender and Affirmative Action* (University of Michigan Press, 1992).

ISSUE 13

Should Handguns Be Banned?

YES: Nicholas Dixon, from "Handguns, Violent Crime, and Self-Defense," *International Journal of Applied Philosophy* (2000)

NO: Daniel D. Polsby, from "The False Promise of Gun Control," *The Atlantic Monthly* (March 1994)

ISSUE SUMMARY

YES: Philosopher Nicholas Dixon examines the contrast between gun ownership and murders in foreign countries and gun ownership and murders in the United States. He argues that there is a causal relationship between gun ownership and murder and that a ban on handguns would bring more benefit than harm.

NO: Professor of law Daniel D. Polsby asserts that gun control legislation is misguided. He maintains that if there were a ban on handguns, criminals would still arm themselves, but law-abiding citizens would not, resulting in more crime and more innocent victims.

Murder and violence are serious problems in the United States and guns play a significant role. In the wake of recent tragedies such as the Littleton, Colorado, high school killings and the mass murders in Atlanta we are especially conscious of the role guns play. But beyond these striking events is the more routine, day-to-day violence that involves guns and killing.

The resulting question is: What should be done to prevent further killing?

One suggestion is to regulate the traffic in guns, in particular, handguns. It is thought by some that this would have a favorable impact by eliminating some of the violence and killing associated with the possession of guns. It would lessen the ability of career criminals to obtain weapons and use them to commit crimes and it would prevent situations in which noncriminals might cause damage through the use of guns that they later regret but which cannot be undone. Ideally, the number of guns in circulation would be so limited that it would be difficult (or impossible) for a criminal to obtain a gun even through the black market.

Some would argue that these positive results are seriously overestimated. They counter that regulating the traffic in guns does not reduce the number of guns in circulation. Instead, regulations reduce the number of guns that are sold on open markets, where people follow restrictions, while there is little or no impact on the number of guns sold through the black market, where people do not follow restrictions. As a result, law-abiding citizens would not have guns—but criminals would. In this case, with law-abiding people at the mercy of criminals, the situation would be far worse, not better.

Gun control is one of those topics that generally separate political conservatives from political liberals. Conservatives tend to stand by the right of citizens to possess guns, while liberals tend to stand by the right of society to outlaw guns (or to restrict their sale or use). Conservatives tend to think that gun restrictions will have a larger impact on law-abiding citizens (who will follow restrictions) than on criminals (who will not); liberals tend to think that bringing the overall number of guns down will definitely have a beneficial impact on a society that is prone to use guns for the wrong reasons. Conservatives sometimes point out that guns don't kill people: people kill people. They often believe that what is required is personal responsibility and self-control, not gun control. Some liberals state that ideas of "personal responsibility" apply in an ideal world, but not in the real world, which contains excessive violence in the media and inner-city poverty.

In the selections that follow, Nicholas Dixon defends the view that handguns should be banned. He argues that the positive effects will outweigh the negative effects. Daniel D. Polsby counters that gun control will not deliver the positive effects that its proponents hope for.

YES

Nicholas Dixon

Handguns, Violent Crime, and Self-Defense

Over the last twenty years, philosophers have written extensively on such public policy issues as abortion, euthanasia, and the death penalty. I believe that the debate over handgun control in the United States should be added to this list. My goal in this paper is twofold. First, I want to persuade applied ethicists that handgun control is worthy of their attention. Second, drawing in part on data and arguments that I have published elsewhere,[1] I will argue that an outright handgun ban is the best policy.

A. Why Applied Ethicists Should Consider the Handgun Control Debate

From its inception in 1940 through the end of 1998, the *Philosopher's Index* contains only two entries mentioning gun control, and one of these articles is devoted primarily to abortion.[2] In contrast, the death penalty was the topic of thirty-one entries in 1990–98 alone. What explains philosophers' comparative neglect of handgun control?

It certainly cannot be justified by the relative unimportance of handgun control. Between 1980 and 1998, there were roughly twenty-six executions in the United States per year.[3] In 1997 alone, 8,104 homicides were committed with handguns in this country. 1997 also saw over 204,400 aggravated assaults and over 197,600 robberies with firearms, the vast majority of which were handguns.[4]

Perhaps philosophers have ignored the issue because of its apparent lack of philosophical interest. The most plausible argument for handgun control is based on the harm principle: restricting access to handguns will be justifiable only if doing so will prevent substantial harm to others. The heart of my utilitarian argument for handgun prohibition is that it will effect precisely such a reduction of harm. Whether this is the case, one might think, depends on empirical questions that are better studied by social scientists. This contrasts with abortion, which raises conceptual issues, such as those surrounding personhood, that are rich in philosophical import. . . .

[One] aspect of the handgun control debate that is philosophically interesting is whether the Second Amendment should be viewed as protecting private ownership of handguns. In particular, rival theories of constitutional interpretation may result in different views on the extent of "the right to bear arms." This question is beyond the scope of my paper, in which I will confine myself to arguing that a handgun ban is *morally* justifiable.

B. The Initial Case for Restricting Handguns

The following table compares handgun ownership and handgun homicide rates per 100,000 people in selected countries. The left-hand column is an estimate of handgun ownership rates in 1991, roughly the midpoint of the time span under investigation, based on FBI projections and on independent enquiries to the police departments of each country. The handgun homicide rates are calculated from data provided by Handgun Control, Inc., which obtained the information from each country's police department.[5]

	Handgun Ownership	Handgun Homicide Rate							
		1980	1983	1985	1988	1990	1992	1996	Average
U.S.A.	22,696	4.60	3.60	3.23	3.56	4.22	5.28	3.75	4.03
Israel	3,716	0.50	N/A	0.39	0.54	N/A	N/A	N/A	0.48
Sweden	3,700	0.22	0.08	N/A	0.23	0.16	0.43	N/A	0.22
Canada	2,301	0.03	0.02	0.02	0.03	0.26	0.50	0.41	0.18
Australia	1,596	0.02	0.06	0.03	0.07	0.06	0.08	0.08	0.06
U.K.	837	0.01	0.01	0.01	0.01	0.04	0.06	0.05	0.03

The first stage of my argument is to contend that this data is most plausibly explained by a causal relationship between handgun ownership and handgun homicide rates. First, the method of concomitant variation supports this causal assertion, based on the perfect coincidence between the rank orderings in terms of handgun ownership and average handgun homicide rates.[6] Second, and more important, in view of the vast disparity between the United States and all of the other countries in terms of both handgun ownership and handgun homicide, the method of difference supports the claim that the United States' extremely high handgun ownership rate is a cause of its extremely high handgun homicide rate.[7] To complete this stage of my causal argument, and to minimize the liklihood that the correlations I cite are purely coincidental, I need a causal theory to explain how the causation that I assert works. My theory is based on common sense: handguns are necessary for handgun homicides, so a higher ownership rate is likely to lead to a higher homicide rate. Simplistic though my causal theory is, I suggest that the correlations I have produced are so striking that the burden of proof is on those who would deny my causal argument.

I do not claim that the handgun ownership rate is the only determinant of homicide and other violent crimes committed with handguns. Two societies may have identical handgun ownership rates yet very different rates of violent crime, both with and without handguns. Economic and racial inequities, unemployment, and countless historical and cultural factors are doubtless also important causal factors. I claim only that the handgun ownership rate is *one* important determinant of handgun violence rates.

Opponents of handgun prohibition could concede that handgun ownership is causally connected with handgun homicide, while denying that it has any relationship with *overall* homicide rates. The vital second step in my causal argument, then, is showing that a reduction in handgun homicide and violence in the United States would reduce its overall rate of homicide and other violent crime. Note that I do not assert that a reduction in the handgun violence rate in *other* countries will substantially reduce their overall rate of violent crime. Handgun ownership and crime in most other countries is so low as to have a negligible impact on their overall crime rate.

I offer two arguments as to why a reduction in handgun violence in the United States will substantially decrease its overall level of violent crime. First, a huge number and a substantial percentage of its homicides and other violent crimes are committed with handguns. Since 1970, over 50% of homicides in this country have been committed with handguns, standing at 53% in 1997.[8] In the U.S. in 1997, 39.7% of its 497,950 robberies and 20% of its 1,022,492 aggravated assaults involved firearms.[9] Handguns are used in over 80% of firearms-related robberies[10] and 86% of firearms-related aggravated assaults.[11] Second, because of their lethality, their cheapness, their ease of use, and their small size (and hence ease of concealability), handguns are uniquely suited to homicide and other violent crimes. The importance of concealability of weapons for use in crime was reinforced by a study of crime weapons seized by the police done by the Bureau of Alcohol, Tobacco and Firearms:

> Seventy-one percent, or 7,538 of the handguns submitted for tracing, had a barrel length of 3 inches or less. Sixty-one percent, or 6,476, had a caliber of .32 or less. Since both of these factors relate to the size of the weapon, these figures indicate that concealability is an overriding factor in selecting a handgun for use in crime.[12]

The connection between handgun ownership and the overall homicide rate is further confirmed by a comparison of the number of handguns and the overall homicide rate in the United States in the last four decades.

	Handguns	Handguns per 100,000	Homicides per 100,000
1950	12 million	7,931	4.6
1960	16 million	8,924	5.1
1970	27 million	13,281	7.8
1980	48 million	21,192	10.2
1990	66 million	26,358	9.4[13]

From 1950 until 1970, the increase in the handgun ownership rate was matched by a steady increase in the overall homicide rate. Since the early 1970s, the annual homicide rate has become relatively stable, deviating very little from the 8 to 10 per 100,000 range. The likely reason why the homicide rate has not risen appreciably since the early 1970s, even though the handgun ownership rate has continued to rise, is that the United States has become "saturated" with sufficient handguns to supply potential murderers.

I now summarize my main argument. First, the extremely high handgun ownership rate in the United States is a major cause of its high rate of homicides and other violent crimes committed with handguns. A reduction in its handgun ownership rate is therefore likely to reduce its rate of handgun violence. Second, because of the high percentage of violent crimes currently committed in the United States with handguns, and because of the special effectiveness of handguns in committing violent crimes, a reduction in the rate of handgun violence is likely to reduce its overall rate of violent crime. In the next section I argue that an outright ban on handguns is the only realistic way to effect such a reduction.[14]

C. Why the Brady Bill Doesn't Go Far Enough

Arguments such as the foregoing may have played a role in the final passage by Congress of a version of the Brady Bill at the end of 1993. The bill imposes a waiting period of a few days, during which a "background check" is conducted, before a handgun can be purchased. Those found to have criminal records or a history of mental illness will be denied legal access to handguns. It is a "targeted" ban, designed to keep handguns out of the hands of those who are allegedly most likely to abuse them. It is hailed as a compromise that will reduce handgun violence, while respecting law-abiding citizens' right to bear arms. In reality, the one benefit of the Brady Bill is that it may have moved this country slightly closer to considering meaningful handgun control. In itself, the Brady Bill is likely to have little effect in reducing handgun crime.

The only people whose legal access to handguns will be ended will be those who have been convicted of felonies, and those with documented mental illness. While opponents of handgun prohibition point out that a high percentage of murders are committed by people with prior arrest records, they estimate that only 25% of murderers have felony convictions.[15] Seventy-five percent of murderers, then, will be unaffected by the Brady Bill. Moreover, lawbreakers who have thus far eluded conviction will be untouched by the bill, as will those who will buy handguns in order to *begin* a career of violent crime. This is to say nothing of previously law-abiding handgun owners who lose their temper and use their weapon to kill or maim after arguments.

The situation is even worse for supporters of the Brady Bill when we turn to *illegal* access to handguns. Its supporters are vulnerable to an objection often raised against a general handgun prohibition. The objection is that only law-abiding citizens are likely to obey a general handgun ban, while felons are likely to keep the handguns they already own, and have continued access to handguns by theft and illegal transfers. The result of a general handgun ban, then, is alleged to be the disarmament of peaceful citizens, while violent types will maintain or even increase their possession of handguns.[16] However, this argument is more damaging as an objection to a targeted ban, such as the Brady Bill, than it is to my proposal for a general handgun ban.

This is because the bill will do nothing to restrict wrongdoers' access to handguns through the illegal channels that already exist: theft and illegal transfers. Felons will be able to get friends with "clean" records to "buy for" them, with no more difficulty than is currently experienced by teenagers in search of alcohol. Handgun "brokers" have already begun to legally purchase large amounts of handguns, which they then illegally sell on the streets to customers with criminal records. The Brady Bill will allow unlimited access (except for a few days' wait) to unlimited numbers of handguns for the vast majority of people. Since on average well over two million new handguns have been made available for sale in the United States every year since 1980,[17] there is every reason to believe that the United States' arsenal of privately owned handguns, which will remain subject to theft and illegal transfer, will continue to grow rapidly.

In contrast, the outright ban that I propose will immediately stem this influx of handguns, which is especially important in view of the fact that a disproportionate number of handgun crimes are committed with new handguns.[18] The pool of 66 million handguns already in private hands or available for sale can be gradually reduced by voluntary return by their owners, with the aid of amnesty and buyback schemes, and by police seizure of weapons from felons. Of course, a handgun ban will never be completely effective in removing all 66 million handguns from circulation; but "a handgun ban does not need to be perfectly effective to lead to a major decrease in handgun violence."[19]

The Brady Bill is inadequate, then, because it will allow continued legal access to handguns for the majority of future violent criminals, and because it will allow the pool of handguns available for theft and illegal transfer to grow ever larger.

D. Utilitarian Objections to Handgun Prohibition

I present my argument that a handgun ban will reduce violent crime in the United States as an empirical hypothesis supported by striking correlations between handgun ownership and handgun homicide rates, and by a simple, intuitively plausible causal theory. Replies thus far given to my argument for handgun prohibition make the elementary error of treating it and other arguments for prohibition as if they were advanced as deductively valid. These replies consist of thought experiments or conjectures showing how handgun prohibition may conceivably fail to reduce violent crime.[20] While this is indeed sufficient to show that my argument is not deductively valid (a point that I readily concede), it does nothing to undermine my actual claim: handgun prohibition will *probably* reduce violent crime. To refute my actual claim, opponents need to show that it is probably false, not just that it *may* be false.

Both steps of my argument have been contested. I begin with the second step, in which I claim that a reduction in handgun violence in this country will reduce overall violent crime. The most common response is what I call "substitution theory": if handguns are banned, criminals will simply turn to even more lethal long guns and other weapons, with no net reduction in the amount of violent crime. Kates and Benenson argue that if only 30% of potential murderers were to "upgrade" to long guns (rifles and shotguns) in the event of a handgun ban, while the other 70% "downgraded" to knives, there would still be a "substantial increase" in homicide.[21] Based on the results of prisoner surveys, Gary Kleck asserts that an even higher rate of substitution of more lethal guns is likely to occur.[22]

The problem with these arguments for substitution theory is the flimsy nature of their empirical support. First, the responses of prisoners to surveys scarcely establish Kleck's intuitively implausible prediction of widespread use of bulky long guns in crime. Second, Kates and Benenson calculated their 30% "threshold" (which is widely cited in the antigun control literature) by comparing the relative lethality of long gun and handgun wounds, without considering the fact that it is far easier to *inflict* wounds in the first place with small, concealable handguns. Given the fact that substitution theory is advanced by opponents of handgun prohibition in order to deny the intuitively plausible view that a reduction in handgun violence will result in a reduction in overall violence, the burden of proof is on its proponents to provide much better support for it. The weakness of substitution theory is especially damaging for those opponents of handgun prohibition who concede that a ban would reduce the level of *handgun* violence.[23]

Further presumptive evidence against substitution theory is provided by the fact that the United States' *overall* homicide rate is substantially higher than that of the comparison countries. In fact, it is higher, in most cases by several hundred percent, than that of all of the other seventeen countries in a recent study.[24] If substitution of other, more lethal weapons were likely to occur in the United States, then we would expect these other countries with low handgun ownership rates to have high nonhandgun homicide rates to "compensate" for their low handgun homicide rates, but they do not.[25]

I turn next to the first stage of my argument, in which I claim that a handgun ban would reduce the amount of handgun violence in the United States. The usual strategy of opponents is to argue that the extremely high rate of handgun violence in the U.S. is attributable to factors unrelated to its high handgun ownership rate.[26] The weakness of most such arguments is that they give little or no analysis of these alleged factors. The unsupported assertion that there may be causes of handgun violence unrelated to handgun ownership rates fails for two reasons to undercut my argument. First, as explained above, showing the bare logical possibility that my causal hypothesis is false does nothing to undercut it. Second, since I claim only that the high handgun ownership rate is *one* of the causes of our rampant handgun violence rate, the existence of other causes in no way weakens my argument. If anything, the existence of multiple causes of handgun violence makes the striking international correlation between ownership and homicide rates even harder to dismiss as a coincidence. . . .

The strongest objection to handgun prohibition is the claim that it would cause an increase in violent crime by denying peaceful citizens the use of handguns in defense of self and property. Any benefits of a handgun ban have to be weighed against a possible reduction in the defensive use of handguns.[27]

The first weakness of this objection is once again the flimsy nature of the empirical evidence adduced in its support. The sole evidence for the effectiveness and the frequency of the defensive uses of handguns is provided by highly suspect surveys of prisoners[28] and gun owners,[29] and a conjecture that the number of justified self-defensive homicides is underreported by the FBI.[30] Second, the argument that the use of handguns in self-defense causes a net decrease in violent crime is further weakened by the fact that a substantial percentage of the very violent crimes that handgun ownership is supposed to prevent are themselves committed with handguns. Rather than acquiescing in an endless spiral of increasingly heavily armed aggressors and victims, we would do better to strive for a society in which neither aggressors nor victims have handguns. Third, underlying the self-defense argument against handgun prohibition may be the fear that it would leave ordinary law-abiding citizens helpless against gun-wielding predators. In reality, however, this distinction between peaceful handgun owners and predators is suspect. Even a handgun purchased for purely defensive purposes may be used offensively, since we are all capable of heated arguments, which can easily turn lethal when a handgun is available. In about one-half of all murders, the victim is a relative or acquaintance of the murderer, and about one-third of murders result from arguments, which are hardly circumstances that apply only to predators.[31] A recent study directly supports my claim that the risk of offensive abuses of handguns outweighs their defensive utility:

> Despite the widely held belief that guns are effective for protection, our results suggest that they actually pose a substantial threat to members of the household.[32]

The comparative international data cited above also counts against the hypothesis that handgun ownership reduces violence because of the defensive use of handguns. The more handguns that are owned in a given country, we may assume, the more times they will be used defensively and, according to the hypothesis we are considering, the less violent crime will occur. But the data indicates the direct opposite: the higher the handgun ownership rate, the higher the handgun homicide rate. In particular, the United States, which far outstrips its rivals in handgun ownership, is also the clear leader in terms of both the handgun and overall homicide rate.

The objection to handgun prohibition on the ground of the alleged defensive benefits of handguns, then, proves only the logical possibility that prohibition will fail to reduce handgun violence. This bare logical possibility is heavily outweighed by the actual handgun ownership and violence rates on which my central causal argument is based.[33]

Notwithstanding my criticisms of arguments for the defensive value of handguns, we should admit that owning handguns may make people *feel* secure in their homes and on the streets. However, if my criticisms are sound, this feeling is illusory, and a substantial reduction in the rate of homicide and violent crime would outweigh the loss of an illusory feeling of security.

The key theoretical point that is ignored by all of these objections is that not all of the logically possible explanations of any set of evidence are on an equal footing. The Tobacco Institute's denial that smoking causes lung cancer is certainly compatible with the evidence, but it is vastly less plausible than the rival hypothesis, supported by extensive correlations and a strong causal theory, that smoking does cause it. Similarly, . . . opponents of handgun prohibition need to do more than show that my hypothesis might be false. They need to show that it is probably false, by producing a more plausible alternative causal explanation. But this is precisely what they have failed to do.

My argument that opponents have failed to meet the burden of proof that is incumbent on them is *not* an attempt to prove my causal hypothesis by means of an appeal to ignorance. On the contrary, in support of my hypothesis I have produced striking correlations between handgun ownership and homicide rates in various countries, a plausible causal theory explaining the causal mechanism at work, and an argument linking a reduction in handgun violence with an overall reduction in violence. It is the strength of this evidence and the supporting causal theory that places the burden of proof on those who would deny my hypothesis to substantiate their objections.

> [I]t is incumbent on them to produce an alternative causal account proving that the United States' high handgun murder rate is caused by factors unrelated to its high rate of handgun ownership. They must specify what these causes are, quantify their relative presence in the United States as compared to the countries with lower homicide rates, demonstrate that variations in these factors correlate with variations in the murder rate, and provide a plausible theory explaining the causal mechanisms at work.[34]

They must also find an alternative explanation of the correlation I have found between handgun ownership and homicide rates, unless they are willing to dismiss it as a coincidence.

This completes my sketch of my response to utilitarian objections to handgun prohibition. For considerably more detail, I urge readers to consult my earlier papers.[35]

E. Utilitarianism, Handgun Prohibition, and Individual Rights

The objections discussed in the previous section did not challenge the utilitarian framework in which my argument is expressed, and I need to pause to consider rights-based objections to handgun prohibition. The United States' legal system does not regard the prevention of violence as an absolute value. We provide defendants with an extensive array of rights, with the result that some people are acquitted even though they committed the violent act of which they are accused. This indicates that we regard protecting individual rights as an important constraint on the utilitarian goal of reducing violent crime. How do these objections affect my utilitarian argument for banning handguns?

A *general* defense of utilitarianism is both beyond the scope of a paper in applied ethics and unnecessary in order to defend my proposal. My strategy in responding to these objections will be to show that handgun prohibition does *not* violate individual moral rights, so that the overwhelming utilitarian arguments for prohibition prevail.

Handgun prohibition undeniably restricts people's freedom. They are prevented from owning handguns, which they may desire for target shooting, collectors' items, or self-defense. However, the right to life and bodily integrity of innocent victims of handgun violence—which, if my main thesis is sound, are constantly endangered by the prevalence of handguns—is arguably far stronger than any rights that are allegedly violated by banning handguns. Gun collectors would remain free to own other types of firearm, and handguns would still be available for enthusiasts at government-run shooting ranges. The most substantial freedom that would be curtailed by my proposal, and the one to which I devote the rest of this section, is the use of handguns in self-defense; but my arguments in the last section showed that defensive uses of handguns are heavily outweighed by offensive abuses. Of what moral force is an alleged right to defend ourselves with handguns, if (1) exercising this "right" endangers rather than protects gun owners and (2) the widespread handgun ownership necessary for the exercise of this freedom causes the death or wounding of thousands of innocent people, violating their unquestioned right to life and bodily integrity?

Now opponents of prohibition could adopt an "absolutist" stance, and insist that central to the very meaning of the concept of a right is that it *can not* be "trumped" by rival moral considerations. According to this view, my right to defend myself with a handgun is inviolable, regardless of the pernicious consequences that my exercise of this right may have for the rest of society (and, indeed, for myself). However, the implausibility of such an absolutist approach is glaring.

First, we cannot sidestep conflicts of rights by simply declaring one of the rival rights to be absolute. For instance, we cannot solve the abortion debate by a fiat that the fetus's (or the pregnant woman's) rights are inviolable. Instead, arguments are needed to explain why one right takes precedence over another. Thus opponents of handgun prohibition need to explain exactly why my right to defend myself with a handgun outweighs the rights of innocent victims of the violent crimes that occur as a result of widespread ownership of handguns.

Second, while my right to defend myself against harm arguably *is* absolute, in the sense that I may always respond to aggression, it is not unconditional. As discussed in depth in the following section, the right to use violence in self-defense is qualified by such requirements as necessity and proportionality. The general right to self-defense does not entail the right to use any particular method that I happen to desire to use. Thus arguments, and not just a bare assertion, are needed to support the claim that we have a right to use handguns in self-defense. The view that enshrines the use of handguns in self-defense as a right simply because some people desire to do so—i.e., that the right to self-defense is unlimited—is easily reduced to absurdity. Paranoid antigovernment survivalist militias doubtless believe that possessing huge arsenals of automatic weapons and explosives (and quite likely, if they could get their hands on them, nuclear weapons) is necessary to protect themselves against the constant threat of governmental tyranny. Unless we are willing to accept the consequence that militia members would indeed have the right to own such weaponry, we need a more substantial argument for the right to own handguns for defensive purposes than the mere fact that some people desire to do so.

We cannot deny that isolated cases will occur in which someone will be injured or killed when she could have escaped injury had she had a handgun for self-protection. However, we should resist the temptation to say that such people are "sacrificed" by handgun prohibition for the common good, since we cannot know in advance who they will be. Handgun prohibition benefits everyone, in that each person is more likely to be the victim of handgun crime than to successfully use a handgun in self-defense. Similarly, mandatory seat belt laws benefit everyone, even though freakish accidents will occur in which the unfortunate victim would have escaped injury had she *not* been wearing a seat belt. If any talk of sacrifice is appropriate, it is to say that hundreds of thousands of victims of handgun crime are sacrificed every year in the United States in order to allow people to act on the mistaken belief that they are made safer by possessing handguns.

Handgun prohibition is based on the least controversial ground for restricting freedom: preventing harm *to others*. Even the most innocuous laws—for instance, those prohibiting people from driving at speeds over 100 m.p.h., privately owning antitank weapons or nuclear warheads, or making child pornography—restrict people's freedom, on the ground that these activities pose an unacceptable risk or certainty of harm to others. These familiar examples show that, just as we do not regard preventing harm to others as an absolute value, and are prepared to tolerate some such harm in order to preserve individual rights, neither do we regard protecting individual freedom as sacrosanct. We restrict freedom without violating rights when doing so will prevent substantial harm to others, while imposing minimal restraints on people's behavior. Handgun prohibition falls well within this familiar rationale.

F. The Moral Limits of the Use of Handguns in Defense of Self and Property

I have just argued that my utilitarian case for handgun prohibition is compatible with respect for individual rights. In this section, I show that other non-consequentialist arguments actually strengthen my proposal, since they act as restraints on the right to use handguns in self-defense. Specifically, I give deontological considerations to supplement my utilitarian arguments that the proven offensive abuses of handguns outweigh conjectures about their defensive uses. My thesis is that if defensive handgun use is kept within morally justifiable limits, it will be far less widespread than is claimed by its advocates, and its benefits will be even more easily outweighed by abuses of handguns than I claimed in my original argument for prohibition.

1. Necessity and Proportionality in Self-Defense

A prima facie reason against the use of private violence in response to crime is that it circumvents our legal system: the making of law by elected legislators, the enforcement of law by a trained police force, and the imposition of punishments by an impartial judiciary. It runs the risk of excessive, unprincipled vigilantism, notwithstanding the widespread public support it enjoys. However, recognizing that the police force is not always available to defend citizens, most societies allow self-defense as a justification for the use of otherwise prohibited force.

In order to evaluate the use of handguns in self-defense, I will cite only uncontroversial principles from existing theories of self-defense. At least two conditions must be met in order to justify the defensive use of violence: *necessity* and *proportionality*.[36] The necessity requirement prohibits the use of violence when harm could be avoided by less drastic measures, such as simply walking away. The proportionality requirement restricts the infliction of death or serious bodily harm to cases where it is used to prevent substantial harm. The clearest case in which both necessity and proportionality conditions are arguably met is when shooting an assailant is necessary to save the victim's life. This justification may be extended to cases where the victim is threatened with severe bodily harm or rape. The necessity condition also mandates that in all these cases fatally shooting the assailant is justifiable only when wounding would not have been sufficient to stop him.

The most commonly quoted evidence supporting the defensive value of handguns is an estimate by Gary Kleck, based on surveys of gun owners, that handguns are used 645,000 times per year in the United States in response to crimes or attempted crimes.[37] The problem is that Kleck makes no attempt to determine how many of these handgun uses were necessary, and proportionate to the harm they were intended to prevent. Instead, he relies unquestioningly on the word of gun owners, who have a vested interest in exaggerating the defensive efficacy of their weapons. More generally, any credible justification of the defensive use of handguns must address the issues of necessity and proportionality. Unnecessary and disproportionate uses of handguns must not only be subtracted from the legitimate defensive uses of guns; they must also be added to the list of abuses of handguns that support my proposal for prohibition.

A certain lenience is appropriate in applying the necessity condition. Whether shooting was justified depends on whether the shooter really was in danger. However, her action may be partially or fully excused if she *reasonably believed* that she was in danger, even if further investigation reveals that she was not. Underlying the use of a partly subjective standard to determine the excusability of shooting in self-defense is the principle that, in cases of uncertainty, the aggressor should bear the greater risk.[38]

The argument so far permits the defensive use of handguns only when the shooter reasonably believes it necessary in order to preserve her life or bodily integrity. Given the availability of less violent alternative methods of self-defense, shooting assailants will rarely be permissible.[39] . . .

2. The Morality of Threatening to Shoot Nonviolent Assailants

. . . [Supporters] of the defensive use of handguns would stress that the most common such use consists of frightening off robbers and burglars by merely displaying the handgun without firing it.[40] Moreover, public knowledge of the widespread ownership of handguns is also alleged to act as a general deterrent to crime.[41] Consequently, . . . owning and displaying handguns in order to prevent robberies and burglaries can be justified as a bluff, which is compatible with the limitations I have set on the defensive use of handguns, even if actually shooting them would not be. A similar argument can be used to defend mutual assured destruction (MAD) as a nuclear defense strategy. As long as a country does not intend to actually use its nuclear weapons in retaliation, the threat to use them may be justifiable. This attempt to justify bluffing with handguns in order to protect property has two weaknesses.

The first problem arises from the need for threats to be credible, so that potential aggressors believe that their victims would indeed respond violently to an attack. The MAD strategy is subject to the paradox that, once a massive countervalue nuclear attack has been launched, the doomed target nation gains nothing from retaliating, other than the satisfaction of knowing that the aggressor nation, along with most of the rest of the globe, will be annihilated. The resultant lack of credibility in the threat of retaliation may tempt an aggressive nation to launch a first strike, thus defeating the purpose of MAD. Thus far, fortunately, the awesome destructive power of nuclear weapons has prevented any nation from calling its rivals' retaliatory nuclear bluff. Similarly, handguns' effectiveness in scaring off robbers and burglars without being fired requires that assailants believe that their victims are prepared to shoot them. Aggressor nations may be deterred by the mere threat of nuclear retaliation, but in the case of handguns, victims must regularly shoot assailants in order for any victims' threats to be credible. And in the previous section I showed that shooting robbers and burglars is normally immoral, because it is disproportionate to the harm threatened. Consequently, even the deterrence achieved by the "pacifist" handgun owner who threatens aggressors without intending to use his or her weapon is "tainted" by its dependence on the immoral actions of other handgun owners who do actually shoot robbers and burglars.

Second, the bluffs of the pacifist handgun owners are intrinsically problematic, precisely because they are threats to do something immoral. This is not to say that all threats to perform immoral actions are themselves immoral. David Hoekema gives a plausible example in which we are justified in immorally threatening (without intending to carry out the threat) the family of terrorists who have threatened to kill hostages unless the terrorists' unreasonable demands are met.[42] However, those who use handguns to frighten off robbers and burglars fail to meet several of the stringent necessary conditions for immoral threats that Hoekema states.[43] For instance, loss of property hardly qualifies as "a grave and imminent catastrophe." (In contrast, even if killing the terrorists' family would be immoral, this action would at least be proportionate to the threatened harm: killing hostages.) Nor have all alternative means of protecting property been exhausted. And owning a handgun for protection of property is an ongoing policy, as opposed to a temporary measure adopted to deal with an emergency. [44]

The situation is more complex with regard to the generalized deterrent effect created by widespread ownership of handguns. To the extent that this deterrence is created by the threat of using violence only in response to violent aggressors who threaten serious bodily harm, it is morally permissible. To the extent that it is created by the threat of using violence against nonviolent robbers and burglars, it is immoral, even though the result—fewer robberies and burglaries—is desirable. In practice, of course, distinguishing these two elements of deterrence is impossible. Even someone who owns a handgun only for "legitimate" deterrence may inadvertently help to deter nonviolent robbers and burglars, who may fear that *any* handgun may be used against them in defense of property as well as self. But if defensive gun use were confined to legitimate cases, such illegitimate deterrence would soon disappear.

Even if all handgun owners genuinely intend to use their guns only when necessary to prevent death or serious physical harm, some will occasionally overreact and use excessive force. Potential criminals are aware of this, and may thus be deterred from even nonviolent crimes. . . . [If] such overreactions are based on a reasonable but mistaken belief that the handgun owner is in serious danger, they may be excusable. However, if we take seriously the necessity and proportionality restrictions on the defensive use of handguns, we should hesitate to cite the deterrent effect of their violation as a benefit of handguns. We should, in contrast, encourage handgun owners to use their guns defensively only when permitted by the necessity and proportionality requirements, even if these restrictions prevent more widespread deterrence.

We have just seen that shooting assailants is permissible only when the victim either correctly, or mistakenly but reasonably, believes that shooting is necessary to protect her life or bodily integrity. Furthermore, displaying a handgun in order to scare off an assailant is justified only if actually shooting the aggressor would be permissible. Finally, the general deterrent effect of the widespread ownership of handguns is justifiable only to the extent that it is created by potential assailants' fear of *legitimate* defensive uses of handguns.

The effect of these deontological restrictions is to further discredit the estimates of the defensive uses of handguns produced by opponents of handgun prohibition. Their estimates, which I have already criticized on the ground that they are based on the testimony of biased respondents to surveys, make no attempt to discriminate between justified and unjustified defensive uses of handguns, and thus include handgun uses in defense of property, which are condemned by the argument of the current section. Since shooting an assailant is most likely to be permitted by the foregoing guidelines when the assailant himself has a handgun, the best policy is handgun prohibition, which ensures that the assailant is far less likely to have a handgun in the first place. In sum, when restricted to morally justifiable uses, the alleged defensive value of handguns, which is advanced as the major reason against prohibition, provides little ground for opposing my proposal to ban handguns.

In contrast to the flimsy and conjectural arguments that handguns are a useful weapon to use to defend against criminals, my argument for prohibition is based on handgun ownership and crime statistics provided by government agencies. The very strength of my data linking handgun ownership and violence rates indicates that offensive abuses of handguns outweigh legitimate defensive uses. In the absence of plausible responses from opponents, my data and arguments indicate that handgun prohibition will substantially reduce violent crime in the United States, without violating individual rights.

G. Conclusion: Is Handgun Prohibition Realistic?

The most common response that I have encountered to my proposal to ban handguns is that it is too "idealistic." Those who give this response may grant my contention that eradicating handguns would reduce violent crime without violating individual rights, but they insist that handgun prohibition is not a practical goal in the United States. Underlying this scepticism is the belief that we cannot realistically expect the United States Congress to pass legislation to ban handguns, and that, even if such a ban were passed, it would be unenforceable.

I have already addressed the issue of enforceability above in section C. While no legislation will ever completely rid the country of handguns, a federal ban would immediately halt the current legal sale of over two million new handguns per year, while voluntary buyback programs and the seizure of weapons used in crime will gradually reduce the arsenal of handguns in private hands. And this reduction will, in turn, reduce the level of violent crime.

As for whether handgun prohibition legislation could be enacted in the first place, the recent passage of precisely such a measure in the United Kingdom, in response to the Dunblaine massacre, shows that it actually can be done. The only way to maintain the view that handgun prohibition is impossible to enact in the United States is to insist that sociopolitical realities unique to this country make it so. These realities include the powerful influence of the gun lobby in Congress, the long tradition of gun ownership, and the fervent belief held by a significant minority that owning a handgun is necessary for self-protection.

Little doubt exists that such factors do indeed make the passage of a handgun ban in the United States currently unattainable. However, to count this as a refutation of my position is to adopt a truly disturbing view about the role of applied ethics. We surely need to distinguish between prescribing what we *should* do—this is the appropriate role for applied ethicists—and, on the other hand, predicting what Congress actually *will* do, which falls instead into the province of political science. The question of what we should do is prior to the question of what is currently attainable. Compromise and accommodation to practical realities should only be discussed *after* we have first determined what would be the fair and just thing to do.

To allow considerations of realpolitik to influence our judgments about the morality of a practice or policy would effectively lock us into the status quo, and sabotage the role of applied ethics as a vehicle for proposing social change. Absurd consequences are easy to find. For instance, when the abolitionist movement first began, little doubt exists that it had no realistic chance *at that time* of persuading Congress to abolish slavery. Does this mean that its members were wrong to morally condemn slavery and call for its abolition? Similar comments apply to the suffragette movement in its early days. Worse still, if applied ethicists are to confine themselves to defending positions that have a realistic chance of currently being legally enacted, prolife philosophers will have to stop writing papers in which they condemn abortion, since, given the current composition of the Supreme Court, legislation banning "regular" abortion is virtually impossible to enact and defend against constitutional challenges.

Granted, the abolitionist movement did indeed take heed of political realities and worked incrementally to restrict slavery to certain states before finally pushing for its complete abolition. This is because it, like the suffragette movement, was a political movement, whose goal was to bring about concrete social change. Nonetheless, underlying both movements were moral arguments that made no compromise for political realities in their condemnation of slavery and the oppression of women. And this is precisely the role that applied ethicists should play in discussing handgun control: providing a moral vision of the handgun policy that would best reduce violence and respect rights. How to realize that moral vision is an important question, but a secondary one, and one that is best left to political organizations that are more knowledgeable about political realities. It may well turn out that Handgun Control, Inc.'s strategy of proposing moderate restrictions on handgun ownership is a shrewd first step that is a necessary prelude to the more radical proposal advanced here. But moral arguments for handgun prohibition are needed to guide and motivate even incremental change to achieve that goal.

Nor is guiding and motivating those who already share a movement's goal the only role for applied ethicists. Even more important is the ability of cogent moral arguments to convince opponents and the uncommitted of the desirability of social change. The abolitionist, suffragette, and civil rights movements all illustrate this phenomenon. So another error made by those who reject as unrealistic my proposal to ban handguns is to regard one of the realities that do indeed make it difficult to achieve at present—i.e., the widespread belief that handguns make law-abiding citizens safer against crime—as engraved in stone. They overlook the power of striking empirical evidence and clearly presented arguments to persuade the American public that the widespread ownership of handguns is a major cause of violent crime. We need to continue to present this evidence and these arguments until we convince enough people that handgun prohibition is desirable that it will eventually become eminently attainable.

Notes

1. Nicholas Dixon, "Why We Should Ban Handguns in the United States," *Saint Louis University Public Law Review* 12:2 (1993), pp. 243–83, and "Perilous Protection: A Reply to Kopel," ibid., pp. 361–91.

2. Alfred E. Koenig, "Do Guns Kill?" *Contemporary Philosophy* 15:6 (Nov./Dec. 1993), p. 16; and Beverly Combs, "If you liked gun control, you'll love the anti-abortion amendment," in Wendy McElroy (ed.), *Freedom, Feminism, and the State* (Cato Institute, 1982).

3. Bureau of Justice Statistics Web site.

4. *Uniform Crime Reports for the United States 1997* (Washington, D.C.: Federal Bureau of Investigations, U.S. Department of Justice, 1998), pp. 20, 31, 34.

5. For more detail on the derivation of many of these statistics, see Nicholas Dixon, "Why We Should Ban Handguns in the United States," pp. 248–50, and "Perilous Protection: A Reply to Kopel," pp. 372–3.

6. When the amount or rate of the effect E (in this case, handgun homicide) varies according to the amount or rate of antecedent factor X (handgun ownership), the method of concomitant variation indicates that X is probably a cause of E.

7. When the effect E (in this case, an extremely high handgun homicide rate) occurs in the presence of antecedent factor X (an extremely high handgun ownership rate) but not in its absence, the method of difference indicates that X is probably a cause of E.

8. *Uniform Crime Reports* 1970–97.

9. *Uniform Crime Reports 1997*, pp. 31, 34.

10. Franklin E. Zimring, "Firearms, Violence and Public Policy," *Scientific American*, November 1991, p. 50.

11. This statistic, which comes from 1967, is cited by Franklin E. Zimring and Gordon Hawkins, *The Citizen's Guide to Gun Control* (New York: Macmillan, 1987), p. 38.

12. *Project Identification: A Study of Handguns Used in Crime* (Department of Treasury, May 1976), p. 2.

13. Handgun ownership numbers are based on the Bureau of Alcohol, Tobacco and Firearms data on the number of handguns available for sale in the United States since 1899. See "Civilian Firearms—Domestic Production, Importation, Exportation, and Availability for Sale," BATF document, 1991. Overall United States homicide rates are taken from *Uniform Crime Reports*, 1950, 1960, 1970, 1980 and 1990.

14. For detail on the exceptions I propose to handgun prohibition, see "Why We Should Ban Handguns," pp. 244–7.

15. Gary Kleck and David J. Bordua, "The Assumptions of Gun Control," in Don B. Kates, Jr. (ed.), *Firearms and Violence: Issues of Public Policy* (San Francisco: Pacific Institute for Public Policy Research, 1984), p. 42.

16. See David Hardy and Don Kates, "Handgun Availability and the Social Harm of Robbery: Recent Data and Some Projections," in Don B. Kates, Jr. (ed.) *Restricting Handguns: The Liberal Skeptics Speak Out* (North River Press, 1979), pp. 129–30, and Gary Kleck, "Policy Lessons from Recent Gun Control Research," *Law and Contemporary Problems* 49 (Winter 1986), p. 41.

17. "Civilian Firearms—Domestic Production, Importation, Exportation, and Availability for Sale," BATF document.

18. Studies have shown that over half the handguns used in crime were first purchased from retailers within five years of the crime. See Zimring and Hawkins, *The Citizen's Guide to Gun Control*, pp. 39–41. See also Robert J. Spitzer, *The Politics of Gun Control* (Chatham, NJ: Chatham House Publishers, 1995), p. 80.

19. Nicholas Dixon, "Perilous Protection: A Reply to Kopel," p. 379.

20. This parallels the tactic used by the Tobacco Institute, which heroically dismisses the overwhelming evidence that smoking tobacco is a cause of lung cancer, because of the logical possibility that the correlations between smoking and increased rates of lung cancer may be coincidental.

21. See, e.g., Don B. Kates, Jr., and Mark K. Benenson, "Handgun Prohibition and Homicide: A Plausible Theory Meets the Intractible Facts," in Kates (ed.), *Restricting Handguns: The Liberal Skeptics Speak Out*, p. 111.

22. Kleck, "Policy Lessons from Recent Gun Control Research," p. 49.

23. See, e.g., David Kopel, "Peril or Protection? The Risks and Benefits of Handgun Prohibition," *St. Louis University Public Law Review* 12:2, pp. 300, 359.

24. Don B. Kates, Jr., *Guns, Murder, and the Constitution* (Pacific Research Institute for Public Policy, 1990), p. 42.

25. For more detail on my response to substitution theory, see "Why We Should Ban Handguns," pp. 268–72.

26. For instance, Don Kates asserts that "the determinants of violence are . . . fundamental economic, sociocultural, and institutional differences" between the United States and other countries. *Firearms and Violence: Issues of Public Policy*, p. 529.

27. See James D. Wright, "The Ownership of Firearms for Reasons of Self-Defense," in Don B. Kates, Jr. (ed.) *Firearms and Violence: Issues of Public Policy*, pp. 301–27; Gary Kleck, "Policy Lessons from Recent Gun Control Research," pp. 43–48; Don B. Kates, Jr., *Guns, Murder, and the Constitution* (Pacific Research Institute for Public Policy, 1990), pp. 17–36; and David B. Kopel, "Peril or Protection?" pp. 332–8.

28. Kleck, "Policy Lessons from Recent Gun Control Research," p. 46.

29. Gary Kleck, "Guns and Self-Defense: Crime Control Through the Use of Force in the Private Sector," *Social Problems* 35 (Feb. 1988), p. 4.

   Even though I attack the source of these surveys, my objection does not commit an ad hominem fallacy. An ad hominem argument consists of attacking the *person* who presents a position, rather than the *substance* of her position. However, when someone is presenting testimony rather than defending a position, her character, actions or circumstances are directly relevant to her credibility. An example of this is a witness in a trial. Since she is simply asserting what she saw or heard, an attorney commits no fallacy in raising questions about the witness's reliability and integrity. In the same way, the fact that handgun owners have a vested interest in exaggerating the defensive efficacy of their weapons is pertinent to the credibility of surveys based on their testimony. I therefore commit no fallacy in challenging the reliability of gun owners' responses.

30. Kleck, "Guns and Self Defense," p. 5.

31. Nicholas Dixon, "Why We Should Ban Handguns," p. 266.

32. Arthur Kellermann et al., "Gun Ownership as a Risk Factor for Homicide in the Home," *New England Journal of Medicine* 329:15 (1993), p. 1090.

33. For more detail on my criticism of arguments for the defensive value of handguns, see "Why We Should Ban Handguns," pp. 272–83.

34. Nicholas Dixon, "Why We Should Ban Handguns in the United States," p. 253.

35. Ibid., pp. 255–82, and Nicholas Dixon, "Perilous Protection," pp. 361–91.

36. George P. Fletcher, *A Crime of Self-Defense: Bernhard Goetz and the Law on Trial* (Chicago: The University of Chicago Press, 1988), p. 19, and Michael Gorr, "Private Defense," *Law and Philosophy* 9 (1990), pp. 262–3.

37. Kleck, "Guns and Self-Defense," p. 4.

38. Daniel D. Polsby, "Reflections on Violence, Guns, and the Defensive Use of Lethal Force," *Law and Contemporary Problems* 49 (Winter 1986), p. 90.

39. For a discussion of alternative methods of self-defense, see Nicholas Dixon, "Why We Should Ban Handguns," pp. 277, 281–2.

40. Gary Kleck, "Guns and Self-Defense," p. 4.

41. Ibid., pp. 11–6.

42. David A. Hoekema, "The Moral Status of Nuclear Deterrent Threats," *Social Philosophy and Policy* 3:1 (Autumn 1985), pp. 103–4.

43. Ibid., pp. 105–7.

44. For another argument for the immorality of bluffing to do what is immoral, see Jeffrey H. Barker, "The Immorality of Credible Nuclear Bluffs," *Public Affairs Quarterly* 3:3 (July 1989), pp. 1–14.

Daniel D. Polsby  **NO**

The False Promise of Gun Control

During the 1960s and 1970s the robbery rate in the United States increased sixfold, and the murder rate doubled; the rate of handgun ownership nearly doubled in that period as well. Handguns and criminal violence grew together apace, and national opinion leaders did not fail to remark on the coincidence.

It has become a bipartisan article of faith that more handguns cause more violence. Such was the unequivocal conclusion of the National Commission on the Causes and Prevention of Violence in 1969, and such is now the editorial opinion of virtually every influential newspaper and magazine, from *The Washington Post* to *The Economist* to the *Chicago Tribune*. Members of the House and Senate who have not dared to confront the gun lobby concede the connection privately. Even if the National Rifle Association can produce blizzards of angry calls and letters to the Capitol virtually overnight, House members one by one have been going public, often after some new firearms atrocity at a fast-food restaurant or the like. And [in] November [1993] they passed the Brady bill.

Alas, however well accepted, the conventional wisdom about guns and violence is mistaken. Guns don't increase national rates of crime and violence—but the continued proliferation of gun-control laws almost certainly does. Current rates of crime and violence are a bit below the peaks of the late 1970s. . . . The rising generation of criminals will have no more difficulty than their elders did in obtaining the tools of their trade. Growing violence will lead to calls for laws still more severe. Each fresh round of legislation will be followed by renewed frustration.

Gun-control laws don't work. What is worse, they act perversely. While legitimate users of firearms encounter intense regulation, scrutiny, and bureaucratic control, illicit markets easily adapt to whatever difficulties a free society throws in their way. Also, efforts to curtail the supply of firearms inflict collateral damage on freedom and privacy interests that have long been considered central to American public life. Thanks to the seemingly never-ending war on drugs and long experience attempting to suppress prostitution and pornography, we know a great deal about how illicit markets function and how costly to the public attempts to control them can be. It is essential that we make use of this experience in coming to grips with gun control.

From *The Atlantic Monthly*, March 1994, pp. 57–60, 62–64, 68–70. Copyright © 1994 by Daniel D. Polsby. Reprinted by permission of Daniel D. Polsby.

⁓ The thousands of gun-control laws in the United States are of two general types. The older kind sought to regulate how, where, and by whom firearms could be carried. More recent laws have sought to make it more costly to buy, sell, or use firearms (or certain classes of firearms, such as assault rifles, Saturday-night specials, and so on) by imposing fees, special taxes, or surtaxes on them. The Brady bill is of both types: it has a background-check provision, and its five-day waiting period amounts to a "time tax" on acquiring handguns. All such laws can be called scarcity-inducing, because they seek to raise the cost of buying firearms, as figured in terms of money, time, nuisance, or stigmatization.

Despite the mounting number of scarcity-inducing laws, no one is very satisfied with them. Hobbyists want to get rid of them, and gun-control proponents don't think they go nearly far enough. Everyone seems to agree that gun-control laws have some effect on the distribution of firearms. But it has not been the dramatic and measurable effect their proponents desired.

Opponents of gun control have traditionally wrapped their arguments in the Second Amendment to the Constitution. Indeed, most modern scholarship affirms that so far as the drafters of the Bill of Rights were concerned, the right to bear arms was to be enjoyed by everyone, not just a militia, and that one of the principal justifications for an armed populace was to secure the tranquillity and good order of the community. But most people are not dedicated antiquitarians, and would not be impressed by the argument "I admit that my behavior is very dangerous to public safety, but the Second Amendment says I have a right to do it anyway." That would be a case for repealing the Second Amendment, not respecting it.

Fighting the Demand Curve

Everyone knows that possessing a handgun makes it easier to intimidate, wound, or kill someone. But the implication of this point for social policy has not been so well understood. It is easy to count the bodies of those who have been killed or wounded with guns, but not easy to count the people who have avoided harm because they had access to weapons. Think about uniformed police officers, who carry handguns in plain view not in order to kill people but simply to daunt potential attackers. And it works. Criminals generally do not single out police officers for opportunistic attack. Though officers can expect to draw their guns from time to time, few even in big-city departments will actually fire a shot (except in target practice) in the course of a year. This observation points to an important truth: people who are armed make comparatively unattractive victims. A criminal might not know if any one civilian is armed, but if it becomes known that a large number of civilians do carry weapons, criminals will become warier.

Which weapons laws are the right kinds can be decided only after considering two related questions. First, what is the connection between civilian possession of firearms and social violence? Second, how can we expect gun-control laws to alter people's behavior? Most recent scholarship raises serious questions about the "weapons increase violence" hypothesis. The second question is emphasized here, because it is routinely overlooked and often mocked when noticed; yet it is crucial. Rational gun control requires understanding not only the relationship between weapons and violence but also the relationship between laws and people's behavior. Some things are very hard to accomplish with laws. The purpose of a law and its likely effects are not always the same thing. Many statutes are notorious for the way in which their unintended effects have swamped their intended ones.

In order to predict who will comply with gun-control laws, we should remember that guns are economic goods that are traded in markets. Consumers' interest in them varies. For religious, moral, aesthetic, or practical reasons, some people would refuse to buy firearms at any price. Other people willingly pay very high prices for them.

Handguns, so often the subject of gun-control laws, are desirable for one purpose—to allow a person tactically to dominate a hostile transaction with another person. The value of a weapon to a given person is a function of two factors: how much he or she wants to dominate a confrontation if one occurs, and how likely it is that he or she will actually be in a situation calling for a gun.

Dominating a transaction simply means getting what one wants without being hurt. Where people differ is in how likely it is that they will be involved in a situation in which a gun will be valuable. Someone who *intends* to engage in a transaction involving a gun—a criminal, for example—is obviously in the best possible position to predict that likelihood. Criminals should therefore be willing to pay more for a weapon than most other people would. Professors, politicians, and newspaper editors are, as a group, at very low risk of being involved in such transactions, and they thus systematically underrate the value of defensive handguns. (Correlative, perhaps, is their uncritical readiness to accept studies that debunk the utility of firearms for self-defense.) The class of people we wish to deprive of guns, then, is the very class with the most inelastic demand for them—criminals— whereas the people most likely to comply with gun-control laws don't value guns in the first place.

Do Guns Drive Up Crime Rates?

Which premise is true—that guns increase crime or that the fear of crime causes people to obtain guns? . . .

If firearms increased violence and crime, then rates of spousal homicide would have skyrocketed, because the stock of privately owned handguns has increased rapidly since the mid-1960s. But according to an authoritative study of spousal homicide in the *American Journal of Public Health*, by James Mercy and Linda Saltzman, rates of spousal homicide in the years 1976 to 1985 fell. If firearms increased violence and crime, the crime rate should have increased throughout the 1980s, while the national stock of privately owned handguns increased by more than a million units in every year of the decade. It did not. Nor should the rates of violence and crime in Switzerland, New Zealand, and Israel be as low as they are, since the number of firearms per civilian household is comparable to that in the United States. Conversely, gun-controlled Mexico and South Africa should be islands of peace instead of having murder rates more than twice as high as those here. The determinants of crime and law-abidingness are, of course, complex matters, which are not fully understood and certainly not explicable in terms of a country's laws. But gun-control enthusiasts, who have made capital out of the low murder rate in England, which is largely disarmed, simply ignore the counterexamples that don't fit their theory.

If firearms increased violence and crime, Florida's murder rate should not have been falling since the introduction . . . of a law that makes it easier for ordinary citizens to get permits to carry concealed handguns. Yet the murder rate has remained the same or fallen every year since the law was enacted, and it is now lower than the national murder rate (which has been rising). As of November [1993] 183,561 permits had been issued, and only seventeen of the permits had been revoked because the holder was involved in a firearms offense. It would be precipitate to claim that the new law has "caused" the murder rate to subside. Yet here is a situation that doesn't fit the hypothesis that weapons increase violence.

If firearms increased violence and crime, programs of induced scarcity would suppress violence and crime. But—another anomaly—they don't. Why not? A theorem, which we could call the futility theorem, explains why gun-control laws must either be ineffectual or in the long term actually provoke more violence and crime. Any theorem depends on both observable fact and assumption. An assumption that can be made with confidence is that the higher the number of victims a criminal assumes to be armed, the higher will be the risk—the price—of assaulting them. By definition, gun-control laws should make weapons scarcer and thus more expensive. By our prior reasoning about demand among various types of consumers, after the laws are enacted criminals should be better armed, compared with noncriminals, than they were before. Of course, plenty of noncriminals will remain armed. But even if many noncriminals will pay as high a price as criminals will to obtain firearms, a larger number will not.

Criminals will thus still take the same gamble they already take in assaulting a victim who might or might not be armed. But they may appreciate that the laws have given them a freer field, and that crime still pays—pays even better, in fact, than before. What will happen to the rate of violence? Only a relatively few gun-mediated transactions—currently, five percent of armed robberies committed with firearms—result in someone's actually being shot (the statistics are not broken down into encounters between armed assailants and unarmed victims, and encounters in which both parties are armed). It seems reasonable to fear that if the number of such transactions were to increase because criminals thought they faced fewer deterrents, there would be a corresponding increase in shootings. Conversely, if gun-mediated transactions declined—if criminals initiated fewer of them because they feared encountering an armed victim or an armed good Samaritan—the number of shootings would go down. The magnitude of these effects is, admittedly, uncertain. Yet it is hard to doubt the general tendency of a change in the law that imposes legal burdens on buying guns. The futility theorem suggests that gun-control laws, if effective at all, would unfavorably affect the rate of violent crime. . . .

Are there empirical studies that can serve to help us choose between the futility theorem and the hypothesis that guns increase violence? Unfortunately, no: the best studies of the effects of gun-control laws are quite inconclusive. Our statistical tools are too weak to allow us to identify an effect clearly enough to persuade an open-minded skeptic. But it is precisely when we are dealing with undetectable statistical effects that we have to be certain we are using the best models available of human behavior.

Sealing the Border

Handguns are not legally for sale in the city of Chicago, and have not been since April of 1982. Rifles, shotguns, and ammunition are available, but only to people who possess an Illinois Firearm Owner's Identification [FOID] card. It takes up to a month to get this card, which involves a background check. Even if one has a FOID card there is a waiting period for the delivery of a gun. In few places in America is it as difficult to get a firearm legally as in the city of Chicago.

Yet there are hundreds of thousands of unregistered guns in the city, and new ones arriving all the time. It is not difficult to get handguns—even legally. Chicago residents with FOID cards merely go to gun shops in the suburbs. Trying to establish a city as an island of prohibition in a sea of legal firearms seems an impossible project.

Is a state large enough to be an effective island, then? Suppose Illinois adopted Chicago's handgun ban. Same problem again. Some people could just get guns elsewhere: Indiana actually borders the city, and Wisconsin is only forty miles away. Though federal law prohibits the sale of handguns in one state to residents of another, thousands of Chicagoans with summer homes in other states could buy handguns there. And, of course, a black market would serve the needs of other customers.

When would the island be large enough to sustain a weapons-free environment? In the United States people and cargoes move across state lines without supervision or hindrance. Local shortages of goods are always transient, no matter whether the shortage is induced by natural disasters, prohibitory laws, or something else.

Even if many states outlawed sales of handguns, then, they would continue to be available, albeit at a somewhat higher price, reflecting the increased legal risk of selling them. Mindful of the way markets work to undermine their efforts, gun-control proponents press for federal regulation of firearms, because they believe that only Congress wields the authority to frustrate the interstate movement of firearms.

Why, though, would one think that federal policing of illegal firearms would be better than local policing? The logic of that argument is far from clear. Cities, after all, are comparatively small places. Washington, D.C., for example, has an area of less than 45,000 acres. Yet local officers have had little luck repressing the illegal firearms trade there. Why should federal officers do any better watching the United States' 12,000 miles of coastline and millions of square miles of interior? Criminals should be able to frustrate federal police forces just as well as they can local ones. Ten years of increasingly stringent federal efforts to abate cocaine trafficking, for example, have not succeeded in raising the street price of the drug. . . .

In firearms regulation, translating theory into practice will continue to be difficult, at least if the objective is to lessen the practical availability of firearms to people who might abuse them. On the demand side, for defending oneself against predation there is no substitute for a firearm. Criminals, at least, can switch to varieties of law-breaking in which a gun confers little or no advantage (burglary, smash-and-grab), but people who are afraid of confrontations with criminals, whether rationally or (as an accountant might reckon it) irrationally, will be very highly motivated to acquire firearms. . . . [P]eople's demand for personal security and for the tools they believe provide it will remain strong.

On the supply side, firearms transactions can be consummated behind closed doors. Firearms buyers, unlike those who use drugs, pornography, or prostitution, need not recurrently expose themselves to legal jeopardy. One trip to the marketplace is enough to arm oneself for life. This could justify a consumer's taking even greater precautions to avoid apprehension, which would translate into even steeper enforcement costs for the police. . . .

Administering Prohibition

. . . Unless people are prepared to surrender their guns voluntarily, how can the U.S. government confiscate an appreciable fraction of our country's nearly 200 million privately owned firearms? We know that it is possible to set up weapons-free zones in certain locations—commercial airports and many courthouses and, lately, some troubled big city high schools and housing projects. The sacrifices of privacy and convenience, and the costs of paying guards, have been thought worth the (perceived) gain in security. No doubt it would be possible, though it would probably not be easy, to make weapons-free zones of shopping centers, department stores, movie theaters, ball parks. But it is not obvious how one would cordon off the whole of an open society.

Voluntary programs have been ineffectual. From time to time community-action groups or police departments have sponsored "turn in your gun" days, which are nearly always disappointing. Sometimes the government offers to buy guns at some price. . . . If the price offered exceeds that at which a gun can be bought on the street, one can expect to see plans of this kind yield some sort of harvest—as indeed they have. But it is implausible that these schemes will actually result in a less-dangerous population. Government programs to buy up surplus cheese cause more cheese to be produced without affecting the availability of cheese to people who want to buy it. So it is with guns.

One could extend the concept of intermittent roadblocks of the sort approved by the Supreme Court for discouraging drunk driving. Metal detectors could be positioned on every street corner, or ambulatory metal-detector squads could check people randomly, or hidden magnetometers could be installed around towns, to detect concealed weapons. As for firearms kept in homes (about half of American households), warrantless searches might be rationalized on the well-established theory that probable cause is not required when authorities are trying to correct dangers to public safety rather than searching for evidence of a crime. . . .

Ignoring the Ultimate Sources of Crime and Violence

The American experience with prohibition has been that black marketeers— often professional criminals—move in to profit when legal markets are closed down or disturbed. In order to combat them, new laws and law-enforcement techniques are developed, which are circumvented almost as soon as they are put in place. New and yet more stringent laws are enacted, and greater sacrifices of civil liberties and privacy demanded and submitted to. But in this case the problem, crime and violence, will not go away, because guns and ammunition (which, of course, won't go away either) do not cause it. One cannot expect people to quit seeking new weapons as long as the tactical advantages of weapons are seen to outweigh the costs imposed by prohibition. Nor can one expect large numbers of people to surrender firearms they already own. The only way to make people give up their guns is to create a world in which guns are perceived as having little value. This world will come into being when criminals choose not to use guns because the penalties for being caught with them are too great, and when ordinary citizens don't think they need firearms because they aren't afraid of criminals anymore.

Neither of these eventualities seems very likely without substantial departures in law-enforcement policy. Politicians' nostrums—increasing the punishment for crime, slapping a few more death-penalty provisions into the code—are taken seriously by few students of the crime problem. The existing penalties for predatory crimes are quite severe enough. The problem is that they are rarely meted out in the real world. The penalties formally published by the code are in practice steeply discounted, and criminals recognize that the judicial and penal systems cannot function without bargaining in the vast majority of cases.

This problem is not obviously one that legislation could solve. . . .

The problem is not simply that criminals pay little attention to the punishments in the books. Nor is it even that they also know that for the majority of crimes, their chances of being arrested are small. The most important reason for criminal behavior is this: the income that offenders can earn in the world of crime, as compared with the world of work, all too often makes crime appear to be the better choice.

. . . More prisons means that fewer violent offenders will have to be released early in order to make space for new arrivals; perhaps fewer plea bargains will have to be struck—all to the good. Yet a moment's reflection should make clear that one more criminal locked up does not necessarily mean one less criminal on the street. The situation is very like one that conservationists and hunters have always understood. Populations of game animals readily recover from hunting seasons but not from loss of habitat. Mean streets, when there are few legitimate entry level opportunities for young men, are a criminal habitat, so to speak, in the social ecology of modern American cities. Cull however much one will, the habitat will be reoccupied promptly after its previous occupant is sent away. So social science has found.

Similarly, whereas increasing the number of police officers cannot hurt, and may well increase people's subjective feelings of security, there is little evidence to suggest that doing so will diminish the rate of crime. Police forces are basically reactive institutions. . . .

There is a challenge here that is quite beyond being met with tough talk. Most public officials can see the mismatch between their tax base and the social entropies they are being asked to repair. There simply isn't enough money; existing public resources, as they are now employed, cannot possibly solve the crime problem. But mayors and senators and police chiefs must not say so out loud: too-disquieting implications would follow. For if the authorities are incapable of restoring public safety and personal security under the existing ground rules, then obviously the ground rules must change. . . .

Communities must, in short, organize more effectively to protect themselves against predators. No doubt this means encouraging properly qualified private citizens to possess and carry firearms legally. It is not morally tenable—nor, for that matter, is it even practical—to insist that police officers, few of whom are at a risk remotely as great as are the residents of many city neighborhoods, retain a monopoly on legal firearms. It is needless to fear giving honest men and women the training and equipment to make it possible for them to take back their own streets.

Over the long run, however, there is no substitute for addressing the root causes of crime—bad education and lack of job opportunities and the disintegration of families. Root causes are much out of fashion nowadays as explanations of criminal behavior, but fashionable or not, they are fundamental. *The root cause of crime is that for certain people, predation is a rational occupational choice.* Conventional crime-control measures, which by stiffening punishments or raising the probability of arrest aim to make crime pay less, cannot consistently affect the behavior of people who believe that their alternatives to crime will pay virtually nothing. Young men who did not learn basic literacy and numeracy skills before dropping out of their wretched public schools may not [be] worth hiring at the minimum wage. . . . Their legitimate opportunities, always precarious in a society where race and class still matter, often diminish to the point of being for all intents and purposes absent. . . .

The solution to the problem of crime lies in improving the chances of young men. Easier said than done, to be sure. No one has yet proposed a convincing program for checking all the dislocating forces that government assistance can set in motion. One relatively straightforward change would be reform of the educational system. Nothing guarantees prudent behavior like a sense of the future, and with average skills in reading, writing, and math, young people can realistically look forward to constructive employment and the straight life that steady work makes possible.

But firearms are nowhere near the root of the problem of violence. As long as people come in unlike sizes, shapes, ages, and temperaments, as long as they diverge in their taste for risk and their willingness and capacity to prey on other people or to defend themselves from predation, and above all as long as some people have little or nothing to lose by spending their lives in crime, dispositions to violence will persist.

This is what makes the case for the right to bear arms, not the Second Amendment. It is foolish to let anything ride on hopes for effective gun control. As long as crime pays as well as it does, we will have plenty of it, and honest folk must choose between being victims and defending themselves.

POSTSCRIPT

Should Handguns Be Banned?

Dixon asserts that there are good reasons to ban handguns. But we must also consider whether there are equally good reasons *not* to ban handguns. Dixon considers, for example, the idea that handguns are a useful part of self-defense. But, in keeping with Dixon's overall utilitarian argument, he questions whether the benefits of such self-defense—if properly conducted—outweigh the benefits that he believes will follow from handgun prohibition.

One thing that utilitarianism often overlooks is the extent to which things are connected one to another. For example, we know from experience with the environment that changing one thing may lead to changes in something else. For instance, the introduction of wolves on one island in Alaska led to the decline of the seabird population, as the wolves preyed on them; this led to a lack of bird droppings, which led to a lack of nutrients for plants, which in turn destroyed the habitat for yet other species of animals. Just as the introduction of wolves on the island did not leave everything else unchanged, Polsby argues that the removal of handguns will not necessarily result in life continuing much as it did before only without the crime and violence that is associated with handguns; instead, Polsby argues that by removing legal handguns, incentives for criminals to obtain guns through other channels (such as smuggling) are created.

Some amount of speculation is necessary to both the "pro" and the "con" side here. *Will* the removal of handguns bring about greater positive result? Will it only make matters worse? And is it even possible to remove handguns? (We have some experience of black markets in other areas. Illegal drugs, for example, can still be obtained by people who seek them.)

Polsby takes a position that is rather unusual for opponents of gun control. He emphasizes that the root cause of crime lies in social conditions such as the breakdown of families, poor schooling, and lack of occupational opportunities—especially in the case of young men. According to his view, these are social conditions that have to be addressed, possibly in the form of social programs. It is here, he suggests—and not in laws and regulations about guns—that we can come to grips with the real problems. Polsby goes so far as to say that, for certain people, the decision to prey on others (and, presumably, use a handgun in order to facilitate their preying) is a *rational* one. That is, given the facts of their situation, using a handgun and committing crimes may be a more rational thing for them to do than to seek a minimum-wage job—which, realistically, they may never even be able to find.

The problem of guns and violent crime is immense, and many-sided. Recent publications that deal with the matter of gun control, gun rights, and gun ownership are John R. Lott, Jr., *More Guns, Less Crime: Understanding Crime and Gun-Control Laws* (University of Chicago Press, 1998); Philip J. Cook and Jens Ludwig, *Gun Violence: The Real Costs* (Oxford University Press, 2002); Richard Poe, *The Seven Myths of Gun Control: Reclaiming the Truth About Guns, Crime, and the Second Amendment* (Three Rivers Press, 2003); and Warren LaPierre, *Guns, Freedom, and Terrorism* (WND Books, 2003).

ISSUE 14

Should the Death Penalty Be Abolished?

YES: Michael Welch, from *Punishment in America: Social Control and the Ironies of Imprisonment* (Sage, 1999)

NO: Ernest van den Haag, from "The Death Penalty Once More," *U.C. Davis Law Review* (Summer 1985)

ISSUE SUMMARY

YES: Criminologist Michael Welch argues that the death penalty encourages murder and is applied in a biased and mistake-laden way to growing groups of people. Much of the recent popular support of capital punishment is due to ignorance of the facts.

NO: Professor of law Ernest van den Haag argues that the death penalty is entirely in line with the U.S. Constitution and that although studies of its deterrent effect are inconclusive, the death penalty is morally justified and should not be abolished.

Since punishment involves the intentional infliction of harm upon another person, and since the intentional infliction of harm is generally wrong, the idea of punishment itself is somewhat problematic. Punishment requires some strong rationale if it is not to be just another form of wrongdoing; capital punishment requires an especially strong rationale.

Consider some actual cases of capital punishment: Socrates was tried in ancient Athens and condemned to die (by drinking poison) for not believing in the gods of the state and for corrupting young people. In 1977 a princess and her lover were executed (by firing squad and beheading, respectively) in Saudi Arabia for adultery. Also in 1977 Gary Gilmore insisted that he receive the death penalty and was executed by a firing squad in Utah for murder.

Justification for capital punishment usually comes down to one of two different lines of reasoning. One is based on the idea of justice, the other on the idea of deterrence.

Justice, it is said, demands that certain criminal acts be paid for by death. The idea is that some people deserve death and have to pay for their criminal acts with their lives.

There are several objections to this view. One of the most important of these focuses on the idea of a person "paying" for a crime by death (or even in some other way). What concept of "paying" is being used here? It does not seem like an ordinary case of paying a debt. It seems to be a kind of vengeance, as when one person says to another "I'll make you pay for that," meaning "I'll make you suffer for that." Yet one of the ideas behind state-inflicted punishment is that it is supposed to be very official, even bureaucratic, and it is designed to eliminate private vendettas and personal vindictiveness. The state, in a civilized society, is not supposed to be motivated by revenge or vindictiveness. The state's only intent is to support law and order and to protect its citizens from coming to harm at the hands of wrongdoers.

The other major line of reasoning in support of capital punishment is based on the idea of deterrence. According to this view, capital punishment must be retained in order to deter criminals and potential criminals from committing capital crimes. An old joke reflects this view: A Texan tells a visitor that in the old days the local punishment for horse-stealing was hanging. The visitor is shocked. "You used to hang people just for taking horses?" "Nope," says the Texan, "horses never got stolen."

Unlike the argument about "paying," the logic behind deterrence is supposed to be intuitively easy to understand. However, assertions concerning deterrence do not seem to be clearly borne out by actual statistics and empirical evidence.

Your intuition may support the judgment that the death penalty deters crime, but the empirical evidence is not similarly uniform and clear, and in some cases the evidence even points to the opposite conclusion. (For example, some people may be more likely to murder an innocent victim if they are reasonably certain of achieving their own death and perhaps some notoriety.) Or consider the example of the failure of deterrence that occurred in England when public hanging was the punishment for the crime of pickpocketing. Professional pickpockets, undeterred by the activity on the gallows, circulated among the crowd of spectators, aware that a good time to pick pockets was when everyone's attention was focused on something else—in this case, when the rope tightened around the neck of the convicted pickpocket.

Further thought about this matter of deterrence raises more questions. Consider this scenario: Two men get into an argument while drinking, and one pulls a gun and shoots the other, who dies. Do we suppose that this killer is even aware of the punishment for murder when he acts? Would he be deterred by the prospect of capital punishment but be willing to shoot if the punishment were only 20 years or life in prison?

In the following selection, Michael Welch argues for the abolition of the death penalty. He refers to its brutalizing effects and to a host of difficulties involving who actually receives the punishment. Then Ernest van den Haag argues against its abolition, discussing the constitutionality, possible deterrent effect, and moral justification of the death penalty.

YES

Michael Welch

The Machinery of Death: Capital Punishment and the Ironies of Social Control

Mechanical terms abound in criminal justice, connoting efficiency, stability, and equilibrium. Consider, for instance, the depiction of criminal justice as a *system* with law *enforcement*. Even critics rely on mechanical metaphors while describing criminal justice as a social control *apparatus* whose *mechanisms* function as *tools* of the ruling class (Lynch & Groves, 1989; Welch, 1996a, 1996b). Contributing to this lexicon, Justice Harry A. Blackmun referred to capital punishment as a *machinery* of death (also see Harlow, Matas, & Rocamora, 1995). The momentum behind executions has increased dramatically since the late 1970s due to several social forces, including political pandering to—and manipulation of—public opinion, the expansion of capital crimes, and the reduction of appeals, which hastens executions . . . .

The efficiency of the machinery of death has been streamlined recently in accordance with the principles of Frederick Taylor's "scientific management."[1] For example, in Arkansas, a triple execution was carried out in 1997 (the second of its kind since capital punishment was resumed). It has been said by prison officials that "such multiple executions minimize overtime costs and reduce stress on prison employees" (Kuntz, 1997, p. E-7). . . .

Although the death penalty is portrayed by its supporters as a precise, reliable, and necessary armament of criminal justice, in reality this machinery of death has proven to be imprecise, unreliable, and reckless. Opponents criticize capital punishment for perpetuating injustice because it is fraught with errors, contradictions, and various ironies. . . . [Here,] we apply Marx's (1981) notions of escalation, nonenforcement, and covert facilitation to capital punishment to illuminate its contradictions. In addition to exploring how the machinery of death produces counterdeterrent effects, creates new categories of violators and victims, and falsely convicts the innocent, we shall remain mindful of the significance of racism and classism in shaping the patterns of executions.

Escalation

. . . [Escalation] implies that "by taking enforcement action, authorities unintentionally encourage rule breaking" (Marx, 1981, p. 222). In this analysis of capital punishment, murder is one type of rule breaking we shall examine; thus, it is argued that executions not only fail to deter homicide but, ironically, promote violence. To support this claim, there is an emerging body of research documenting that capital punishment may indeed have counterdeterrent effects.

Brutalization Versus Deterrence

Despite the volume of empirical studies demonstrating that there is *no* conclusive evidence linking deterrence with capital punishment, the myth persists. Walker (1994) characterized the myth of deterrence as a crime control theology, a belief that resembles a religious conviction more than an intellectual position because it rests on faith rather than on facts. But the issue is not whether the death penalty offers greater deterrence than no penalty at all—of course it does. Rather, the issue is whether the death penalty deters more than other severe penalties, such as life imprisonment without parole. . . .

Proponents of deterrence theory argue that publicizing executions is a necessary component of capital punishment because it is through such publicity that the tough "law and order" message of death sentences is widely communicated. Conversely, a competing theory about publicized executions has challenged the notion of deterrence. Brutalization theory suggests that publicized executions not only fail to deter violence but, paradoxically, increase it. To appreciate fully brutalization theory, we must deconstruct the central element of deterrence theory, namely the assumption that potential killers are restrained from committing murder because they *identify* with those who have been executed. Brutalization theory suggests that *some* persons, rather than identifying with the condemned, identify with the executioner (Bowers & Pierce, 1980). It is crucial here to return to the principal message inherent in capital punishment: Those who commit heinous crimes *deserve* to die. Supporting this perspective, advocates of the death penalty view executions as a "public service" performed by the state, ridding society of its despicable members.

According to brutalization theory, however, publicized executions create an *alternative identification process* that promotes imitation, not deterrence. Bowers and Pierce (1980) found an increase in homicides soon after well-publicized executions, suggesting that some murderers liken their victims to the condemned. This finding was presented as evidence of a counterdeterrent effect (also see Bailey, 1983, 1998; Bowers, 1988; Cochran, Chamlin, & Seth, 1994; Decker & Kohfeld, 1990; Forst, 1983; King, 1978). It is important to emphasize that Bowers and Pierce specified that the brutalization effect has an impact on individuals who are prone to violence, not persons who are generally nonviolent; in such cases, the publicized execution reinforces the belief that lethal vengeance is justified. Executions devalue human life and "demonstrate that it is appropriate to kill those who have gravely offended us" (Bowers & Pierce, 1980, p. 456). In the context of social control, evidence engendered by brutalization studies supports the claim that capital punishment produces an ironic and escalating effect by promoting, rather than deterring, murder.

The Creation of New Categories and Net Widening

. . .

Juvenile Offenders

Increasingly, the application of the death penalty has expanded to include juveniles. Although eight states do not specify a minimum age at which the death penalty may be imposed, 14 states and the federal system require a minimum age of 18, and 16 states indicate an age of eligibility between 14 and 17 (Snell, 1996; see Table 1). In 1997, California Governor Pete Wilson reported that he would consider a state law allowing executions of 14-year olds, and Cruz M. Bustamante said he might support executions for "hardened criminals" as young as 13 (Verhovek, 1998, p. A-7). Texas State Representative Jim Pitts in 1998 proposed the death penalty for 11-year-old killers. Pitts reasoned: "This is a drastic step. . . . But some of the kids are growing up today, they just aren't the 'Leave it to Beaver' kids that I grew up with" (Verhovek, 1998, p. A-7). Reacting to the 1998 Arkansas schoolyard killings, Pitts argued that the state needs to "send a message to our kids that they can't do these kinds of crimes"(Verhovek, 1998, p. A-7).

Table 1

Minimum Age Authorized for Capital Punishment, 1996

Age 16 or Less	Age 17	Age 18	None Specified
Alabama (16)	Georgia	California	Arizona
Arkansas (14)[a]	New Hampshire	Colorado	Idaho
Delaware (16)	North Carolina[b]	Connecticut[c]	Montana
Florida (16)	Texas	Federal system	Louisiana
Indiana (16)		Illinois	Pennsylvania
Kentucky (16)		Kansas	South Carolina
Mississippi (16)[d]		Maryland	South Dakota[e]
Missouri (16)		Nebraska	Utah
Nevada (16)		New Jersey	
Oklahoma (16)		New Mexico	
Virginia (14)[f]		New York	
Wyoming (16)		Ohio	
		Oregon	
		Tennessee	
		Washington	

Source: Snell (1997, p. 5).
Note: Reporting by states reflects interpretations by state attorney general offices and may differ from previously reported ages.
a. See Arkansas Code Ann. 9-27-318(b)(1)(Repl. 1991).
b. The age required is 17 unless the murderer was incarcerated for murder when a subsequent murder occurred; then the age may be 14.
c. See Conn. Gen. Stat. 53a-46a(g)(1).
d. The minimum age defined by statute is 13, but the effective age is 16, based on a Mississippi Supreme Court decision.
e. Juveniles may be transferred to adult court. Age can be a mitigating factor.
f. The minimum age for transfer to adult court is 14 by statute, but the effective age for a capital sentence is 16, based on interpretation of a U.S. Supreme Court decision by the state attorney general's office.

Mentally Handicapped Offenders
The new categories of offenders eligible for the death penalty also include the emotionally and mentally handicapped. Although in recent memory the U.S. Supreme Court has prohibited the execution of emotionally disturbed capital defendants (*Ford v. Wainwright,* 1986; Miller & Radelet, 1993; Paternoster, 1991), such restrictions have been not been uniformly enforced. In 1995, Varnall Weeks, a convicted murderer diagnosed by psychiatric experts as a paranoid schizophrenic, was executed in Alabama. Weeks was clearly disturbed: Living in a maze of delusions, he believed that "he would come back to life as a giant flying tortoise that would rule the world" (Bragg, 1995, p. 7). At one of his hearings, Weeks described himself as God, wore a domino on a band around his shaved head, and responded to the court's question with a "rambling discourse on serpents, cybernetics, albinos, Egyptians, the Bible, and reproduction. . . . [He also] sat in his cell naked in his own feces, mouthing senseless sounds" (Shapiro, 1995, p. A-29). Although prosecution and defense acknowledged that he suffered from paranoid schizophrenia, the courts contended that he was sane enough to be executed. The U.S. Supreme Court unanimously rejected his appeal. To date, legislators and the courts have not established a consistent or humane definition of how sane or competent a capital defendant needs to be in order to be executed.

Whereas the death penalty for mentally ill murderers is characterized by inconsistent court rulings, there are no such obstacles interfering with the execution of mentally retarded capital defendants (those scoring below 70 on a standardized intelligence test). It has been speculated that throughout history, mildly retarded offenders have been commonly executed but that their level of intelligence was never known to the courts because such tests were not conducted. Today, defendants are routinely administered intelligence tests; thus, the courts are fully aware of the defendant's level of intelligence. In 1989, the High Court ruled in *Penry v. Lynaugh* that states have the right to execute mentally retarded persons convicted of capital murder.

Critics point out that executing mentally retarded (even mildly retarded) offenders raises serious moral and ethical issues, especially because mental retardation constitutes a serious liability affecting every dimension of that person's life. "Many individuals who are sentenced to death and executed in this country have mental retardation" (Harlow et al., 1995, p. 1; Reed, 1993). Persons with mental retardation are quite susceptible to suggestion and have serious difficulty in logic, planning, and understanding consequences. With this in mind, Professor of Special Education Ruth Luckasson asked, "Can you imagine anyone easier to execute?" (quoted in Harlow et al., 1995, p. 1). Luckasson added, "I have seen people with mental retardation sitting in their own capital trials, with their lives at stake, who had absolutely no understanding of what was going on" (quoted in Harlow et al., 1995, p. 1). In 1992, Bill Clinton, then governor of Arkansas, refused to halt the execution of Ricky Ray Rector, who had blown away part of his brain in a suicide attempt just after he had killed a police officer. At the time of his trial, Rector was so mentally retarded that "he did not understand that death was permanent"

(Ridgeway, 1994, p. 23). On the day of his death, he told his lawyer that "he planned to vote for Mr. Clinton that November" (Shapiro, 1995, p. A-29) and asked the guards to "save his dessert for a snack before bedtime" (Terry, 1998, p. 22).

In 1995, Mario Marquez was executed by the state of Texas after being convicted of double murder and rape. Marquez, a grade-school dropout with an IQ of 65, was the 10th of 16 children born to a migrant farmworker. As a child, he was beaten with a horsewhip by his father and abandoned to the streets and a life of drug abuse at the age of 12. During the trial, Marquez asked his lawyer "if he [Marquez] was going to have a good job when he goes to heaven" and wanted his lawyer to tell him "if he could get a job being a gardener, or taking care of animals" (Hentoff, 1995, p. 30). . . .

In sum, capital punishment generates an escalating, counterdeterrent effect because, by taking enforcement action (i.e., performing executions), authorities unintentionally encourage a type of rule breaking, namely homicide. The irony of this form of social control is supported by brutalization research. To reiterate, a particularly important analytic element of escalation is the creation of new categories of violators and victims. Such categories are the products of legislation, driven by relentless political pandering to the public on crime. Not only do these self-serving political activities widen the net of capital punishment, but they tend to snare violators—juveniles, the mentally handicapped, the emotionally disturbed—who paradoxically become vulnerable victims of an overzealous criminal justice apparatus.

Nonenforcement

. . . [Nonenforcement] constitutes another irony of social control in that authorities, by taking no enforcement action, intentionally permit rule breaking (Marx, 1981). Arguably one of the more tragic examples of nonenforcement can be found in America's history of vigilante "justice," particularly lynching. Authorities deliberately encouraged these travesties of justice by refusing to impose sanctions on persons who carried them out. In addition, many of these incidents of nonenforcement were motivated by racism, in that blacks served as convenient scapegoats.

Contemporary examinations of racism and the death penalty should not neglect the history of formal (executions) and informal (lynchings) penalties imposed on black defendants and suspects. Following the Civil War, black codes were *formally* established to perpetuate the economic subordination of former slaves. Such codes employed harsher penalties for crimes committed by blacks and led to a disproportionate number of black executions. *Informally*, black men also were subject to lynching (illegal execution) by vigilante mobs. Bowers (1984) reported that in the 1890s there were more lynchings (1,540) than legal executions (1,098). Though lynchings gradually declined, nearly 2,000 illegal executions occurred in the early part of the 20th century: Between 1900 and 1909 there were 885 reported lynchings, between 1910 and 1919, 621 lynchings, and in the 1920s, 315 (Bowers, 1984; also see Brundage, 1993; Jackson, 1996; Tolnay & Beck, 1992, 1994).[2]

Nowadays, a long-standing criticism of the death penalty is that despite efforts to guard against arbitrariness (as enumerated in *Gregg v. Georgia*, 1976), it continues to be administered in ways that are racially biased. Casual observers of the death penalty controversy might assume that the death penalty is racially discriminatory because black murderers, compared to white murderers, are disproportionately sentenced to death. This assumption, however, would be too simplistic. To clarify the extent of racism evident in the death penalty, one must look at the race of the victim as well as the race of the offender. In the United States, approximately half of those murdered each year are black. However, since 1977, about 85% of capital defendants who have been executed had killed a white person, whereas only 11% had murdered a black person (Baldus, Woodworth, & Pulaski, 1990). Research continues to demonstrate that killers of whites are more likely than killers of blacks to be sentenced to death: Paternoster (1983) revealed that blacks who kill whites have a 4.5 times greater chance of facing the death penalty than blacks who kill blacks. When the race of the victim is ignored, the chances of blacks' and whites' receiving a death sentence are almost equal. Furthermore, Keil and Vito (1989) found that when controlling for seriousness of the murder (in Kentucky), "Prosecutors were more likely to seek the death penalty in cases in which blacks killed whites and . . . juries were more likely to sentence to death blacks who killed whites" (p. 511). Baldus et al. (1990) concluded that when the murder victim was white, the chance of a death penalty was roughly doubled in certain kinds of cases: in particular, those cases catalogued as "middle-ground" incidents in which the victim was killed during the commission of a felony (e.g., homicide during a robbery).[3] In a recent study on racial disparities in capital punishment, Baldus (in press) reported that in Philadelphia, black defendants in murder cases are four times more likely than other defendants to be sentenced to death, even when the circumstances of the killings are the same (see Butterfield, 1998). . . .

The racial bias in capital punishment should be viewed as another irony of social control, especially in the realm of nonenforcement. Given that only 11% of all executions involve capital defendants convicted of killing a black person, there is the appearance that the lives of white victims are more valuable than black victims. From 1977 to 1995, 88 black men were executed for murdering whites, whereas only 2 white men have been executed for killing blacks (Eckholm, 1995). To date, Texas—the all-time leader of executions with 404 at year end 1996—has never executed *anyone* for killing a black person. . . .

Incidentally, in Virginia in 1998, Louis Ceparano pleaded guilty to burning alive a black man, Garnett P. Johnson, and chopping off his head with an ax. Ceparano was one of two white men accused of soaking Johnson with gasoline and subjecting him to racial slurs, then setting fire to him. Ceparano was spared the death penalty and received two consecutive life terms without possibility of parole ("White Man Pleads Guilty," 1998).

Advocates who believe that the death penalty can be modified to eliminate its racial bias (van den Haag & Conrad, 1983) are likely to encounter an even greater irony. Because in most murders, the assailant and the victim are of the same race, eliminating the disparity linked to the race of the victim would be likely to result in a higher proportion of blacks sentenced to death.

> If killers of black people were executed at the rate of killers of whites, many more blacks would receive death sentences. If, on the other hand, killers of whites were executed at the same rate as killers of blacks, many whites would be spared. (Eckholm, 1995, p. B-4)

The history of black lynchings in America serves as a reminder of egregious acts of nonenforcement that authorized and perpetuated the racist practice of unlawful executions. Nowadays, incidents of nonenforcement are not as clear-cut and obvious. Admittedly, it is unlikely that authorities *intentionally* encourage lethal violence against blacks. Still, executions remain significantly patterned by the race of the victim, thereby suggesting that in the eyes of the state, white murder victims are inherently more valuable than their black counterparts. Thus, racial disparities in capital punishment contradict fundamental principles of justice in a democratic society.

Covert Facilitation

Although sentencing disparities according to the race of murder victims violate basic ideals of fairness, such contradictions are compounded when innocent people are falsely convicted, and worse, executed. False convictions in capital crimes may be the result of error, wrongdoing, or a combination of the two. Whereas the former serves as evidence of an imperfect criminal justice system, the latter reveals an insidious side of the machinery of death. The deliberate prosecution of innocent people typically emerges in the form of covert facilitation: hidden or deceptive enforcement action in which authorities intentionally encourage rule breaking (Marx, 1981). In this context, *rule breaking* refers to wrongdoing by the prosecutors and police that is encouraged by the state for the purpose of securing capital convictions, even if the suspect is innocent (e.g., framing a suspect, prosecutorial misconduct, allowing perjured testimony). Cases of false conviction shed additional light on racism and classism because people of color and the impoverished are more vulnerable to these miscarriages of justice.

Capital punishment experts have long speculated that numerous innocent persons have been convicted, and in some instances, executed; still, a general understanding of such injustices was previously based on anecdotal and unsystematic research. Then, in 1987, Hugo Bedau and Michael Radelet published a systematic study of 350 defendants believed to have been wrongly convicted in capital (or potential capital) cases between the years 1900 and 1985. It is important to note that Bedau and Radelet did not simply include any case that appeared suspect. Rather, they applied strict standards of miscarriages of justice and accepted cases only on the basis of *overwhelming* evidence that an innocent person had been falsely convicted. In an expanded volume of their work, Radelet, Bedau and Putnam released *In Spite of Innocence: Erroneous Convictions in Capital Cases* (1992), cataloguing 416 cases of falsely convicted capital defendants between 1900 and 1991. Approximately one-third of these defendants were sentenced to death, and the authors persuasively documented 23 cases in which innocent people were executed. Most of the remaining defendants, though initially trapped in the machinery of justice, fortunately escaped execution. Radelet et al. referred to them as the lucky ones. Nevertheless, they still experienced years of incarceration along with the agony of uncertainty; consequently, their lives were virtually ruined (also see Dieter, 1997; Huff, Rattner, & Sagarin, 1996).

Covert facilitation is commonly found in the most egregious cases of false convictions, and as we shall see, racism and classism also permeate many such travesties of justice. Consider Walter McMillian, who, after spending 6 years on Alabama's death row, was released in 1993. Upon further scrutiny, different prosecutors conceded that the state had withheld evidence from his lawyers and had relied on perjured testimony to falsely convict McMillian. In a case that fits the "middle-ground" category of homicide, Ronda Morrison, an 18-year-old white female clerk, was murdered by a black male during a robbery in Monroeville, Alabama—coincidentally, the home town of Harper Lee, author of *To Kill a Mockingbird* (1960), a story of race and justice in the Jim Crow South. While being interrogated in connection to another killing, Ralph Myers, an ex-con with a lengthy criminal record, accused McMillian of murdering Morrison. In an unusual move, McMillian was assigned to death row before his trial. After a one-and-a-half day trial, McMillian was convicted on the testimony of three witnesses, including that of Myers and another criminal suspect. The defense lawyer called a dozen witnesses who each testified that McMillian was at home the day of the murder, socializing with friends at a fish fry. The prosecution offered no physical evidence linking McMillian to the murder; thus, critics insist that the trial was driven by racism. It was well known that McMillian was dating a white woman and that one of his sons had married a white woman; both McMillian and his attorney believed that these interracial relationships motivated the prosecution (Dieter, 1997).

The Alabama Bureau of Investigation eventually discredited the prosecution's case against McMillian. All three witnesses recanted their testimony, and Myers also reported that he was pressured by law officers to accuse McMillian. The case emerged at a time when federal appeals for capital defendants were becoming increasingly restricted, a reminder of how flawed—and corrupt—the machinery of death can be. Bryan Stevenson, McMillian's attorney, said, "It's clear that he had nothing to do with this crime. There are other folks in prison who don't have the money or the resources or the good fortune to have folks come in and help them" (Applebome, 1993, p. B-11).

In another recent case, all charges were dropped against three black men who were incarcerated in an Illinois prison from 1978 to 1996 for a double murder they did not commit. Dennis Williams spent much of that sentence waiting on death row, as did Verneal Jimerson, a fourth black inmate whose charges were dismissed a month earlier. Their case not only underscores the flaws of the criminal justice system but sheds additional light on the controversy over the restriction of federal death penalty appeals recently affirmed by the U.S. Supreme Court. The reduction of federal appeals for capital defendants is expected to cut in half the time between conviction and execution (from approximately 8 to 4 years). Richard C. Dieter, director of the Death Penalty Information Center, warns that these restrictions mean that the length of appeals would "fall well below the average time it takes to discover new evidence of innocence. . . . This rush to get on with the death penalty by shortening the appeals process will raise the danger of executing innocent people" (Terry, 1996, p. A-14).

The case against Williams, Jimerson, and their codefendants, Willie Rainge and Kenneth Williams, stems from the murder of a white couple in suburban Chicago in 1978, but new DNA evidence, witness recantations, and a jailhouse confession led to their release. Cook County State's Attorney Jack O'Malley said his office was trying to determine how the original investigation "got derailed and why it is the wrong people were charged" (Terry, 1996, p. A-14). To this, Dennis Williams quickly responded *racism*: "The police just picked up the first young black men they could and that was it. . . . They didn't care if we were guilty or innocent. . . . We are victims of this crime too" (Terry, 1996, p. A-14). In a strange turn of events, Jimerson had been previously released when the only witness connecting him to the crime recanted; later, in a deal to get released from prison, the witness changed her testimony again. Jimerson was then rearrested, convicted, and sentenced to die. Jimerson and his codefendants believe they were indeed *framed* by the prosecution.

Contrary to popular belief, capital cases often are not meticulously litigated. Indigent defendants assigned court-appointed attorneys stand a good chance of being consumed by the machinery of death. . . .

Although the term *presumed innocence* rings of democratic notions of justice, many prosecutors smugly overlook its importance. Even Edwin R. Meese, while serving as U.S. Attorney General, stated that "suspects who are innocent of a crime should [have the right to have lawyer present during police questioning]. But the thing is, you don't have many suspects who are innocent of a crime. That's contradictory. If a person is innocent of a crime, he is not a suspect" ("Attorney General Speaks," 1985, p. 67). . . .

[The] concept covert facilitation is useful in analyzing the complex ironies of capital punishment. From this perspective, we can look beyond *honest* mistakes occurring in capital cases and examine activities that are truly pernicious. In these cases, capital defendants not only face a flawed criminal justice process but also risk being falsely convicted by unethical prosecutors willing to frame suspects to advance their political aspirations. Again, minorities, the impoverished, and the mentally handicapped remain easy targets of covert facilitation.

Conclusion

Despite clear and compelling evidence that the system of capital punishment has glaring biases and errors, its popularity continues to rise. Approximately 80% of the U.S. population favors the death penalty for offenders convicted of first-degree murder (Moore, 1994), and this level of support is the highest since 1936 (Bohm, 1991).[4] Researchers have found, however, that Americans are greatly misinformed about capital punishment (Bohm, 1991, 1996; Bowers, 1993). Ironically, then, the enormous public support for the death penalty is based, not on a sophisticated understanding of the facts, but on beliefs rooted in popular myths of criminal justice.

[Here] we explored the machinery of death as it pertains to the ironies of social control, namely escalation, nonenforcement, and covert facilitation. To summarize, [we] confronted significant contradictions apparent in American capital punishment. The United States is the only Western industrialized democracy to execute offenders, and this practice continues to violate contemporary standards of decency, especially the execution of juveniles and the mentally retarded. Contradictions also are found in the death penalty's failure to offer a deterrent effect, protect the community (including police; Bailey & Peterson, 1987), eliminate racial and socioeconomic biases, and ensure that innocent people are not falsely convicted or executed. In addition, the death penalty is confounded by several other problems that reveal deep structural contradictions in the social control apparatus, including financial costs, the alliance between the state and certain physicians and psychiatrists who facilitate the execution protocol, and the recent restriction of appeals, all of which paradoxically make errors more likely. . . .

The nation's enthusiasm for the death penalty has become a "fatal attraction" insofar as its contradictions and ironies lead to a self-defeating form of social control. In addition to producing a counterdeterrent effect (i.e., brutalization), a greater commitment to capital punishment creates more categories of violators (and victims), resulting in a higher volume of death sentences. A greater commitment to expediting capital cases by eliminating appeals also means more mistakes are likely to occur.[5] In the end, capital punishment policy is reckless and unjust—especially for people of color, the impoverished, and the mentally handicapped.

Notes

1. Frederick Taylor (1856–1915) promoted the "efficiency movement" in managing the industrial workforce, emphasizing the optimum use of time and motion.
2. A discussion of racism and the death penalty ought to include references to *racial hoaxes* in which black men are easily targeted as criminal suspects. Consider the cases of Charles Stuart, Susan V. Smith, and Jesse Anderson, all of whom committed premeditated murder and falsely reported to police that their crimes were the acts of a black man (Russell, 1998; Welch, 1996a).
3. Baldus et al. (1990) showed that disparities in the death penalty are more clearly understood by classifying murders into three types. The first category includes crimes of passion and killings in barroom brawls; these rarely draw the death penalty. The second category includes grisly murders such as mass and serial killings; these are typically sanctioned by capital punishment, regardless of race. However, racial disparities most commonly arise in the third category, known as "middle-ground" incidents in which homicide occurs during the commission of a felony (e.g., armed robbery); in this type of murder, the race of the victim is a crucial factor in determining the penalty. The killing of a white victim under these circumstances, especially when the perpetrator is black, has the highest chance of drawing capital punishment.
4. Researchers also conclude that the support for the death penalty may not be as deep as the polls suggest. When given the choice between favoring

the death penalty and life imprisonment with absolutely no possibility of parole, support for the death penalty drops to less than half (Bohm, 1991, 1996; Bowers, 1993; Gallup & Newport, 1991; McGarrell & Sandys, 1996).

5. Opponents of the death penalty are alarmed and enraged over Congress's passing of the Anti-Terrorism and Effective Death Penalty Act of 1996, which sharply limits the prisoner's ability to file more than one habeas corpus petition. In 1996, Congress also voted to stop funding ($20 million) the Post-Conviction Defender Organizations that have played a vital role in representing death row inmates. In reaction to this move and to Congress's curtailing of federal habeas corpus protections, the American Bar Association in 1997 called for the suspension of the death penalty until the system is changed to afford adequate due process ("A Lawyerly Cry of Conscience," 1997). Regarding the defender's program, the *New York Times* editorialized, "It deserves to live. A Congress committed to the death penalty cannot in good conscience deny competent legal counsel. Abolishing the Defender Organizations harms the causes of economy, speed, and justice" ("Shortchanging Inmates," 1995, p. A-32).

References

Applebome, P. (1993, March 3). Alabama releases man held on death row for six years. *New York Times*, pp. A-1, B-11.

Attorney General speaks. (1985, October 14). *U.S. News and World Report*, p. 67.

Bailey, W. C. (1983). Disaggregation in deterrence and death penalty research: The case of murder in Chicago. *Journal of Criminal Law and Criminology, 74*, 827–859.

Bailey, W. C. (1998). Deterrence and brutalization, and the death penalty. *Criminology, 36*, 711–734.

Bailey, W. C., & Peterson, R. D. (1987). Police killings and capital punishment. The post-Furman period. *Criminology, 25*, 1–26.

Baldus, D. (in press). The death penalty in black and white: Who lives, who dies, who decides. *Cornell Law Review*.

Baldus, D., Woodworth, G., & Pulaski, C. (1990). *Equal justice and the death penalty: A legal and empirical analysis*. Boston: Northeastern University Press.

Bohm, R. (1991). American death penalty opinion, 1936–1986: A critical examination of the Gallup polls. In R. Bohm (Ed.), *The death penalty in America: Current research* (pp. 113–145). Cincinnati, OH: Anderson.

Bohm, R. (1996). Understanding and changing public support for capital punishment. *Corrections Now, 1*(1), 1–4.

Bowers, W. J. (1984). *Legal homicide: Death as punishment in America, 1864–1982*. Boston: Northeastern University Press.

Bowers, W. J. (1988). The effect of execution is brutalization, not deterrence. In K. Hass & J. Inciardi (Eds.), *Challenging capital punishment: Legal and social science approaches* (pp. 49–90). Newbury Park, CA: Sage.

Bowers, W. J. (1993). Capital punishment and contemporary values: People's misgivings and the court's misperceptions. *Law and Society Review, 27*, 157–175.

Bowers, W. J., & Pierce, G. (1980). Deterrence or brutalization: What is the effect of executions. *Crime and Delinquency, 26*, 453–484.

Bragg, R. (1995, May 13). A killer racked by delusions dies in Alabama's electric chair. *New York Times*, p. 7.

Brundage, W. (1993). *Lynching in the New South: Georgia and Virginia, 1880–1930*. Champaign: University of Illinois Press.

Butterfield, F. (1998, June 7). New study adds to evidence of bias in death sentences. *New York Times*, p. 20.

Cochran, J. K., Chamlin, M., & Seth, M. (1994). Deterrence or brutalization? An impact assessment of Oklahoma's return to capital punishment. *Criminology, 32*, 107–134.

Decker, S., & Kohfeld, C. (1990). The deterrent effect of capital punishment in the five most active execution states: A time series analysis. *Criminal Justice Review, 15*, 173–191.

Dieter, R. (1997). *Innocence and the death penalty: The increasing danger of executing the innocent.* Washington, DC: Death Penalty Information Center.

Eckholm, E. (1995, February 25). Studies find death penalty tied to race of the victims. *New York Times*, pp. B-1, B-2.

Ford v. Wainwright, 477 U.S. 699 (1986).

Forst, B. (1983). Capital punishment and deterrence: Conflicting evidence? *Journal of Criminal Law and Criminology, 74*, 927–942.

Gallup, A., & Newport, F. (1991, June). Death penalty support remains strong. *Gallup Monthly Report*, No. 321, pp. 3–5.

Gregg v. Georgia, 428 U.S. 153 (1976).

Harlow, E., Matas, D., & Rocamora, J. (1995). *The machinery of death: A shocking indictment of capital punishment in the United States.* New York: Amnesty International.

Hentoff, N. (1995, February 21). Executing the retarded in our name. *Village Voice*, pp. 30–31.

Huff, C. R., Rattner, A., & Sagarin, E. (1996). *Convicted but innocent: Wrongful conviction and public policy.* Thousand Oaks, CA: Sage.

Jackson, J. (1996). *Legal lynching: Racism, injustice, and the death penalty.* New York: Marlowe.

Keil, T., & Vito, G. (1989). Race, homicide severity, and application of the death penalty: A consideration of the Barnett Scale. *Criminology, 27*, 511–536.

King, D. (1978). The brutalization effect: Execution publicity and the incidence of homicide in South Carolina. *Social Forces, 57*, 683–687.

Kuntz, T. (1997, January 12). Banality, nausea, triple execution: Guards on inmates' final hours. *New York Times*, p. E-7.

A lawyerly cry of conscience. (1997, February 22). *New York Times*, p. 20.

Lee, H. (1960). *To kill a mockingbird.* New York: HarperCollins.

Lynch, M., & Groves, W. B. (1989). *A primer in radical criminology.* New York: Harrow & Heston.

Marx, G. (1981). Ironies of social control: Authorities as contributors to deviance through escalation, nonenforcement, and covert facilitation. *Social Problems, 28*, 221–233.

McGarrell, E. F., & Sandys, M. (1996). Misperception of public opinion toward capital punishment: Examining the spuriousness explanation of death penalty support. *American Behavioral Scientist, 39*, 500–513.

Miller, K., & Radelet, M. (1993). *Executing the mentally ill: The criminal justice system and the case of Alvin Ford.* Newbury Park, CA: Sage.

Moore, D. W. (1994, September). Majority advocate death penalty for teenage killers. *Gallup Poll Monthly*, No. 321, pp. 2–5.

Paternoster, R. (1983). Race of the victim and location of crime: The decision to seek the death penalty in South Carolina. *Journal of Criminal Law and Criminology, 74*, 754–785.

Paternoster, R. (1991). *Capital punishment in America.* New York: Lexington.

Penry v. Lynaugh, 57 U.S.L.W. 4958 (1989).

Radelet, M., Bedau, H., & Putnam, C. (1992). *In spite of innocence: Erroneous convictions in capital cases.* Boston: Northeastern University Press.

Reed, E. (1993). *The Penry penalty: Capital punishment and offenders with mental retardation.* Landam, MD: University Press of America.

Ridgeway, J. (1994, October 11). Slaughterhouse justice: Race, poverty, and politics: The essential ingredients for a death penalty conviction. *Village Voice*, pp. 23–24.

Russell, K. (1998). *The color of crime: Racial hoaxes, white fear, black protectionism, police aggression and other macroaggressions.* New York: New York University Press.

Shapiro, A. (1995, May 11). An insane execution. *New York Times*, p. A-29.

Shortchanging inmates on death row. (1995, October 13). *New York Times*, p. A-32.

Snell, T. (1997). *Capital punishment 1996*. Washington, DC: Bureau of Justice Statistics.

Terry, D. (1996, July 3). After 18 years in prison, 3 are cleared of murders. *New York Times*, p. A-14.

Terry, D. (1998, April 12). Jury to decide if condemned man comprehends his fate. *New York Times*, p. 22.

Tolnay, S., & Beck, E. (1994). Lethal social control in the South: Lynchings and executions between 1880 and 1930. In G. Bridges & M. Myers (Eds.), *Inequality, crime, and social control* (pp. 176–194). Boulder, CO: Westview.

van den Haag, E., & Conrad, J. (1983). *The death penalty: A debate*. New York: Plenum.

Verhovek, S. (1998, April 18). Texas legislator proposes the death penalty for murderers as young as 11. *New York Times*, p. A-7.

Walker, S. (1994). *Sense and nonsense about crime and drugs: A policy guide* (3rd ed.). Belmont, CA: Wadsworth.

Welch, M. (1996a). *Corrections: A critical approach*. New York: McGraw-Hill.

Welch, M. (1996b). Critical criminology, social justice, and an alternative view of incarceration. *Critical Criminoloy: An International Journal, 7*(2), 43–58.

White man pleads guilty to killing a black man. (1998, May 31). *New York Times*, p. 22.

Ernest van den Haag  **NO**

The Death Penalty Once More

People concerned with capital punishment disagree on essentially three questions: (1) Is it constitutional? (2) Does the death penalty deter crime more than life imprisonment? (3) Is the death penalty morally justifiable?

Is the Death Penalty Constitutional?

The fifth amendment, passed in 1791, states that "no person shall be deprived of life, liberty, or property, without due process of law." Thus, with "due process of law," the Constitution authorizes depriving persons "of life, liberty or property." The fourteenth amendment, passed in 1868, applies an identical provision to the states. The Constitution, then, authorizes the death penalty. It is left to elected bodies to decide whether or not to retain it.

The eighth amendment, reproducing almost verbatim a passage from the English Bill of Rights of 1689, prohibits "cruel and unusual punishments." This prohibition was not meant to repeal the fifth amendment since the amendments were passed simultaneously. "Cruel" punishment is not prohibited unless "unusual" as well, that is, new, rare, not legislated, or disproportionate to the crime punished. Neither the English Bill of Rights, nor the eighth amendment, hitherto has been found inconsistent with capital punishment.

Evolving Standards

Some commentators argue that, in *Trop v. Dulles*, the Supreme Court indicated that "evolving standards of decency that mark the progress of a maturing society" allow courts to declare "cruel and unusual," punishments authorized by the Constitution. However, *Trop* was concerned with expatriation, a punishment that is not specifically authorized by the Constitution. The death penalty is. *Trop* did not suggest that "evolving standards" could de-authorize what the Constitution repeatedly authorizes. Indeed, Chief Justice Warren, writing for the majority in *Trop*, declared that "the death penalty . . . cannot be said to violate the constitutional concept of cruelty."[1] Furthermore, the argument based on "evolving standards" is paradoxical: the Constitution would be redundant if current views, enacted by judicial fiat, could supersede what it plainly says. If "standards of decency" currently invented or evolved could, without formal amendment, replace or repeal the standards authorized by the Constitution, the Constitution would be superfluous.

It must be remembered that the Constitution does not force capital punishment on the population but merely authorizes it. Elected bodies are left to decide whether to use the authorization. As for "evolving standards," how could courts detect them without popular consensus as a guide? Moral revelations accepted by judges, religious leaders, sociologists, or academic elites, but not by the majority of voters, cannot suffice. The opinions of the most organized, most articulate, or most vocal might receive unjustified deference. Surely the eighth amendment was meant to limit, but was not meant to replace, decisions by the legislative branch, or to enable the judiciary [to] do what the voters won't do.[2] The general consensus on which the courts would have to rely could be registered only by elected bodies. They favor capital punishment. Indeed, at present, more than seventy percent of the voters approve of the death penalty. The state legislatures reflect as much. Wherefore, the Supreme Court, albeit reluctantly, rejected abolition of the death penalty by judicial *fiat*. This decision was subsequently qualified by a finding that the death penalty for rape is disproportionate to the crime,[3] and by rejecting all mandatory capital punishment.

Caprice

Laws that allowed courts too much latitude to decide, perhaps capriciously, whether to actually impose the death penalty in capital cases also were found unconstitutional. In response, more than two-thirds of the states have modified their death penalty statutes, listing aggravating and mitigating factors, and imposing capital punishment only when the former outweigh the latter. The Supreme Court is satisfied that this procedure meets the constitutional requirements of non-capriciousness. However, abolitionists are not.

In *Capital Punishment: The Inevitability of Caprice and Mistake*,[4] Professor Charles Black contends that the death penalty is necessarily imposed capriciously, for irremediable reasons. If he is right, he has proved too much, unless capital punishment is imposed more capriciously now than it was in 1791 or 1868, when the fifth and fourteenth amendments were enacted. He does not contend that it is. Professor Black also stresses that the elements of chance, unavoidable in all penalizations, are least tolerable when capital punishment is involved. But the irreducible chanciness inherent in human efforts does not constitutionally require the abolition of capital punishment, unless the framers were less aware of chance and human frailty than Professor Black is. (I shall turn to the moral as distinguished from the legal bearing of chanciness anon.)

Discrimination

Sociologists have demonstrated that the death penalty has been distributed in a discriminatory pattern in the past: black or poor defendants were more likely to be executed than equally guilty others. This argues for correction of the distributive process, but not for abolition of the penalty it distributes, unless constitutionally excessive maldistribution ineluctably inheres in the penalty. There is no evidence to that effect. Actually, although we cannot be sure that it has disappeared altogether, discrimination has greatly decreased compared to the past.[5]

However, recently the debate on discrimination has taken a new turn. Statistical studies have found that, *ceteris paribus*, a black man who murders a white has a much greater chance to be executed than he would have had, had his victim been black.[6] This discriminates against black *victims* of murder: they are not as fully, or as often, vindicated as are white victims. However, although unjustified per se, discrimination against a class of victims need not, and here does not, amount to discrimination against their victimizers. The pattern discriminates *against* black murderers of whites and *for* black murderers of blacks. One may describe it as discrimination for, or discrimination against, just as one may describe a glass of water as half full or half empty. Discrimination against one group (here, blacks who kill whites) is necessarily discrimination in favor of another (here, blacks who kill blacks).

Most black victims are killed by black murderers, and a disproportionate number of murder victims is black. Wherefore the discrimination in favor of murderers of black victims more than offsets, numerically, any remaining discrimination against other black murderers.[7]

Comparative Excessiveness

Recently lawyers have argued that the death penalty is unconstitutionally disproportionate if defendants, elsewhere in the state, received lesser sentences for comparable crimes. But the Constitution only requires that penalties be appropriate to the gravity of the crime, not that they cannot exceed penalties imposed elsewhere. Although some states have adopted "comparative excessiveness" reviews, there is no constitutional requirement to do so.

Unavoidably, different courts, prosecutors, defense lawyers, judges and juries produce different penalties even when crimes seem comparable. Chance plays a great role in human affairs. Some offenders are never caught or convicted, while others are executed; some are punished more than others guilty of worse crimes. Thus, a guilty person, or group of persons, may get away with no punishment, or with a light punishment, while others receive the punishment they deserve. Should we let these others go too, or punish them less severely? Should we abolish the penalty applied unequally or discriminatorily?[8]

The late Justice Douglas suggested an answer to these questions:

> A law that . . . said that blacks, those who never went beyond the fifth grade in school, those who made less than $3,000 a year, or those who were unpopular or unstable should be the only people executed [would be wrong]. A law which in the overall view reaches that result in practice has no more sanctity than a law which in terms provides the same.[9]

Justice Douglas' answer here conflates an imagined discriminatory law with the discriminatory application of a non-discriminatory law. His imagined law would be inconsistent with the "equal protection of the laws" demanded by the fourteenth amendment, and the Court would have to invalidate it *ipso facto*.

But discrimination caused by uneven application of non-discriminatory death penalty laws may be remedied by means other than abolition, as long as the discrimination is not intrinsic to the laws.

Consider now, albeit fleetingly, the moral as distinguished from the constitutional bearing of discrimination. Suppose guilty defendants are justly executed, but only if poor, or black and not otherwise. This unequal justice would be morally offensive for what may be called tautological reasons:[10] if any punishment for a given crime is just, then a greater or lesser punishment is not. Only one punishment can be just for all persons equally guilty of the same crime.[11] Therefore, different punishments for equally guilty persons or group members are unjust: some offenders are punished more than they deserve, or others less.

Still, equality and justice are not the same. "Equal justice" is not a redundant phrase. Rather, we strive for two distinct ideals, justice and equality. Neither can replace the other. We want to have justice and, having it, we want to extend it equally to all. We would not want equal injustice. Yet, sometimes, we must choose between equal injustice and unequal justice. What should we prefer? Unequal justice is justice still, even if only for some, whereas equal injustice is injustice for all. If not every equally guilty person is punished equally, we have unequal justice. It seems preferable to equal injustice—having no guilty person punished as deserved.[12] Since it is never possible to punish equally all equally guilty murderers, we should punish, as they deserve, as many of those we apprehend and convict as possible. Thus, even if the death penalty were inherently discriminatory—which is not the case—but deserved by those who receive it, it would be morally just to impose it on them. If, as I contend, capital punishment is just and not inherently discriminatory, it remains desirable to eliminate inequality in distribution, to apply the penalty to all who deserve it, sparing no racial or economic class. But if a guilty person or group escaped the penalty through our porous system, wherein is this an argument for sparing others?

If one does not believe capital punishment can be just, discrimination becomes a subordinate argument, since one would object to capital punishment even if it were distributed equally to all the guilty. If one does believe that capital punishment for murderers is deserved, discrimination against guilty black murderers and in favor of equally guilty white murderers is wrong, not because blacks receive the deserved punishment, but because whites escape it.

Consider a less emotionally charged analogy. Suppose traffic police ticketed all drivers who violated the rules, except drivers of luxury cars. Should we abolish tickets? Should we decide that the ticketed drivers of nonluxury cars were unjustly punished and ought not to pay their fines? Would they become innocent of the violation they are guilty of because others have not been ticketed? Surely the drivers of luxury cars should not be exempted. But the fact that they were is no reason to exempt drivers of nonluxury cars as well. Laws could never be applied if the escape of one person, or group, were accepted as ground for not punishing another. To do justice is primarily to punish as deserved, and only secondarily to punish equally.

Guilt is personal. No one becomes less guilty or less deserving of punishment because another was punished leniently or not at all. That justice does not catch up with all guilty persons understandably is resented by those caught. But it does not affect their guilt. If some, or all, white and rich murderers escape the death penalty, how does that reduce the guilt of black or poor murderers, or make them less deserving of punishment, or deserving of a lesser punishment?

Some lawyers have insisted that the death penalty is distributed among those guilty of murder as though by a lottery and that the worst may escape it.[13] They exaggerate, but suppose one grants the point. How do those among the guilty selected for execution by lottery become less deserving of punishment because others escaped it? What is wrong is that these others escaped, not that those among the guilty who were selected by the lottery did not.

Those among the guilty actually punished by a criminal justice system unavoidably are selected by chance, not because we want to so select them, but because the outcome of our efforts largely depends on chance. No murderer is punished unless he is unlucky enough both to be caught and to have convinced a court of his guilt. And courts consider evidence not truth. They find truth only when the evidence establishes it. Thus they may have reasonable doubts about the guilt of an actually guilty person. Although we may strive to make justice as equal as possible, unequal justice will remain our lot in this world. We should not give up justice, or the death penalty, because we cannot extend it as equally to all the guilty as we wish. If we were not to punish one offender because another got away because of caprice or discrimination, we would give up justice for the sake of equality. We would reverse the proper order of priorities.

Is the Death Penalty More Deterrent Than Other Punishments?

Whether or not the death penalty deters the crimes it punishes more than alternative penalties—in this case life imprisonment with or without parole—has been widely debated since Isaac Ehrlich broke the abolitionist ranks by finding that from 1933–65 "an additional execution per year . . . may have resulted on the average in seven or eight fewer murders."[14] Since his article appeared, a whole cottage industry devoted to refuting his findings has arisen.[15] Ehrlich, no slouch, has been refuting those who refuted him.[16] The result seems inconclusive.[17] Statistics have not proved conclusively that the death penalty does or does not deter murder more than other penalties.[18] Still, Ehrlich has the merit of being the first to use a sophisticated statistical analysis to tackle the problem, and of defending his analysis, although it showed deterrence. (Ehrlich started as an abolitionist.) His predecessors cannot be accused of mathematical sophistication. Yet the academic community uncritically accepted their abolitionist results. I myself have no contribution to make to the mathematical analyses of deterrent effects. Perhaps this is why I have come to believe that they may becloud the issue, leading us to rely on demonstrable deterrence as though decisive.

Most abolitionists believe that the death penalty does not deter more than other penalties. But most abolitionists would abolish it, even if it did.[19] I have discussed this matter with prominent abolitionists such as Charles Black, Henry Schwarzchild, Hugo Adam Bedau, Ramsey Clark, and many others. Each told me that, even if every execution were to deter a hundred murders, he would oppose it. I infer that, to these abolitionist leaders, the life of every murderer is more valuable than the lives of a hundred prospective victims, for these abolitionists would spare the murderer, even if doing so would cost a hundred future victims their lives.

Obviously, deterrence cannot be the decisive issue for these abolitionists. It is not necessarily for me either, since I would be for capital punishment on grounds of justice alone. On the other hand, I should favor the death penalty for murderers, if probably deterrent, or even just possibly deterrent. To me, the life of any innocent victim who might be spared has great value; the life of a convicted murderer does not. This is why I would not take the risk of sacrificing innocents by not executing murderers.

Even though statistical demonstrations are not conclusive, and perhaps cannot be, I believe that capital punishment is likely to deter more than anything else. They fear most death deliberately inflicted by law and scheduled by the courts. Whatever people fear most is likely to deter most. Hence, I believe that the threat of the death penalty may deter some murderers who otherwise might not have been deterred. And surely the death penalty is the only penalty that could deter prisoners already serving a life sentence and tempted to kill a guard, or offenders about to be arrested and facing a life sentence. Perhaps they will not be deterred. But they would certainly not be deterred by anything else. We owe all the protection we can give to law enforcers exposed to special risks.

Many murders are "crimes of passion" that, perhaps, cannot be deterred by any threat. Whether or not they can be would depend on the degree of passion; it is unlikely to be always so extreme as to make the person seized by it totally undeterrable. At any rate, offenders sentenced to death ordinarily are guilty of premeditated murder, felony murder, or multiple murders. Some are rape murderers, or hit men, but, to my knowledge, no one convicted of a "crime of passion" is on death row. Whatever the motive, some prospective offenders are not deterrable at all, others are easily deterred, and most are in between. Even if only some murders were, or could be, deterred by capital punishment, it would be worthwhile. . . .

Almost all convicted murderers try to avoid the death penalty by appeals for commutation to life imprisonment. However, a minuscule proportion of convicted murderers prefer execution. It is sometimes argued that they murdered for the sake of being executed, of committing suicide via execution. More likely, they prefer execution to life imprisonment. Although shared by few, this preference is not irrational per se. It is also possible that these convicts accept the verdict of the court, and feel that they deserve the death penalty for the crimes they committed, although the modern mind finds it hard to imagine such feelings. But not all murderers are ACLU humanists. . . .

Is the Death Penalty Moral?

Miscarriages

Miscarriages of justice are rare, but do occur. Over a long enough time they lead to the execution of some innocents.[20] Does this make irrevocable punishments morally wrong? Hardly. Our government employs trucks. They run over innocent bystanders more frequently than courts sentence innocents to death. We do not give up trucks because the benefits they produce outweigh the harm, including the death of innocents. Many human activities, even quite trivial ones, forseeably cause wrongful deaths. Courts may cause fewer wrongful deaths than golf. Whether one sees the benefit of doing justice by imposing capital punishment as moral, or as material, or both, it outweighs the loss of innocent lives through miscarriages, which are as unintended as traffic accidents.

Vengeance

Some abolitionists feel that the motive for the death penalty is an un-Christian and unacceptable desire for vengeance. But though vengeance be the motive, it is not the purpose of the death penalty. Doing justice and deterring crime are the purposes, whatever the motive. Purpose (let alone effect) and motive are not the same.

The Lord is often quoted as saying "Vengeance is mine." He did not condemn vengeance. He merely reserved it to Himself—and to the government. For, in the same epistle He is also quoted as saying that the ruler is "the minister of God, a revenger, to execute wrath upon him that doeth evil." The religious notion of hell indicates that the biblical God favored harsh and everlasting punishment for some. However, particularly in a secular society, we cannot wait for the day of judgment to see murderers consigned to hell. Our courts must "execute wrath upon him that doeth evil" here and now.

Charity and Justice

Today many religious leaders oppose capital punishment. This is surprising, because there is no biblical warrant for their opposition. The Roman Catholic Church and most Protestant denominations traditionally have supported capital punishment. Why have their moral views changed? When sharing secular power, the churches clearly distinguished between justice, including penalization as deserved, a function of the secular power, and charity, which, according to religious doctrine, we should feel for all those who suffer for whatever reasons. Currently, religious leaders seem to conflate justice and charity, to conclude that the death penalty and, perhaps, all punishment, is wrong because uncharitable. Churches no longer share secular power. Perhaps bystanders are more ready to replace justice with charity than are those responsible for governing.

Human Dignity

Let me return to the morality of execution. Many abolitionists believe that capital punishment is "degrading to human dignity" and inconsistent with the "sanctity of life." Justice Brennan, concurring in *Furnam*, stressed these phrases repeatedly.[21] He did not explain what he meant.

Why would execution degrade human dignity more than life imprisonment? One may prefer the latter; but it seems at least as degrading as execution. Philosophers, such as Immanuel Kant and G. F. W. Hegel, thought capital punishment indispensable to redeem, or restore, the human dignity of the executed. Perhaps they were wrong. But they argued their case, whereas no one has explained why capital punishment degrades. Apparently those who argue that it does degrade dignity simply define the death penalty as degrading. If so, degradation (or dehumanization) merely is a disguised synonym for their disapproval. Assertion, reassertion, or definition, do not constitute evidence or argument, nor do they otherwise justify, or even explain, disapproval of capital punishment.

Writers, such as Albert Camus, have suggested that murderers have a miserable time waiting for execution and anticipating it.[22] I do not doubt that. But punishments are not meant to be pleasant. Other people suffer greatly waiting for the end, in hospitals, under circumstances that, I am afraid, are at least as degrading to their dignity as execution. These sufferers have not deserved their suffering by committing crimes, whereas murderers have. Yet, murderers suffer less on death row, unless their consciences bother them.

Lex Talionis

Some writers insist that the suffering the death penalty imposes on murderers exceeds the suffering of their victims. This is hard to determine, but probably true in some cases and not in other cases. However, the comparison is irrelevant. Murderers are punished, as are all offenders, not just for the suffering they caused their victims, but for the harm they do to society by making life insecure, by threatening everyone, and by requiring protective measures. Punishment, ultimately, is a vindication of the moral and legal order of society and not limited by the *Lex Talionis*, meant to limit private retaliation for harms originally regarded as private.

Sanctity of Life

We are enjoined by the Declaration of Independence to secure life. How can this best be achieved? The Constitution authorizes us to secure innocent life by taking the life of murderers, so that any one who deliberately wants to take an innocent life will know that he risks forfeiting his own. The framers did not think that taking the life of a murderer is inconsistent with the "sanctity of life" which Justice Brennan champions. He has not indicated why they were wrong.[23]

Legalized Murder?

Ever since Cesare Bonesana, Marchese di Beccaria, wrote *Dei Delitti e Delle Pene*, abolitionists have contended that executing murderers legitimizes murder by doing to the murderer what he did to his victim. Indeed, capital punishment retributes, or pays back the offender. Occasionally we do punish offenders by doing to them what they did to their victims. We may lock away a kidnapper who wrongfully locked away his victim, and we may kill the murderer who wrongfully killed his victim. To lawfully do to the offender what he unlawfully did to his victim in no way legitimizes his crime. It legitimizes (some) killing, and not murder. An act does not become a crime because of its physical character, which, indeed, it may share with the legal punishment, but because of its social, or, better, antisocial, character—because it is an unlawful act.

Severity

Is the death penalty too severe? It stands in a class by itself. But so does murder. Execution is irreparable. So is murder. In contrast, all other crimes and punishments are, at least partly or potentially, reparable. The death penalty thus is congruous with the moral and material gravity of the crime it punishes.[24]

Still, is it repulsive? Torture, however well deserved, now is repulsive to us. But torture is an artifact. Death is not, since nature has placed us all under sentence of death. Capital punishment, in John Stuart Mills' phrase, only "hastens death"—which is what the murderer did to his victim. I find nothing repulsive in hastening the murderer's death, provided it be done in a nontorturous manner. Had he wished to be secure in his life, he could have avoided murder.

To believe that capital punishment is too severe for any act, one must believe that there can be no act horrible enough to deserve death.[25] I find this belief difficult to understand. I should readily impose the death penalty on a Hitler or a Stalin, or on anyone who does what they did, albeit on a smaller scale.

Conclusion

The death penalty has become a major issue in public debate. This is somewhat puzzling, because quantitatively it is insignificant. Still, capital punishment has separated the voters as a whole from a small, but influential, abolitionist elite. There are, I believe, two reasons that explain the prominence of the issue.

First, I think, there is a genuine ethical issue. Some philosophers believe that the right to life is equally imprescriptible for all, that the murderer has as much right to live as his victim. Others do not push egalitarianism that far. They believe that there is a vital difference, that one's right to live is lost when one intentionally takes an innocent life, that everyone has just the right to one life, his own. If he unlawfully takes that of another he, *eo ipso*, loses his own right to life.

Second, and perhaps as important, the death penalty has symbolic significance. Those who favor it believe that the major remedy for crime is punishment. Those who do not, in the main, believe that the remedy is anything but punishment. They look at the causes of crime and conflate them with compulsions, or with excuses, and refuse to blame. The majority of the people are less sophisticated, but perhaps they have better judgment. They believe that everyone who can understand the nature and effects of his acts is responsible for them, and should be blamed and punished, if he could know that what he did was wrong. Human beings are human because they can be held responsible, as animals cannot be. In that Kantian sense the death penalty is a symbolic affirmation of the humanity of both victim and murderer.

Notes

1. 356 U.S. 99 (1958).
2. The courts have sometimes confirmed the obsolescence of non-repealed laws or punishments. But here they are asked to invent it.
3. In Coker v. Georgia, 433 U.S. 584, 592 (1977), the Court concluded that the eighth amendment prohibits punishments that are "'excessive' in relation to the crime committed." I am not sure about this disproportion. However, threatening execution would tempt rapists to murder their victims who, after all, are potential witnesses. By murdering their victims, rapists would increase their chances of escaping execution without adding to their risk. Therefore, I agree with the court's conclusion, though not with its argument.
4. C. BLACK, CAPITAL PUNISHMENT: THE INEVITABILITY OF CAPRICE AND MISTAKE (2d ed. 1981).
5. Most discrimination occurred in rape cases and was eliminated when the death penalty for rape was declared unconstitutional.
6. For a survey of the statistical literature, see, e.g., Bowers, *The Pervasiveness of Arbitrariness and Discrimination under Post-*Furman *Capital Statutes*, 74 J. CRIM. L. & CRIMINOLOGY 1067 (1983). His article is part of a "Symposium on Current Death Penalty Issues" compiled by death penalty opponents.
7. Those who demonstrated the pattern seem to have been under the impression that they had shown discrimination against black murderers. They were wrong. However, the discrimination against black victims is invidious and should be corrected.
8. The capriciousness argument is undermined when capriciousness is conceded to be unavoidable. But even when capriciousness is thought reducible, one wonders whether releasing or retrying one guilty defendant, because another equally guilty defendant was not punished as much, would help reduce capriciousness. It does not seem a logical remedy.
9. Furman v. Georgia, 408 U.S. 238, 256 (1971) (Douglas, J., concurring).
10. I shall not consider here the actual psychological motives that power our unending thirst for equality.
11. If courts impose different punishments on different persons, we may not be able to establish in all cases whether the punishment is just, or (it amounts to the same) whether the different persons were equally guilty of the same crime, or whether their crimes were identical in all relevant respects. Thus, we may not be able to tell which of two unequal punishments is just. Both may be, or neither may be. Inequality may not entail more injustice than equality, and equality would entail justice only if we were sure that the punishment meted out was the just punishment.

12. Similarly, it is better that only some innocents suffer undeserved punishment than that all suffer it equally.

13. It would be desirable that all of the worst murderers be sentenced to death. However, since murderers are tried in different courts, this is unlikely. Further, sometimes the testimony of one murderer is needed to convict another, and cannot be obtained except by leniency. Morally, and legally it is enough that those sentenced to death deserve the penalty for their crimes, even if others, who may deserve it as much, or more, were not sentenced to death.

14. Ehrlich, *The Deterrent Effect of Capital Punishment: A Question of Life or Death*, 65 AM. ECON. REV. 397, 414 (1975).

15. *See, e.g.,* Baldus & Cole, *A Comparison of the Work of Thorsten Sellin and Isaac Ehrlich on the Deterrent Effect of Capital Punishment*, 85 YALE L. J. 170 (1975); Bowers & Pierce, *Deterrence or Brutalization: What is the Effect of Executions?*, 26 CRIME & DELINQ. 453 (1980); Bowers & Pierce, *The Illusion of Deterrence in Isaac Ehrlich's Research on Capital Punishment*, 85 YALE L. J. 187 (1975).

16. Ehrlich, *Fear of Deterrence*, 6 J. LEGAL STUD. 293 (1977); Ehrlich & Gibbons, *On the Measurement of the Deterrent Effect of Capital Punishment and the Theory of Deterrence*, 6 J. LEGAL STUD. 35 (1977).

17. At present there is no agreement even on whether the short run effects of executions delay or accelerate homicides. *See* Phillips, *The Deterrent Effect of Capital Punishment: New Evidence on an Old Controversy*, 86, AM. J. Soc. 139 (1980).

18. As stated in Gregg v. Georgia, 428 U.S. 153, 185 (1976), "Although some of the studies suggest that the death penalty may not function as a significantly greater deterrent than lesser penalties, there is no convincing empirical evidence either supporting or refuting this view."

19. Jeffrey Reiman is an honorable exception. *See* Reiman, *Justice, Civilization, and the Death Penalty: Answering van den Haag*, 14 PHIL. & PUB. AFF. 115 (1985).

20. Life imprisonment avoids the problem of executing innocent persons to some extent. It can be revoked. But the convict also may die in prison before his innocence is discovered.

21. "[T]he Cruel and Unusual Punishments Clause prohibits the infliction of uncivilized and inhuman punishments. The State, even as it punishes, must treat its members with respect for their intrinsic worth as human beings." Furman v. Georgia, 408 U.S. 238, 270 (1972) (Brennan, J., concurring). "When we consider why [certain punishments] have been condemned, . . . we realize that the pain involved is not the only reason. The true significance of these punishments [that have been condemned] is that they treat members of the human race as nonhumans, as objects to be toyed with and discarded." *Id*. at 272–73.

> In determining whether a punishment comports with human dignity, we are aided also by a second principle inherent in the Clause—that the State must not arbitrarily inflict a severe punishment. This principle derives from the notion that the State does not respect human dignity when, without reason, it inflicts upon some people a severe punishment that it does not inflict upon others.

Id. at 274. "Death is truly an awesome punishment. The calculated killing of a human being by the State involves, by its very nature, a denial of the executed person's humanity." *Id*. at 290. "In comparison to all other punishments today, then, the deliberate extinguishment of human life by the State is uniquely degrading to human dignity." *Id*. at 291.

22. In *Reflections on the Guillotine*, Camus stated that "[t]he parcel [the condemned person] is no longer subject to the laws of chance that hang over

the living creature but to mechanical laws that allow him to foresee accurately the day of his beheading. . . . The Greeks, after all, were more humane with their hemlock." A. CAMUS, RESISTANCE, REBELLION AND DEATH 175, 202 (1960).

23. "Sanctity of life" may mean that we should not take, and should punish taking innocent life: "*homo homini res sacra.*" In the past this meant that we should take the life of a murderer to secure innocent life, and stress its sacredness. Justice Brennan seems to mean that the life of the murderer should be sacred too—but no argument is given for this premise.

24. Capital punishment is not inconsistent with Weems v. United States, 217 U.S. 349 (1910), which merely held that punishment cannot be excessive, that is, out of proportion to the gravity of the crime. Indeed, if life imprisonment suffices for anything else, it cannot be appropriate for murder.

25. The notion of deserving is strictly moral, depending exclusively on our sense of justice, unlike the notion of deterrence, which depends on the expected factual consequences of punishment. Whilst deterrence alone would justify most of the punishments we should impose, it may not suffice to justify all those punishments that our sense of justice demands. Wherefore criminal justice must rest on desert as well as deterrence, to be seen as morally justified.

POSTSCRIPT

Should the Death Penalty Be Abolished?

The argument is sometimes made that even if capital punishment is not a deterrent (or, more radically, even if capital punishment actually encourages crime), justice demands that certain criminals be executed. For example, former Nazis who killed many innocent people are today tracked down and brought to trial. Usually, these are elderly men who have lived many years without killing anyone. If the death penalty is demanded for these people, would this demand receive support from the deterrence line of reasoning? Probably not. First, these people have already stopped killing and so do not need to be deterred. Second, should we suppose that executing them will deter potential future Nazis, Aryan supremacists, and other racists from murder? More likely, in these cases, the argument is that these former Nazis should die for what they have done as a matter of justice.

A special issue for Americans is whether or not the death penalty is constitutional—in particular, whether or not it is cruel and unusual punishment. In a series of important legal cases (including *Furman v. Georgia*, 1972, and *Gregg v. Georgia*, 1976), the U.S. Supreme Court found that capital punishment *as then applied* was indeed unconstitutional. The main problem was that a lack of explicit standards in applying the death penalty gave much room for discretion, which in turn allowed prejudice and racism to hide behind legality. But the Court allowed the development of procedures of administering capital punishment that did not violate the Constitution.

One of the major points on which Welch and van den Haag seem to differ is over the extent to which we can separate and correct the bias, error, and other negative features to which Welch draws our attention from the death penalty itself. Van den Haag would argue that all the negative features that Welch has identified can be addressed without the moral acceptability of the death penalty being brought into question. Welch would probably respond that the moral acceptability of the death penalty is not its moral acceptability in an ideal world but in the real world that we live in.

Much has been written about the death penalty. Useful recent sources are Mark Grossman, *Encyclopedia of Capital Punishment* (ABC-CLIO, 1998); Hugo Bedau and Paul Cassell, eds., *Debating the Death Penalty: Should America Have Capital Punishment?* (Oxford University Press, 2004); and Bill Kurtis, *The Death Penalty on Trial: Crisis in American Justice* (Public Affairs, 2004).

ISSUE 15

Is Torture Ever Justified?

YES: Mirko Bagaric and Julie Clarke, from "Not Enough Official Torture in the World?" *University of San Francisco Law Review* (Spring 2005)

NO: Desmond Manderson, from "Another Modest Proposal," *Deakin Law Review* (vol. 10, no. 2, 2005)

ISSUE SUMMARY

YES: Bagaric and Clarke remind us, first of all, that torture, although prohibited by international law, is nevertheless widely practiced. A rational examination of torture, and a consideration of hypothetical (but realistic) cases shows that torture is justifiable in order to prevent great harm. Torture should be regulated and carefully practiced as an information-gathering technique in extreme cases.

NO: Manderson argues against the "regulated torture" idea of Bagaric and Clarke and affirms the idea of an absolute prohibition against torture. Manderson stresses that Bagaric and Clarke are writing—and torture is allegedly being used—in the real-world social context of "the war on terror." Yet (he says) these writers act as if their own arguments are merely a harmless exercise of reason, detached from actual events in Guantanamo, Abu Graib, etc.

This is a question that might not even have arisen in a serious way if it were not for current events and the War on Terrorism. Actually, philosophers had been talking about questions like this before 9/11, but only in a purely hypothetical way. No one anticipated that seemingly crazy ideas about buildings being blown up in New York and thousands of people being killed would actually become a reality.

But times have changed. And the question is now asked as a reflection of the times. Yet, to ask the question does not mean that one is considering torture as a possibility. For some of those who address this very question would insist that the answer is no and would further insist that in this day of terrorism one of the important values that distinguishes us from the terrorists is that our answer should be that torture is absolutely out of the question. We should not try to imagine situations or conditions under which we torture people. So, on this view, we should not try to "draw a line," for one side of the line will be the side where torture is justified. Part of what we would be doing is determining an area in which we believed that torture is justified. But, in order to stay faithful to a negative answer to the issue question, there should not be any such area.

Opponents of the view that torture is never justified might construct various scenarios. Suppose, for example, that there was a ticking bomb that was hidden in a secret location and was set to go off at a certain time and would be sure to kill hundreds or thousands of innocent people. And suppose that the authorities had in their custody an individual who had detailed information about the bomb, including its location and the time it was set to go off. If this person were unwilling to disclose the information voluntarily, would torture be justified? After all, so much is at stake. If that one person were tortured, the very lives of a great many innocent people lie in the balance. How, it might be asked, could his well-being outweigh theirs?

The opponents of torture would probably respond that the question of torturing the person does not really have to do with his well-being but rather with our own actions. The imagined scenario seems to suggest that so much is (potentially) at stake that we must be prepared to torture people. If so, we can't lay claim to ideas about human rights, the sacredness of life, etc. And if we really are going to be prepared to torture people, we have to have trained torturers who know how to do their job well. Even in the imagined "ticking bomb" scenario, the innocent people wouldn't be saved if we used an incompetent torturer who bungled the job and did something that resulted in the person's death. But the torturer has to cause some serious pain nevertheless. Proponents of torture seem to need someone who is a trained torturer, someone who is not doing this for the first time. So one question is whether we should initiate action now to produce such people in case they might be used.

In the first reading, Bagaric and Clarke argue that torture is already being practiced widely—although unmonitored and "underground." Their idea is to acknowledge it, endorse it, but draw lines. In the second reading, Desmond Manderson acknowledges that torture takes place, but does not wish to condone it. On Manderson's view, the current situation in which we abhor torture is a civilized achievement that should not be lost.

YES

Mirko Bagaric and
Julie Clarke

Not Enough Official Torture in the World? The Circumstances in Which Torture Is Morally Justifiable

Recent events stemming from the "war on terrorism" have highlighted the prevalence of torture, both as an interrogation technique and as a punitive measure. Torture is almost universally deplored. It is prohibited by international law and is not officially sanctioned by the domestic laws of any state. The formal prohibition against torture is absolute—there are no exceptions to it. This is not only pragmatically unrealistic, but unsound at a normative level. Despite the absolute ban on torture, it is widely used. Contrary to common belief, torture is not the preserve of despot military regimes in third world nations. For example, there are serious concerns regarding the treatment by the United States of senior Al Qaeda leader Khalid Shaikh Mohammad. There is also irrefutable evidence that the United States tortured large numbers of Iraqi prisoners, as well as strong evidence that it tortured prisoners at Guantanamo Bay prison in Cuba, where suspected Al Qaeda terrorists are held. More generally Professor Alan Dershowitz has noted, "[C]ountries all over the world violate the Geneva Accords [prohibiting torture]. They do it secretly and hypothetically, the way the French did it in Algeria."

Dershowitz has also recently argued that torture should be made lawful. His argument is based on a harm minimization rationale from the perspective of victims of torture. He said, "Of course it would be best if we didn't use torture at all, but if the United States is going to continue to torture people, we need to make the process legal and accountable." Our argument goes one step beyond this. We argue that torture is indeed morally defensible, not just pragmatically desirable. The harm minimization rationale is used to supplement our argument.

While a "civilized" community does not typically condone such conduct, this Article contends that torture is morally defensible in certain circumstances, mainly when more grave harm can be avoided by using torture as an interrogation device. The pejorative connotation associated with torture should be abolished. A dispassionate analysis of the propriety of torture indicates that it is morally justifiable. At the outset of this analytical discussion, this Article requires readers to move from the question of whether torture is *ever* defensible to the issue of the circumstances in which it is morally permissible.

From *University of San Francisco Law Review*, vol. 39, Spring 2005, pp. 581–616. Copyright © 2005 by University of San Francisco Law Review. Reprinted by permission.

Consider the following example: A terrorist network has activated a large bomb on one of hundreds of commercial planes carrying over three hundred passengers that is flying somewhere in the world at any point in time. The bomb is set to explode in thirty minutes. The leader of the terrorist organization announces this intent via a statement on the Internet. He states that the bomb was planted by one of his colleagues at one of the major airports in the world in the past few hours. No details are provided regarding the location of the plane where the bomb is located. Unbeknown to him, he was under police surveillance and is immediately apprehended by police. The terrorist leader refuses to answer any questions of the police, declaring that the passengers must die and will do so shortly.

Who in the world would deny that all possible means should be used to extract the details of the plane and the location of the bomb? The answer is not many. The passengers, their relatives and friends, and many in society would expect that all means should be used to extract the information, even if the pain and suffering imposed on the terrorist resulted in his death.

Although the above example is hypothetical and is not one that has occurred in the real world, the force of the argument cannot be dismissed on that basis. As C.L. Ten notes, "fantastic examples" that raise fundamental issues for consideration, such as whether it is proper to torture wrongdoers, play an important role in the evaluation of moral principles and theories. These examples sharpen contrasts and illuminate the logical conclusions of the respective principles to test the true strength of our commitment to the principles. Thus, fantastic examples cannot be dismissed summarily merely because they are "simply" hypothetical.

Real life is, of course, rarely this clear cut, but there are certainly scenarios approaching this degree of desperation, which raise for discussion whether it is justifiable to inflict harm on one person to reduce a greater level of harm occurring to a large number of blameless people. Ultimately, torture is simply the sharp end of conduct whereby the interests of one agent are sacrificed for the greater good. As a community, we are willing to accept this principle. Thus, although differing in degree, torture is no different in nature from conduct that we sanction in other circumstances. It should be viewed in this light.

Given this, it is illogical to insist on a blanket prohibition against torture. Therefore, the debate must turn to the circumstances when torture is morally appropriate. This is the topic of this Article.

International law defines torture as severe pain and suffering, generally used as an interrogation device or as a punitive measure. This Article focuses on the use of torture as an interrogation device and poses that the device is only permissible to prevent significant harm to others. In these circumstances, there are five variables relevant in determining whether torture is permissible and the degree of torture that is appropriate. The variables are (1) the number of lives at risk; (2) the immediacy of the harm; (3) the availability of other means to acquire the information; (4) the level of wrongdoing of the agent; and (5) the likelihood that the agent actually does possess the relevant information.

This Article analyzes the meaning of torture and the nature and scope of the legal prohibition against torture [and] examines whether torture is morally defensible. It is argued that torture is no different than other forms of morally permissible behavior and is justifiable on a utilitarian ethic. It is also argued that, on close reflection, torture is also justifiable against a backdrop of a non-consequentialist rights-based ethic, which is widely regarded as prohibiting torture in all circumstances. Thus, the Article concludes that torture is morally justifiable in rare circumstances, irrespective of which normative theory one adopts. [We] examine the circumstances in which torture is justifiable. Finally, [we] debunk the argument that torture should not be legalized because it will open the floodgates to more torture.

Torture: Reality and Legal Position

The Law on Torture

Pursuant to international law, "torture" is defined as:

> Any act by which severe pain or suffering, whether physical or mental, is intentionally inflicted on a person for such purposes as obtaining from him or a third person information or a confession, punishing him for an act he or a third person has committed or is suspected of having committed, or intimidating or coercing him or a third person, or for any reason based on discrimination of any kind, when such pain or suffering is inflicted by or at the instigation of or with the consent or acquiescence of a public official or other person acting in an official capacity. It does not include pain or suffering arising only from, inherent in or incidental to lawful sanctions.

Torture is prohibited by a number of international documents. It is also considered to carry a special status in customary international law, that of *jus cogens,* which is a "peremptory norm" of customary international law. The significance of this is that customary international law is binding on all states, even if they have not ratified a particular treaty. At the treaty level, there are both general treaties that proscribe torture and specific treaties banning the practice.

In terms of general treaties, torture is prohibited by a number of international and regional treaties. . . .

The rigidity of the rule against torture is exemplified by the fact that it has a non-derogable status in human rights law. That is, there are no circumstances in which torture is permissible. This prohibition is made clear in Article 2(2) of the U.N. Convention Against Torture, which states, "No exceptional circumstances whatsoever, whether a state of war or a threat of war, internal political instability or any other public emergency, may be invoked as a justification of torture." Thus, the right not to be tortured is absolute. . . .

This absolute prohibition is frequently highlighted by Amnesty International and other human rights organizations. For example, Amnesty International states, "The law is unequivocal—torture is absolutely prohibited in all circumstances. . . . The right to be free from torture is absolute. It cannot be denied to anyone in any circumstances."

Torture is also prohibited as a war crime, pursuant to humanitarian law. In addition, torture is considered to be a crime against humanity when the acts are perpetrated as part of a widespread or systematic attack against a civilian population, whether or not they are committed in the course of an armed conflict.

The Reality of Torture

As with many legal precepts, the black letter law must be considered against the context of reality. As this part shows, various forms of torture are used despite the legal prohibition of it.

1. Forms of Torture

As is noted by Dershowitz, torture comes in many different forms and intensities:

> Torture is a continuum and the two extremes are on the one hand torturing someone to death—that is torturing an enemy to death so that others will know that if you are caught, you will be caused excruciating pain—that's torture as a deterrent. . . . At the other extreme, there's non-lethal torture which leaves only psychological scars. The perfect example of this is a sterilised needle inserted under the fingernail, causing unbearable pain but no possible long-term damage. These are very different phenomena. What they have in common of course is that they allow the government physically to come into contact with you in order to produce pain.

Various methods of torture have and continue to be applied in a multitude of countries. The most common methods are beating, electric shock, rape and sexual abuse, mock execution or threat of death, and prolonged solitary confinement. Other common methods include sleep and sensory deprivation, suspension of the body, "shackling interrogees in contorted painful positions" or in "painful stretching positions," and applying pressure to sensitive areas, such as the "neck, throat, genitals, chest and head."

2. The Benefits of Torture: An Effective Information Gathering Device

The main benefit of torture is that it is an excellent means of gathering information. Humans have an intense desire to avoid pain, no matter how short term, and most will comply with the demands of a torturer to avoid the pain. Often even the threat of torture alone will evoke cooperation. To this end, Dershowitz cites a recent kidnapping case in Germany in which the son of a distinguished banker was kidnapped. The eleven-year-old boy had been missing for three days. The police had in their custody a man they were convinced had perpetrated the kidnapping. The man was taken into custody after being seen collecting a ransom that was paid by the boy's family. During seven hours of interrogation the man "toyed" with police, leading them to one false location after another. After exhausting all lawful means of interrogation, the deputy commissioner of the Frankfurt police instructed his officers, in writing, that they could try to extract information "by means of the infliction of pain, under medical supervision and subject to prior warning." Ten minutes after the warning was given the suspect told the police where the boy was; unfortunately the boy was already dead, having been killed shortly after the kidnapping.

3. The Widespread Use of Torture

a. Torture Around the World Despite the contemporary abhorrence against it, dozens of countries continue to use torture. A study of 195 countries and territories by Amnesty International between 1997 and mid-2000 found reports of torture or ill-treatment by state officials in more than 150 countries and in more than seventy countries that torture or ill-treatment was reported as "widespread or persistent." It is also clear that torture is not limited to military regimes in third world nations. Amnesty International recently reported that in 2003 it had received reports of torture and ill-treatment from 132 countries, including the United states, Canada, Japan, France, Italy, Spain, and Germany. . . .

The Circumstances in Which Torture Is Acceptable

The only situation where torture is justifiable is where it is used as an information gathering technique to avert a grave risk. In such circumstances, there are five variables relevant in determining whether torture is permissible and the degree of torture that is appropriate. The variables are (1) the number of lives at risk; (2) the immediacy of the harm; (3) the availability of other means to acquire the information; (4) the level of wrongdoing of the agent; and (5) the likelihood that the agent actually does possess the relevant information. Where (1), (2), (4) and (5) rate highly and (3) is low, all forms of harm may be inflicted on the agent—even if this results in death.

The Harm to Be Prevented

The key consideration regarding the permissibility of torture is the magnitude of harm that is sought to be prevented. To this end, the appropriate measure is the number of lives that are likely to be lost if the threatened harm is not alleviated. Obviously, the more lives that are at stake, the more weight that is attributed to this variable.

Lesser forms of threatened harm will not justify torture. Logically, the right to life is the most basic and fundamental of all human rights—non-observance of it would render all other human rights devoid of meaning. Every society has some prohibition against taking life, and "the intentional taking of human life is . . . the offence which society condemns most strongly." The right to life is also enshrined in several international covenants. For example, Article 2 of the European Convention on Human Rights (which in essence mirrors Article 6 of the International Covenant on Civil and Political Rights) provides that "everyone's right to life shall be protected by law. No one shall be deprived of his life intentionally save in the execution of a sentence of a court following his conviction of a crime for which this penalty is provided by law."

Torture violates the right to physical integrity, which is so important that it is only a threat to the right to life that can justify interference with it. Thus, torture should be confined to situations where the right to life is imperiled.

Immediacy of Harm and Other Options to Obtain Information

Torture should only be used as a last resort and hence should not be utilized where there is time to pursue other avenues of forestalling the harm. It is for this reason that torture should only be used where there is no other means to obtain the relevant information. Thus, where a terrorist has planted a bomb on a plane, torture will not be permissible where, for example, video tapes of international airports are likely to reveal the identity of the plane that has been targeted.

The Likelihood of Knowledge or Guilt

As a general rule torture should normally be confined to people that are responsible in some way for the threatened harm. This is not, however, invariably the case. People who are simply aware of the threatened harm, that is "innocent people," may in some circumstances also be subjected to torture.

Regardless of the guilt of the agent, it is most important that torture is only used against individuals who actually possess the relevant information. It will be rare that conclusive proof is available that an individual does, in fact, possess the required knowledge; for example, potential torturees will not have been through a trial process in which their guilt has been established. This is not a decisive objection, however, to the use of torture. The investigation and trial process is simply one means of distinguishing wrongdoers from the innocent. To that end, it does not seem to be a particularly effective process. There are other ways of forming such conclusions. One is by way of lie-detector tests. The latest information suggests that polygraphs are accurate about eighty to ninety per cent of the time. There has been little empirical research done to ascertain the number of innocent people who are ultimately convicted of criminal offenses. As one example, however, research carried out in the United Kingdom for the Royal Commission on Criminal Justice suggests that up to eleven percent of people who plead guilty claim innocence. The wrongful acquittal rate would no doubt be even higher than this.

Moreover, it is important to note that even without resort to polygraphs there will be many circumstances where guilt or relevant knowledge is patently obvious. A clear example is where a person makes a relevant admission that discloses information that would only be within the knowledge of the wrongdoer. Another example occurred in the recent German kidnapping case, referred to earlier, where the man in custody had been witnessed collecting a ransom and had indicated to the police that the kidnapped boy was still alive. Where lesser forms of evidence proving guilt are available, the argument in favor of torture is lower.

The Formula

Incorporating all these considerations, the strength of the case in favor of torture can be mapped as follows:

$$\frac{W + L + P}{T \times O}$$

Where:

W = whether the agent is the wrongdoer

L = the number of lives that will be lost if the information is not provided

P = the probability that the agent has the relevant knowledge

T = the time available before the disaster will occur ("immediacy of the harm")

O = the likelihood that other inquiries will forestall the risk

W is a weighting that is attributable to whether the agent has had any direct connection with the potential catastrophe. Where the person is responsible for the incident—for example, planted or organized the bomb—more emphasis should be attached. Where the agent is innocent and has simply stumbled on the relevant information—for example, she saw the bomb being planted or overheard the plan to plant the bomb—this should be reduced by a certain amount. The prohibition against inflicting harm on the innocent is certainly strong, but it is not inviolable.

Torture should be permitted where the application of the variables exceeds a threshold level. Once beyond this level, the higher the figure the more severe the forms of torture that are permissible. There is no bright line that can be drawn concerning the point at which the "torture threshold" should be set. More precision can, however, be obtained by first ascribing unit ranges to each of the above variables (depending on their relative importance), then applying the formula to a range of hypothetical situations, and then making a judgment about the numerical point at which torture is acceptable.

There is obviously a degree of imprecision attached to this process and considerable scope for discussion and disagreement regarding the *exact* weight that should be attached to each variable. It is important to emphasize, however, that this is not an argument against our proposal. Rather it is a signal for further discussion and refinement. This is a call that we are confident other commentators will take up. The purpose of this Article is not to set in stone the full range of circumstances where torture is justifiable. Our aim is more modest—to convince readers that torture is justifiable in some circumstances and to set out the variables that are relevant to such an inquiry.

Regulation Better Than Prohibition

In addition to the moral argument for torture as an interrogation device, Dershowitz has argued that torture should be legalized for harm minimization reasons. Dershowitz has pushed for the introduction of "a torture warrant," which would place a "heavy burden on the government to demonstrate by factual evidence the necessity to administer this horrible, horrible technique of torture." He further adds:

> I think that we're much, much better off admitting what we're doing or not doing it at all. I agree with you, it will much better if we never did it. But if we're going to do it and subcontract and find ways of circumventing, it's much better to do what Israel did. They were the only country in the world ever directly to confront the issue, and it led to a supreme court decision, as you say, outlawing torture, and yet Israel has been criticized all over the world for confronting the issue directly. Candor and accountability in a democracy is very important. Hypocrisy has no place.

The obvious counter to this is the slippery slope argument. "If you start opening the door, making a little exception here, a little exception there, you've basically sent the signal that the ends justify the means," resulting in even more torture. The slippery slope argument is often invoked in relation to acts that in themselves are justified, but which have similarities with objectionable practices, and urges that in morally appraising an action we must not only consider its intrinsic features but also the likelihood of it being used as a basis for condoning similar, but in fact relevantly different undesirable practices. The slippery slope argument in the context of torture holds that while torture might be justified in the extreme cases, legalizing it in these circumstances will invariably lead to torture in other less desperate situations.

This argument is not sound in the context of torture. First, the floodgates are already open—torture is widely used, despite the absolute legal prohibition against it. It is, in fact, arguable that it is the existence of an unrealistic absolute ban on torture that has driven torture "beneath the radar screen of accountability" and that the legalization of torture in very rare circumstances would, in fact, reduce the instances of torture because of the increased level of accountability.

Second, there is no evidence to suggest that the *lawful* violation of fundamental human interests will necessarily lead to a violation of fundamental rights where the pre-conditions for the activity are clearly delineated and controlled. Thus, in the United States the use of the death penalty has not resulted in a gradual extension of the offenses for which people may be executed or an erosion in the respect for human life. Third, promulgating the message that the "means justifies the ends [sometimes]" is not inherently undesirable. Debate can then focus on the precise means and ends that are justifiable.

Conclusion

The absolute prohibition against torture is morally unsound and pragmatically unworkable. There is a need for measured discussion regarding the merits of torture as an information gathering device. This would result in the legal use of torture in circumstances where there are a large number of lives at risk in the immediate future and there is no other means of alleviating the threat. While none of the recent high profile cases of torture appear to satisfy these criteria, it is likely that circumstances will arise in the future where torture is legitimate and desirable. A legal framework should be established to properly accommodate these situations.

Desmond Manderson  **NO**

Another Modest Proposal

Professor Mirko Bagaric and Julie Clarke, writing from the comfort of Deakin University School of Law, have attracted widespread media attention by arguing that torture is a "permissible" and "moral" action in certain circumstances. Within days, Peter Faris, one-time head of the now defunct National Crime Authority, was reported as supporting the "call." Government sanctioned torture is apparently back on the agenda.

This issue is by no means hypothetical. We are familiar with the dismal story of Abu Ghraib. But it was by no means an isolated instance. In pursuit of the so-called "global war against terrorism," the United States has not only been involved in cases of torture themselves, but has routinely sent—the term used is "rendered"—suspects to third countries in order that they might be tortured there. So too rumours of the kind of practices and calculated cruelties that take place at Guantanamo Bay have surfaced this year with worrying regularity.

Above all, the United States Government has over the past several years clearly indicated its desire to claim an absolute sovereignty befitting the Sun King. The Bush Administration insists on its right to act as *it* sees fit in the "war on terror," including by the use of torture and unconstrained by either domestic or international law. The Working Group Report on Detainee Interrogations in the Global War on Terrorism, authorized by Secretary of Defense Rumsfeld, argues that the President's "ultimate authority" in a time of self-proclaimed and self-defined war is not inhibited by any laws including United States statutes against torture. Consequently "the prohibition against torture must be construed as inapplicable to interrogations undertaken pursuant to his Commander-in-Chief Authority." Alberto Gonzales, at the time Legal Counsel to the White House, is on record as advising that the "new paradigm" of counterterrorism "renders obsolete Geneva [Convention]'s strict limitations on questioning of enemy prisoners and renders quaint some of its provisions." For his sins, Alberto Gonzales was appointed United States Attorney General in the second Bush administration. A legal black hole has been created in two ways. On the one hand, an untrammelled sovereignty is now claimed in interrogating terror suspects. On the other, the United States President has himself declared that the detainees at Guantanamo and elsewhere (over 70,000 people at last count) fall into no recognizable international category and are therefore uncovered by any international law. In the vacuum caused by the infinity of sovereignty and the nullity of its targets, anything is now possible.

From *Deakin Law Review*, vol. 10, no. 2, 2005, pp. 642–652. Copyright © 2005 by Deakin Law Review. Reprinted by permission.

Trained lawyers that they are, Bagaric and Clarke ignore this social context. They studiously protect themselves against allegations of their complicity in these trends. Torture, they say, is only justifiable where "torturing a wrongdoer" "is the only means, due to the immediacy of the situation, to save the life of an innocent person." "Recent high-profile incidents of torture, apparently undertaken as punitive measures or in a bid to acquire information where there was no evidence of an immediate risk to the life of an innocent person, were reprehensible." Well isn't that nice to know. Moreover, the authors even concede that there may be *no* such real-life situations at all. So the question is presented as a harmless thought experiment designed to help us interrogate, and indeed to think more carefully about, our moral instincts. The effort taken to present their argument as theoretical rather than grounded in a specific event; and concomitantly as reasoned, rather than grounded in an emotional response, is central to the defensive strategy that underscores their analysis.

This attempt to escape responsibility for their words is complete nonsense. Is there a single victim of torture anywhere in the world who will be relieved to learn that the head of Deakin University Law School has at last injected a bit of sanity and balance into a terribly overwrought "debate"? Let us be clear about this: the only reason Bagaric and Clarke's article was worth publishing—in the *University of San Francisco Law Review*, and certainly on the opinion pages of *The Age* and the *Sydney Morning Herald*—is because their subject is topical and *relevant*. Despite all their protestations to the contrary, their argument matters because, no matter how much they attempt to distance themselves from it, there is a real social context in which they have intervened. Can they seriously deny that their argument will be seized upon by those who wish to justify or practice torture around the world? Bagaric and Clarke refer to a hypothetical case in which the extraction of information from a suspect must be accomplished urgently to avoid the execution of a hostage; Peter Faris refers to the imminent explosion of a bomb. The very same hypotheticals were used by Attorney General Gonzales to justify discarding the Geneva Convention. "The nature of the new war places a high premium on other factors, such as the ability to quickly obtain information from captured terrorists and their sponsors in order to avoid further atrocities against . . . civilians." Yet as we know, this "torture memo" encouraged the very practices that Bagaric and Clarke themselves judge "reprehensible." These practices include not only Abu Ghraib, but a wide range of interrogation techniques through which, according to Amnesty International's most recent report, the US government is even now engaging in torture dressed up in bureaucratic newspeak "in pursuit of unchecked executive power."

The authors dismiss this as a "slippery slope" argument. But the use made of arguments like those of Bagaric and Clarke to justify ever-expanding practices of torture is not hypothetical but a demonstrable fact, engineered, according to US government sources, as part of "a calculated effort to create an atmosphere of legal ambiguity." These Australian academics are seriously implicated in the creation of that atmosphere: that too is not just my fear or my opinion, but a fact. Just as we cannot understand what Voltaire meant by *infâme* without looking at the events to which he was responding, the context in which an argument is made must be read as part of its meaning. This is not a complex point. One is responsible not only for one's words but also for their necessary and predictable effects.

Neither do the authors *themselves* sincerely believe that the argument they make is either limited or purely hypothetical. They attack the "misguided," "alarmist," "reflexive," "absolutist" and "short-sighted" "moral indecency" of our belief that torture is always wrong. . . . Whatever else we may say of Bagaric and Clarke, their argument is rich in emotion and rhetoric. True enough, they say that their defence of torture is so cautiously phrased that "a real-life situation where torture is justifiable [might] not eventuate." But in the very next paragraph they conclude: "the argument in favour of torture in limited circumstances needs to be made because it will encourage the community to think more carefully about moral judgments we collectively hold that are the cause of an enormous amount of suffering in the world." I wonder what hasty moral judgments they have in mind as being responsible for "enormous injustice and suffering"? The sole example they provide is our crazy, woolly-headed prohibition of torture. So this is what their argument must mean: the prohibition against torture is doing our society enormous harm *not only* in some hypothetical thought-world, but right now.

Even if we take Bagaric and Clarke's very modest proposal for torture at face value, it is logically inseparable from the real-world practices they disavow. Torture by its very nature deals with uncertainty; ignorance is the problem that it claims to solve through the exercise of violence. Yet torture produces such exceptionally unreliable information that it is generally thought to be useless. All Western legal systems acknowledge this by excluding, because of its inherent unreliability, evidence and confessions obtained through torture. But the authors do not once address their assumption that torture produces enough reliable information, enough of the time, to justify it. The central reason that Australian suspect Mamdouh Habib was recently released from US custody is that he had been tortured, and therefore any confession he had made was legally inadmissible in any court. Having been tortured, Habib could never be put on trial. Bagaric and Clarke provide no evidence as to why we should think that torture will produce good evidence. On the contrary, under current law, it produces no evidence at all.

Now let us look at the problem of ignorance and uncertainty from the torturer's point of view. A licensed torturer cannot *know* that a supposed terrorist (for example) is the only way to locate a bomb; or that there is a bomb; or that he will tell the truth; or even that he is a terrorist. The torturer suspects these things or rather he says he suspects these things, and of course he has every reason to say he suspects these things, because that is what justifies his actions. It is human nature to see the confused and ambiguous world in the way that is most convenient to us. Suppose our supposed terrorist denies knowing anything. Do we let him go . . . or torture him some more? When exactly do we stop? When exactly do we believe what the victim is telling us when the justification of torture is precisely that we only believe them when they tell us what we want to know, without already knowing it? If I have not put this point clearly it is because I can't. There is a paradox here which must lead to the kind of grey areas or "slippery slope" that Bagaric and Clarke attempt unsuccessfully to exclude. Given criteria under which torture is presumed acceptable, such as that which Bagaric and Clarke offer, the pressure on someone in a volatile and violent situation to see his enemy in a way that *will* justify torture is irresistible. The authors concede that their modest proposal may not lead to torture that saves a life. But they don't tell you the logical corollary: it will lead to torture, and therefore by their own reasoning it will lead to torture that does *not* save a life. Voltaire said, "doubt is not a pleasant condition, but certainty is an absurd one." He was not wrong.

Torture in Practice

Bagaric and Clarke therefore cannot avoid considering the modern world, where torture is not so uncommon. In the real world, it is duplicitous to describe torture, as Bagaric and Clarke do, as "inflicting a relatively small level of harm on a wrong-doer." This must be some kind of joke. In the first place, there seems to be a real lack of understanding as to how the physical aspects of torture work. How effective would regulated, prescribed, and "relative small" dose of torture be? Torture is not like paying a parking fine. The terror and the threat of torture does not come only from the pain by itself. Many of us can tolerate a finite dose of pain, even if it is severe: ask a woman what childbirth is like. There is surely no reason to think that highly motivated terrorists would find the suffering of a specific "level of harm" impossible to bear. The power of torture, in most instances, comes instead from the promise that the torturer makes that the pain will not stop unless you talk. It is a logical contradiction to imagine that torture can be regulated, as Bagaric and Clarke seem to imagine, because it is part of its essence as torture that the victim is beyond protection and that resistance is futile. In addition, it is fundamental to its psychology that the torturer is the sole arbitrator of life and death. The whole power of torture comes from the absolute reduction of one party to pure power and the other to pure powerlessness. In short, and I believe this is a central point that the authors have not understood, torture gets people to talk (not, of course, to tell the truth, but certainly to talk) if and only if the *torture* is sovereign. A torturer-cum-bureaucrat is a contradiction in terms.

It is appalling that these lawyers—Faris too minimizes torture as "pulling out a fingernail"—trivialize the very practice they advocate. Perhaps Bagaric and Clarke have read nothing about the nature of pain, memory, and fear. Perhaps they have not read a single thing about the experience of torture and its implications on those who suffer it and those around them. Perhaps they just have no imagination. They do not appear to understand that torture is not simply pain. It is the experience of absolute powerlessness that reduces the victim, in their own eyes as well as their torturer's, to an animal, a body without will or dignity of any kind. It is the destruction of identity. Torture is rape just as rape is torture. It is not something to shrug off or even, most of the time, to get over.

Neither can we limit our analysis to a single tortured individual. In the world we live in and in which Bagaric and Clarke's argument actually matters, torture is never about the emergency rescue of an innocent life. It is used to extract a wide range of information about the functioning of many outlaw groups. But because of the inherent unreliability of its evidence, this is not its main purpose. Torture is used to punish and humiliate dissidents, terrorists, and members of ethnic minorities. It is used as a calibrated dose of cruelty through which to terrorize whole communities. . . . torture is a demonstration of what the State can do to you and what it can get you to do. The effect is to create a generalized fear about the infinite and random power of the State to destroy lives, and an intense sense of vulnerability in victim populations.

To try and talk about torture as an act practiced on isolated individuals without considering its effects on the families and societies around them, who all live under its constant and unavoidable shadow, is either foolish or duplicitous. Torture does not just affect individuals. It affects whole societies: it terrorizes them and ultimately . . . the powerlessness it communicates shifts from passivity to rage. The turning point in the lives of many Al Qaeda operatives was their imprisonment and torture in Egyptian, Syrian, and other middle eastern prisons: this same Egypt to which the United States *still* "renders" suspects in order to soften them up. Torture produces terrorists: whole families and villages of them. That too is a necessary implication of even the apologists' pale fiction of torture. It is one reason that there is a growing suspicion that the prisoners in Guantanamo Bay—according to the Secretary General of Amnesty International, part of the "gulag of our times"—may never be released. How can they be? Bystanders or warriors, they are much greater risks to us now.

To these real and necessary consequences, which our society would have to understand, accept, and somehow combat if we were ever to accept Bagaric and Clarke's argument, the authors have paid no attention at all.

Defending It

I have argued, first logically and then practically, that it is impossible to accept this modest proposal for torture as being confined to its own strict terms. We are inevitably led to imagine the actual physical and social consequences of such a principle. But for the sake of argument let us look a little closer at the ways in which Bagaric and Clarke attempt to defend an entitlement to torture. According to Bagaric and Clarke, the illegality of torture has only served, by its unnecessary absolutism, to drive it "beneath the radar screen of accountability"; legalization might "reduce the instances of it." It is difficult to see why this assertion would be true. Our societies are not without experience of legal torture. Was there less of it then? Moreover, the emotions that lead to real torture assure—fear, crisis, hatred—will not be reduced by legality, In what sense will "accountability" make a difference to these practices except to provide a helpful framework in which they can be organized, carried out and justified?

The radar argument sounds initially plausible: it is certainly true that illegality does not always work and sometimes only serves to make matters worse. This is particularly the case, for example, in relation to victimless crimes. But torture is hardly victimless. Let us look a little closer to see how the analogy falls down. With drug use or prostitution, the argument is that legalization will clean up the secretive conditions under which they operate and therefore not lessen their incidence but ameliorate their effects, In general, the scholars of what is called "harm minimization" do not dare to contend that a more open approach to drugs will lead to less use; only that it will dramatically improve the social and health conditions of users. But it is not the *conditions* under which torture is practiced that are the problem. Danger and pain are not a by-product of torture (as they are, for example, to a considerable degree a by-product of the current regime of drug prohibition); they are intrinsic to it. Were torture done in public, were it supervised by a qualified medical practitioner in a hygienic environment, were it made respectable—tell me, would any of this make torture better? . . . Voltaire comes to mind: "If we believe absurdities, we shall commit atrocities."

The centre-piece of Bagaric and Clarke's defence offers as obvious example of begging the question as I have seen. They argue by analogy to "the right of self-defence, which of course extends to the defence of another." Let us leave aside that rather hasty "of course" which is far from evident. Just as we are entitled to respond with violence to a murderous attack, they say, we are entitled to protect others; if the only way to protect them is by torturing somebody for information, then torture must be legitimate too. But the analogy falls down in at least three ways. First, the principle of self-defence recognizes a reality: when it's "him or me" a law that said I could not respond to an attacker would be simply unenforceable. Here the violence of torture is a choice deliberately made and carried out, and not purely responsive.

Secondly, their analogy assumes the only point it needs to prove. One can legally defend oneself; one can even kill an attacker if necessary; but what legal system has *ever* authorized a case of torture "in self-defence"? Why do the authors assume that self-defence, which is strictly limited to a direct, minimal and reasonable response to threat, is in any way equivalent to torture, which is by its very nature indirect and maximal? In fact, our societies have, at least since the Enlightenment, feared pain more than death, believed that human dignity requires absolute protection under all circumstances, and thought torture a more serious act than execution. Legal systems throughout the world outlawed torture long, long before capital punishment. In the United States, torture has always been contrary to the 8th Amendment; it is the paradigmatic example of "cruel and unusual punishment." Yet the death penalty continues to be applied—as painlessly as possible. So clearly in the United States, and in fact throughout the world, it is generally considered worse to torture than to kill. Bagaric and Clarke think it obvious that if we can kill someone in self-defence, *therefore* it must be all right to torture them. But this is precisely what the absolute prohibition of torture rejects. It is not that Bagaric and Clarke could not make an argument against this orthodoxy. But they do not attempt to do so. They simply assert their position as self-evident. It is nothing of the kind.

There is a third, and to my mind even more important, way in which the analogy between self-defence and torture fails. Self-defence is about individual action, torture is about government action: the limits we believe ought to apply to each are not necessarily the same. There is a profound difference between individual acts of cruelty and a system of government-regulated torture. There is a difference between kidnapping and a government policy of taking Aboriginal children from their families. There is a difference between murder—even mass murder—and genocide. The difference is the government sanction and the government power that stands behind it in each case. Government action—law—carries a mark of legitimacy with it. Self-defence which leads to murder, or even revenge, might elicit our sympathy. But it is not the same thing as a government program which establishes, institutionalizes, organizes, and legitimizes torture. No matter how limited, torture is thereby made *right* in a way that no act of personal self-defence ever makes murder right. It seems a little surprising that one has to say this to members of a faculty of law. The standards we expect of governments are different from the behaviour we anticipate from individuals. We hold governments to higher standards for a reason.

So too, the reach and mechanisms of government power make torture a weapon from which no member of the community will feel immune. If the State could torture any one of us—they probably wouldn't, but they *could*—what sort of a society would we live in? Now Bagaric and Clarke attempt to avoid this problem by implying that torture would only effect the very few that in some sense deserved it. They insist that it is "verging on moral indecency" "to favour the interests of wrongdoers over those of the innocent." The word "wrongdoer" is used throughout their argument. Although it makes us feel morally superior to the victim of torture, it is another question-begging term, since the authors again simply assume that we can happily identify the wrongdoers. Perhaps they are only associates of terrorists, or family members; and in any case any torture that takes place will very probably precede a trial that might establish whether or not they are innocent. After all, as both Bagaric and Clarke along with Gonzales insist, the whole point of the argument in favour of torture is our need "to *quickly* obtain information from captured terrorists and their sponsors." So much for the rule of law: another suspicion of 'wrongdoing' has been miraculously converted into a certainty.

In the real world, . . . there are many reasons why we might all live in fear of a government which had reserved to itself some kind of right to torture suspects. Perhaps it might just be a case of mistaken identity, or maybe you happened to be born with a foreign sounding name, or maybe you look suspicious or are the wrong colour, or come from a country with a violent history, or are otherwise associated with the wrong people, or perhaps you were just known for holding unpopular opinions at one time or other. How much torture might it take to clear your name? In the face of all these nagging fears, would even a Professor at a law school feel truly safe? And what effect would that endemic, nagging fear have on all our lives and our relationship to the State? Peter Faris, former head of the National Crime Authority, says it would be all right "to pull out a fingernail of a terrorist in order to save a couple of million lives." But the government legitimization of torture, whatever the reason, would ultimately serve only to cripple a few million lives.

Opposing It

The apologists cannot see the difference between self-defence and torture because they are concerned only about outcomes and never about means. For Bagaric and Clarke, it is simply a calculation: one tortured terrorist versus an innocent life or many. Their argument is a rather crude example of utilitarianism, except for the fact that they have not seriously attempted to take into account the actual costs and benefits of the balancing act they propose. In their version of the utilitarian calculus, the benefits are a sheer fantasy and the costs are completely ignored.

Against utilitarianism, there is not much to say that has not been said many times before. Ethics means that there are some things you do not do *even though* it would advantage you (or the whole society) to do them. Ethics means that we impose limits on our actions which cannot be reduced to a calculation about winners and losers. Slavery, for example, would not be less wrong if more people gained from it than lost. It would not be less wrong even if we only enslaved "wrongdoers." The wrong is intrinsic and irredeemable. It is not negotiable in terms of costs and benefits.

So too, human rights protect not just good people but all people, and not just some of the time but all of the time: they are not to be weighed up, or sacrificed. It is in the nature of a human right that it is incalculable. We might feel that certain people have acted in such a way that they no longer *deserve* to be treated humanely, and if society as a whole were to gain by torturing them a little, then we should be allowed to do so. But human rights are not something we deserve. They are something that protects each of us from abuse by protecting us all of us unconditionally. These rights recognize as inviolable the core of our autonomy as human beings, *regardless* of the temptation or the need to violate them. And as partial and problematic as this argument undoubtedly is, if there is anything at all that we have a right to protect against the government and against all of society, it is our bodily integrity, indeed our sanity, our very self. That is the absolute right of which torture threatens to deprive us. Rather more than a fingernail is at stake.

Torture is wrong under all circumstances, not because it leads to certain bad outcomes, but for no reason: simply and inherently. This is not a perverse argument. Love, for example, is good not because it might lead us to wealth or happiness, but for no reason. It just is. In fact, to look for reasons, to ask "what is love good *for*" or "how does loving someone benefit *me*"? is a sign of psychopathy. If Bagaric and Clarke, and Faris, cannot see the inherent wrong of torture, it is hard to see how to communicate with them. But let me suggest two possible approaches intended to communicate what I see as intrinsically true to those who clearly don't see it that way.

The first approach is literary. . . . Jonathan Swift, author of *Gulliver's Travels,* wrote "A Modest Proposal" of his own. What will we do about the poor children of Ireland, he asked, who are such a burden to their parents?

> I have been assured by a very knowing American of my acquaintance in London, that a young healthy child well nursed is at a year old a most delicious, nourishing, and wholesome food, whether stewed, roasted,

baked, or boiled; and I make no doubt that it will equally serve in a fricassee or a ragout.

There's a solution to famine for you, and what after all is wrong with it? If children seem too innocent, we could just eat those in the reformatories, wrongdoers each and every one. Without a sense of our limits, the calibration of costs and benefits is unstoppable: and we *shall* be led to commit atrocities. It strikes me that the current modest proposal for torture makes the same mistakes: slipping seamlessly and without argument across fundamental distinctions, attempting to rationalize a repugnant argument, ignoring the social context it echoes and blind to the horrific practical implications of the system it envisages. But Swift's modest proposal was satire, while Bagaric and Clarke's is farce.

The second approach is historical. Both proposals, above all, display that dangerous human quality of arrogance which somehow assumes that we can and should weigh up a person's pain or a community's fear, against a life or lives. It is the economists' approach to life and the tyrant's approach to politics: everything is about numbers, and no calculation is too dangerous to be attempted. This offers an easy answer to all our problems, but the easy answers are usually wrong. We know all about the Western history of State-sanctioned torture, *l'amende honorable* and the Inquisition. It is not a tradition worth reviving.

Finally, our repugnance is not simply the instinctive and "reflex rejection of torture" that Bagaric and Clarke disparage. A great deal of effort and thought has been expended towards making torture as unacceptable as it is today. We have *learnt* this feeling of disgust as a response to torture over time, and it is rather easier to argue that the world might benefit from more of it than less. Disgust, like shame, is not a pointless emotion. On the contrary, it is an exceptionally powerful way to change the behaviour of people and of communities.

POSTSCRIPT

Is Torture Ever Justified?

Bagaric and Clarke first remind us that torture is a widespread reality. Just because treaties are signed and international agreements are made, we should not assume that there is no torture (or that what little torture there may be is practiced only by rogue states, dictators, international pariahs, etc.). To this, however, there may be two sorts of responses. One is to seek to get a handle on torture, to regulate it in some way, so that the harm is reduced. (Think of a similar response to the situation in which hard drugs are a social problem: Here a harm reduction strategy may involve the distribution of clean needles. The problem isn't solved in such a way that it no longer exists. Rather, the harm that may result—e.g., the transmission of HIV—is minimized.) Another sort of response is wanting to reinforce the prohibition of torture and not to regulate it. On this view, the occurrence of torture is not something that we have to take into account and come to grips with—it is considered to be in a category like crime: We know that it goes on, but we don't want to *regulate* it. We want to *stamp it out*. We try as hard as we can to prevent others from torturing, but we have ultimate control only over our own actions. So the first move in stamping it out is that we ourselves do not practice it.

One problem is that this second approach leaves an opening for "the bad guys" to act in ways that we say and show by our actions that we will not act. So, if we follow this path, some will say that we are really being negligent of our duty, for we have to protect and take care of those near and dear to us. We have to protect innocent people from "the bad guys." Here we face one of the major problems in politics: How to act right in a world in which other people do not act right. For, in the end, this is the kind of world that we live in—the real world, rather than an ideal world.

Further resources on torture are Sam Levinson, *Torture: A Collection* (Oxford University Press, new edition, 2006); Karen J. Greenberg, *The Torture Debate in America* (Cambridge University Press, 2005); Alfred A. McCoy, *A Question of Torture: CIA Interrogation, from the Cold War to the War on Terror (American Empire Project)* (Owl Books, reprint edition, 2007); Jennifer K. Harbury, *Truth, Torture, and the American Way: The History and Consequences of U.S. Involvement in Torture* (Beacon Press, 2005); and Karen J. Greenberg and Joshua L. Dratel, eds., *The Torture Papers: The Road to Abu Ghraib* (Cambridge University Press, 2005).

ISSUE 16

Is Physician-Assisted Suicide Wrong?

YES: Richard Doerflinger, from "Assisted Suicide: Pro-Choice or Anti-Life?" *Hastings Center Report* (January/February 1989)

NO: David T. Watts and Timothy Howell, from "Assisted Suicide Is not Voluntary Active Euthanasia," *Journal of the American Geriatrics Society* (October 1992)

ISSUE SUMMARY

YES: Admitting that religiously based grounds for the wrongness of killing an innocent person are not convincing to many people, Doerflinger argues on mainly secular grounds having to do with inconsistencies in the arguments of supporters of physician-assisted suicide. He examines the idea of autonomy, and the tendency for something like physician-assisted suicide to spread once it becomes initially accepted in a limited way.

NO: Watts and Howell first claim that it is very important to distinguish between *assisted suicide* and *voluntary active euthanasia*. Basically, the first of these is suicide or killing oneself; the second involves being killed by someone else (e.g., a physician). Watts and Howell argue that most of the opposition to physician-assisted suicide turns out to be really opposition to voluntary active euthanasia; furthermore, they argue that physician-assisted suicide would not have the dire consequence that its opponents predict.

The initial situation here is that someone—usually a terminally ill patient—wishes to die and requests physician assistance. (After all, the doctor knows what drugs will do the job, and there have been cases of laypeople botching a suicide attempt and ending up alive but paralyzed.) But a physician who agrees to this request seems to be going against all his or her training and experience (including the Hippocratic Oath and a career devoted to the preservation of life and health). Not only that but, according to the ordinary understanding of murder (as well according to the legal definition and most religious views), to participate in purposely bringing about the death of an innocent person would be murder. (It is no defense to a charge of murder that the victim asked you to do it—contrast the case of killing in self-defense where such killing is indeed a defense against the charge of murder, and is generally considered not to be wrong anyway.)

Consider one particular case that was reported a few years ago. A physicist who had long been exposed to X-rays in his scientific practice had cancer. The disease was at an advanced stage. During the course of the cancer, the physicist had lost his left hand and two of the fingers on the right hand; he had lost other body parts as well; and he had lost his sight. Hospitalized, and in great pain, he was given about a year to live. He was not able to kill himself and begged his brothers to kill him. The first two brothers refused. But the third brother agreed, brought a gun to the hospital, and shot his dying brother.

Many people would be quite sympathetic in a case like this, but nevertheless warn us of a slippery slope. If we allow physician-assisted suicide, it might be said, the policy would expand. Even if we grant that in fact a case like the physicist is the most appropriate case for physician-assisted suicide, most cases won't be like that. What about a physicist who lapses into a coma and can't express his wishes? Or a person who is still at the early stages of some fatal disease and is not in great pain at the moment, but has nothing to look forward to but death? What about a great athlete who wants to die because he now finds himself confined to a wheelchair? What about elderly people who request that they be killed through physician-assisted suicide because they are not well and do not wish to be "a burden" on their offspring? Perhaps family members who wish to inherit something (rather than see it go for fruitless medical expenses) and will subtly get the message across to their aged relatives that "it's time to go"? The list goes on. The problem, opponents to physician-assisted suicide might say, is that once you begin to allow this in some cases, it's easy to begin sliding down a slippery slope and ending up with results that are not at all what was desired in the first place.

In the following essays, Richard Doerflinger first argues that physician-assisted suicide is wrong and that the whole idea of there being such a thing as "rational suicide" is flawed. Then David Watts and Timothy Howell distinguish between various categories of euthanasia and suicide, and conclude that there really are cases of rational suicide and that physician-assisted suicide is not necessarily wrong.

# YES

Richard Doerflinger

Assisted Suicide:
Pro-Choice or Anti-Life?

The intrinsic wrongness of directly killing the innocent, even with the victim's consent, is all but axiomatic in the Jewish and Christian worldviews that have shaped the laws and mores of Western civilization and the self-concept of its medical practitioners. This norm grew out of the conviction that human life is sacred because it is created in the image and likeness of God, and called to fulfillment in love of God and neighbor.

With the pervasive secularization of Western culture, norms against euthanasia and suicide have to a great extent been cut loose from their religious roots to fend for themselves. Because these norms seem abstract and unconvincing to many, debate tends to dwell not on the wrongness of the act as such but on what may follow from its acceptance. Such arguments are often described as claims about a "slippery slope," and debate shifts to the validity of slippery slope arguments in general.

Since it is sometimes argued that acceptance of assisted suicide is an outgrowth of respect for personal autonomy, and not lack of respect for the inherent worth of human life. I will outline how autonomy-based arguments in favor of assisting suicide do entail a statement about the value of life. I will also distinguish two kinds of slippery slope argument often confused with each other, and argue that those who favor social and legal acceptance of assisted suicide have not adequately responded to the slippery slope claims of their opponents.

Assisted Suicide versus Respect for Life

Some advocates of socially sanctioned assisted suicide admit (and a few boast) that their proposal is incompatible with the conviction that human life is of intrinsic worth. Attorney Robert Risley has said that he and his allies in the Hemlock Society are "so bold" as to seek to "overturn the sanctity of life principle" in American society. A life of suffering, "racked with pain," is "not the kind of life we cherish."[1]

Others eschew Risley's approach, perhaps recognizing that it creates a slippery slope toward practices almost universally condemned. If society is to help terminally ill patients to commit suicide because it agrees that death is

Doerflinger: © The Hastings Center. Reprinted by permission. This article originally appeared in the *Hastings Center Report Special Supplement,* vol. 19, no. 1 (1989).

objectively preferable to a life of hardship, it will be difficult to draw the line at the seriously ill or even at circumstances where the victim requests death.

Some advocates of assisted suicide therefore take a different course, arguing that it is precisely respect for the dignity of the human person that demands respect for individual freedom as the noblest feature of that person. On this rationale a decision as to when and how to die deserves the respect and even the assistance of others because it is the ultimate exercise of self-determination—"ultimate" both in the sense that it is the last decision one will ever make and in the sense that through it one takes control of one's entire self. What makes such decisions worthy of respect is not the fact that death is chosen over life but that it is the individual's own free decision about his or her future.

Thus Derek Humphry, director of the Hemlock Society, describes his organization as "pro-choice" on this issue. Such groups favor establishment of a constitutional "right to die" modeled on the right to abortion delineated by the U.S. Supreme Court in 1973. This would be a right to choose *whether or not* to end one's own life, free of outside government interference. In theory, recognition of such a right would betray no bias toward choosing death.

Life versus Freedom

This autonomy-based approach is more appealing than the straight-forward claim that some lives are not worth living, especially to Americans accustomed to valuing individual liberty above virtually all else. But the argument departs from American traditions on liberty in one fundamental respect.

When the Declaration of Independence proclaimed the inalienable human rights to be "life, liberty, and the pursuit of happiness," this ordering reflected a long-standing judgment about their relative priorities. Life, a human being's very earthly existence, is the most fundamental right because it is the necessary condition for all other worldly goods including freedom; freedom in turn makes it possible to pursue (without guaranteeing that one will attain) happiness. Safeguards against the deliberate destruction of life are thus seen as necessary to protect freedom and all other human goods. This line of thought is not explicitly religious but is endorsed by some modern religious groups:

> The first right of the human person is his life. He has other goods and some are more precious, but this one is fundamental—the condition of all the others. Hence it must be protected above all others.[2]

On this view suicide is not the ultimate exercise of freedom but its ultimate self-contradiction: A free act that by destroying life, destroys all the individual's future earthly freedom. If life is more basic than freedom, society best serves freedom by discouraging rather than assisting self-destruction. Sometimes one must limit particular choices to safeguard freedom itself, as when American society chose over a century ago to prevent people from selling themselves into slavery even of their own volition.

It may be argued in objection that the person who ends his life has not truly suffered loss of freedom, because unlike the slave he need not continue to exist under the constraints of a loss of freedom. But the slave does have some freedom, including the freedom to seek various means of liberation or at least the freedom to choose what attitude to take regarding his plight. To claim that a slave is worse off than a corpse is to value a situation of limited freedom less than one of no freedom whatsoever, which seems inconsistent with the premise of the "pro-choice" position. Such a claim also seems tantamount to saying that some lives (such as those with less than absolute freedom) are objectively not worth living, a position that "pro-choice" advocates claim not to hold.

It may further be argued in objection that assistance in suicide is only being offered to those who can no longer meaningfully exercise other freedoms due to increased suffering and reduced capabilities and lifespan. To be sure, the suffering of terminally ill patients who can no longer pursue the simplest everyday tasks should call for sympathy and support from everyone in contact with them. But even these hardships do not constitute total loss of freedom of choice. If they did, one could hardly claim that the patient is in a position to make the ultimate free choice about suicide. A dying person capable of making a choice of that kind is also capable of making less monumental free choices about coping with his or her condition. This person generally faces a bewildering array of choices regarding the assessment of his or her past life and the resolution of relationships with family and friends. He or she must finally choose at this time what stance to take regarding the eternal questions about God, personal responsibility, and the prospects of a destiny after death.

In short, those who seek to maximize free choice may with consistency reject the idea of assisted suicide, instead facilitating all choices *except* that one which cuts short all choices.

In fact proponents of assisted suicide do *not* consistently place freedom of choice as their highest priority. They often defend the moderate nature of their project by stating, with Derek Humphry, that "we do not encourage suicide for any reason except to relieve unremitting suffering." It seems their highest priority is the "pursuit of happiness" (or avoidance of suffering) and not "liberty" as such. Liberty or freedom of choice loses its value if one's choices cannot relieve suffering and lead to happiness; life is of instrumental value, insofar as it makes possible choices that can bring happiness.

In this value system, choice as such does not warrant unqualified respect. In difficult circumstances, as when care of a suffering and dying patient is a great burden on family and society, the individual who chooses life despite suffering will not easily be seen as rational, thus will not easily receive understanding and assistance for this choice.

In short, an unqualified "pro-choice" defense of assisted suicide lacks coherence because corpses have no choices. A particular choice, that of death, is given priority over all the other choices it makes impossible, so the value of choice as such is not central to the argument.

A restriction of this rationale to cases of terminal illness also lacks logical force. For if ending a brief life of suffering can be good, it would seem that ending a long life of suffering may be better. Surely the approach of the California "Humane and Dignified Death Act"—where consensual killing of a patient expected to die in six months is presumably good medical practice, but killing the same patient a month or two earlier is still punishable as homicide—is completely arbitrary.

Slippery Slopes, Loose Cannons

Many arguments against sanctioning assisted suicide concern a different kind of "slippery slope": Contingent factors in the contemporary situation may make it virtually inevitable in practice, if not compelling at the level of abstract theory, that removal of the taboo against assisted suicide will lead to destructive expansions of the right to kill the innocent. Such factors may not be part of euthanasia advocates' own agenda; but if they exist and are beyond the control of these advocates, they must be taken into account in judging the moral and social wisdom of opening what may be a Pandora's box of social evils.

To distinguish this sociological argument from our dissection of the conceptual *logic* of the rationale for assisted suicide, we might call it a "loose cannon" argument. The basic claim is that socially accepted killing of innocent persons will interact with other social factors to threaten lives that advocates of assisted suicide would agree should be protected. These factors at present include the following:

The psychological vulnerability of elderly and dying patients. Theorists may present voluntary and involuntary euthanasia as polar opposites; in practice there are many steps on the road from dispassionate, autonomous choice to subtle coercion. Elderly and disabled patients are often invited by our achievement-oriented society to see themselves as useless burdens on younger, more vital generations. In this climate, simply offering the *option* of "self-deliverance" shifts a burden of proof, so that helpless patients must ask themselves why they are *not* availing themselves of it. Society's offer of death communicates the message to certain patients that they *may* continue to live if they wish but the rest of us have no strong interest in their survival. Indeed, once the choice of a quick and painless death is officially accepted as rational, resistance to this choice may be seen as eccentric or even selfish.[3]

The crisis in health care costs. The growing incentives for physicians, hospitals, families, and insurance companies to control the cost of health care will bring additional pressures to bear on patients. Curt Garbesi, the Hemlock Society's legal consultant, argues that autonomy-based groups like Hemlock must "control the public debate" so assisted suicide will not be seized upon by public officials as a cost-cutting device. But simply basing one's own defense of assisted suicide on individual autonomy does not solve the problem. For in the economic sphere also, offering the option of suicide would subtly shift burdens of proof.

Adequate health care is now seen by at least some policymakers as a human right, as something a society owes to all its members. Acceptance of assisted suicide as an option for those requiring expensive care would not only offer health care providers an incentive to make that option seem attractive—it would also demote all other options to the status of strictly private choices by the individual. As such they may lose their moral and legal claim to public support—in much the same way that the U.S. Supreme Court, having protected abortion under a constitutional "right of privacy," has quite logically denied any government obligation to provide public funds for this strictly private choice. As life-extending care of the terminally ill is increasingly seen as strictly elective, society may become less willing to appropriate funds for such care, and economic pressures to choose death will grow accordingly.

Legal doctrines on "substituted judgment." American courts recognizing a fundamental right to refuse life-sustaining treatment have concluded that it is unjust to deny this right to the mentally incompetent. In such cases the right is exercised on the patient's behalf by others, who seek either to interpret what the patient's own wishes might have been or to serve his or her best interests. Once assisted suicide is established as a fundamental right, courts will almost certainly find that it is unjust not to extend this right to those unable to express their wishes. Hemlock's political arm, Americans Against Human Suffering, has underscored continuity between "passive" and "active" euthanasia by offering the Humane and Dignified Death Act as an amendment to California's "living will" law, and by including a provision for appointment of a proxy to choose the time and manner of the patient's death. By such extensions our legal system would accommodate nonvoluntary, if not involuntary, active euthanasia.

Expanded definitions of terminal illness. The Hemlock Society wishes to offer assisted suicide only to those suffering from terminal illnesses. But some Hemlock officials have in mind a rather broad definition of "terminal illness." Derek Humphry says "two and a half million people alone are dying of Alzheimer's disease."[4] At Hemlock's 1986 convention, Dutch physician Pieter Admiraal boasted that he had recently broadened the meaning of terminal illness in his country by giving a lethal injection to a young quadriplegic woman—a Dutch court found that he acted within judicial guidelines allowing euthanasia for the terminally ill, because paralyzed patients have difficulty swallowing and could die from aspirating their food at any time.

The medical and legal meaning of terminal illness has already been expanded in the United States by professional societies, legislatures, and courts in the context of so-called passive euthanasia. A Uniform Rights of the Terminally Ill Act proposed by the National Conference of Commissioners on Uniform State Laws in 1986 defines a terminal illness as one that would cause the patient's death in a relatively short time if life-preserving treatment is *not* provided—prompting critics to ask if all diabetics, for example, are "terminal" by definition. Some courts already see comatose and vegetative states as "terminal" because they involve an inability to swallow that will lead to death unless artificial feeding is instituted. In the *Hilda Peter* case, the New Jersey Supreme Court declared that the traditional state interest in "preserving life" referred only to "cognitive and sapient life" and not to mere "biological" existence, implying that unconscious patients are terminal, or perhaps as good as dead, so far as state interests are concerned. Is there any reason to think that American law would suddenly resurrect the older, narrower meaning of "terminal illness" in the context of *active* euthanasia?

Prejudice against citizens with disabilities. If definitions of terminal illness expand to encompass states of severe physical or mental disability, another social reality will increase the pressure on patients to choose death: long-standing prejudice, sometimes bordering on revulsion, against people with disabilities. While it is seldom baldly claimed that disabled people have "lives not worth living," able-bodied people often say they could not live in a severely disabled state or would prefer death. In granting Elizabeth Bouvia a right to refuse a feeding tube that preserved her life, the California Appeals Court bluntly stated that her physical handicaps led her to "consider her existence meaningless" and that "she cannot be faulted for so concluding." According to disability rights expert Paul Longmore, in a society with such attitudes toward the disabled, "talk of their 'rational' or 'voluntary' suicide is simply Orwellian newspeak."[5]

Character of the medical profession. Advocates of assisted suicide realize that most physicians will resist giving lethal injections because they are trained, in Garbesi's words, to be "enemies of death." The California Medical Association firmly opposed the Humane and Dignified Death Act, seeing it as an attack on the ethical foundation of the medical profession.

Yet California appeals judge Lynn Compton was surely correct in his concurring opinion in the *Bouvia* case, when he said that a sufficient number of willing physicians can be found once legal sanctions against assisted suicide are dropped. Judge Compton said this had clearly been the case with abortion, despite the fact that the Hippocratic Oath condemns abortion as strongly as it condemns euthanasia. Opinion polls of physicians bear out the judgment that a significant number would perform lethal injections if they were legal.

Some might think this division or ambivalence about assisted suicide in the medical profession will restrain broad expansions of the practice. But if anything, Judge Compton's analogy to our experience with abortion suggests the opposite. Most physicians still have qualms about abortion, and those who perform abortions on a full-time basis are not readily accepted by their colleagues as paragons of the healing art. Consequently they tend to form their own professional societies, bolstering each other's positive self-image and developing euphemisms to blunt the moral edge of their work.

Once physicians abandon the traditional medical self-image, which rejects direct killing of patients in all circumstances, their new substitute self-image may require ever more aggressive efforts to make this killing more widely practiced and favorably received. To allow killing by physicians in certain circumstances may create a new lobby of physicians in favor of expanding medical killing.

The human will to power. The most deeply buried yet most powerful driving force toward widespread medical killing is a fact of human nature: Human beings are tempted to enjoy exercising power over others; ending another person's life is the ultimate exercise of that power. Once the taboo against killing has been set aside, it becomes progressively easier to channel one's aggressive instincts into the destruction of life in other contexts. Or as James Burtchaell has said: "There is a sort of virginity about murder; once one has violated it, it is awkward to refuse other invitations by saying, 'But that would be murder!'"[6]

Some will say assisted suicide for the terminally ill is morally distinguishable from murder and does not logically require termination of life in other circumstances. But my point is that the skill and the instinct to kill are more easily turned to other lethal tasks once they have an opportunity to exercise themselves. Thus Robert Jay Lifton has perceived differences between the German "mercy killings" of the 1930s and the later campaign to annihilate the Jews of Europe, yet still says that "at the heart of the Nazi enterprise . . . is the destruction of the boundary between healing and killing."[7] No other boundary separating these two situations was as fundamental as this one, and thus none was effective once it was crossed. As a matter of historical fact, personnel who had conducted the "mercy killing" program were quickly and readily recruited to operate the killing chambers of the death camps.[8] While the contemporary United States fortunately lacks the anti-Semitic and totalitarian attitudes that made the Holocaust possible, it has its own trends and pressures that may combine with acceptance of medical killing to produce a distinctively American catastrophe in the name of individual freedom.

These "loose cannon" arguments are not conclusive. All such arguments by their nature rest upon a reading and extrapolation of certain contingent factors in society. But their combined force provides a serious case against taking the irreversible step of sanctioning assisted suicide for any class of persons, so long as those who advocate this step fail to demonstrate why these predictions are wrong. If the strict philosophical case on behalf of "rational suicide" lacks coherence, the pragmatic claim that its acceptance would be a social benefit lacks grounding in history or common sense.

References

1. Presentation at the Hemlock Society's Third National Voluntary Euthanasia Conference, "A Humane and Dignified Death," September 25–27, 1986, Washington, DC. All quotations from Hemlock Society officials are from the proceedings of this conference unless otherwise noted.

2. Vatican Congregation for the Doctrine of the Faith, *Declaration on Procured Abortion* (1974), para. 11.

3. I am indebted for this line of argument to Dr. Eric Chevlen.

4. Denis Herbstein, "Campaigning for the Right to Die," *International Herald Tribune,* 11 September 1986.

5. Paul K. Longmore, "Elizabeth Bouvia, Assisted Suicide and Social Prejudice," *Issues in Law & Medicine* 3:2 (1987), 168.

6. James T. Burtchaell, *Rachel Weeping and Other Essays on Abortion* (Kansas City: Andrews & McMeel, 1982), 188.

7. Robert Jay Lifton, *The Nazi Doctors: Medical Killing and the Psychology of Genocide* (New York: Basic Books, 1986), 14.

8. Yitzhak Rad, *Belzec, Sobibor, Treblinka* (Bloomington, IN: Indiana University Press, 1987), 11, 16–17.

David T. Watts
and Timothy Howell

 **NO**

Assisted Suicide Is Not Voluntary Active Euthanasia

Ongoing developments continue to spotlight the controversial issues of voluntary active euthanasia and assisted suicide. In November 1991, Washington State's Initiative 119, which would have allowed physicians, in certain circumstances, to aid terminally ill patients' dying, was defeated by 56% to 44%.[1] Dr. Jack Kevorkian assisted in the suicides of two non-terminally ill women in October 1991, leading to the suspension of his Michigan medical license.[2] Murder charges were later brought against Kevorkian by a grand jury. In New Hampshire, a bill has been introduced which would allow physicians to assist patients' suicides but not perform active euthanasia.[3,4]

Such developments highlight some of the confusion emerging from discussions of voluntary active euthanasia (V.A.E.) and assisted suicide. A significant source of confusion has been the tendency to join these concepts or even to consider them synonymous. For example, the AGS Position Statement on V.A.E. and a recent article by Teno and Lynn in the *Journal of the American Geriatrics Society* both reject easing restrictions on V.A.E. and assisted suicide while making arguments *only* against euthanasia.[5,6] The National Hospice Organization also opposes euthanasia and assisted suicide, but it, too, appears to blur the distinction between them in stating that "euthanasia encompasses . . . in some settings, physician-assisted suicide."[7] Others appear to use the terms euthanasia and assisted suicide synonymously in arguing against both.[8]

In contrast, the AMA Ethics and Health Policy Counsel argues against physician-assisted suicide and distinguishes this from euthanasia.[9] The AMA Council on Ethical and Judicial Affairs also acknowledges there is "an ethically relevant distinction between euthanasia and assisted suicide that makes assisted suicide a more attractive option." Yet it then goes on to assert that "the ethical concerns about physician-assisted suicide are similar to those of euthanasia since both are essentially interventions intended to cause death."[10]

In order to weigh and appreciate the merits of the different arguments for and against V.A.E. and physician-assisted suicide, it is critical that appropriate distinctions be made. For example, we believe the arguments made in the references cited above and by others[11,12] against euthanasia are telling. However, we find that these same arguments are substantially weaker when used against assisted suicide. And while we agree with the AMA Council on Ethical and Judicial Affairs that an ethically relevant distinction exists between euthanasia and assisted

From *Journal of the American Geriatrics Society*, vol. 40, no. 10, October 1992, pp. 1043–1046.

suicide, we think it is important to distinguish further between different forms of assisted suicide. Only by doing so can we begin to sort out some of the apparent confusion in attitudes toward these issues. We caution our readers that the literature on this topic, while growing, remains preliminary, with little empirical research yet completed.[13] Our arguments, however, are philosophical in nature and do not ultimately stand or fall on empirical data.

Definitions

Voluntary active euthanasia: Administration of medications or other interventions intended to cause death at a patient's request.

Assisted suicide: Provision of information, means, or direct assistance by which a patient may take his or her own life. Assisted suicide involves several possible levels of assistance: *providing information,* for example, may mean providing toxicological information or describing techniques by which someone may commit suicide; *providing the means* can involve written prescriptions for lethal amounts of medication; *supervising or directly aiding* includes inserting an intravenous line and instructing on starting a lethal infusion.

These levels of assistance have very different implications. Providing only information or means allows individuals to retain the greatest degree of control in choosing the time and mode of their deaths. Physician participation is only indirect. This type of limited assistance is exemplified by the widely reported case of Dr. Timothy Quill, who prescribed a lethal quantity of barbiturates at the request of one of his patients who had leukemia.[14] By contrast, supervising or directly aiding is the type of physician involvement characterizing the case of Dr. Jack Kevorkian and Janet Adkins. Adkins was a 54-year-old woman with a diagnosis of Alzheimer-type dementia who sought Kevorkian's assistance in ending her life. Dr. Kevorkian inserted an intravenous catheter and instructed Mrs. Adkins on activating a lethal infusion of potassium following barbiturate sedation, a process personally monitored by Kevorkian.[15] This form of assisted suicide carries significant potential for physician influence or control of the process, and from it there is only a relatively short step to physician initiation (i.e., active euthanasia). We therefore reject physician-supervised suicide for the arguments commonly made against V.A.E., namely, that legalization would have serious adverse consequences, including potential abuse of vulnerable persons, mistrust of physicians, and diminished availability of supportive services for the dying.[6, 7, 10–12] We find each of these arguments, however, insufficient when applied to more limited forms of physican-assisted suicide (i.e., providing information or means).

Will Assisted Suicide Lead to Abuse of Vulnerable Persons?

A major concern is that some patients will request euthanasia or assisted suicide out of convenience to others.[6, 9] It is certainly possible that a patient's desire to avoid being a burden could lead to such a request. With euthanasia, there is danger that a patient's request might find too ready acceptance. With assisted suicide, however, the ultimate decision, and the ultimate action, are the patient's, not the physician's. This places an important check and balance on physician initiation or patient acquiescence in euthanasia. As the AMA Council on Ethical and Judicial Affairs acknowledges, a greater level of patient autonomy is afforded by physician-assisted suicide than by euthanasia.[10]

Culturally or socially mediated requests for assisted suicide would remain a significant concern. Patients might also request aid in suicide out of fear, pain, ambivalence, or depression.[16] The requirement that patients commit the ultimate act themselves cannot alone provide a sufficient safeguard. It would be incumbent on physicians to determine, insofar as possible, that requests for assisted suicide were not unduly influenced and that reversible conditions were optimally treated. As to how physicians might respond to such requests, data from the Netherlands indicate that about 75% of euthanasia requests in that country are refused.[17] It is our impression that most requests for assisted suicide, therefore, appear to represent opportunities for improved symptom control. We believe most serious requests would likely come from patients experiencing distressing symptoms of terminal illness.[18] By opening the door for counseling or treatment of reversible conditions, requests for assisted suicide might actually lead to averting some suicides which would have otherwise occurred.

Another concern regarding euthanasia is that it could come to be accepted without valid consent and that such a practice would more likely affect the frail and impoverished. The Remmelink Commission's investigation of euthanasia in the Netherlands appeared to justify such concerns in estimating that Dutch physicians may have performed 1,000 acts of involuntary euthanasia involving incompetent individuals.[19] But while euthanasia opens up the possibility of invalid consent, with assisted suicide consent is integral to the process. Because the choice of action clearly rests with the individual, there is substantially less likelihood for the abuse of assisted suicide as a societal vehicle for cost containment. And there is little basis for assuming that requests for assisted suicide would come primarily from frail and impoverished persons. Prolonged debilitation inherent in many illnesses is familiar to an increasing number of patients, family members, and health professionals. Such illnesses represent a greater financial threat to the middle- and upper-middle class, since the poor and disenfranchised have less to spend down to indigency. Thus, we suspect requests to assisted suicide might actually be more common from the educated, affluent, and outspoken.

Patients diagnosed with terminal or debilitating conditions are often vulnerable. We agree that such patients might request assisted suicide out of fear of pain, suffering, or isolation, and that too ready acceptance of such requests could be disastrous. Yet, we believe that patients' interests can be safeguarded by requirements for persistent, competent requests as well as thorough assessments for conditions, such as clinical depression, which could be reversed, treated, or ameliorated. Foley recently outlined an approach to the suicidal cancer patient.[20] We share her view that many such patients' requests to terminate life are altered by the availability of expert, continuing hospice services. We concur with Foley and others in calling for the wider availability of such services,[5,6] so that requests for assisted suicide arising from pain, depression, or other distressing symptoms can be reduced to a minimum.

Would Assisted Suicide Undermine Trust Between Patients and Physicians?

The cardinal distinction between V.A.E. and assisted suicide is that V.A.E. is killing by physicians, while suicide is self-killing. Prohibiting both euthanasia and physician-supervised suicide (i.e., with direct physician involvement) should diminish worries that patients might have about physicians wrongly administering lethal medicine. At present, physician-patient trust is compromised by widespread concern that physicians try too hard to keep dying patients alive. The very strength of the physician-patient relationship has been cited as a justification for physician involvement in assisted suicide.[21]

A number of ethicists have expressed concern that both euthanasia and assisted suicide, if legalized, would have a negative impact on the way society perceives the role of physicians.[6,9,11,12] Limited forms of assisted suicide, however, have been viewed more positively.[22] Public and professional attitudes appear to be evolving on this issue. A 1990 Gallup poll found that 66% of respondents believed someone in great pain, with "no hope of improvement," had the moral right to commit suicide; in 1975 the figure was 41%.[23] A panel of distinguished physicians has stated that it is not immoral for a physician to assist in the rational suicide of a terminally ill person.[24] The recent publication of a book on techniques of committing or assisting suicide evoked wide interest and significant support for the right of people to take control of their dying.[25] For a significant segment of society, physician involvement in assisted suicide may be welcomed, not feared. Furthermore, while relatively few might be likely to seek assistance with suicide if stricken with a debilitating illness, a substantial number might take solace knowing they could request such assistance.

There is another argument raised against V.A.E. that we believe also falters when used to object to assisted suicide. It has been maintained that prohibiting euthanasia forces physicians to focus on the humane care of dying patients, including meticulous attention to their symptoms.[6,18] This argument implies that physicians find it easier to relieve the suffering of dying patients by ending their lives rather than attempting the difficult task of palliating their symptoms. But for some patients, the suffering may not be amenable to even the most expert palliation. Even in such instances, some argue that limited forms of assisted suicide should be prohibited on the grounds that not to forbid them would open the door for more generalized, less stringent applications of assisted suicide.

To us, this "slippery slope" argument seems to imply that the moral integrity of the medical profession must be maintained, even if at the cost of prolonged, unnecessary suffering by at least some dying patients. We believe such a posture is itself inhumane and not acceptable. It contradicts a fundamental principle that is an essential ingredient of physician-patient trust: that patient comfort should be a primary goal of the physician in the face of incurable illness.

Furthermore, by allowing limited physician involvement in assisted suicide, physicians can respect both the principle of caring that guides them and the patients for whom caring alone is insufficient. We concede that there is another alternative: terminally ill patients who cannot avoid pain while awake may be given continuous anesthetic levels of medication.[6] But this is exactly the sort of dying process we believe many in our society want to avoid.

Will Assisted Suicide and Euthanasia Weaken Societal Resolve to Increase Resources Allocated to Care of the Dying?

This argument assumes that V.A.E. and assisted suicide would both be widely practiced, and that their very availability would decrease tangible concern for those not choosing euthanasia or suicide. However, euthanasia is rarely requested even by terminal cancer patients.[6] In the Netherlands, euthanasia accounts for less than 2% of all deaths.[17] These data suggest that even if assisted suicide were available to those with intractable pain or distressing terminal conditions, it would likely be an option chosen by relatively few. With assisted suicide limited to relatively few cases, this argument collapses. For with only a few requesting assisted suicide, the vast number of patients with debilitating illnesses would be undiminished, and their numbers should remain sufficient to motivate societal concern for their needs. Furthermore, to withhold assisted suicide from the few making serious, valid requests would be to subordinate needlessly the interests of these few to those of the many. Compounding their tragedy would be the fact that these individuals could not even benefit from any increase in therapeutic resources prompted by their suffering, insofar as their conditions are, by definition, not able to be ameliorated.

Conclusion

We have argued that assisted suicide and voluntary active euthanasia are different and that each has differing implications for medical practice and society. Further discussion should consider the merits and disadvantages of each, a process enhanced by contrasting them. We have further argued that different forms of assisted suicide can be distinguished both clinically and philosophically. Although some may argue that all forms of assisted suicide are fundamentally the same, we believe the differences can be contrasted as starkly as a written prescription and a suicide machine.

We do not advocate ready acceptance of requests for suicide, nor do we wish to romanticize the concept of rational suicide.[26] In some situations, however, where severe debilitating illness cannot be reversed, suicide may represent a rational choice. If this is the case, then physician assistance could make the process more humane. Along with other geriatricians, we often face dilemmas involving the management of chronic illnesses in late life. We believe we can best serve our patients, and preserve their trust, by respecting their desire for autonomy, dignity, and quality, not only of life, but of dying.

References

1. Caplan A. Patient rights measure needs push from Bush. Wis State J November 13, 1991, p 11A.

2. Holyfield J. Doctor who helped suicides has his license suspended. Wis State J November 21, 1991, p 5A.

3. Beresford L., ed. Euthanasia movement may be helping spur new additional attention to pain relief. Hospice News Serv 1992;3:1–3.

4. Anonymous. New Hampshire: Lawmakers file suicide bill. Wis State J November 13, 1991, p 3A.

5. AGS Public Policy Committee. Voluntary active euthanasia. J Am Geriatr Soc 1991;39:826.

6. Teno J. Lynn J. Voluntary active euthanasia: The individual case and public policy. J Am Geriatr Soc 1991;39:827–830.

7. National Hospice Organization. Statement of the National Hospice Organization Opposing the Legalization of Euthanasia and Assisted Suicide. Arlington, VA: National Hospice Organization, 1991.

8. Travis R. Two arguments against euthanasia (letter). Gerontologist 1991; 31:561–562.

9. Orentlicher D. Physician participation in assisted suicide. JAMA 1989; 262; 1844–1845.

10. AMA. Report of the Council on Ethical and Judicial Affairs: Decisions Near the End of Life. Chicago, IL: American Medical Association. 1991.

11. Singer PA. Should doctors kill patients? Can Med Assoc J 1988;138:1001–1001.

12. Singer PA, Siegler M. Euthanasia—a critique. N Engl J Med 1990; 322:1881–1883.

13. Watts DT, Howell T, Priefer BA. Geriatricians' attitudes toward assisting suicide of dementia patients. J Am Geriatr Soc 1992, September 40:878–885.

14. Quill TE. Death and dignity: A case of individualized decision making. N Engl J Med 1991;324:691–694.

15. Cassel CK, Meier DE. Morals and moralism in the debate over euthanasia and assisted suicide. N Engl J Med 1990;323:750–752.

16. Jackson DL, Youngner S. Patient autonomy and "death with dignity": Some clinical caveats. N Engl J Med 1979;301:404–408.

17. Van der Maas PJ, Van Delden JJM, Pijnenborg L. Looman CWN. Euthanasia and other medical decisions concerning the end of life. Lancet 1991; 338:669–74.

18. Palmore EB. Arguments for assisted suicide (letter). Gerontologist 1991; 31:854.

19. Karel R. Undertreatment of pain, depression needs to be addressed before euthanasia made legal in U.S. Psychiatric News. December 20, 1991, pp 5, 13, 23.

20. Foley KM. The relationship of pain and symptom management to patient requests for physician-assisted suicide. J Pain Symptom Manag 1991; 6:289–297.

21. Jecker NS. Giving death a hand. When the dying and the doctor stand in a special relationship. J Am Geriatr Soc 1991;39:831–835.

22. American College of Physicians ACP to DA, Grand Jury: Dr. Quill acted "humanely." ACP Observer, September, 1991, p 5.

23. Ames K. Wilson L. Sawhill R et al. Last rights. Newsweek August 26, 1991, pp 40–41.

24. Wanzer SH, Federman DD, Adelstein SJ et al. The physician's responsibility toward hopelessly ill patients: A second look. N Engl J Med 1989;320:844–849.

25. Humphry D. Final Exit: The Practicalities of Self-Deliverance and Assisted Suicide for the Dying. Eugene, OR: The Hemlock Society, (distributed by Carol Publishing, Secaucus, NJ). 1991.

26. Conwell Y, Caine ED. Rational suicide and the right to die: Reality and myth. N Engl J Med 1991;325:1100–1103.

POSTSCRIPT

Is Physician-Assisted Suicide Wrong?

We normally understand that physician-assisted suicide, if adopted as a matter of policy, will bring with it certain regulations and safeguards. Clearly, not just asking a physician for assistance is going to be sufficient. Even ordinary people are sometimes depressed, and it is understandable that people with a serious illness are even more likely to be depressed. So, at a minimum, people who request physician-assisted suicide would have to be screened for depression.

Moreover, as Watts and Howell, explain, levels of physician-assistance can vary from merely providing information, writing prescriptions, and so on, all the way up to the methods practiced by Dr. Kevorkian, including the use of his "suicide machines." In fact, while much of the public gets its ideas about what physician-assisted suicide is from Dr. Kevorkian, most proponents of physician-assisted suicide regard what he does as an example of what can happen if we *don't* have regulations and safeguards in place.

It is sometimes difficult for young and healthy people to imagine themselves at the end of life. But some people will have lived through their own relative's deaths. And the very fact that we are all going to die—although no one knows the exact circumstances and whether we will go peacefully or in pain—makes this a real issue for all of us. The uncertainty that exists might make some people lean toward the side of the issue that provides the greater scope for leeway, allowing some provision for physician-assisted suicide, perhaps as a sort of "insurance" that may not even be needed.

Some of the opposition to the idea of physician-assisted suicide might come from a general repulsion against taking life. This is a good reaction to have. But it doesn't mean that the reaction is a substitute for judgment. Likewise, some of the opposition might come from a negative association of this with the Nazis. Again, the negative reaction is good one. What is required here though is an ability to get past purely emotional responses and mental associations. What we need are reasons and careful thinking.

Further resources on this issue can be found in James H. Ondrey, *Physician-Assisted Suicide* (Greenhaven Press, 2006); Gerald Dworkin, R.G. Frey, and Sissela Bok *Euthanasia and Physician-Assisted Suicide (For and Against)* (Cambridge University Press, 2005); and Ian Dowbiggin, *A Merciful End: The Euthanasia Movement in Modern America* (Oxford University Press, 2007).

Perhaps of unique interest is Derek Humphrey's *Final Exit: The Practicalities of Self-Deliverance and Assisted Suicide for the Dying,* 3rd ed. (Delta, 2003). This book was written by a founder of the Hemlock Society (now merged into the Compassion & Choices organization); the book contains useful information and is also a practical "how-to" guide so that "self-deliverance" (suicide) can be successfully achieved.

Internet References . . .

Animal Rights and Vegetarianism

http://www.peta.org/
http://ar.vegnews.org/Animal_Rights.html

Human Beings and Other Species

*N*owadays we recognize that human beings are part of nature and that we share the planet with other species. In former times, human beings and nature were thought to be two entirely different things. Even then, it was realized of course that we shared the planet with other species, but there was little or no question that eating their meat was morally acceptable. Now that we have become accustomed to seeing animals as fellow inhabitants of the natural world, the question arises about our proper relation to them.

* Does Morality Require Vegetarianism?

ISSUE 17

Does Morality Require Vegetarianism?

YES: Jordan Curnutt, from "A New Argument for Vegetarianism," *Journal of Social Philosophy* (Winter 1997)

NO: Holmes Rolston III, from *Environmental Ethics: Duties to and Values in the Natural World* (Temple University Press, 1988)

ISSUE SUMMARY

YES: Jordan Curnutt specifically rejects the two major lines of thought that have led to the philosophical support of vegetarianism, utilitarian ideas (based on animal suffering) and deontological ideas (based on animal rights). Curnutt offers what he calls a new argument for vegetarianism, based on the harm of killing animals, and the weakness of the reasons that people might propose for causing that harm.

NO: Environmental thinker Holmes Rolston III maintains that meat eating by humans is a natural part of the ecosystem. He states that it is important that animals do not suffer needlessly, but it would be a mistake to think that animals, like humans, are members of a culture. Rolston concludes that people too readily project human nature on animal nature.

T his issue comes about because humans are rational beings and, at least to some extent, we are able to control our actions. Many other living things eat meat but are not rational beings. Lions, for example, eat meat—but a male lion will often kill all the lion cubs of his new mate, which would certainly seem by human standards to be unreasonable. The idea that we are just following nature when we eat meat may not exactly be true, say many who recognize that some animal behaviors are not to be used as models by people. Instead we must pick and choose the behaviors that we follow.

Moreover, unlike lions, most people do not *have* to eat meat in order to survive. Indeed, some entire cultures are vegetarian. Individual vegetarians can be found in other cultures as well, for example, in American culture. On the other hand, in American culture the practice of meat eating is the norm and is quite widespread—just look at all the McDonald's and Burger Kings!

As a justification for eating meat, some conclude that it is not quite right to say that we are just doing what the other living things do—for we do not follow animal behavior if we think it would be wrong to do so. But if meat eating is a cultural practice, then, like any other cultural practice, it is subject to rational judgment and moral critique. We know that in the past, many socially accepted practices have been condoned at the time they were practiced but later found to be morally wanting. We can look back now in amazement at the practice of slavery in the South in the early part of the 1800s or the way great poverty was ignored in Victorian England while some people lived lives of luxury. One wonders, "How could people *do* that?" Could it be that future generations will look back at the Americans who thought nothing of consuming Big Macs and likewise wonder, "How could people *do* that?"

Many find the basic problem with meat eating to be the conditions under which animals who are raised for food live. The people who eat meat bring about these deplorable conditions, some argue, because high consumer demand dictates that the supermarkets are well stocked with meat, that fast food outlets sell meat, and therefore make it easier to obtain a meal with meat than one without. Animal husbandry is big business, and it is big business because the customers demand the product. Because of this huge demand, it can be said that many people look the other way when farmers raise animals under conditions that many vegetarians find appalling.

In the following selections, Jordan Curnutt argues that morality does in fact require vegetarianism. The argument, he claims, is a new one, based on harm rather than on either animal suffering or animal rights. Holmes Rolston III then maintains that the human consumption of meat is part of our human interaction with the natural (as opposed to the cultural) environment. He asserts that it is important that animals do not suffer needlessly, of course, but it would be a mistake to think that animals are members of a culture in the same way that humans belong to a culture. People too readily project human nature on animal nature, he contends.

YES

Jordan Curnutt

A New Argument for Vegetarianism

Philosophical discussion of vegetarianism has been steadily decreasing over the last ten years or so. This follows a prolific period in the 1970s and 1980s when a veritable flood of books and journal articles appeared, devoted wholly or in part to various defenses and rejections of vegetarianism. What has happened? Have the relevant problems have been solved? Have philosophers simply lost interest in the topic? I don't think so. My hypothesis is that the major theoretical approaches to the issue which have been most rigorously pursued have produced a stalemate: appeal to some form of utilitarian theory, or to rights-based theories, or to pain and suffering, have not proved fruitful for resolving the problems.

I would like to present an alternative to these traditional approaches. This alternative avoids the difficulties which result in the stalemate, successfully eludes subsequent objections, and justifies a moral requirement to refrain from eating animals. I will first briefly explain why the old argu- ments have not been helpful. The remainder of the paper is devoted to the explanation and defense of a new argument for vegetarianism, one which does not depend on calculations of utility, any particular conception of rights, or the imposition of pain and suffering.[1]

Old Arguments for Vegetarianism

Peter Singer has been the leading utilitarian defender of vegetarianism for more than twenty years.[2] He has often cited the vast amounts of pain and suffering experienced by domesticated animals "down on the factory farm" as they await and inevitably succumb to their fate as food for human consumption.[3] A utilitarian of any species is required to produce that state of affairs in which aggregations of certain positive and negative mental states exceed (or at least equal) such aggregations of any alternative state of affairs. Singer has argued that factory farming woefully fails to meet this standard. Vegetarianism is morally obligatory simply because it maximizes utility, precisely what utilitarians say we are supposed to do. Animal-eating promotes disutility, precisely what we are supposed to avoid.

But several philosophers have urged that utilitarianism is a perilous ally for the vegetarian. One major problem is that the end of animal-eating produces

From *Journal of Social Philosophy*, vol. 28, no. 3, Winter 1997, pp. excerpts from 153–157, 162–163, 165–172. Copyright © 1997 by Blackwell Publishing, Ltd. Reprinted by permission.

disutilities which must be accounted for in the utilitarian ledger. When that is done, animal-eating may not emerge as morally wrong after all. For example, R.G. Frey has claimed that the demise of the meat industry and its satellites which would attend a wholesale conversion to vegetarianism would be catastrophic to human welfare, and so could not be given a utilitarian justification.[4] Frey lists fourteen different ways in which rampant vegetarianism would deleteriously affect human affairs, mainly in the form of economic losses for those employed in the industry. In the face of this, his utilitarian calculation yields the result that we are permitted to eat animals at will, but we must strive to reduce the amount of suffering they experience.[5]

Not only does vegetarianism produce disutilites, but animal-eating can actually maximize utility: utilitarianism may *require* animal-eating. Roger Crisp contends that this theory leads to what he calls the "Compromise Requirement view."[6] According to Crisp, "nonintensively-reared animals lead worthwhile lives" and humans derive gustatory pleasure, satisfaction, or some other positive mental state from eating them. Vegetarianism would put an end to these two sources of utility. Thus, given the requirement to maximize utility, raising and eating animals in these circumstances becomes a utilitarian obligation.[7]. . .

The leading contender to utilitarian theory in this area has been the rights-based perspective of Tom Regan. His dedication to defending animals in general and vegetarianism in particular nearly matches Singer's in duration and production.[8] In brief, Regan's position is that mammals of at least one year old are "subjects-of-a-life": they are conscious beings with a wide variety of mental states, such as preferences, beliefs, sensations, a sense of self and of the future. These features identify animals as rightsholders and possessors of "inherent" value. One implication of this view is that killing animals for food, whether or not this is done painlessly and independently of the quality of the animals' life, is a violation of their right to respectful treatment, since it uses them as a means to our own ends. Hence, vegetarianism is morally required.

Regan is one of many philosophers who advocate the view that nonpersons in general or animals in particular (or both) qualify as moral rightsholders.[9] These philosophers tend to identify rightsholders according to their possession of certain affective capacities, such as interests or desires, and a number of them argue that animals do have these capacities. On the other hand, many other philosophers prefer cognitive criteria, confining rightsholders to beings with certain more advanced mental capacities—rationality and autonomy are the favorites—and explicitly or by implication disqualifying animals from this category.[10]

The Case for Animal Rights represents the *opus classicus* of the deontological approach to animal issues. Through more than four hundred pages of dense and tightly argued text, Regan has canvassed the philosophical problems of human-animal relationships more thoroughly than anyone has ever done. Even so, his view has been subjected to some quite damaging criticisms, ranging from concern over the mysterious and controversial nature of "inherent value" to charges of inconsistency and implausibility when the rights of humans and those of animals come into conflict.[11] This fact, along with the formidable arguments marshaled by those who champion cognitive requirements for rightsholding, suggest that basing a case for vegetarianism upon the foundation of moral rights is an onerous task. The major problem is that the topic is exceedingly complex. A study of rights must address such daunting questions as: What are rights? Are they real independently existing entities (natural rights) or human inventions (political, legal) or both? What is needed to qualify as a rightsholder? Exactly what rights are held by whom and why? How are conflicts among rights settled?

Thus we have a very complicated theoretical endeavor marked by profound differences, yielding an area of philosophical debate which is highly unsettled. This tells us that a new argument for vegetarianism should traverse a relatively uncontroversial theoretical region which is stable and fixed.

A New Argument for Vegetarianism (NEW)

NEW makes no appeal to utility, rights, or pain and suffering:

1. Causing harm is prima facie morally wrong.
2. Killing animals causes them harm.
3. Therefore, killing animals is prima facie morally wrong.
4. Extensive animal-eating requires the killing of animals.
5. Therefore, animal-eating is prima facie morally wrong.
6. The wrongness of animal eating is not overridden.
7. Therefore, animal eating is ultima facie morally wrong.

Premise [1] is an assumption: harming is wrong, not because it violates some right or because it fails to maximize utility, but simply because it is wrong. As "prima facie," however, the wrongness may be overridden in certain cases. I discuss premise [6] in the last section of the paper, and there I argue that the wrongness of the harm which eating animals causes them is not overridden, that it is "all things considered" or ultima facie wrong.

The term "extensive" in premise [4] indicates that the target of NEW is the industrialized practice of killing billions of animals as food for hundreds of millions of people, what has been referred to as "factory farming." NEW allows small-scale subsistence hunting, and eating animals who died due to accidents, natural causes, or other sources which do not involve the deliberate actions of moral agents.

The term "animal" used here and throughout this paper refers to any vertebrate species. For reasons I will make clear, NEW is more tentative with regard to invertebrate species. NEW is concerned with the harm caused by the killing and eating of animals, so it does not prohibit uses of animals which do not directly result in their deaths, in particular, those characteristic of the egg and dairy industries. Thus, the argument claims that "ovolacto vegetarianism" is morally required.

I now proceed to defend the remainder of NEW: how killing animals causes them harm (premise [2]); why the prima facie wrongness of killing animals (conclusion [3]) means that eating animals is also prima facie wrong (conclusion [5]); and why the wrongness is not overridden (premise [6]).

Killing and Harm

The claim that killing animals causes them harm might seem too obvious to warrant much discussion. However, its importance here is to distance NEW more clearly from other defenses of vegetarianism. As we will see, killing is harmful—and therefore morally wrong—whether or not any rights are violated, and whether or not any pain or suffering occurs or some other conception of utility fails to be maximized.

Joel Feinberg's analysis of harm is especially useful here. To harm a being is to do something which adversely affects that individual's *interests*. According to Feinberg, harming amounts to "the thwarting, setting back or defeating of an interest."[12] Interests are not univocal. Some interests are more important than others depending on their function in maintaining the basic well-being or welfare of the individual concerned. The most critical and essential interests that anyone can have are what Feinberg calls "welfare interests":

> In this category are the interests in the continuance for a foreseeable interval of one's life, the interests in one's own physical health and vigor, the integrity and normal functioning of one's body; the absence of absorbing pain and suffering . . . emotional stability, the absence of groundless anxieties and resentments, the capacity to engage normally in social intercourse . . . a tolerable social and physical environment, and a certain amount of freedom from interference and coercion.[13]

Welfare interests are "the very most important interests . . . cry[ing] out for protection" not only because they are definitive of basic well-being, but also because their realization is necessary before one can satisfy virtually any other interest or do much of anything with one's life. We cannot achieve our (ulterior) interests in a career or personal relationships or material goods if we are unhealthy, in chronic pain, emotionally unstable, living in an intolerable social and physical environment, and are constantly interfered with and coerced by others. Feinberg concludes that when welfare interests are defeated, a very serious harm indeed has been done to the possessor of those interests.[14]

What does it take to have an interest? Feinberg points out that there is a close connection between interests and desires: if A does in fact have an interest in x, we would typically not deny that A wants x.[15] However, we do speak of x *being in* A's interest, whether A wants x or not; this seems to be especially so when we are considering the welfare interests described above. We believe that normally an individual's life, physical and mental health, and personal freedom are in his or her interest even if these things are not wanted by that individual. This suggests to Feinberg that interests of this kind obtain independently of and are not derived from desires.[16]

We have here all that is needed to defend the claim that killing an animal causes it harm and is therefore (by the moral principle assumed in premise [1]) morally wrong. Moreover, killing is perhaps the most serious sort of harm that can be inflicted upon an animal by a moral agent; this is so not only because of the defeat of an animal's welfare interests—in life, health, and bodily integrity—but also because these are likely the only kind of interests animals have. One understanding of such interests appeals to the desire the animal has to live in a healthy, normal state of well-being. On Feinberg's analysis, another understanding of these interests makes no appeal to any such desire. This implies that killing defeats welfare interests independently of whether or not animals have a desire for life and well-being. They have an interest in this which is defeated when agents cause their deaths.

Some might object here that this is much too fast. Although it is true that x can be in A's interest even when A does not desire x, still x cannot be in A's interest if A has no desires whatever. Otherwise, we would be allowing that plants have interests, and that, some might think, is clearly absurd. Therefore, in order for this analysis of harm to be applicable to animals, it must be shown that they have some desires, preferably desires for that which agents are defeating.

Desire

Let us agree that the morally relevant sense of interest we want here is one constituted by certain desires. So why would anyone think that animals do not have desires? We attribute desires to animals routinely on much the same basis that we attribute desires to other people: as an explanation of their behavior. To say that some animal A wants x, uttered because A is doing something, is an extremely common locution for those who are in contact with animals everyday and seems to cause no problem for those who rarely ever encounter an animal. This creates a strong presumption in favor of animal desire. . . .

Recapitulation and Elaboration

At this point in the defense of NEW, we have firmly established the following:

1. Causing harm is prima facie morally wrong.
2. Killing animals causes them harm.
3. Therefore, killing animals is prima facie morally wrong.

We have seen why killing animals harms them, and we have successfully countered challenges to the analysis of animal harms. We understand why this is one of the worst harms an animal can undergo, which indicates that this is a very serious (though prima facie) wrong when perpetrated by a moral agent. We can also now see the advantages of NEW over the old arguments for vegetarianism. NEW is not contingent upon any current or possible methods of raising animals for humans to eat: no matter how it is done, supplying food for millions of animal-eaters means the defeat of animal welfare interests. NEW does not employ any theoretical contructs which are unsettled and divisive: the analysis of harm in terms of interests and desires which are exhibited by certain behaviors is widely accepted and intuitively appealing. NEW does not introduce any indeterminacy or unwieldy ratiocination into the discussion: the desires and interests of animals, and the wrongness of defeating them, are plainly evident for all those who would simply look and see.

We can also now understand two further aspects of the vegetarianism required by NEW. Killing any creature with certain desires defeats its welfare interests, and is therefore harmful, but not all living things have such desires and interests. The judgment that some being has the requisite mental states must be formed on the basis of behavior and physiological evidence. Since invertebrates and plants either do not exhibit the appropriate behavior or they do not possess the appropriate physiological equipment (or both), consuming them is permitted. Although I do not hold that "interest-less" forms of life have no moral status whatever, I cannot here develop the notion of degrees of moral value or consider what else besides interests would qualify an entity for a moral status. It will have to suffice to say that beings with certain mental states are of greater moral worth than those without them, from the moral point of view it is better (*ceteris paribus*) to kill and eat a plant than an animal. Moreover, much vegetable matter can be eaten without killing anything: most vegetarian fare consists of the fruits and flowers of plants which are not killed or are harvested at the end of annual life cycles.

The Moral Wrongness of Eating Animals

The next step is to link the wrongness of *killing* animals with the wrongness of *eating* them:

3. Therefore, killing animals is prima facie morally wrong.
4. Animal eating requires the killing of animals.
5. Therefore, animal-eating is prima facie morally wrong.

Many might regard this step as especially problematic. All that has been shown so far is that moral agents who kill animals are engaged in actions which are prima facie wrong; how can it follow from this that different actions, done by different agents, are also prima facie wrong? After all, very few of those who consume animal flesh have personally killed the animals they eat. Those who actually do the killing—slaughterhouse workers—act impermissibly, while those who merely eat the body parts of dead animals supplied by those workers do not. How could the wrongness of one set of agents and actions *transfer* to an entirely different set?

One response would point out that purchasing and consuming the products of "factory farming" contributes to a morally abhorrent practice and thus perpetuates future wrongdoing. So although it is the killing which constitutes what is wrong with the practice of animal-eating, and conceding that very few animal-eaters actually kill what they eat, this contribution to and perpetuation of the killing should prompt us to act *as if* eating the animals is itself wrong. . . .

[But] we must not make this concession. Animal-eating is itself wrong, but this is not due to any "transference" of wrongness from the act of killing to the act of purchasing and eating animal flesh. The purchasing and consuming are two parts of the same wrong.

To see this, consider this modification of the objection which concerns us now:

> This is a lovely lamp. You say its base is made from the bones and its shade from the skin of Jews killed in concentration camps? Well, so what? I didn't kill them. Of course what the Nazis did was wrong, a very great moral evil. But my not buying the lamp is obviously not going to bring any of them back. Nor will it prevent any future harm: this sort of thing doesn't even occur any more, so there is no future wrongdoing to prevent even if my refusal to buy were effective in this way, which of course it wouldn't be. So what's wrong with buying and using the lamp?

. . . We do not need to find some way to understand this activity which will allow it to be construed "as if" it were wrong (but really isn't). Animal-eating is wrong for much the same reason that purchasing and using the products of a concentration camp or those of slave labor generally is wrong; it is wrong for the same reason that buying stolen property or accepting any of the ill-gotten gains of another is wrong: a person who eats animals, or buys and uses lamps from Auschwitz or cotton clothing from the antebellum South, or a hot stereo from a hoodlum is profiting from, benefiting from a morally nefarious practice. Doing so, and especially doing so when morally innocuous alternatives are readily available, not only indicates support for and the endorsement of moral evil, it is also to participate in that evil. It is an act of complicity, partaking in condemnable exploitation, reaping personal advantages at a significant cost to others. This is so whether or not an individual's abstinence from the practice has any effect whatsoever on its perpetuation. It strikes me as quite uncontroversial to say that one who concurs and cooperates with wrongdoing, who garners benefits through the defeat of the basic welfare interests of others, is himself doing something which is seriously morally wrong.

Overriding the Moral Wrongness of Eating Animals

The final step in the defense of NEW is to support premise [6]: the prima facie wrongness of animal-eating is not defeated by additional factors which serve as overriding reasons; from this it will follow that animal-eating is ultima facie morally wrong (the conclusion [7]). There are at least four grounds for overriding this wrong: [1] traditional-cultural; [2] esthetic; [3] convenience; [4] nutrition. Do any of these supply an overriding reason which would morally justify the very serious harm that killing animals for food causes them?

[1] People eat animals because they have been raised on that diet, as have their parents and grandparents and on back through the generations. Animal-eating is a social practice which is deeply embedded into modern culture. Slavery, the oppression of women, and institutionalized racism also once had this status; however, few if any suppose that this status is what makes practices morally right or wrong. Slavery, for example, is wrong because it requires the persistent exploitation, coercion, and degradation of innocent people, not because it happens to be extinct in our society. The fact that a practice has the

weight of tradition on its side and a prominent place in a given culture does not in itself carry any moral weight.[17]

[2] Animal flesh is regarded by most people as esthetically pleasing. Animal body parts are prepared for consumption in hundreds of different ways, employing many cooking techniques, spices, and accompaniments. Yet the esthetic attractions of other practices are regarded as irrelevant to their moral appraisal. Heliogabalus had masses of people gathered in fields, only to be mercilessly slaughtered solely for the pleasing effect he found in the sight of red blood on green grass.[18] Or consider "snuff films," whose "plot" is centered around the filming of an actual murder of a person apparently chosen at random. Who would not condemn such cinema in the strongest possible terms, even if it were directed by Orson Wells or Martin Scorcese and starred Dustin Hoffman or Meryl Streep? Yet one has only to enter the nearest slaughterhouse with a video camera on any given day of the week to produce a movie every bit as horrific as the most polished "snuff film."

[3] The convenience of animal-eating is largely a function of the other two factors. The pervasiveness of the desire to eat animals and its prominence within a variety of social functions naturally provokes free market economies to supply meat relatively cheaply and easily. Again, this seems to say nothing about whether or not animal-eating is morally permissible. It is often quite inconvenient and very difficult to keep a promise or discharge a parental duty or make a sacrifice for a stranger—or a friend; it is often quite convenient and very easy to conceal the truth or pocket merchandise without paying or take advantage of powerless persons. Few of us believe that convenience and ease have much of anything to do with whether these actions are morally right or wrong. Why should it be any different when it comes to killing animals for food?

It might be said that the difference is that human interests in convenience, in tradition, and esthetic pleasure override animal interests in life and well-being. This is because the defeat of an *animal* welfare interest, though morally wrong, is not a serious moral wrong. But what is it about humans which gives these nonbasic interests a moral priority over the most basic and important interests an animal can have? And what is it about animals which prevents a severe harm to them from being a serious moral problem? Certainly the nonbasic interests of some humans do not have a moral priority over the welfare interests of other humans, and there is no question that the gravity of a wrong increases with the severity of harm caused to humans. So in order to sustain the objection, some feature, unique to our species, must be identified which accounts for the disparity between human and animal harms and wrongs. Two such distinguishing features, already encountered, immediately present themselves as possibilities: rationality and language. However, appeal to one or both of these capacities raises two immediate problems. First, neither feature is uniquely absent in animal species. No one would seriously contend that a taste for human baby flesh morally overrides anything, nor would anyone claim that the defeat of a child's welfare interest was not a serious moral wrong. Second, why does the proposed feature make such an enormous moral difference? The suggestion is that rationality or language justifies a gap in treatment so vast that it means utmost respect and consideration for humans but allows killing animals out of habit and pleasure. This seems very implausible. The lack of the requisite capacities might reasonably justify *some* difference in treatment, but not a difference which requires a dignified life for those who are favored and permits an ignominious death for those who are not.

[4] Nutrition. Most recent debate about vegetarianism has focused on the question of the adequacy of a meatless diet for human nutrition. This could provide the best reason for overriding the wrongness of killing animals. Let us assume as a fundamental principle that no moral agent can be required to destroy his or her own health and basic welfare for the sake of others; therefore, a diet having this consequence is not morally justified. Does vegetarianism seriously endanger an individual's heath and well-being?

Kathryn Paxton George has argued that a vegetarian diet would make large numbers of humans worse off than they would otherwise be if they ate animals. She lists seven groups of people for whom such abstinence posses a significant risk to personal health.[19] Evelyn Pluhar has disputed many of George's findings, especially those regarding the benefits of iron and the threat of osteoporosis. Supported by numerous nutrition studies, she argues that vitamin and mineral supplementation, as well as the utilization of appropriate plant sources, will alleviate any deficiencies; furthermore, Pluhar contends that the correlation between consuming animal products and meeting certain health requirements is a dubious one.[20] George responded that Pluhar had either misinterpreted or willfully ignored certain facts of the studies she had herself cited.[21] The exchange continues; a journal has devoted an entire issue to their disagreement.[22]

Fortunately, we need not enter this particular debate; George's target is what she calls "strict vegetarianism," the vegan diet totally devoid of any animal product. Both George and Pluhar admit that eggs and dairy products, which are allowed by NEW, would fulfill all or most of the required protein, vitamin, and mineral intake. I am not aware of any humans who, as a matter of basic welfare, must consume animal flesh in addition to eggs and dairy products, but if there are any such people, NEW would allow them to eat animals: we are under no moral requirement to significantly harm ourselves so that others, human or nonhuman, may benefit. . . .

I conclude that none of [1]–[4] serve as a sufficiently compelling reason to override the wrongness of harming the animals eaten. If there are any individuals who must eat animal flesh (rather than just eggs and dairy products) in order to avoid a pronounced deterioration of their health, they are not prohibited from doing so by NEW. This possible case notwithstanding, the eating of animal flesh is ultima facie morally wrong.

Notes

1. There is another defense of vegetarianism based on the value of ecosystems, for example Peter Wenz' "An Ecological Argument for Vegetarianism," *Ethics and Animals* 5 (1984): 2–9. This approach is rare even though the ecologically destructive effects of raising cattle and sheep have been frequently noted in the scientific literature and are not uncommon in philosophical discussions of the environment. Such ecological arguments (as Wenz acknowledges, p. 2)

depend on accepting that an ecosystem itself has a moral status. Here I assume the view is mistaken, so we need not consider the argument. The best cases for the moral value of ecosystems can be found in J. Baird Callicott, *In Defense of the Land Ethic,* State University of New York Press, 1989, and Holmes Rolston, *Environmental Ethics,* Temple University Press, 1989. However, both Callicott and Rolston reject vegetarianism.

2. In many works, but most notably *Animal Liberation,* Avon, 1st ed., 1975, 2nd ed., 1990; and *Practical Ethics,* Cambridge, 1st ed., 1979, 2nd ed., 1993.

3. For example, *Animal Liberation,* chap. 3. See also *Animal Factories,* Harmony Books, rev. ed., 1990, coauthored with Jim Mason.

4. *Rights, Killing, and Suffering,* Basil Blackwell, 1983.

5. Frey: 197–202.

6. "Utilitarianism and Vegetarianism," *International Journal of Applied Philosophy* 4 (1988): 41–49.

7. Crisp: 44. However, utility is not maximized by eating the products of factory farming. Crisp argues, against Frey, that utilitarian considerations do not permit us to eat "intensively-reared" animals. But Frey asserts that "millions upon millions" of animals are not intensively-reared anyway (pp. 33–34).

8. Principally in a series of papers beginning with "The Moral Basis of Vegetarianism," *Canadian Journal of Philosophy* 5 (1975): 181–214, and culminating in *The Case for Animal Rights,* University of California Press, 1983.

9. For example: Joel Feinberg, "The Rights of Animals and Unborn Generations" *Philosophy & Environmental Crisis,* William T. Blackstone, ed., University of Georgia, 1974: 43–68, and "Human Duties and Animal Rights," *On the Fifth Day,* R. Morris and M. Fox, eds., Acropolis Books, 1978: 45–69; James Rachels, "Do Animals Have a Right to Liberty?" *Animal Rights and Human Obligations,* T. Regan and P. Singer, eds., Prentice Hall, 1976: 205–223; Stephen R.L. Clark, "The Rights of Wild Things," *Inquiry* 22 (1979): 171–78; Robert Elliot, "Moral Autonomy, Self-Determination and Animal Rights," *The Monist* 70 (1987): 83–97; Bernard Rollin, *Animal Rights and Human Morality,* Prometheus Books, rev. ed., 1990.

10. For example: H.J. McCloskey, "Rights," *Philosophical Quarterly* 15 (1965): 113–27; "Moral Rights and Animals," *Inquiry* 22 (1979); 23–54; John Passmore, *Man's Responsibility for Nature,* Scribner's, 1974; Jan Narveson, "Animal Rights," *Canadian Journal of Philosophy* 7 (1977): 161–78; and "Animal Rights Revisited," *Ethics and Animals,* H. Miller and W. Williams, eds., Humana Press, 1983; Richard A. Watson, "Self-Consciousness and the Rights of Nonhuman Animals," *Environmental Ethics* 1 (1979): 99–129; Philip Montague, "Two Concepts of Rights," *Philosophy and Public Affairs* 9 (1980): 372–84; L.W. Sumner, *The Moral Foundations of Rights,* Oxford, 1987; Tibor Machan, "Do Animals Have Rights?" *Public Affairs Quarterly* 5 (1991): 163–73.

11. For example: Paul Taylor, "Inherent Value and Moral Rights," and Jan Narveson, "On a Case for Animal Rights," both in *The Monist* 70 (1987): 15–49; David Ost, "The Case Against Animal Rights," *The Southern Journal of Philosophy* 24 (1986): 365–73; Mary Anne Warren, "Difficulties with the Strong Animal Rights Position," *Between the Species* 2 (1987): 163–73; and J. Baird Callicott, "Review of Tom Regan, *The Case For Animal Rights*" repr. in *In Defense of the Land Ethic,* State University of New York Press, 1989: 39–47.

12. *Harm to Others,* Oxford University Press, 1984: 33.

13. Feinberg: 37. Welfare interests are contrasted with "ulterior interests," which presuppose but also require as a necessary condition that certain welfare interests are satisfied. Feinberg lists raising a family, building a dream house, advancing a social cause, and others as examples of ulterior interests.

14. Ibid.

15. Ibid.: 38.

16. Ibid.: 42.

17. A point forcefully made by means of a macabre device in the classic short story by Shirley Jackson, "The Lottery."

18. As reported by R.M. Hare in *Freedom and Reason,* Clarendon Press, 1963: 161.

19. "So Animal a Human . . . , or the Moral Relevance of Being An Omnivore," *Journal of Agricultural Ethics* 3 (1990): 172–86. Her list (pp. 175–78) includes children, pregnant and lactating women, the elderly, the poor, and the "undereducated."

20. "Who Can be Morally Obligated to be a Vegetarian?" *Journal of Agricultural and Environmental Ethics* 5 (1992): 189–215.

21. "The Use and Abuse of Scientific Studies," *Journal of Agricultural and Environmental Ethics* 5 (1992): 217–33.

22. *Journal of Agricultural and Environmental Ethics* 7 (1994).

Higher Animals: Duties to Sentient Life

Domestic and Hunted Animals

Domestic Food Animals

Animal agriculture is tangential to an environmental ethic, yet there is a carry-over connecting the one to the other. Domestic animals are breeds, no longer natural kinds. They are "living artifacts,"[1] kept in culture for so long that it is often not known precisely what their natural progenitors were. They fit no environmental niche; the breeding of them for traits that humans desire has removed them from the forces of natural selection. Without human interest in these animals they would soon cease to exist. Most domestic breeds would go extinct; a few might revert to feral conditions; fewer still might resettle homeostatically into environmental niches. Most feral forms, unchecked by predators, competitors, and diseases, are misfits that cause heavy environmental degradation.

But domestic animals cannot enter the culture that maintains them. By all behavioral evidence, sheep, cows, and pigs are oblivious to the economy for which they are reared, much less to the cultural context of the persons who care for them. They cannot live in the world ethically, cognitively, and critically in those superior human ways. Pet dogs may join the life of the family, enthusiastically eating hot dogs at a picnic; nevertheless, pets are not in culture. Although food animals are taken out of nature and transformed by culture, they remain uncultured in their sentient life, cultural objects that cannot become cultural subjects. They live neither in nature nor in culture but in the peripheral rural world. Meanwhile, they can suffer.

This *is* the case, descriptive of their condition. What *ought* to be? . . . [W]e recognize the wild condition from which such animals were once taken and recognize also that they can neither return to the wild nor enter cultural subjectivity. Although tamed, they can have horizons, interests, goods no higher than those of wild subjectivity, natural sentience. They ought to be treated, by the homologous, baseline principle, with no more suffering than might have been their lot in the wild, on average, adjusting for their modified capacities to care for themselves. In taking an interest in them, humans have assumed a responsibility for them. (Whether modern industrial farming introduces suffering in excess of ecological norms will have to be investigated elsewhere.)

From ENVIRONMENTAL ETHICS: DUTIES TO AND VALUES IN THE NATURAL WORLD, 1999, pp. 78–84, 358, 373. Copyright © 1988 by Temple University Press. Reprinted by permission.

By a weaker (but significant) hedonist principle, domestic animals ought to be spared pointless suffering, but they have no claim to be spared innocent suffering. The killing and the eating of animals, when they occur in culture, are still events in nature; they are ecological events, no matter how superimposed by culture. Humans are claiming no superiority or privilege exotic to nature. Analogous to predation, human consumption of animals is to be judged by the principles of environmental ethics, not those of interhuman ethics. We step back from culture into agriculture, toward the wild, and fit the ecological pattern. What *is* in nature may not always imply *ought* (and it may seldom do so in inter-human ethics), but *ought* in environmental ethics seldom negates what *is* in wild nature. Humans eat meat, and meat-eating is a natural component of ecosystems, one to which we do not object in nature nor try to eliminate from our cultural interactions with nature.

A troop of half a dozen chimpanzees, our nearest relatives, will kill and eat about a hundred medium-sized animals a year. Hunter-gatherer cultures are the earliest known, and when agricultural cultures replace them, humans have no duty to cease to be omnivores and become herbivores. They might elect to become vegetarians, perhaps on grounds of more efficient food production or better nutrition, but they have no duty to sentient life to do so.

A characteristic argument for vegetarianism runs as follows:

1. Pain is a bad thing, whether in humans or in animals.
2. Humans (at least most of them) can live nutritiously without causing animal pain.
3. It is immoral for humans to kill and eat humans, causing them pain.
4. Food animals suffer pain, similarly to the way humans do, if killed and eaten.
5. There are no morally relevant differences between humans and food animals.
6. It is immoral for humans to kill and eat animals, causing them pain.

Appealing to sentiment and logically attractive in its charitable egalitarianism, such argument fails to distinguish between nature and culture, between environmental ethics and interhuman ethics. We simply see ourselves in fur. But there are morally relevant differences that distinguish persons in culture from food animals in agriculture, where quasi-ecosystemic processes remain. Whether or not there are differences in pain thresholds between sheep and humans, the value destruction when a sheep is eaten is far less, especially since the sheep have been bred for this purpose and would not otherwise exist. Because animals cannot enter culture, they do not suffer the *affliction* (a heightened, cognitively based pain, distinct from physical pain) that humans would if bred to be eaten.

Chickens can live in ignorant bliss of their forthcoming slaughter (until the moment of execution); persons in such a position could not, because they are in the world culturally and critically. Even if such a fate could be kept secret from persons, the value destruction in their killing would still be greater. The fact that there are twilight zones (humans who are pre-persons or failed persons) does not challenge the existence of morally relevant class differences. In recognizing the human superiority, nothing should be subtracted from the natural condition of animals. But we have no strong duty to deny their original ecology, and only a weaker duty to make their lot better by avoiding pointless pain.

It is not "unfair" or "unjust" to eat a pig. Even an alligator that eats humans is not being unfair or unjust (although humans will be reprehensible if they do not try to prevent it). Humans in their eating habits follow nature; they can and ought to do so. But humans do not eat other humans because such events interrupt culture; they destroy those superior ways in which humans live in the world. The eating of other humans, even if this were shown to be an event in nature, would be overridden by its cultural destructiveness. Cannibalism destroys interpersonal relations. But in nature no such relations obtain, or can obtain. (Human cannibalism has been rare and virtually always a cultural event with religious overtones, not a natural event.)

It may be objected that the differences in rules for those with superior gifts means here that the only moral animals should refuse to participate in the meat-eating phase of their ecology, just as they refuse to play the game merely by the rules of natural selection. Humans do not look to the behavior of wild animals as an ethical guide in other matters (marriage, truth-telling, promise keeping, justice, charity). Why should they justify their dietary habits by watching what animals do? But these other matters are affairs of culture. Marriage, truth-telling, promise-keeping, justice, charity—these are not events at all in spontaneous nature. They are person-to-person events. By contrast, eating is omnipresent in spontaneous nature; humans eat because they are in nature, not because they are in culture. Eating animals is not an event between persons but a human-to-animal event, and the rules for it come from the ecosystems in which humans evolved and which they have no duty to remake. Humans, then, can model their dietary habits on their ecosystems, but they cannot and should not model their interpersonal justice or charity on ecosystems.

It may seem that while animals are not to be treated like persons in all respects, both they and persons have about equally the capacity to feel pain, and so both ought to be treated equally in this relevant respect involving the pain-pleasure scale. But this is not the only relevant scale, because it does not catch the full scale of value destructions at stake. The eating of persons would destroy cultural values, which the eating of animals does not. The eating of animals, though it does destroy values, reallocates such values when humans gain nutrition and pleasure at the sacrifice of animal lives in a manner wholly consistent with the operation of the natural ecosystem in which such animals were once emplaced and are still quasi-placed in their agricultural stations. Different rules do apply to persons, to persons in exchange with persons, and even to persons in exchange with nature. These rules do require that animals lives count morally, but they do not require humans to deny their ecology and replace it with a charity or justice appropriate to culture.

Sentience in nature and sentience in culture are not really the same thing, despite their common physiology and origin. Sentience in nature belongs with food chains and natural selection; sentience in culture has been transformed into another gestalt, that of self-reflective personality and moral agency. Eating an animal implies no disrespect for animal life . . . ; to the contrary, it respects that ecology. Eating a person would disrupt personal life as set in a cultural pattern; it would reduce personal life to the level of animal life in an ecology. It insults persons to treat them as food objects by the criteria of animal ecology; persons may and must treat nonhuman lives as food objects, but it respects animals to treat them so.

Pain is a bad thing in humans or in animals. But this fools us until we distinguish between intrinsic and instrumental pain. Instrumental pain has contributory reference to further goods; intrinsic pain has no such reference. Intrinsic pain is a bad thing, absolutely; but only instrumental pain is characteristic of nature, where intrinsic pain is a nonfunctional anomaly. Pain is routinely instrumental in ecological defenses, captures, and transfers of goods, and the pains imposed in agriculture are homologous. They are not intrinsic pains; they must be judged in their instrumentality and with no presumption against innocent suffering.

Enjoying pleasure and escaping pain are of value, and evolutionary ecosystems are full of devices for accomplishing both. But much pain remains, and much thwarted pleasure. In nature, the pain-pleasure axis is not the only spectrum of value; indeed, it is not the highest value in either human or nonhuman life. It might be said, for instance, that knowing the meaning of life is more important for humans than leading a painless life, that a life with courage and sacrificial charity in it, which requires the presence of some pain, is a richer life than one without it. Similarly, the evolution of a world with carnivorous mammals, primates, humans, and culture is a richer world than one without them, and the presence of pain seems to have been necessary for such evolution. In that sense, advanced values are frequently built on suffering.

Perhaps it is not merely the pain but the indignity of domestication that is deplorable. A gazelle is pure wild grace, but a cow is a meat factory, pure and simple; a cow might even suffer less than a gazelle but be greatly disgraced. Cows cannot know they are disgraced, of course, and the capture of values in nature is not undignified. A lioness destroys a gazelle, and there is nothing unworthy here. Likewise, in domestication, humans parallel ecosystems and capture agriculturally the values in a cow. There is nothing undignified in this event, even though the once-natural values in the cow, like those in the gazelle, have to be destroyed by the predator.

Although we have defended eating animals as a primary, natural event, we have also said, secondarily, that there is an obligation to avoid pointless pain. Consider, for instance, the following case. There are more than 2,000,000 Muslims in Britain; the Jewish community numbers nearly 400,000. Muslims still practice animal sacrifice; a sheep or goat is sacrificed during a feast concluding a month of fasting, and often at the birth of a child. The animal is sacrificed to Allah, and the meat is eaten and enjoyed. Though Jews no longer practice animal sacrifice as they did in former times, they require their meat to be kosher, slaughtered according to religious ritual. Modern secular abattoirs stun animals with a massive blow or an electric shock before butchering them, and this is thought to be more humane. But it makes the animal unacceptable to Jews and Muslims, who must sever the major blood vessels of an unblemished animal. About 1,500,000 sheep and goats and 100,000 cattle are slaughtered by Jews and Muslims each year.

Animal rights activists have pressed to require stunning, and a government report finds that religious methods of slaughter result in a degree of suffering and distress that does not occur in a properly stunned animal. Muslims and Jews have joined forces to defend their practices.[2] But the additional pain that their methods impose, no longer necessary, cannot be interpreted in the context of ecology; it is pain inflicted for culture-based reasons. Unblemished animals make better sacrifices to God; they enhance religious cleanliness. This pain is ecologically pointless; it has point only culturally and, by the account given here, is not justified. This pain is not homologous; it is superfluous. Perhaps both Jews and Muslims can reach reformed religious convictions, in which respect for animal life overrides their previous concepts of cleanliness, or where the mercy of God prohibits pointless suffering.

Notes

1. J. Baird Callicott, "Animal Liberation: A Triangular Affair," *Environmental Ethics* 2, 1980, p. 330.

2. Karen DeYoung, "Ritual Slaughter Sparks Debate," *Washington Post*, 27 December 1985, pp. A19–20.

POSTSCRIPT

Does Morality Require Vegetarianism?

Traditionally, there has been no question with regard to the moral question of eating meat. There is no law against it; it is widely practiced; and it is supported by the biblical idea that God gave people animals to eat. So it is to some extent a great change in the moral climate that this question is even being raised at all.

It is partly due to the views of environmental thinkers such as Rolston that people have begun to think seriously about the place of human beings within the larger biological environment. This naturally leads to questions about animals and human beings and their relationship.

Of course, there is another biblical injunction to the effect that people should exercise stewardship over God's creation. It is, however, not clear how this is to fit in with the other biblical idea (above)—with the secular view that Curnutt and Rolston take here.

From a religious perspective, we might remember that there are millions of people who base vegetarianism on religion. And from a purely cultural perspective, we know that, as widely accepted as meat eating is in our own culture, some cultures practice vegetarianism. Part of the difficulty here stems from our dual role in nature. On the one hand, we use reason to stand apart from nature; on the other hand, reason tells us that we are part of nature. But even if we think of ourselves as part of nature, this does not solve our problem. For now, we have to think again (as we did in the introduction to this issue) and use reason to decide whether we should be like the lions, who hunt and kill animals to eat, or whether such killing and eating—even if culturally traditional for us—should be left behind.

A classic work in this field is Peter Singer, *Animal Liberation* (New York Review of Books, 1990). Bernard E. Rollin, in *Farm Animal Welfare: Social, Bio-ethical, and Research Issues* (Iowa State University Press, 1995), and Howard F. Lyman, in *Mad Cowboy: Plain Truth From the Cattle Rancher Who Won't Eat Meat* (Scribner, 1998), address the conditions under which animals are raised for food, and Lyman in particular is critical of the negative impact that this has on human beings. Carol J. Adams, in *The Sexual Politics of Meat: A Feminist-Vegetarian Critical Theory,* 10th anniversary ed. (Continuum Pub Group, 1999), argues that meat eating is connected with male dominance. Also relevant are Craig B. Stanford et al., eds., *Meat-Eating and Human Evolution* (Oxford University Press, 2001); Eric Schlosser, Fast Food Nation: *The Dark Side of the All-American Meal* (Harper-Collins, 2002); Matthew Scully, *Dominion: The Power of Man, the Suffering of Animals, and the Call to Mercy* (St. Martin's Press, 2002); and Charles Patterson, *Eternal Treblinka: Our Treatment of Animals and the Holocaust* (Lantern Books, 2002).

Contributors to This Volume

EDITOR

STEPHEN SATRIS was born in New York City. He received a B.A. in philosophy from the University of California, Los Angeles, an M.A. in philosophy from the University of Hawaii at Manoa, and a Ph.D. in philosophy from Cambridge University, England. He has written on moral and philosophical issues for professional journals, and he is the author of *Ethical Emotivism* (Martinus Nijhoff, 1987). He has taught at several American universities, and he currently teaches philosophy at Clemson University in Clemson, South Carolina. Professor Satris is a former president of the South Carolina Society for Philosophy and is currently C. Calhoun Lemon Fellow in Clemson University's Rutland Center for Ethics.

STAFF

Larry Loeppke	Managing Editor
Jill Peter	Senior Developmental Editor
Susan Brusch	Senior Developmental Editor
Beth Kundert	Production Manager
Jane Mohr	Project Manager
Tara McDermott	Design Coordinator
Nancy Meissner	Editorial Assistant
Lori Church	Pemissions Coordinator
Julie J. Keck	Senior Marketing Manager
Mary S. Klein	Marketing Communications Specialist
Alice M. Link	Marketing Coordinator
Tracie A. Kammerude	Senior Marketing Assistant

AUTHORS

GEORGE J. ANNAS is the Edward R. Utley Professor of Law and Medicine at Boston University's Schools of Medicine and Public Health in Boston, Massachusetts. He is also director of Boston University's Law, Medicine, and Ethics Program and chair of the department of health law. His publications include *Some Choice: Law, Medicine, and the Market* (Oxford University Press, 1998). He is the author of the third edition of *The Rights of Patients* (Southern Illinois University Press, 2004).

JOHN ARTHUR is a philosopher at the State University of New York at Bingamton. He has published works on social, political, and legal philosophy.

MIRKO BAGARIC is a professor of law at Deakin University's School of Law in Australia. He has published on a wide variety of social issues. His latest book is *How to Live: Being Happy and Dealing with Moral Dilemmas* (University Press of America, 2006).

DAVID BOAZ is executive vice president of the Cato Institute. An expert on such issues as the failure of big government, the politics of the baby-boom generation, drug prohibition, and educational choice, he writes widely on these subjects and others for such publications as *The New York Times, The Washington Post,* and *The Wall Street Journal.* He is the author of *The Libertarian Reader: Classic and Contemporary Writings From Lao-Tzu to Milton Friedman* (Simon & Schuster Trade, 1998). His latest publication is *Toward Liberty* (Cato Institute, 2002).

HILARY BOK teaches philosophy at the Johns Hopkins University in Baltimore, where she is Luce Professor in Bioethics and Moral and Political Theory. Her publications and research interests are in ethics, bioethics, free will, and the philosophy of Kant.

JAMES F. CHILDRESS is the John Allen Hollingsworth Professor of Ethics and Professor of Medical Education at the University of Virginia. Professor Childress is the recipient of several prestigious academic awards, is the author (or co-author) of scores of books and articles, and has served on numerous advisory bodies, including the presidentially appointed National Bioethics Advisory Commission. With Tom L. Beachamp, he is co-author of *Principles of Biomedical Ethics,* 5th ed. (University of Oxford Press, 2001), a classic work in its field.

ROBERT J. CIHAK is board member and senior fellow in the Discovery Institute of Seattle, Washington. He is a physician and past president of the Association of American Physicians and Surgeons.

JULIE CLARKE teaches law at Deakin University's School of Law in Australia.

PETER COLLINS is director of the Centre for the Study of Gambling, Salford University, England. A specialist on the subject of gambling, Collins has advised numerous government bodies in the United Kingdom and other countries.

JORDAN CURNUTT is professor of philosophy at St. Cloud State University in Minnesota. His research interests are in ethics and the environment.

NICHOLAS DIXON is Dykstra Professor and chair of the Philosophy Department at Alma College in Alma, Michigan. He has published extensively in ethics, social philosophy, and the philosophy of sport.

RICHARD DOERFLINGER is deputy director of the secretariat for Pro-Life Activities at the U.S. Conference of Catholic Bishops in Washington, D.C. He is also Adjunct Fellow in Bioethics and Public Policy at the National Catholic Bioethics Center in Boston. Speaking on behalf of the Catholic Bishops, he has prepared policy statements and given congressional testimony on abortion, euthanasia, human embryo research, and other bioethical issues.

THE DRUG ENFORCEMENT ADMINISTRATION's mission is to enforce the controlled substance laws and regulations of the United States and bring to the criminal and civil justice system of the United States, or any other competent jurisdiction, those organizations and principal members of organizations, involved in the growing, manufacture, or distribution of controlled substances appearing in or destined for illicit traffic in the United States; and to recommend and support non-enforcement programs aimed at reducing the availability of illicit controlled substances on the domestic and international markets.

JANE ENGLISH (1947–1978) was a philosopher whose published work was primarily on feminism and social philosophy.

AUTUMN FIESTER is a senior fellow at the Center for Bioethics at the University of Pennsylvania. She teaches and conducts research in moral philosophy, animals and bioethical issues, and clinical professionalism.

MICHAEL A. GLUECK is a physician and writer. He is the author of numerous articles on health care, mental health reform, and many health-related topics.

ALAN H. GOLDMAN is now Kenan Professor of Philosophy at the College of William and Mary. (Previously, he taught for 25 years at the University of Miami in Florida.) He is the author of numerous books and articles on aesthetics, moral knowledge, and the philosophy of law. His most recent book is *Practical Rules: When We Need Them and When We Don't* (Cambridge, 2002).

GILBERT HARMAN is Stuart Professor of Philosophy at Princeton University. He has published extensively in ethics, the epistemology, metaphysics, cognitive science, and the philosophy of language. His most recent book is *Explaining Value and Other Essays in Moral Philosophy* (Clarendon Press, 2000).

TIMOTHY HOWELL is associate professor of psychiatry and director of the geropsychiatry program at UW Health—a health and medical network affiliated with the University of Wisconsin. He is active in both teaching and clinical care.

JEEF JORDAN is a professor of philosophy at the University of Delaware. He works in metaphysics and the philosophy of religion.

C. STEPHEN LAYMAN is professor of philosophy at Seattle Pacific University. He has published in logic, metaphysics, and the philosophy of religion. His books include: *The Shape of the Good* (University of Notre Dame Press, 1991),

The Power of Logic, 2d ed. (McGraw-Hill, 2002), and *Letters to a Doubting Thomas: A Case for the Existence of God* (Oxford University Press, 2007).

DESMOND MANDERSON, a professor of law at McGill University in Montreal, holds a Canada Research Chair in Law and Discourse. He works in many areas of legal study, including legal ethics, law and music, law and literature, and international drug policy.

DON MARQUIS is a professor of philosophy at the University of Kansas in Lawrence, Kansas. He has written on issues in medical ethics.

ALBERT G. MOSLEY, philosopher and musician, is currently at Smith College in Massachusetts. He is the editor of *African Philosophy: Selected Readings* (Pearson Education, 1995) and coauthor, with Nicholas Capaldi, of *Affirmative Action* (Rowman & Littlefied, 1996).

LISA NEWTON teaches philosophy at Fairfield University in Connecticut, where she is director of the Applied Ethics program. She has written on a wide variety of ethical, social, and political topics, including business ethics and the environment.

LOUIS P. POJMAN (1935–2005) was a prolific American philosopher who published (as editor or author) over 30 books and wrote more than 100 articles. His writing extends widely and embraces many areas of philosophy, but Pojman is best remembered as a writer on ethical, social, and political issues. He was particularly concerned to make ideas clear to non-philosophers.

DANIEL D. POLSBY is dean for academic affairs and professor of law at George Mason University's School of Law. Polsby was on the faculty of Northwestern Law School for over 20 years, and for over 10 of those years he was the Kirkland & Ellis Professor of Law. In addition, he has held visiting appointments at the University of Southern California, the University of Michigan, and Cornell University. He has published widely in many areas of law, including voting rights, family law, employment rights, and gun control.

VINCENT C. PUNZO is Professor Emeritus at Saint Louis University in St. Louis, Missouri. His specialties are ethics and political philosophy.

AYN RAND (1905–1982) was born in Russia and emigrated to the United States in 1926. She wrote for a general audience, producing novels (such as the *Fountainhead* and *Atlas Shrugged*) as well as non-fiction (such as *The Virtue of Selfishness* and *Capitalism: The Unknown Ideal*). Rand founded Objectivism, a new philosophical movement that is still strong today.

JONATHAN RAUCH has a regular column in *National Journal* and is a writer in residence at the Brookings Institution in Washington and a correspondent for the *Atlantic Monthly*. Much of his work can also be found on-line at http://www.indegayforum.org/authors/show/116.html.

JOHN A. ROBERTSON holds the Vinson and Elkins Chair at the University of Texas School of Law at Austin. He has written and lectured widely on law and bioethical issues. He is the author of *The Rights of the Critically Ill* (Ballinger, 1983) and *Children of Choice: Freedom and the New Reproductive Technologies* (Princeton University Press, 1994). He is also the author of numerous articles on reproductive rights, genetics, organ transplantation, and human experimentation. Robertson has served on or has been a consultant to many national bioethics advisory bodies and is currently chair of the Ethics Committee of the American Society for Reproductive Medicine.

HOLMES ROLSTON III is an internationally known philosopher of the environment. He is University Distinguished Professor at Colorado State University in Fort Collins, Colorado. He has written extensively and lectured widely on the environment, science, and religion. His works have been translated into many languages.

ERNEST VAN DEN HAAG (1914–2002) was a distinguished lecturer at Columbia University, Yale University, and Harvard University. For many years, he was John M. Olin Professor of Jurisprudence at Fordham University and also a scholar at the Heritage Foundation. van den Haag was both a psychoanalyst and a criminologist. He is coauthor, with John P. Conrad, of *The Death Penalty: A Debate* (Plenum, 1983).

DAVID T. WATTS is a practicing physician, a poet, a radio commentator, and an author. His most recent book is *Bedside Manners: One Doctor's Reflections on the Oddly Intimate Encounters between Patient and Healer* (Three Rivers Press, 2006).

MICHAEL WELCH is a sociologist and professor of criminal justice at Rutgers University. His work focuses on the ideas of punishment and social control. He is the author of *Detained: Immigration Laws and the Expanding I.N.S. Jail Complex* (Temple University Press, 2002). Welch is the author of several books, including, most recently, Scapegoats of September 11th: Hate Crimes and State Crimes in the War on Terror (Rutgers University Press, 2006).

Index

371

TITLES IN THE TAKING SIDES SERIES